MAD®
SPY vs SPY

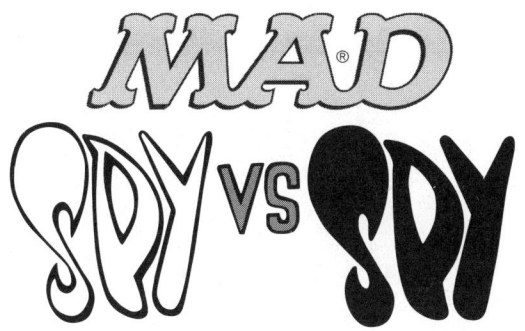

BLACK (AND WHITE) OPS

ANTONIO PROHIAS
▪▅▅• ▪▅▅• ▅▅▅ ▪▪▪▪ ▪▪ ▪▅ ▪▪▪

FALL RIVER PRESS

New York

FALL RIVER PRESS

New York

An Imprint of Sterling Publishing
387 Park Avenue South
New York, NY 10016

FALL RIVER PRESS and the distinctive Fall River Press logo are
registered trademarks of Barnes & Noble, Inc.

Copyright © 1972, 1978, and 1982 by
Antonio Prohias and E.C. Publications.
MAD, "Spy vs Spy," and all related elements ® and © by
E.C. Publications, Inc.

This 2013 compilation published by Fall River Press, by arrangement with MAD Books.

Cartoon Network logo ™ and © by Cartoon Network.

Contents of this compilation appeared originally in slightly different form in
The Third MAD Dossier of Spy vs Spy, *The Sixth MAD Casebook on Spy vs Spy*, and
The Fifth MAD Report on Spy vs Spy.

All rights reserved. No part of this publication may be reproduced, stored in a retrieval
system, or transmitted in any form or by any means (including electronic, mechanical,
photocopying, recording, or otherwise) without prior written permission from the publisher.

ISBN 978-1-4351-5173-4

Distributed in Canada by Sterling Publishing
c/o Canadian Manda Group, 165 Dufferin Street
Toronto, Ontario, Canada M6K 3H6

For information about custom editions, special sales, and premium and corporate purchases,
please contact Sterling Special Sales at 800-805-5489 or specialsales@sterlingpublishing.com.

Manufactured in the United States of America

2 4 6 8 10 9 7 5 3 1

www.sterlingpublishing.com

Visit MAD online at www.madmagazine.com

Though Alfred E. Neuman wasn't the first to say, "A fool and his money are soon parted," here's your chance to
prove the old adage right—subscribe to MAD! Simply call 1-800-4-MADMAG and mention code 5MBN2.
Operators are standing by (the water cooler).

CONTENTS

BLACK (AND WHITE) OPS

Operation: Bomb Site 3
Operation: Altered Ego 13
Operation: Changing of the God 29
Operation: Spell Shock 43
Operation: Safe Conduct 53
Operation: Trojan Horseplay 63
Operation: Mouth Trap 71
Operation: Guided Mischief 87
Operation: Shoe-In 103
Operation: Subversus 109
Operation: Portal to Portal Play 117
Operation: Big Tow 131
Operation: Cigar Store 139
Operation: Operation 147
Operation: One-Way Trick 165
Operation: Maid of Steel 175

THE FATAL FILES

The Bugging Incident 192
The Rat-Fink Case 204
The Splitsville Memorandum 215
The Pool Shark Portfolio 227
The Shell Game Report 237
The One That Got Away Affair 255
Spy Jr. vs Spy Jr. 267
The Air A-Tack Mission 271

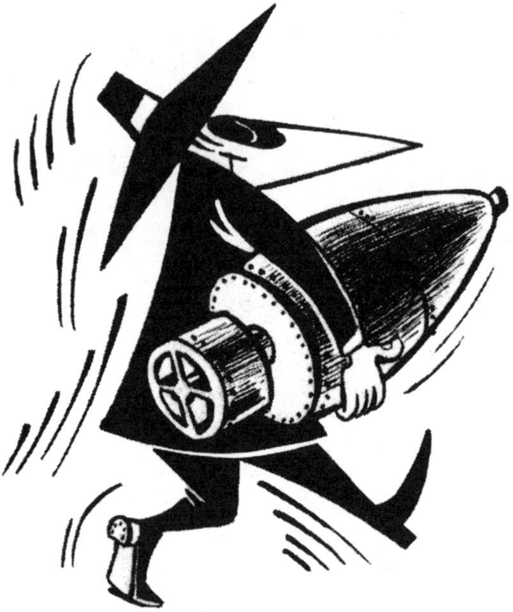

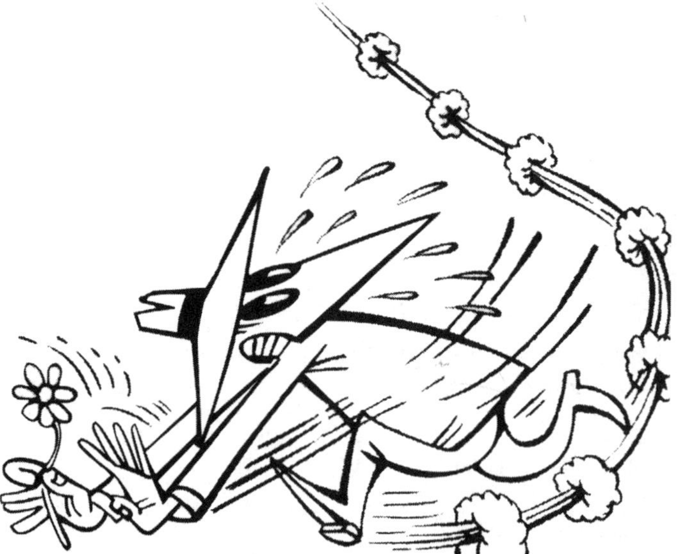

BLACK (AND WHITE) OPS

OPERATION: BOMB SITE

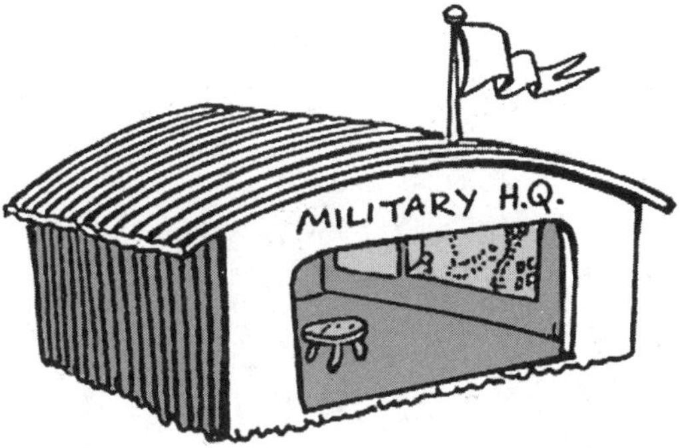
MILITARY H.Q.

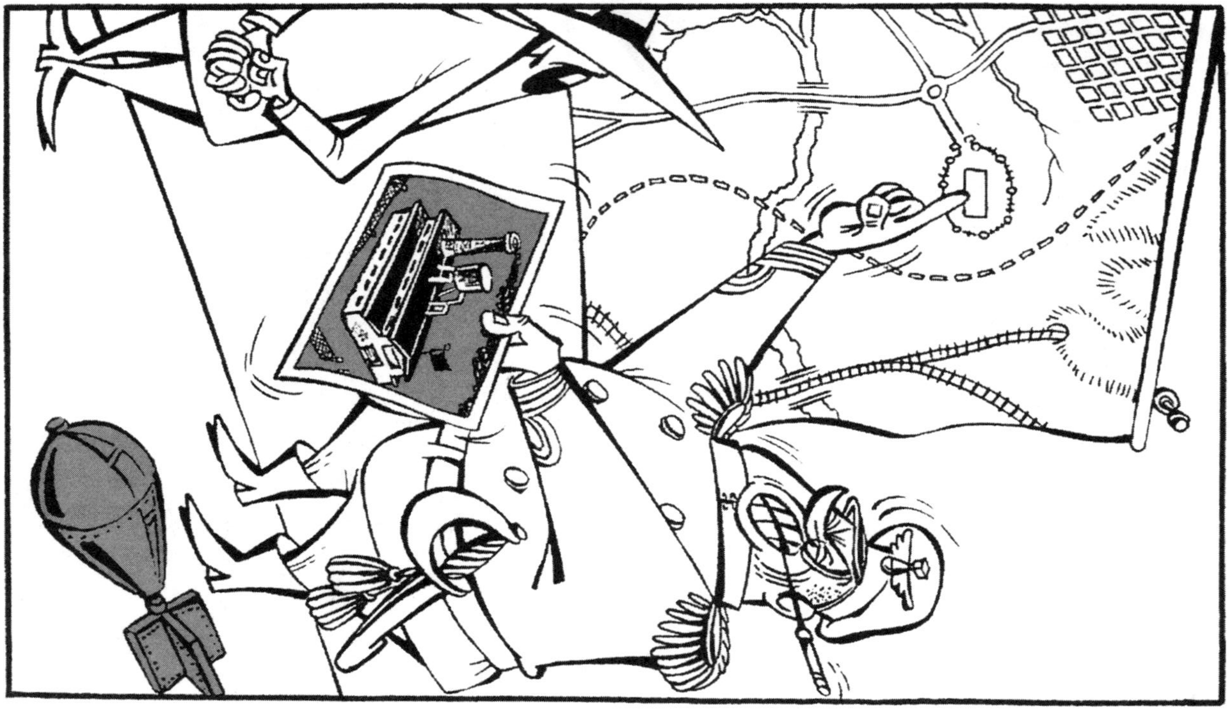

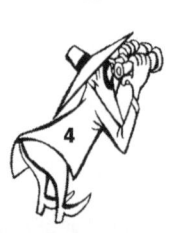

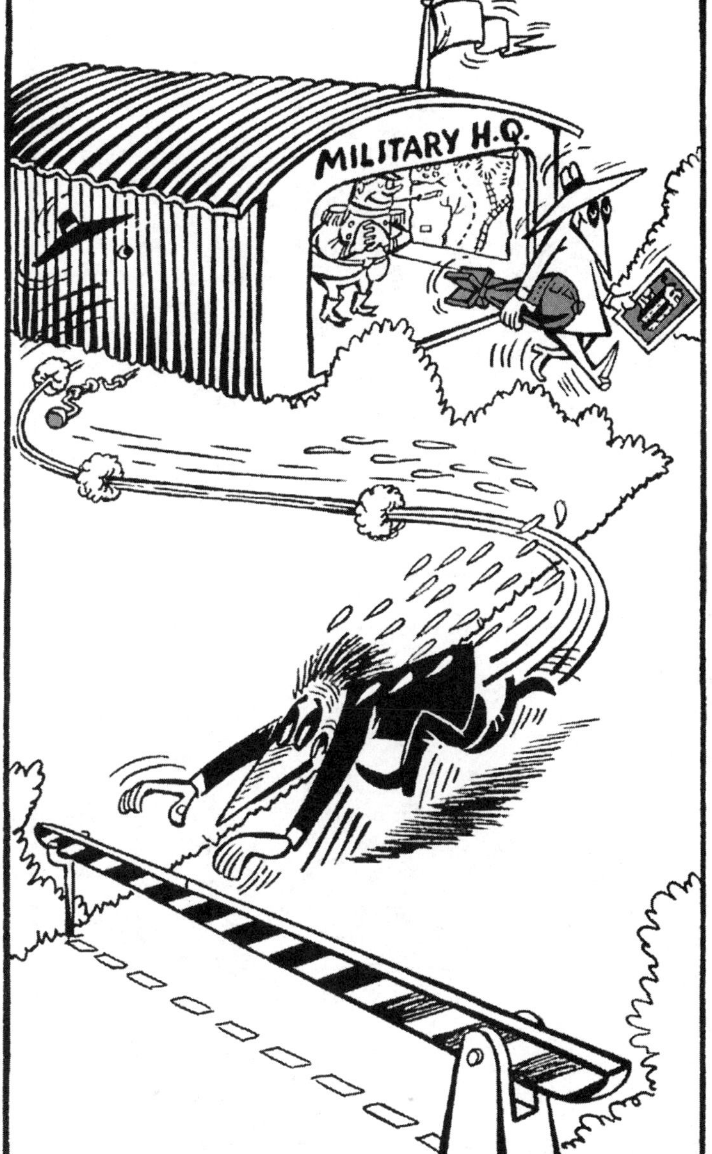
MILITARY H.Q.

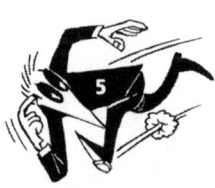

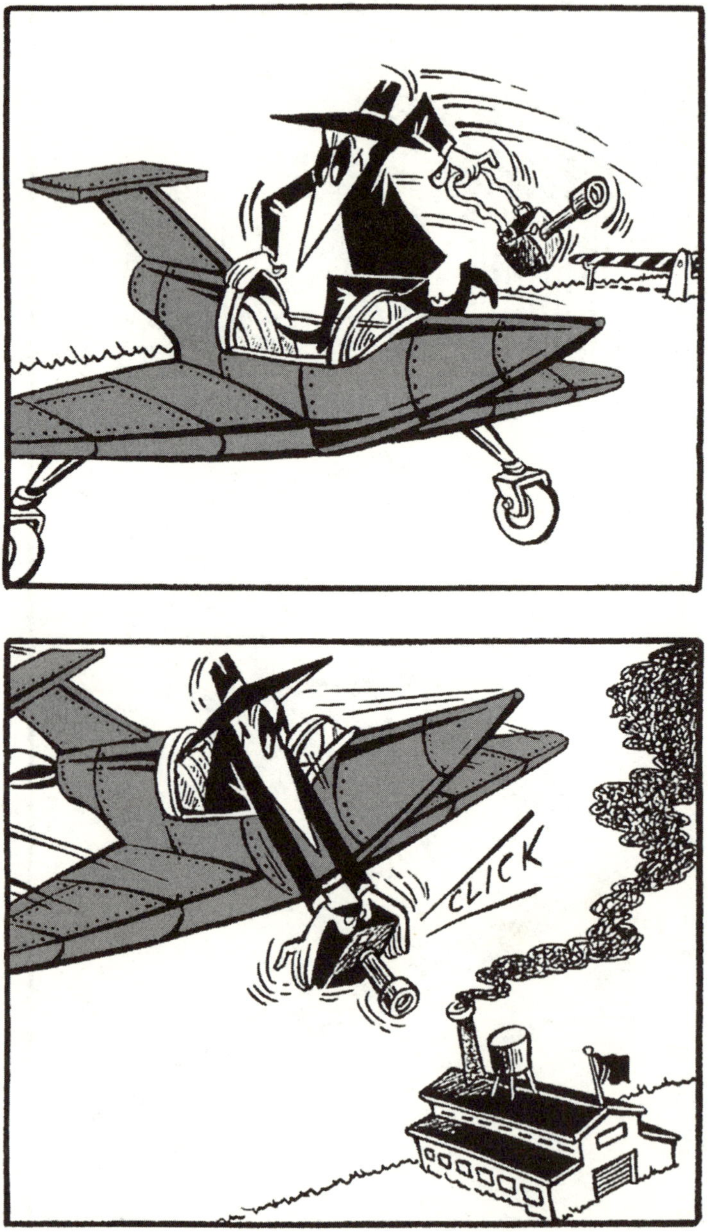
CLICK

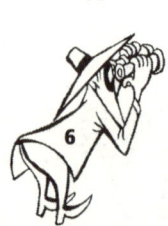

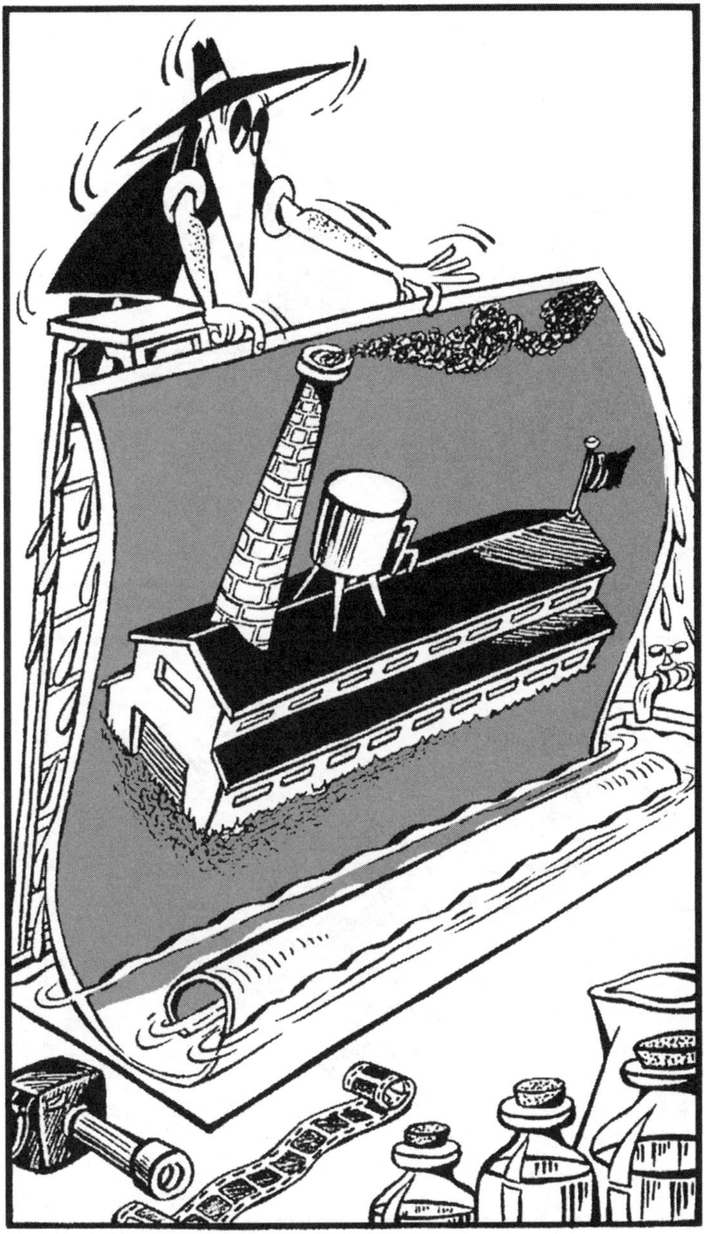

OPERATION: BOMB SITE

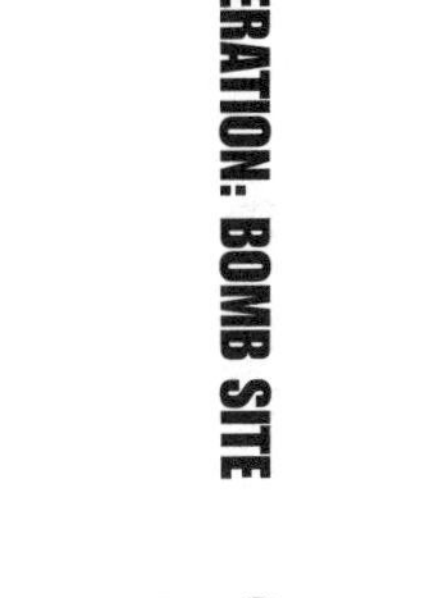

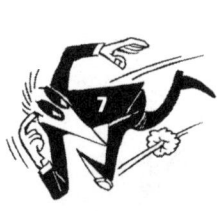

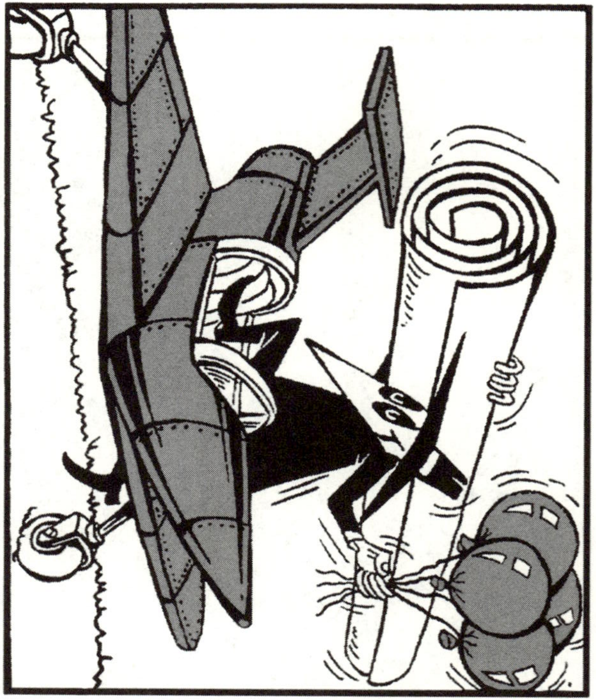

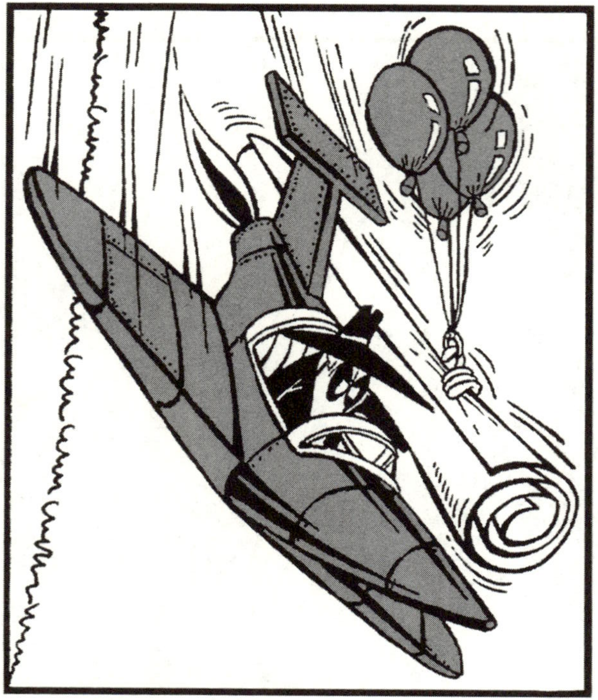

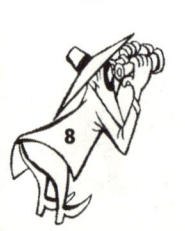

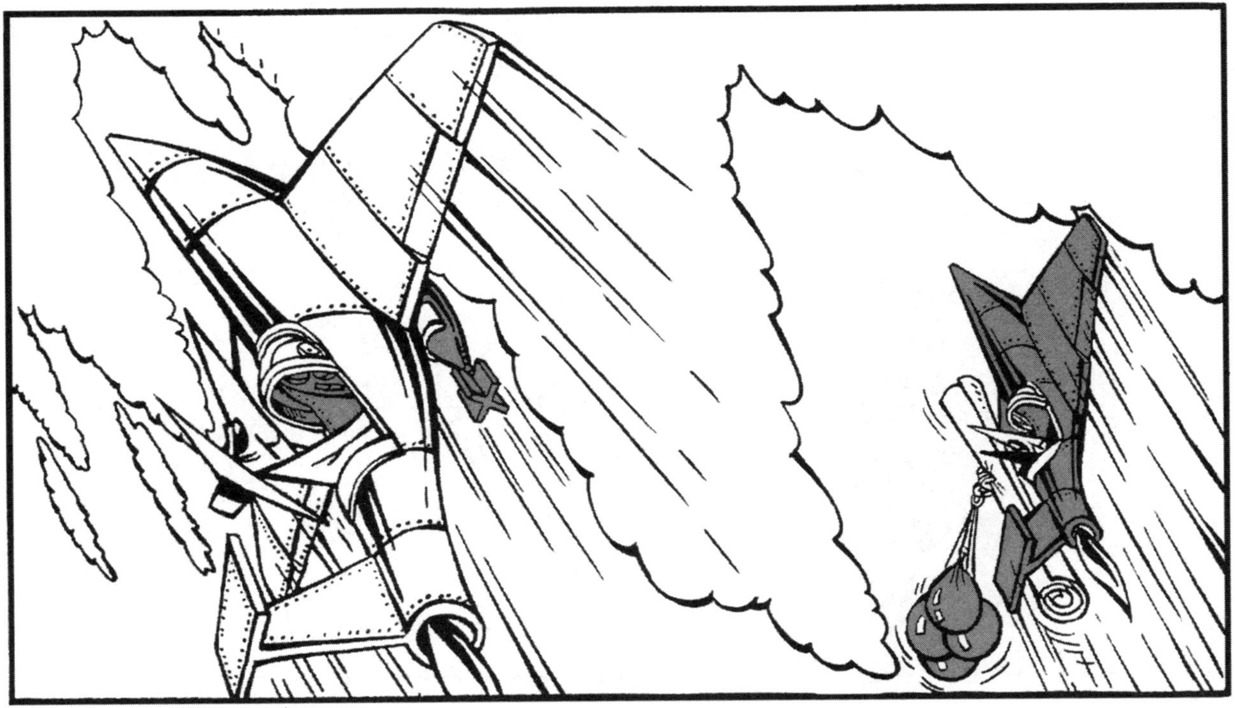

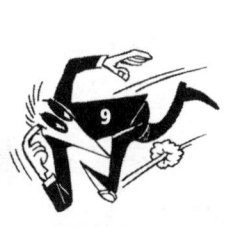

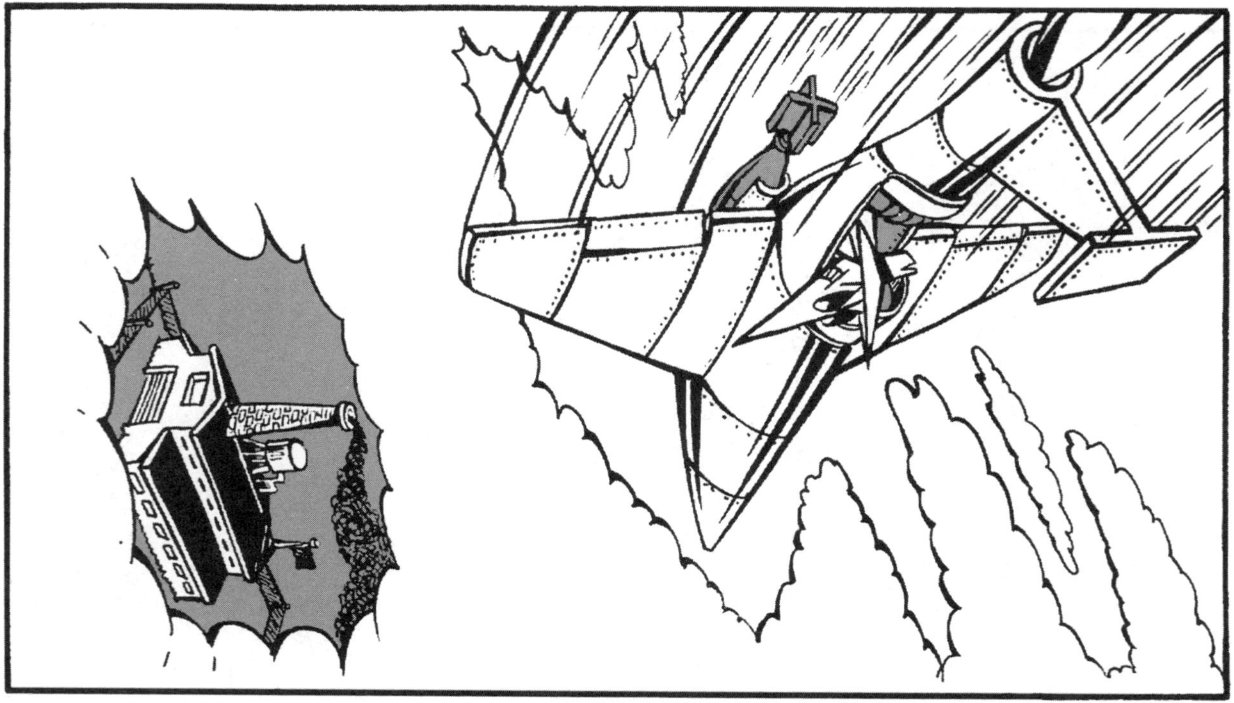

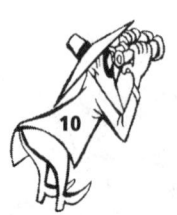

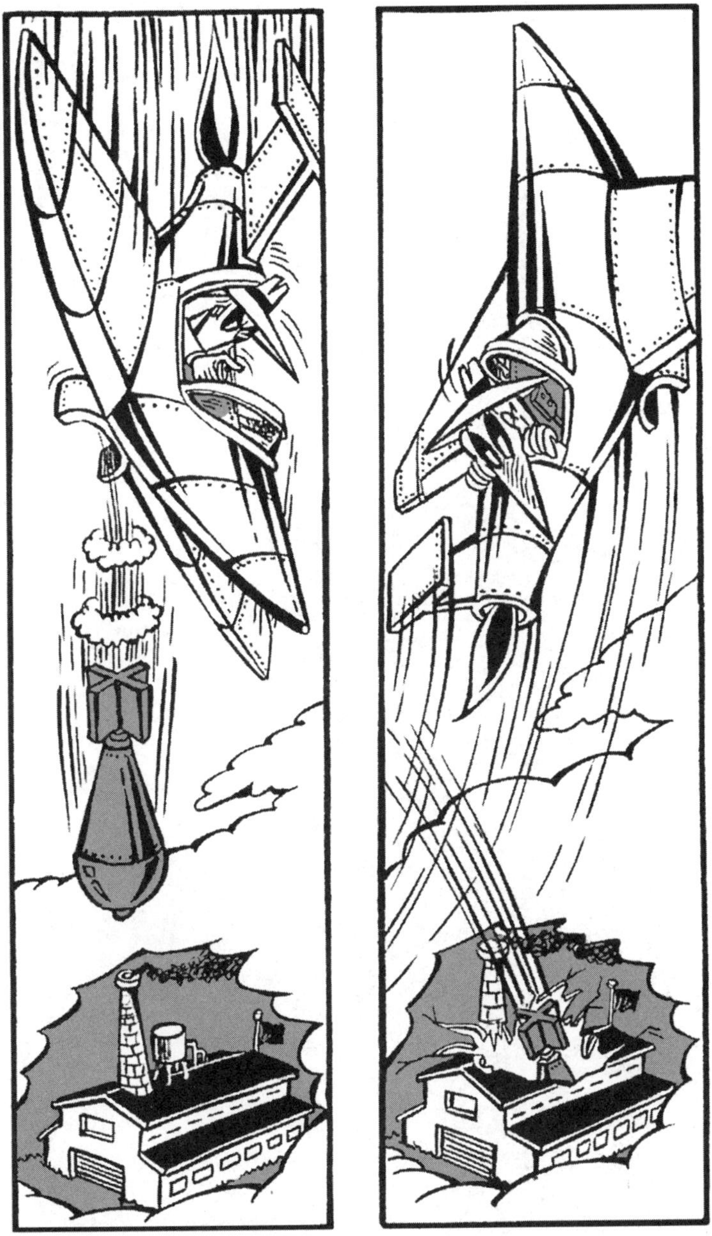

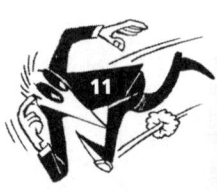

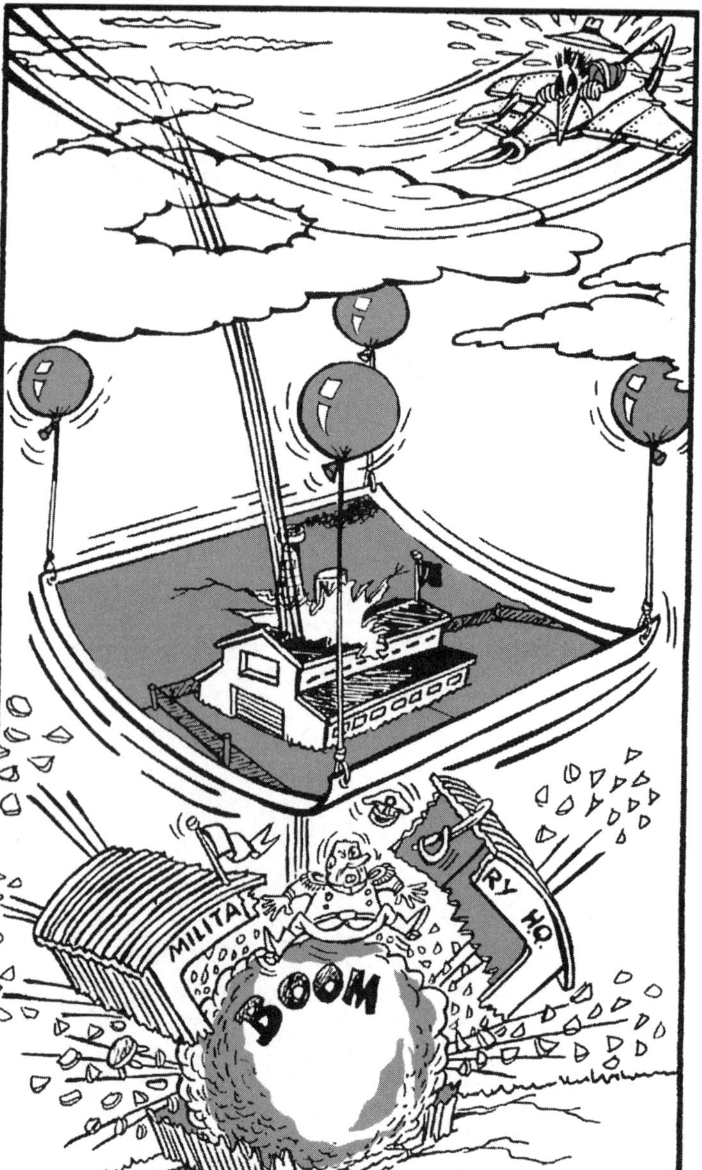
MILITA
RY H.Q.
BOOM

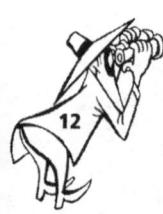

OPERATION: ALTERED EGO

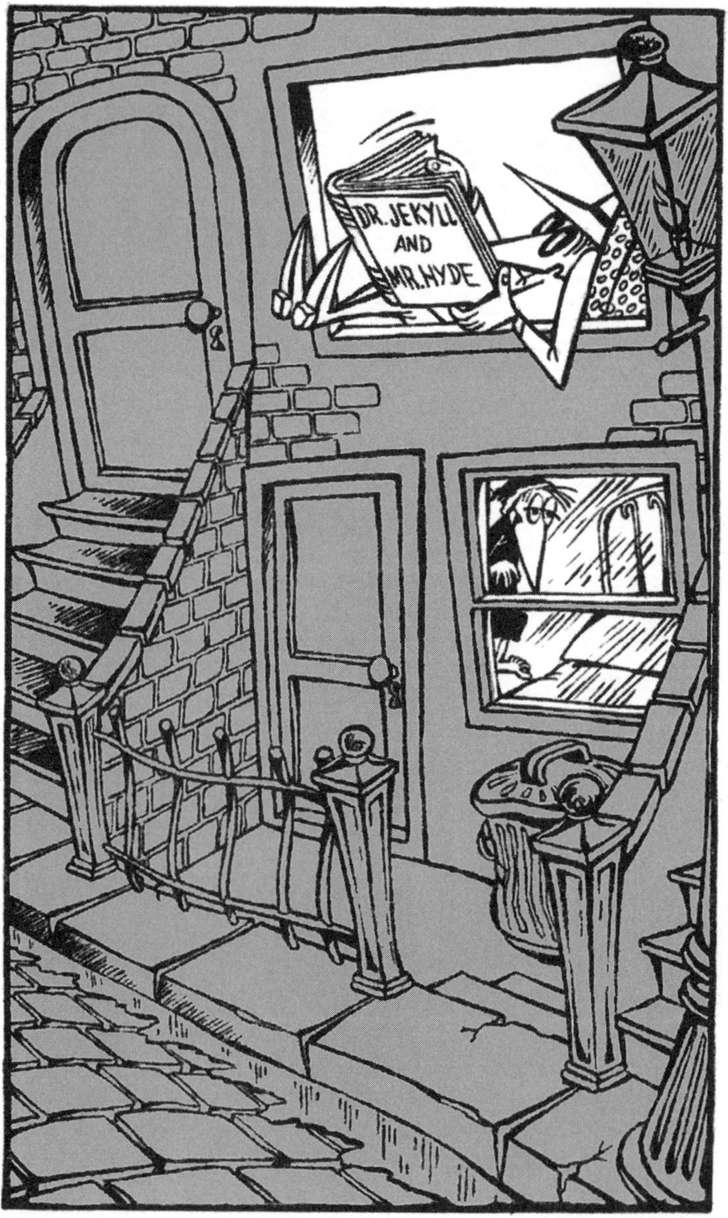
DR. JEKYLL
AND
MR. HYDE

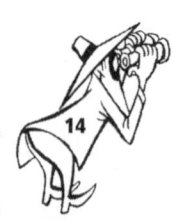

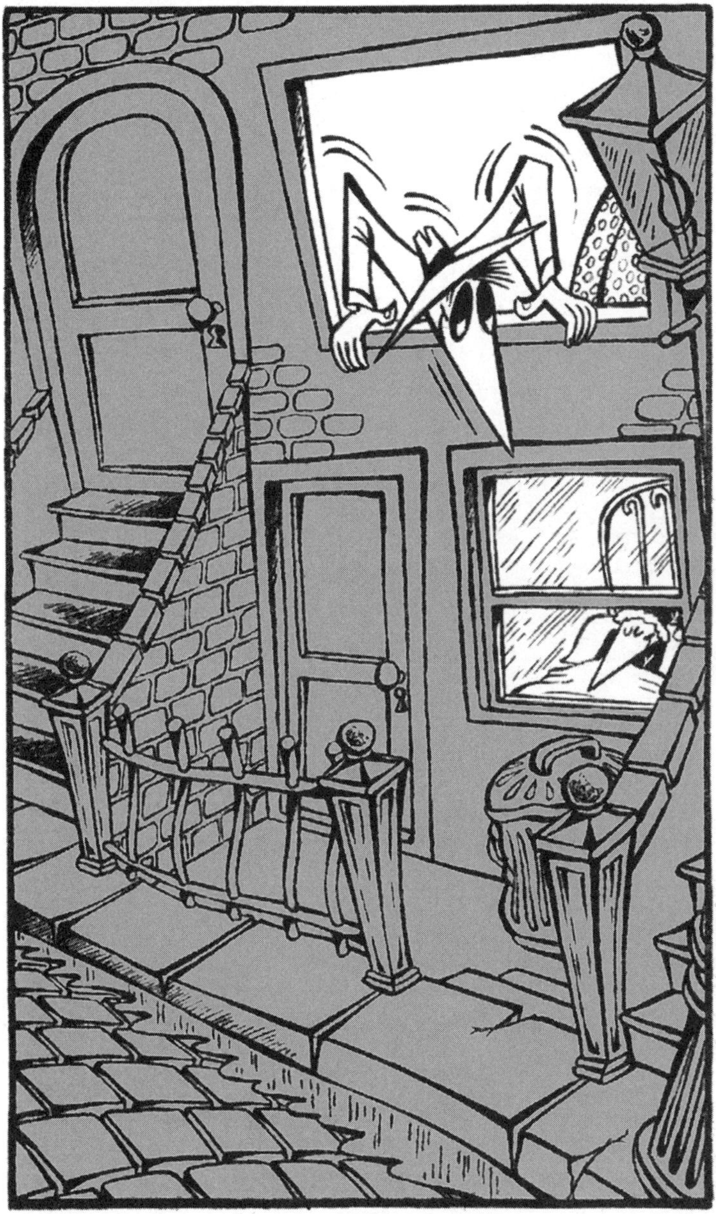

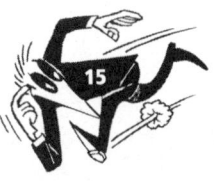

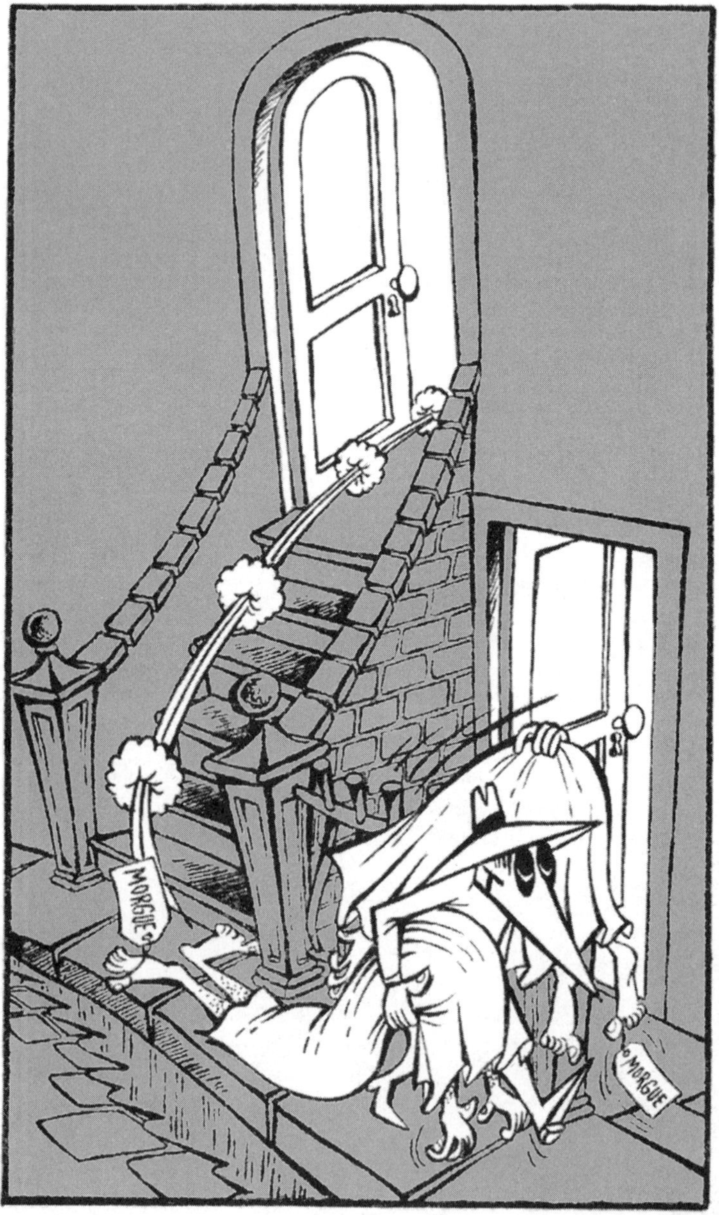
MORGUE
MORGUE

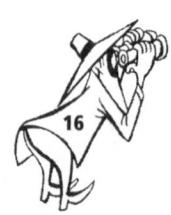

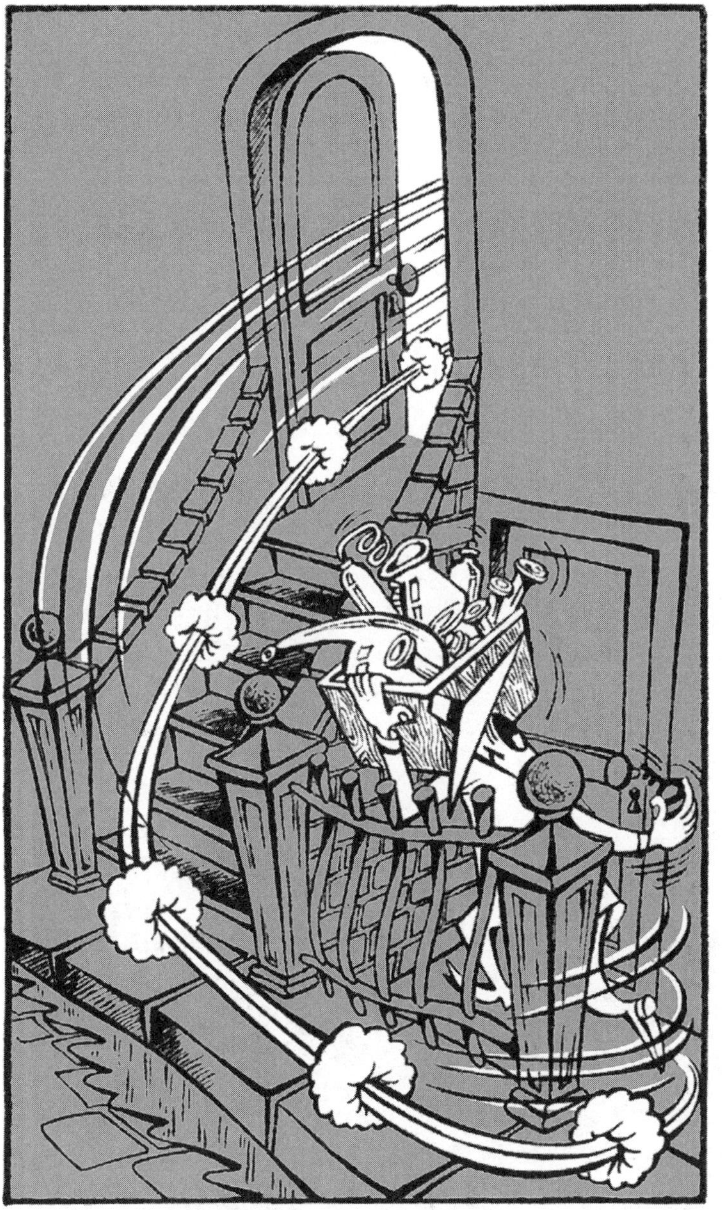

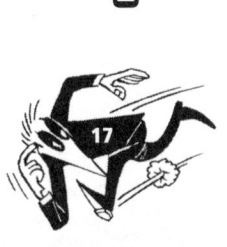

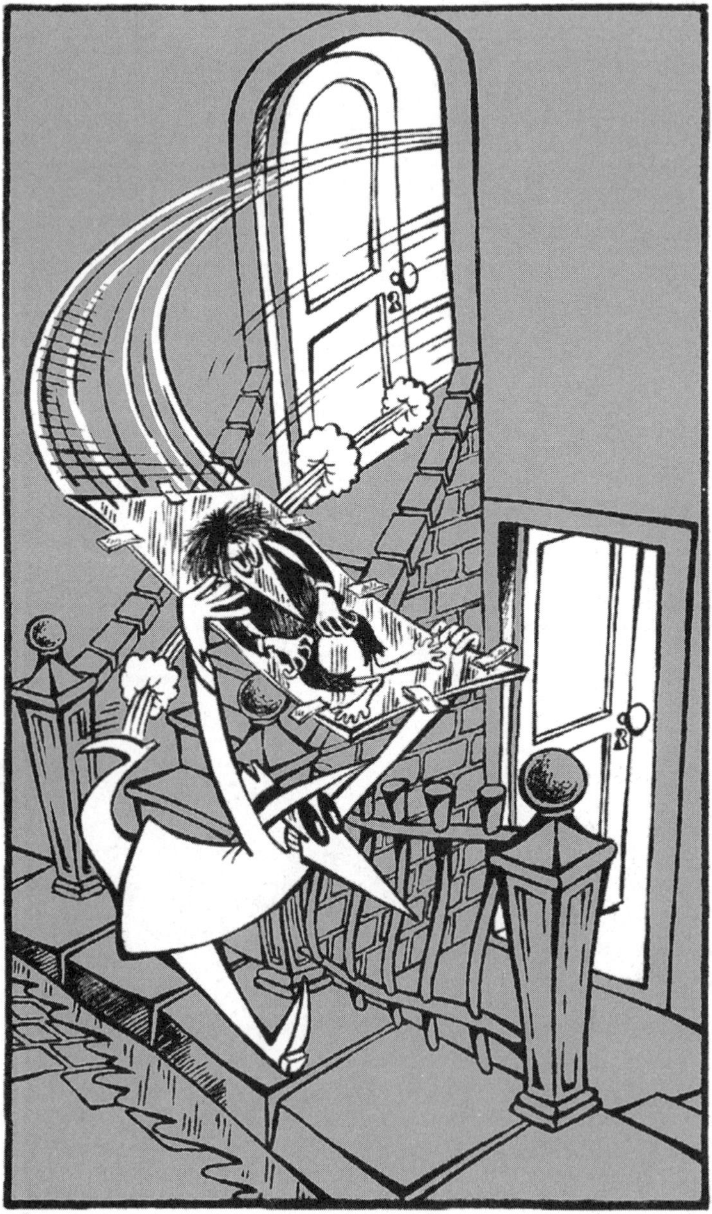

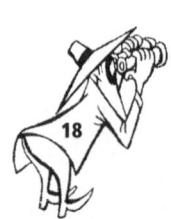

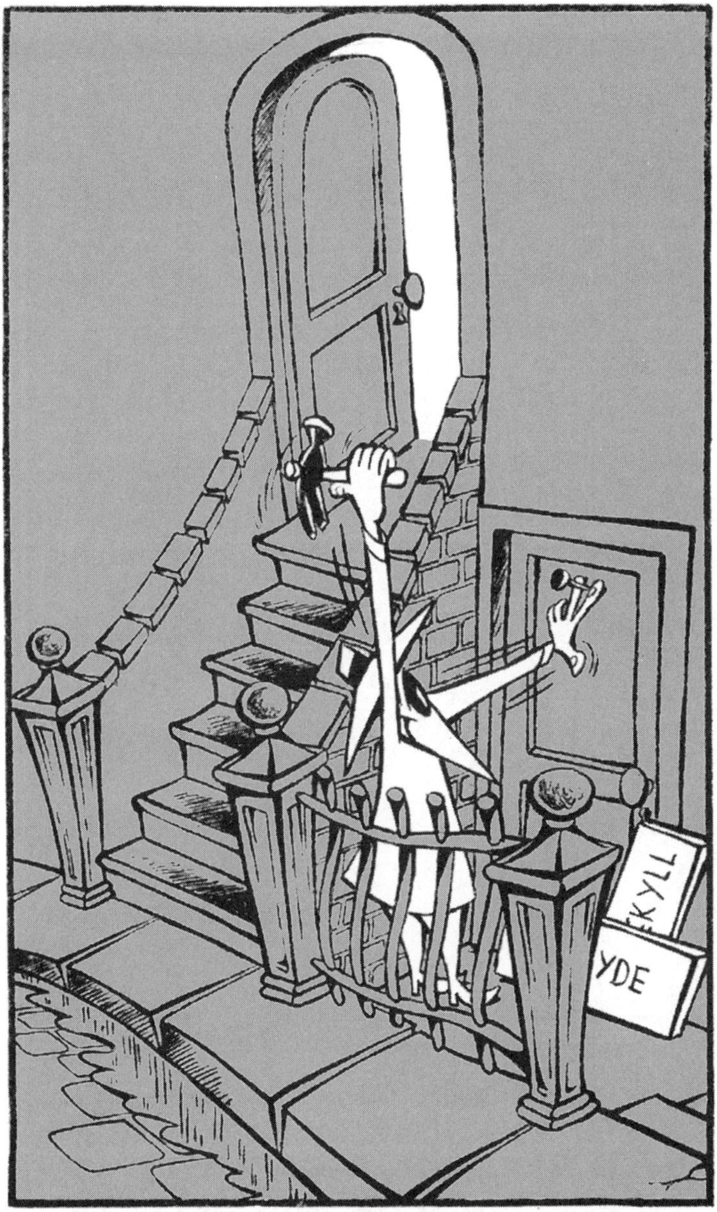
KYLL
YDE

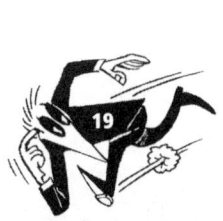

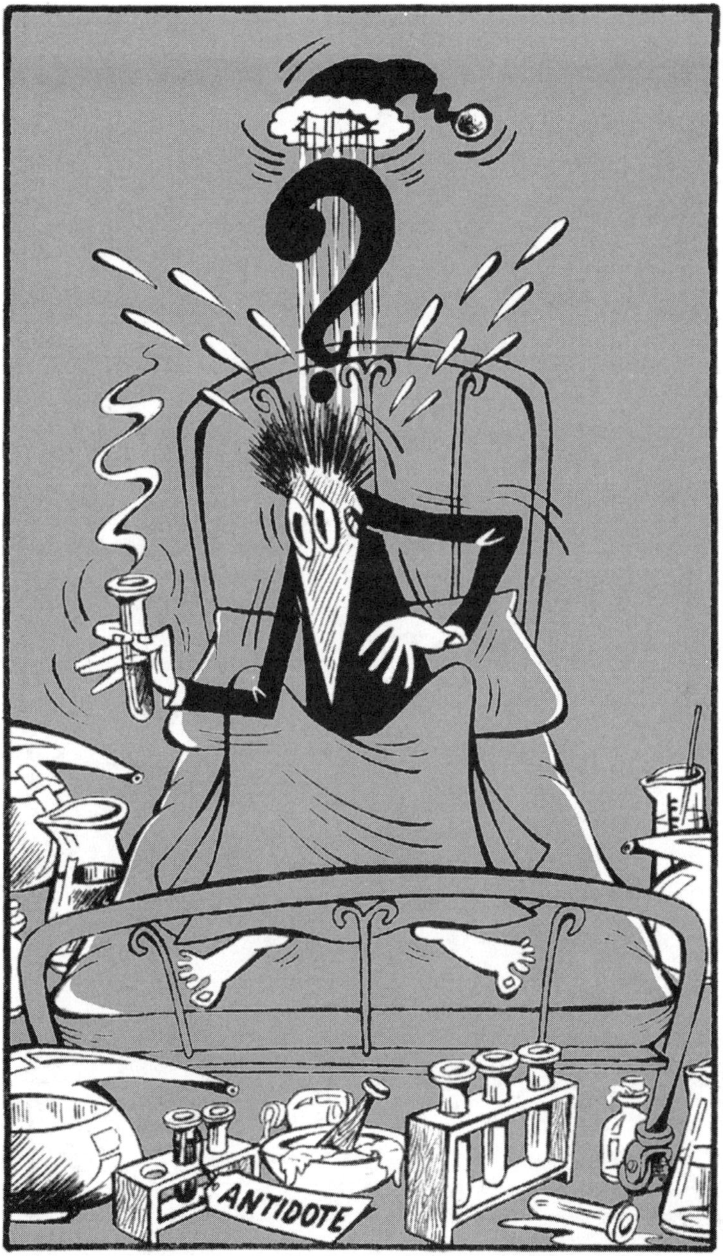
ANTIDOTE

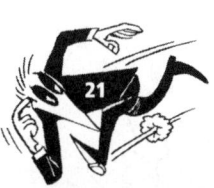

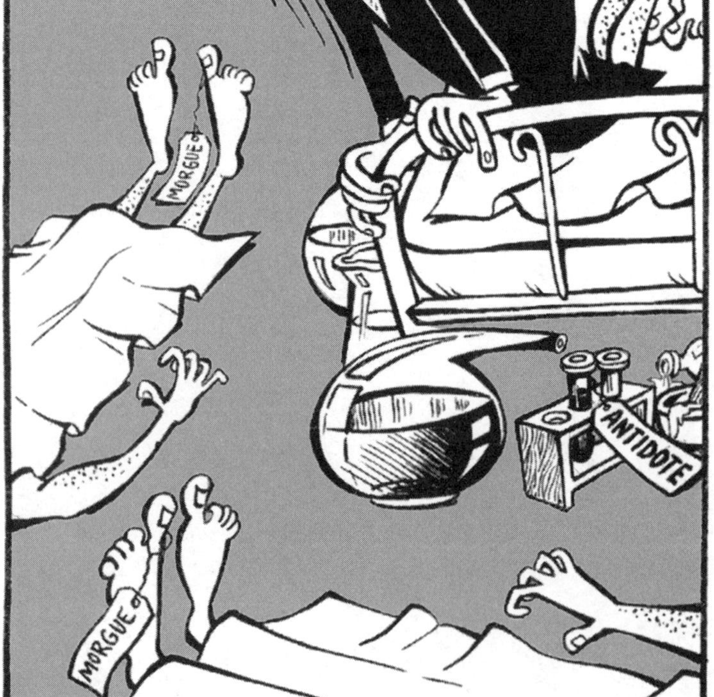
MORGUE
MORGUE
ANTIDOTE

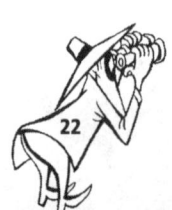

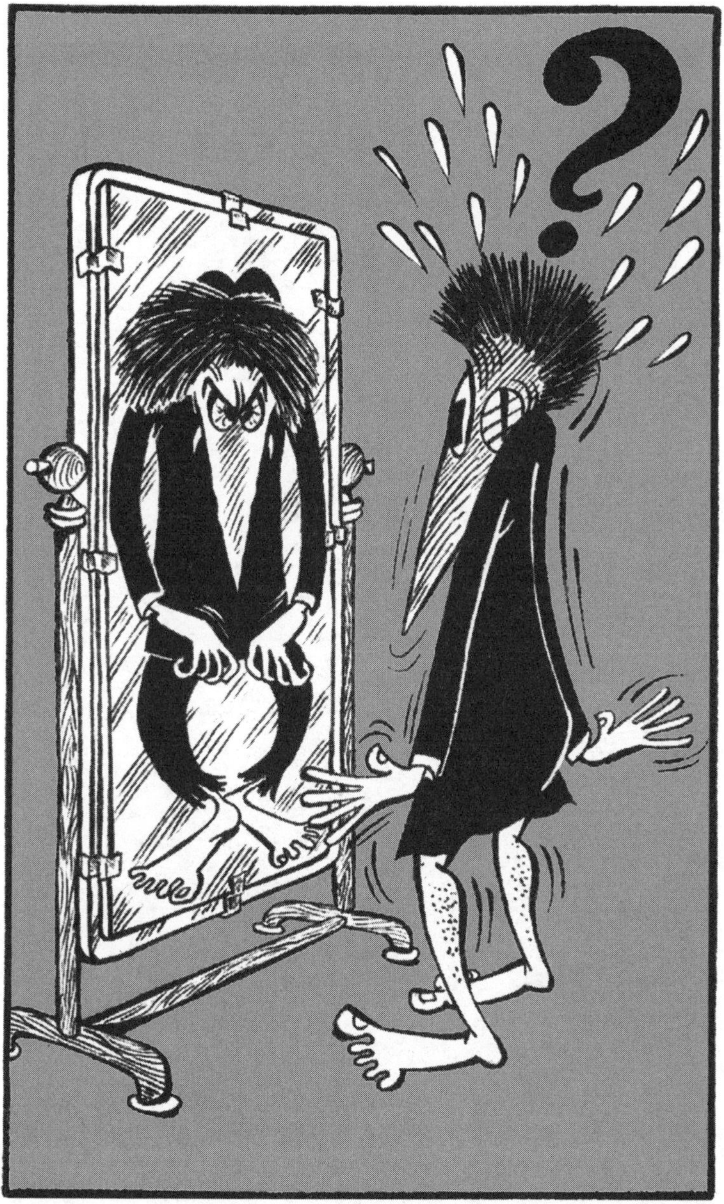

OPERATION: ALTERED EGO

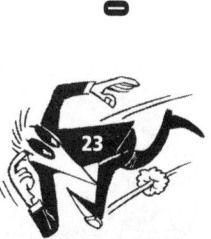

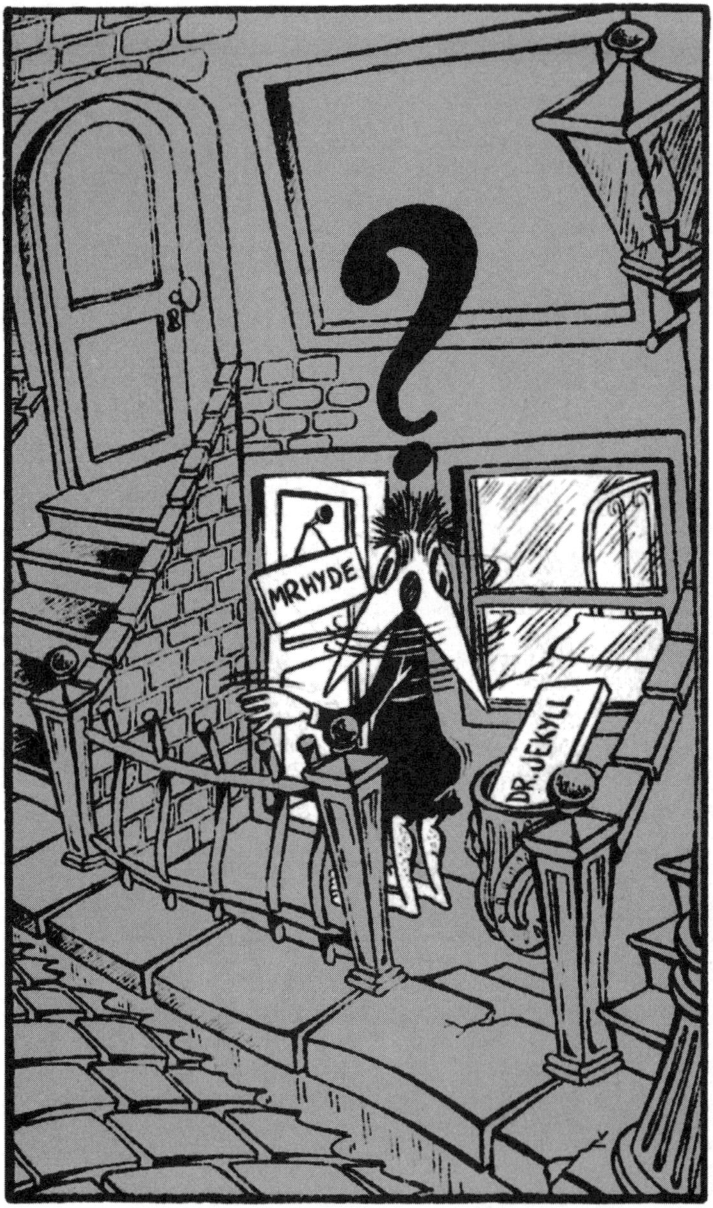
MR HYDE
DR. JEKYLL

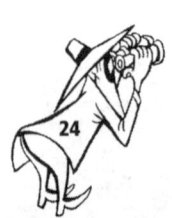

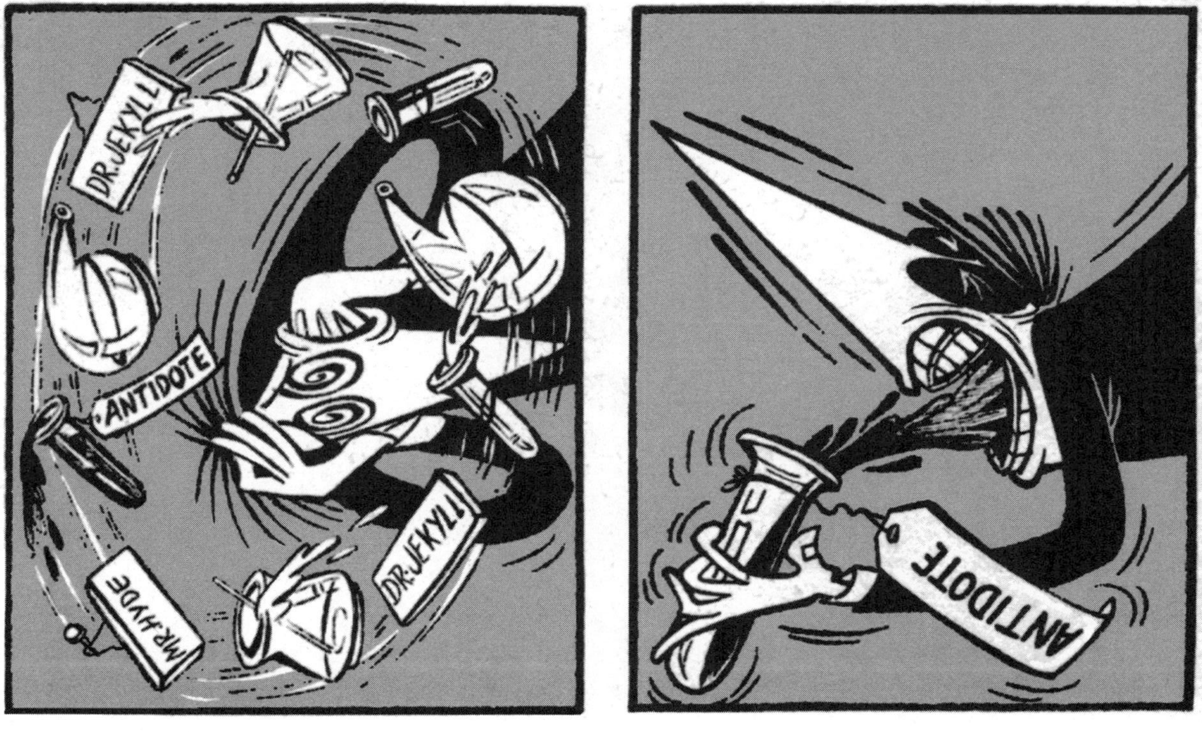
DR. JEKYLL
ANTIDOTE
MR. HYDE
DR. JEKYLL
ANTIDOTE

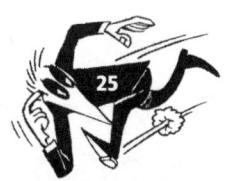

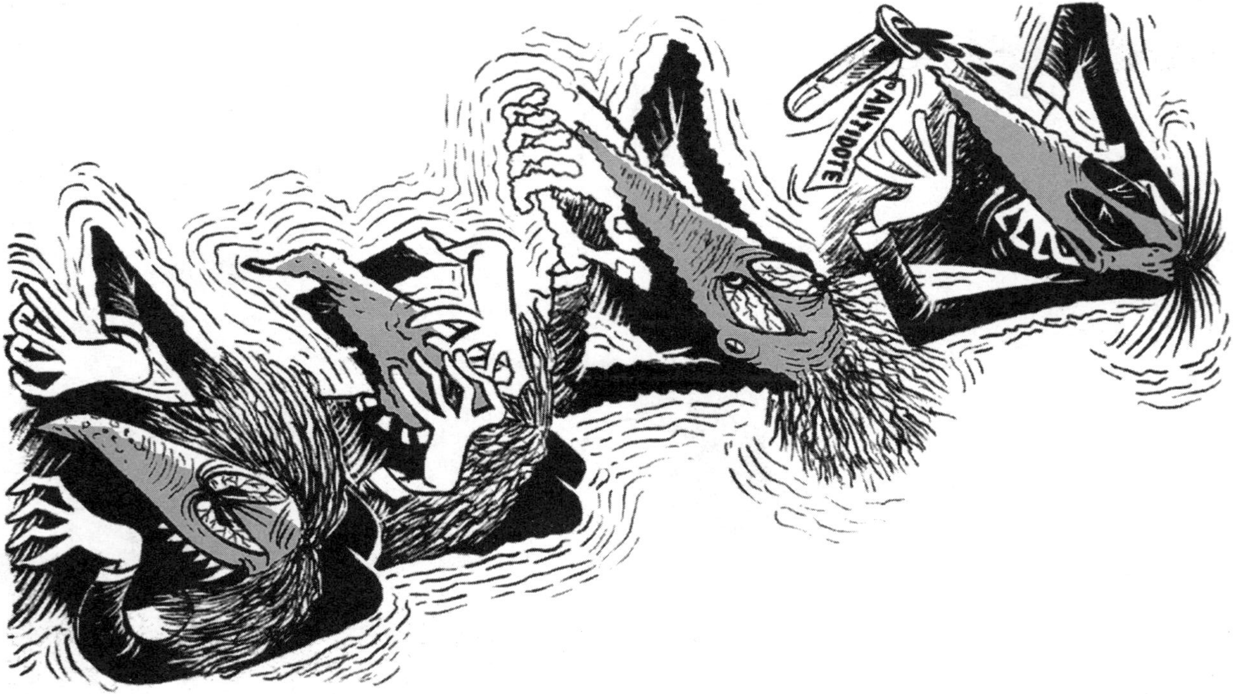
ANTIDOTE

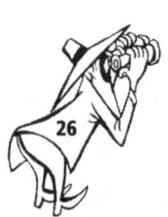

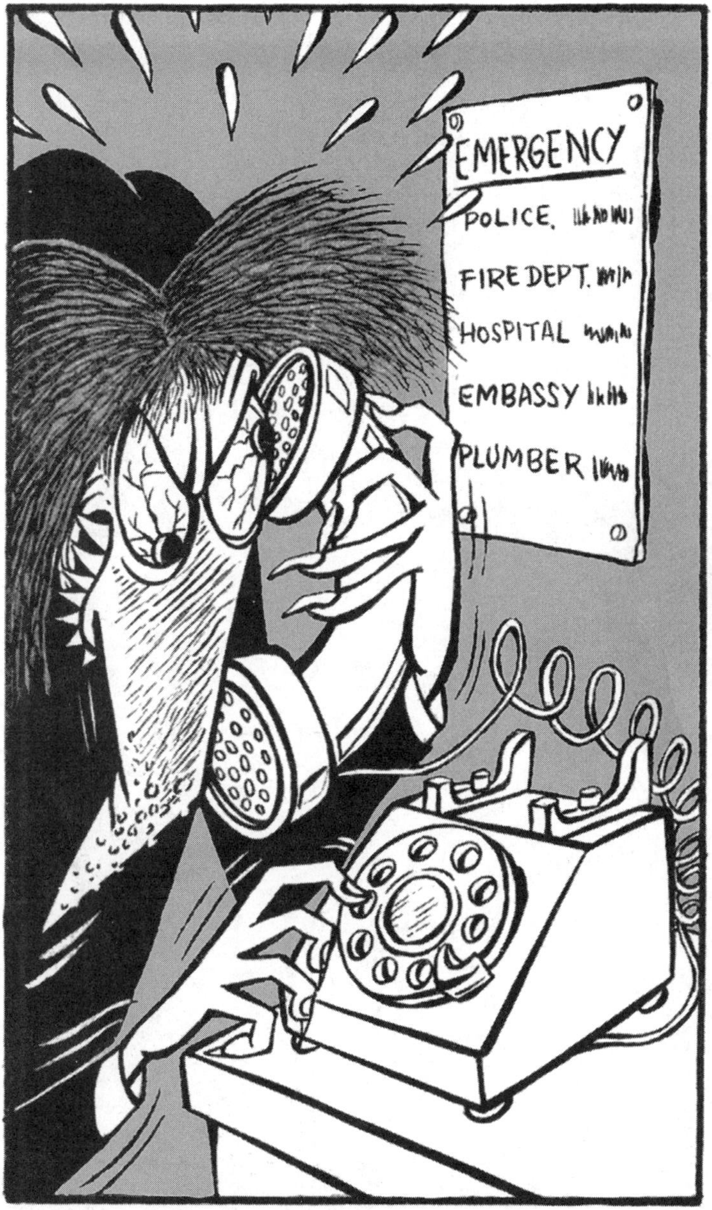
EMERGENCY
POLICE.
FIRE DEPT.
HOSPITAL
EMBASSY
PLUMBER

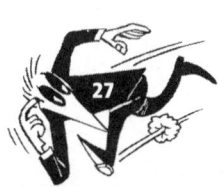

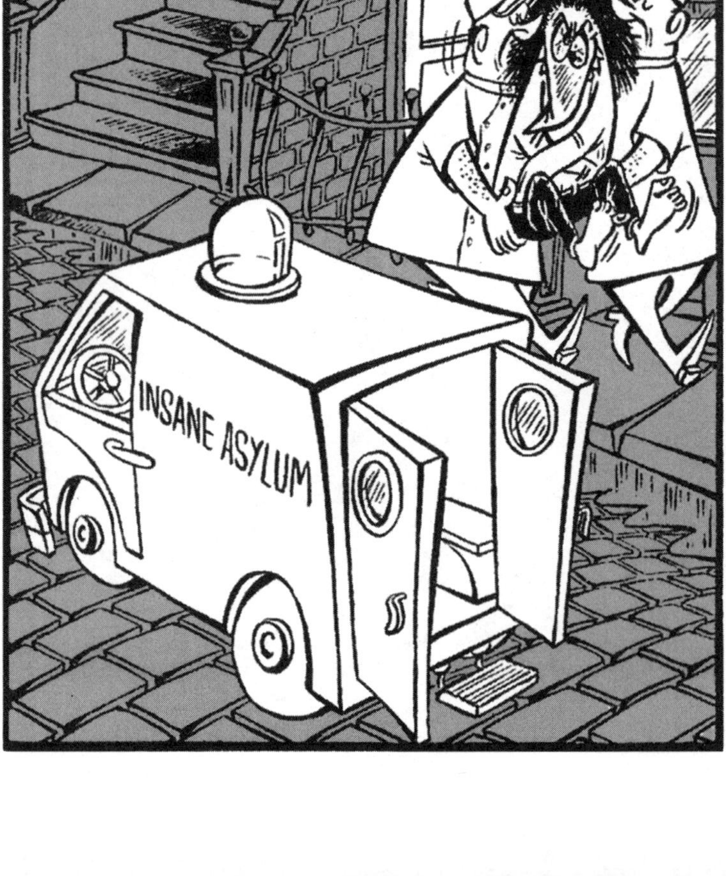
MR HYDE
INSANE ASYLUM

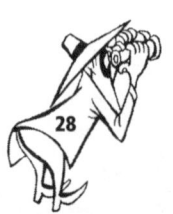

OPERATION: CHANGING OF THE GOD

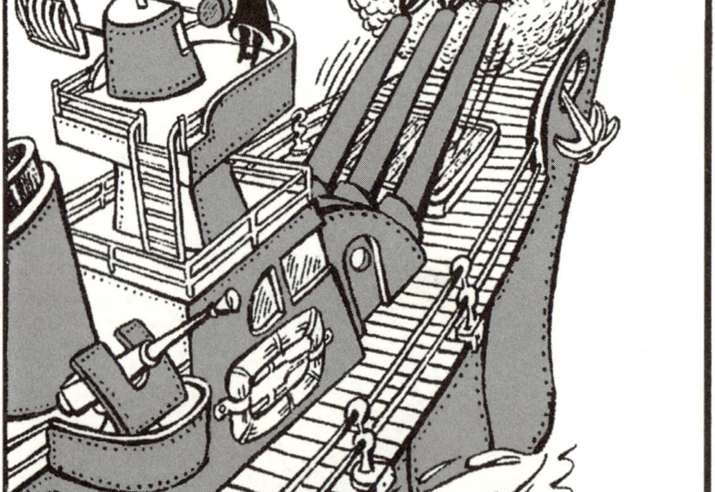
BOOM

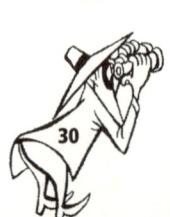

OPERATION: CHANGING OF THE GOD

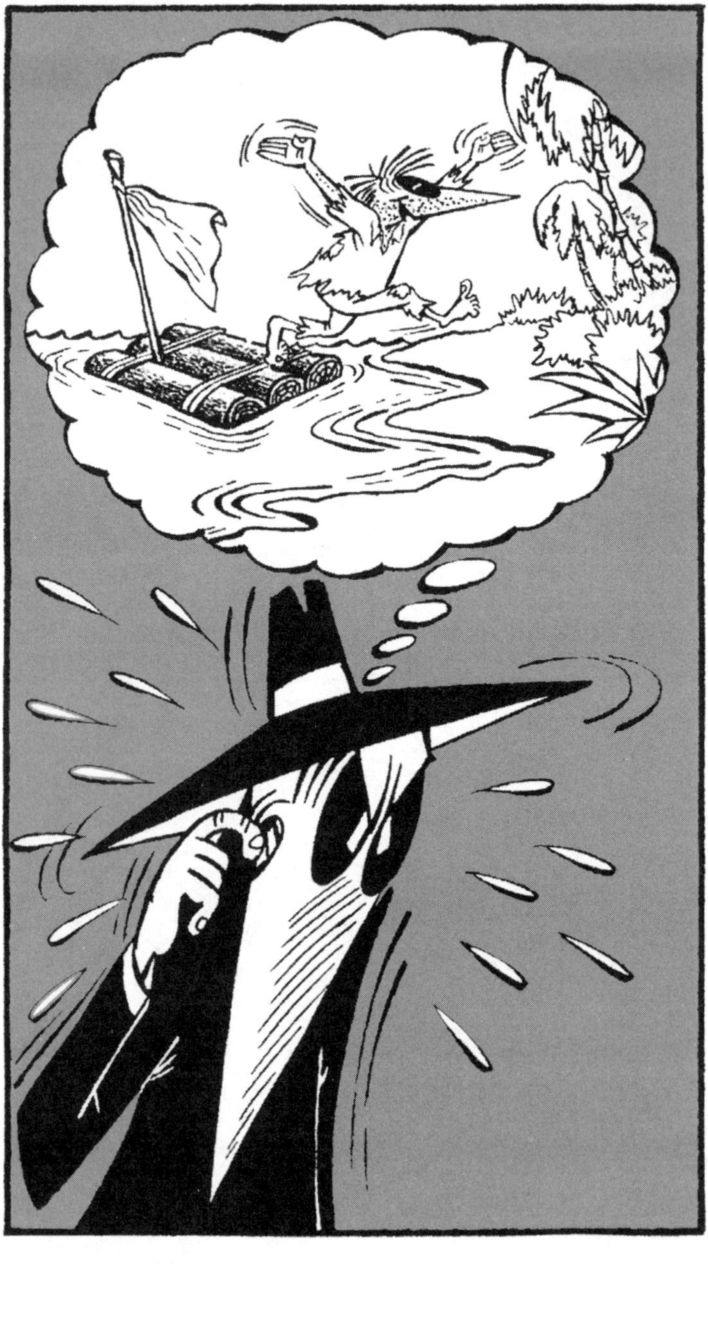

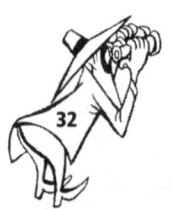

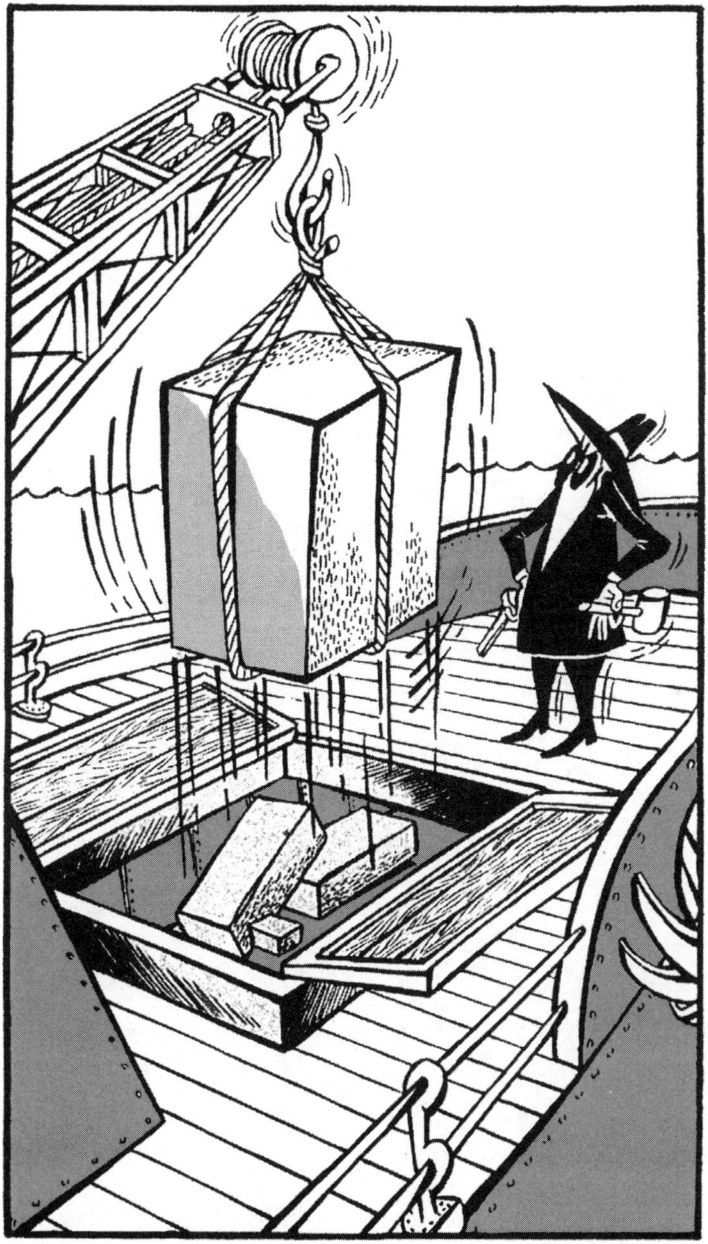

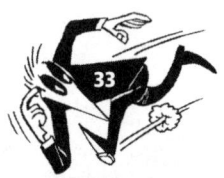

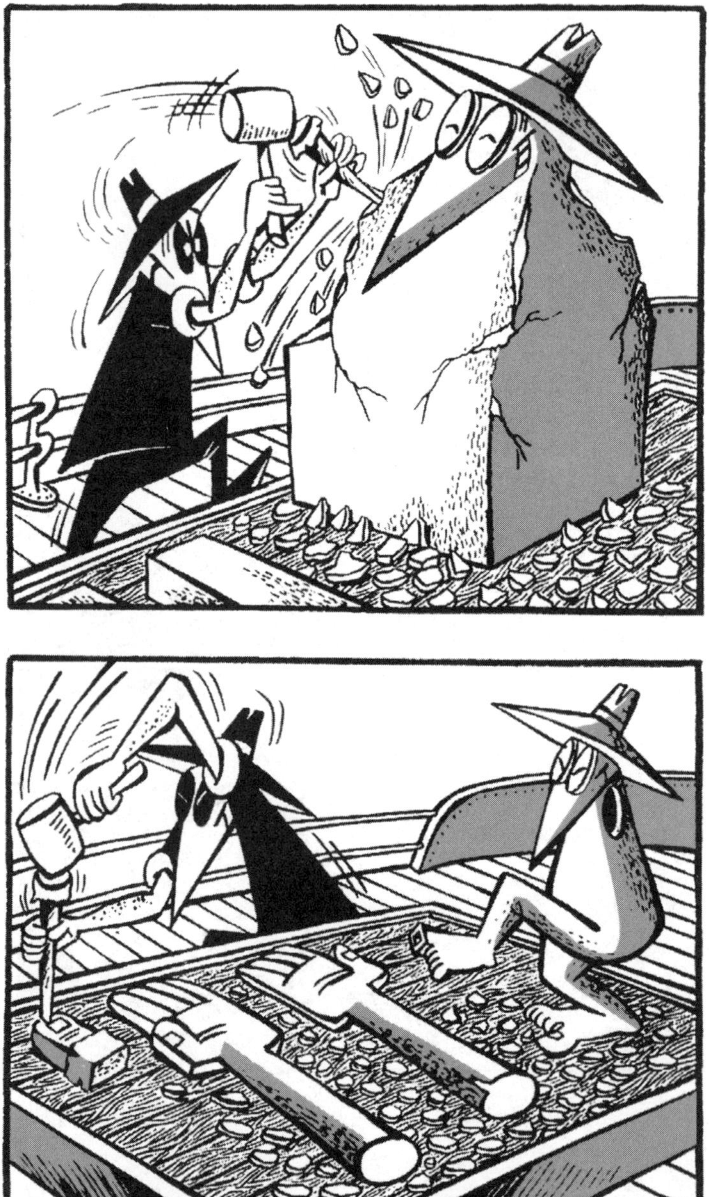

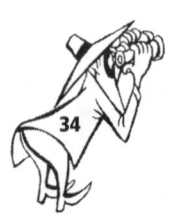

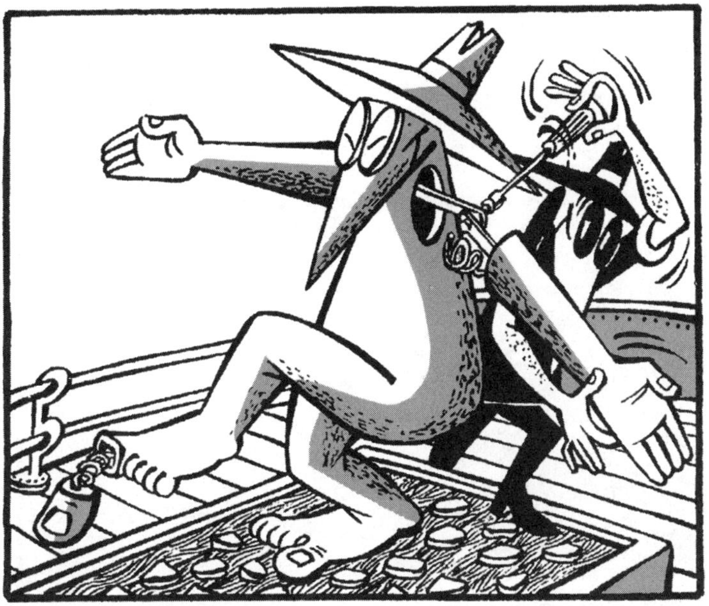

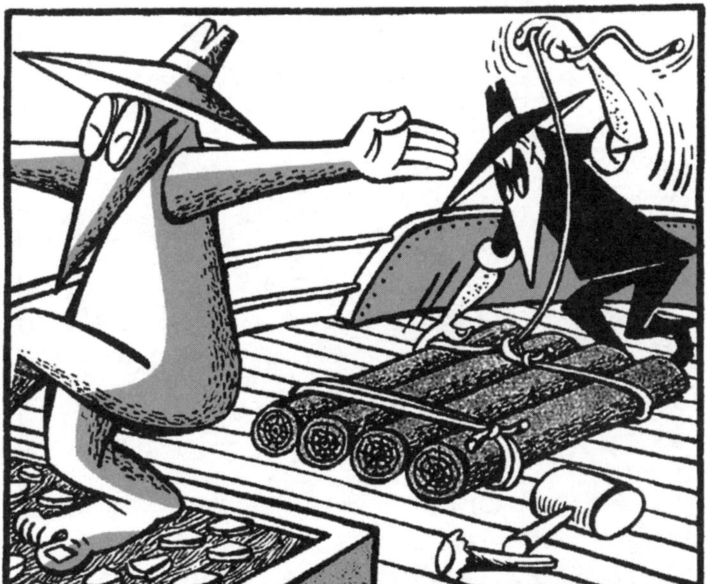

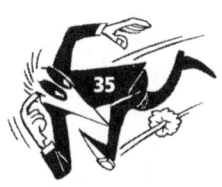

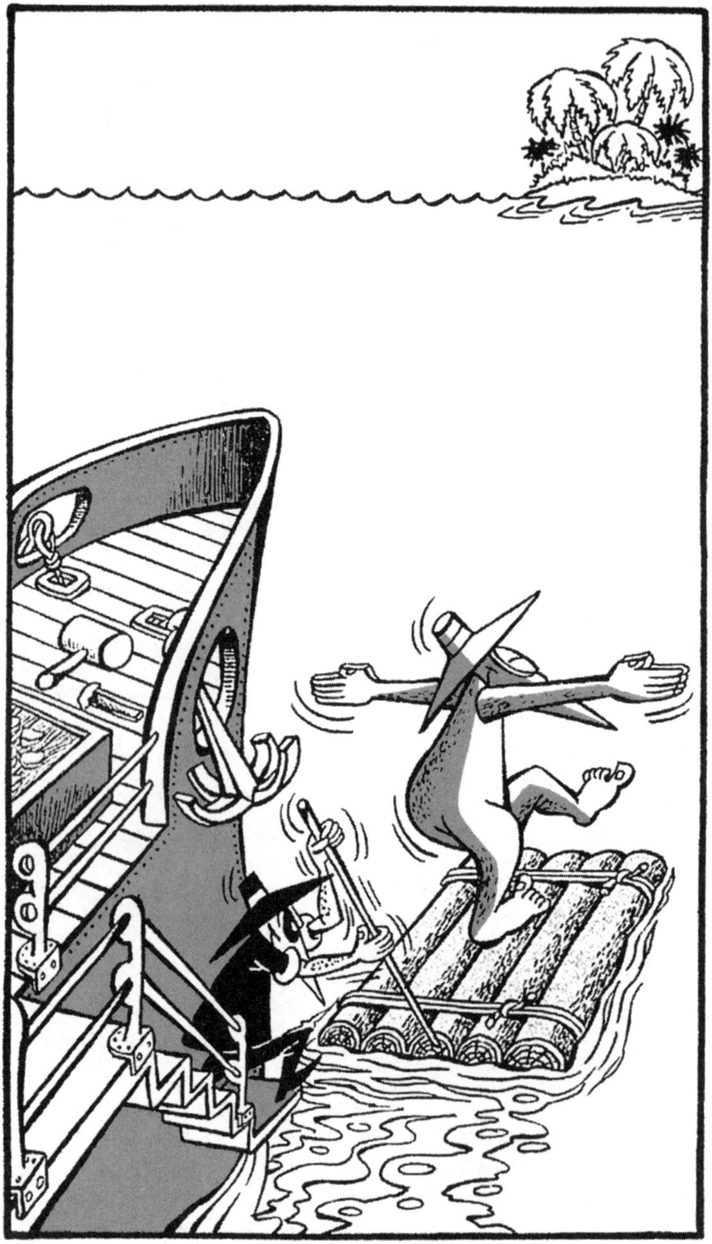

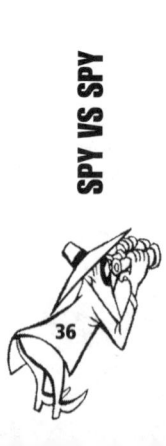

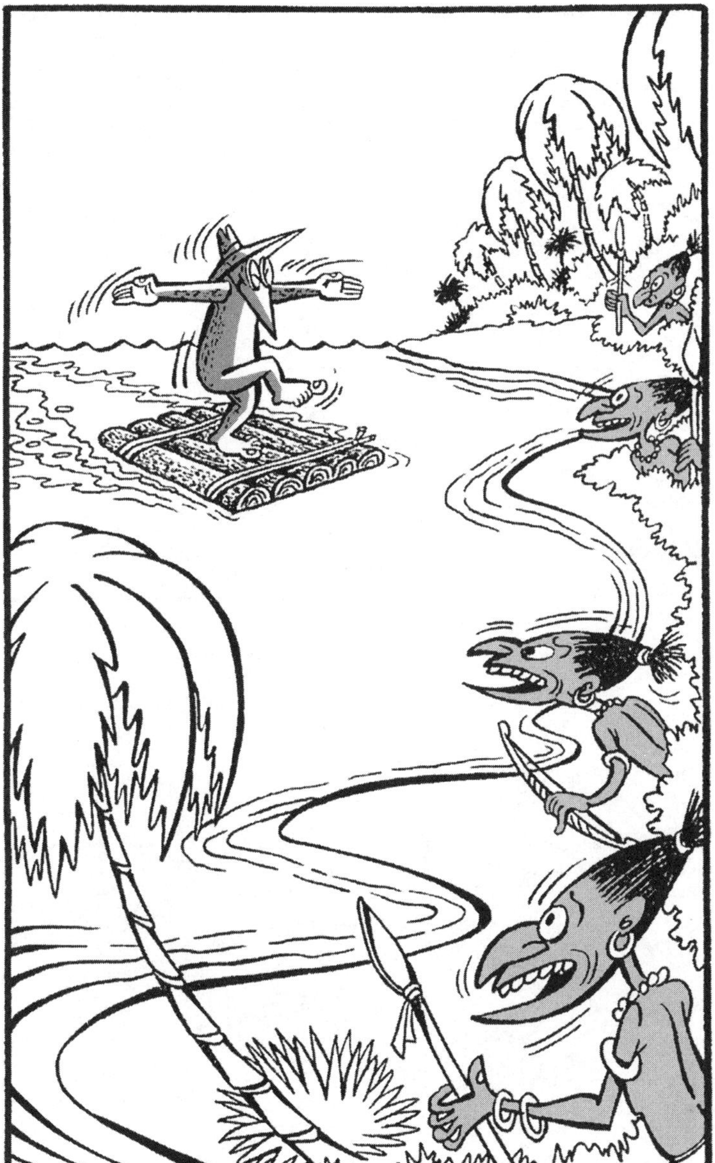

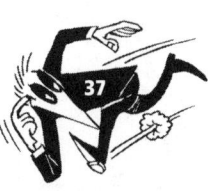

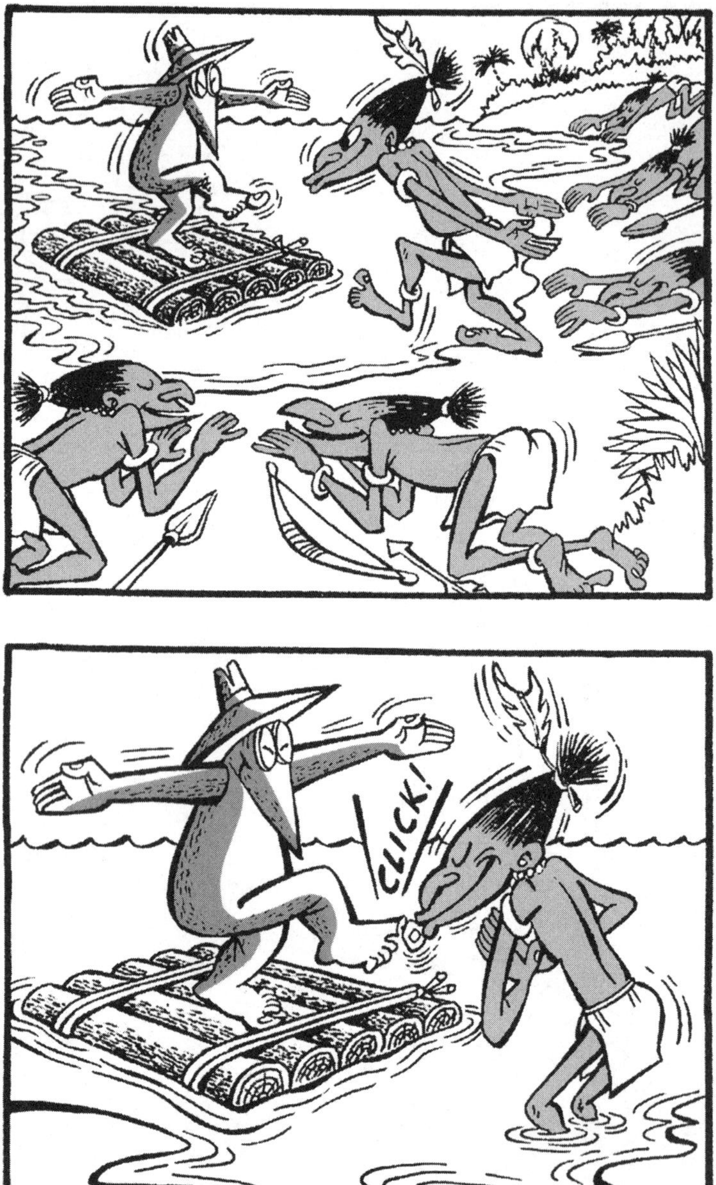
CLICK!

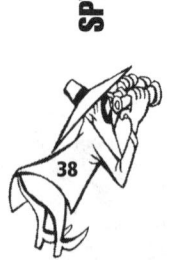

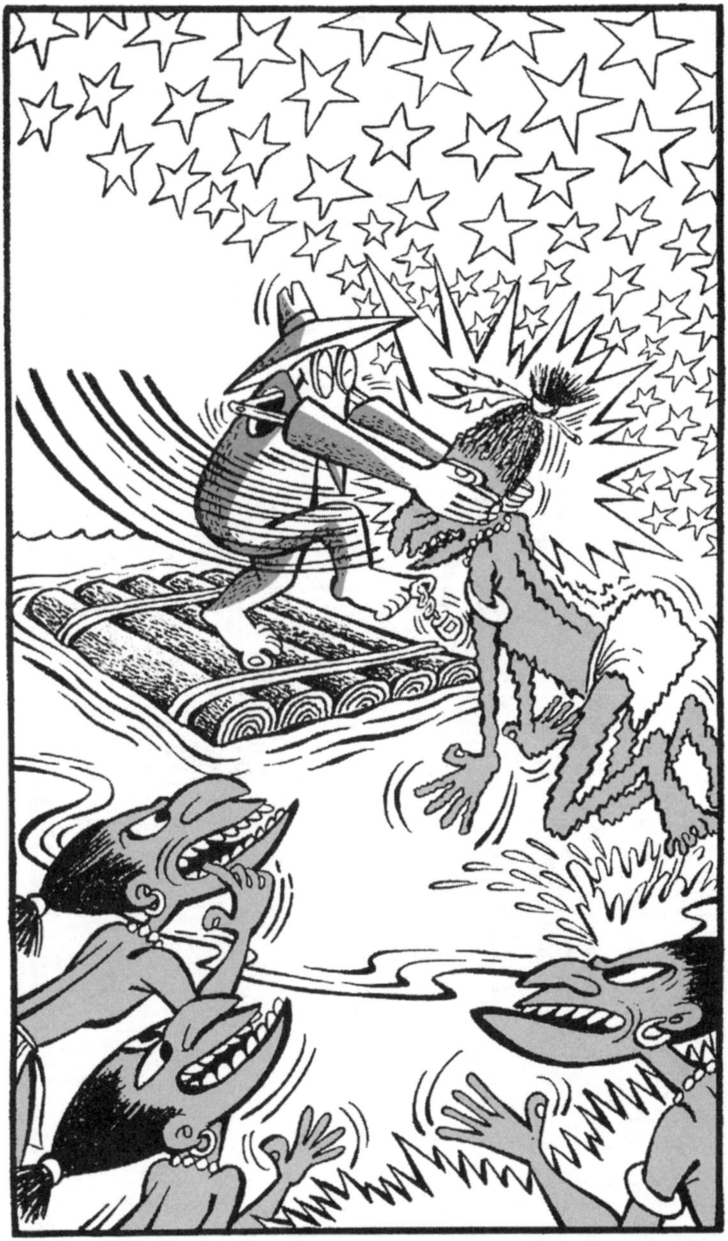

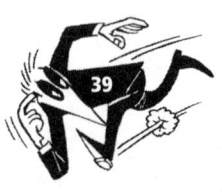

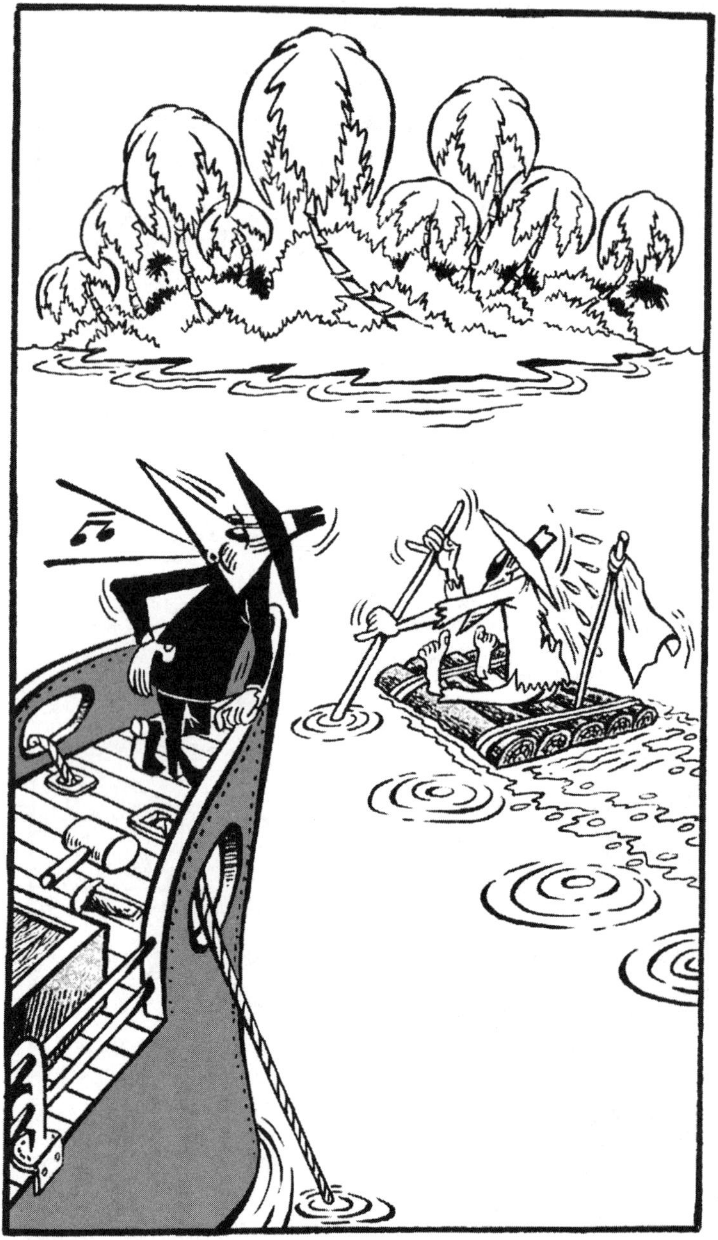

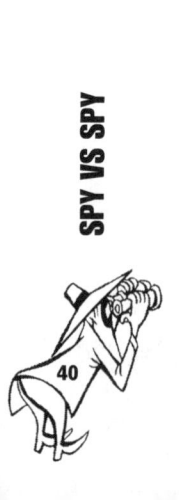

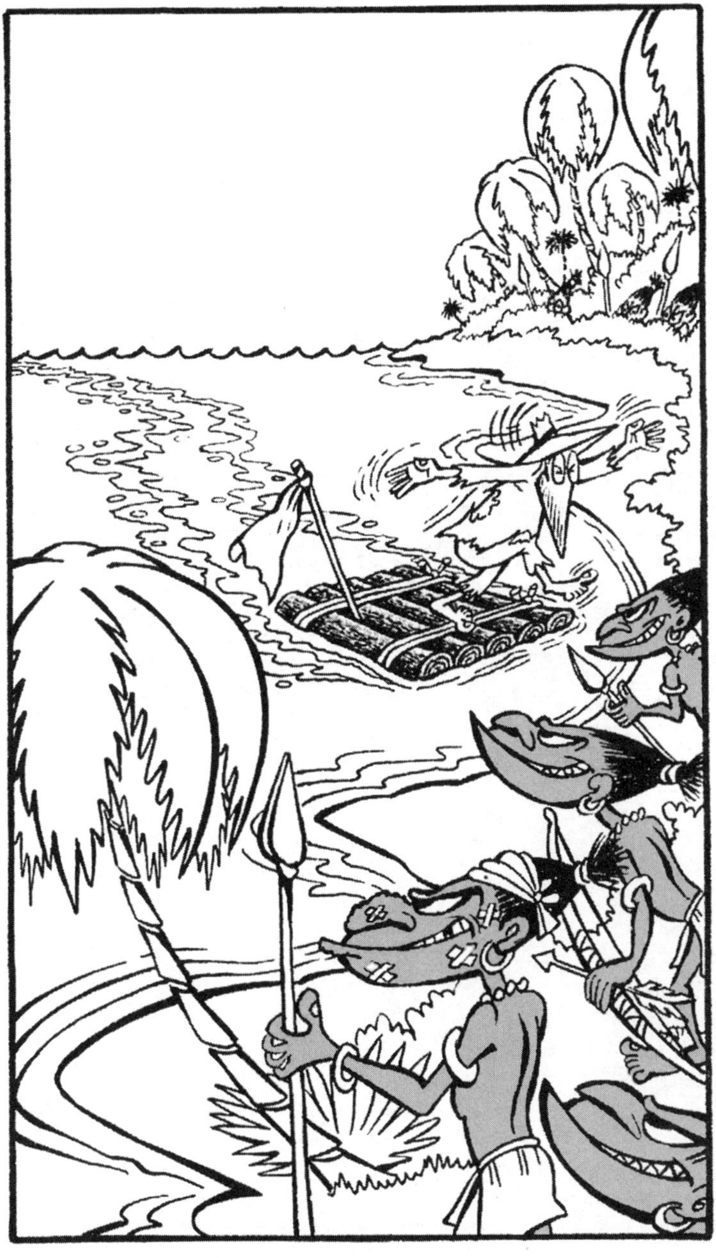

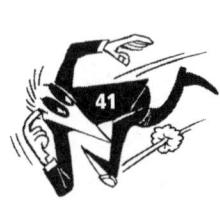

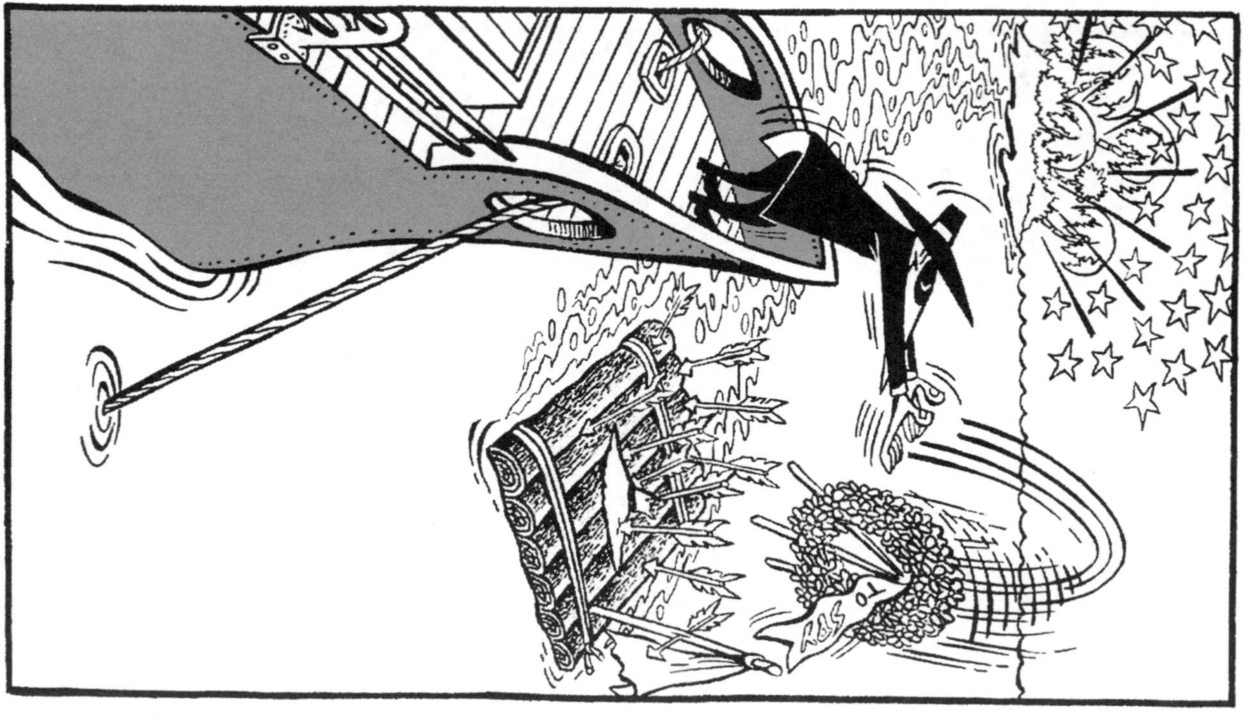
TO SPY

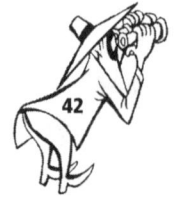

OPERATION: SPELL SHOCK

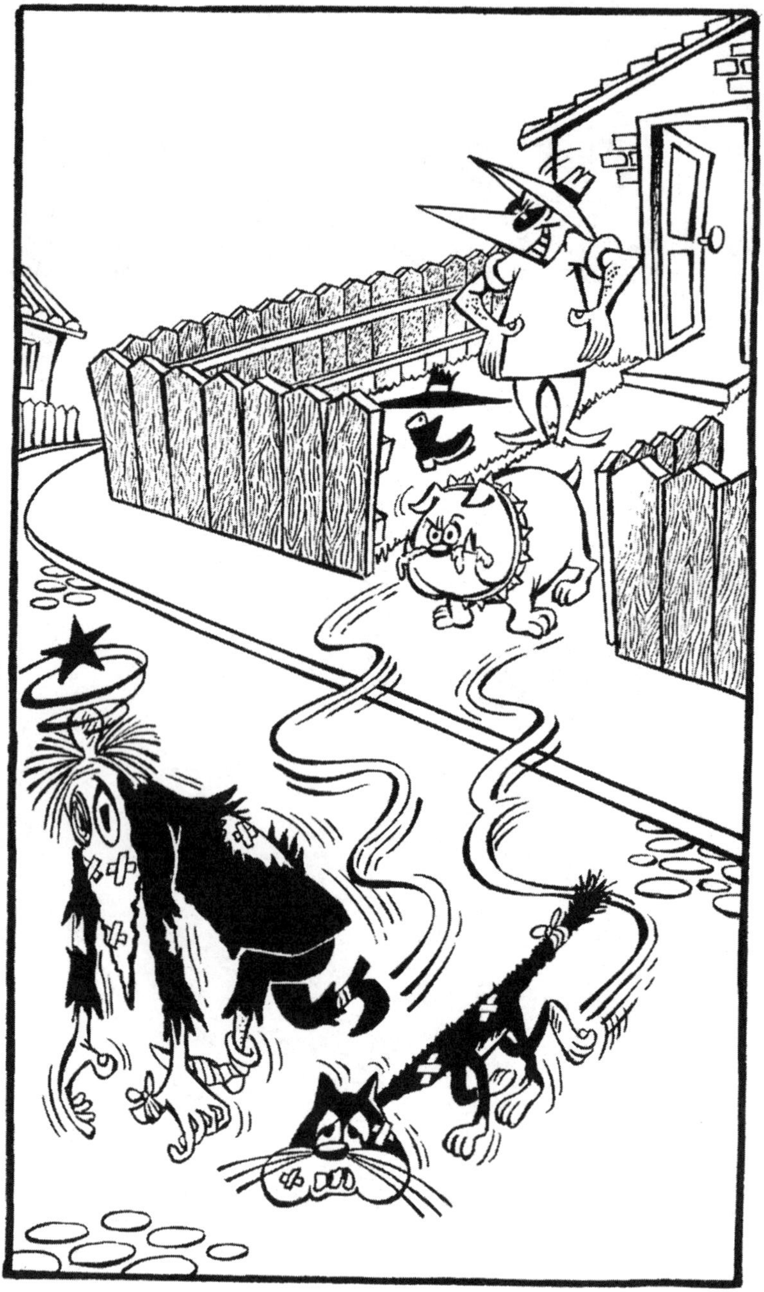

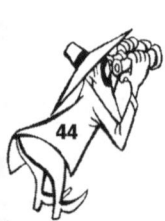

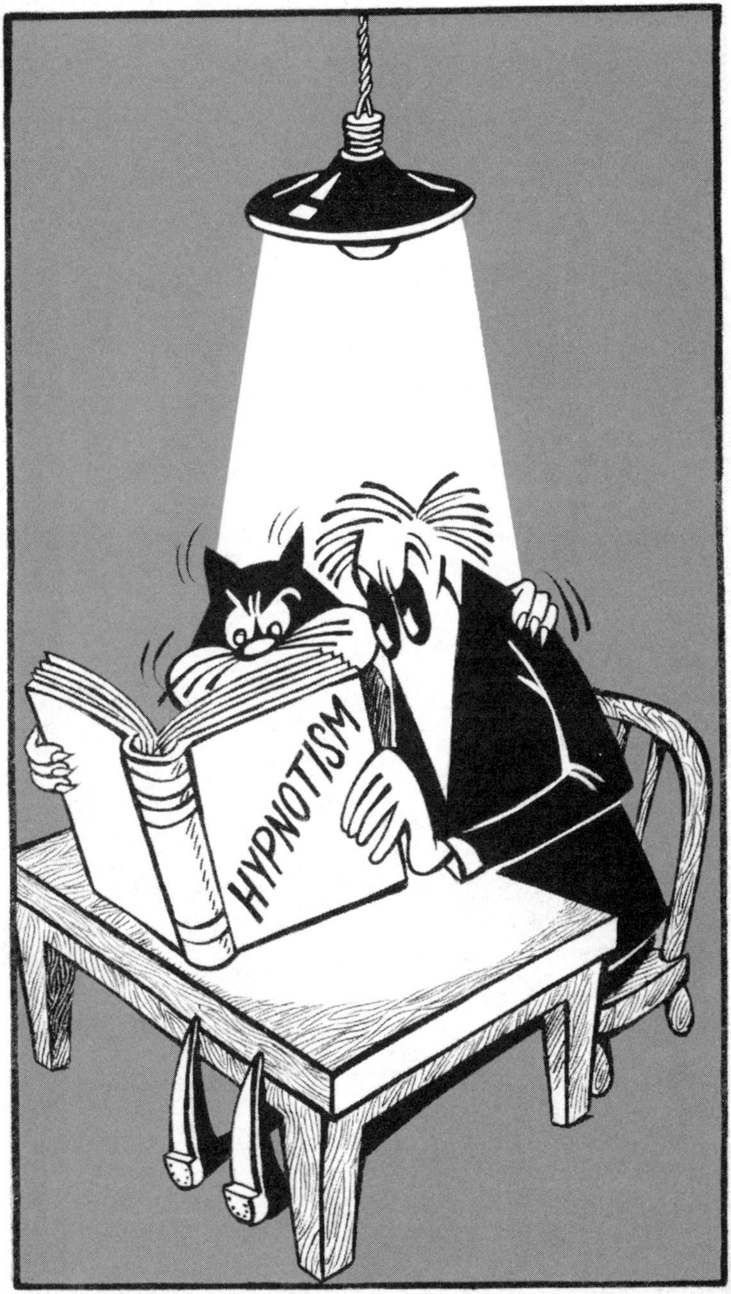
HYPNOTISM

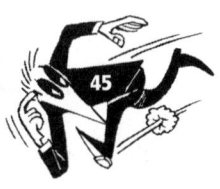

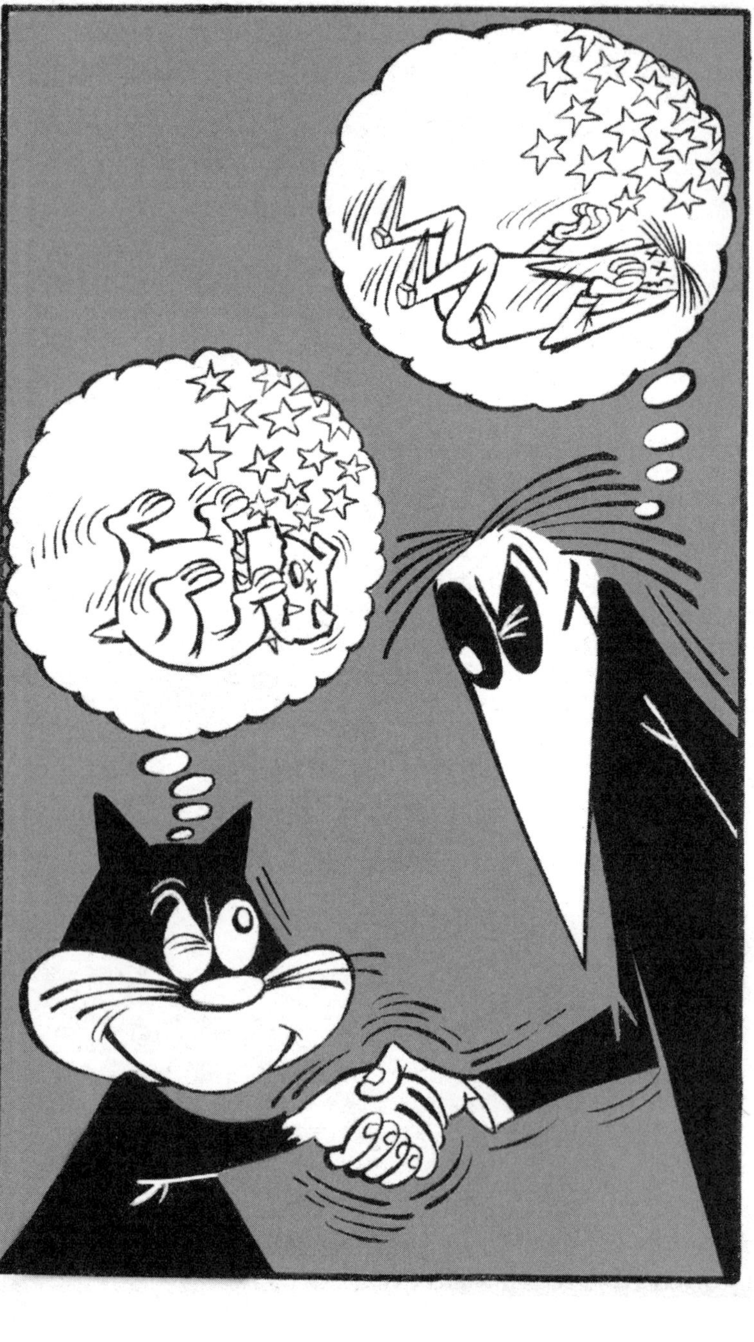

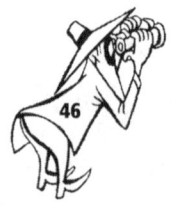

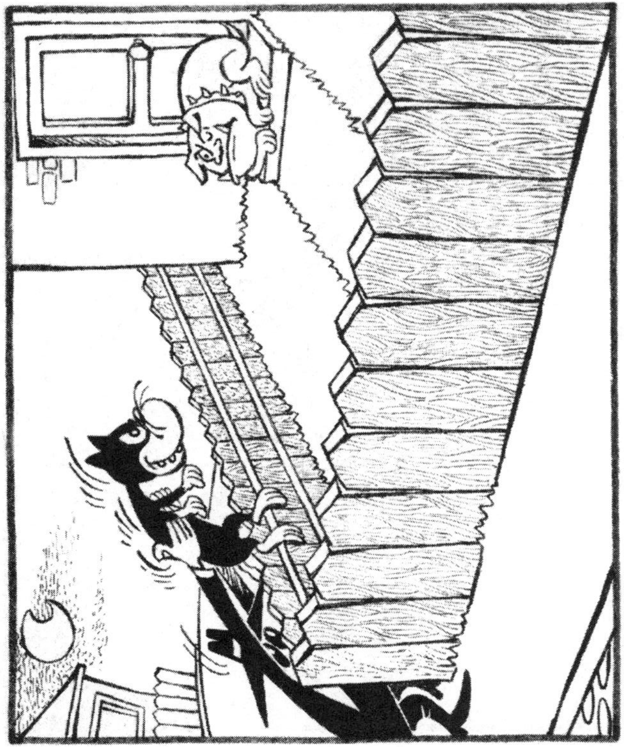

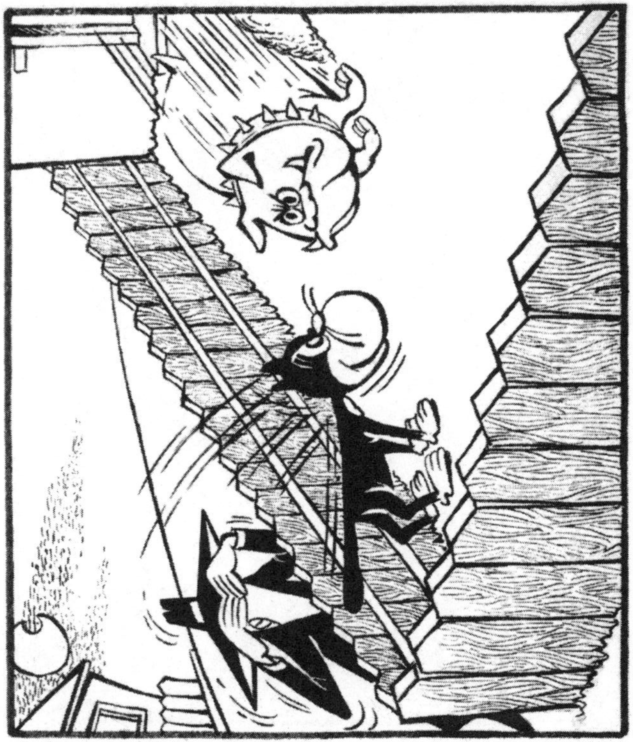

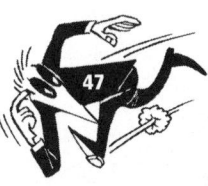

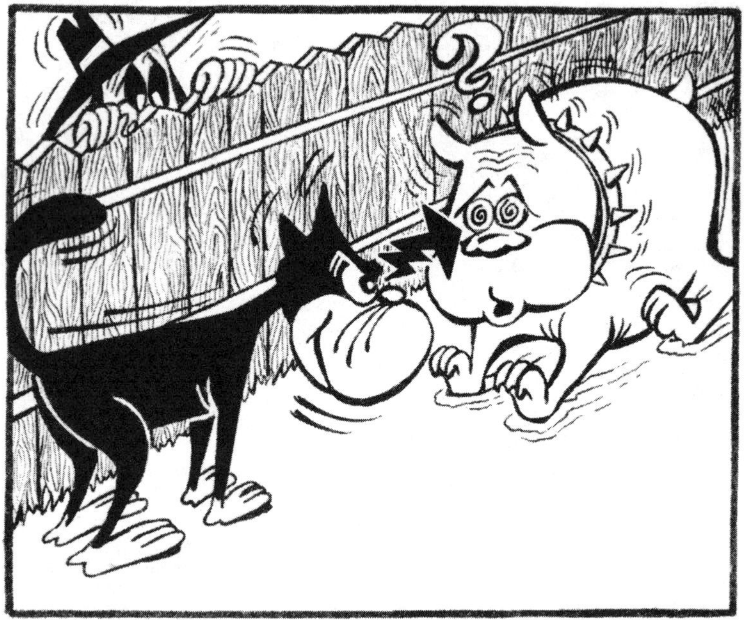

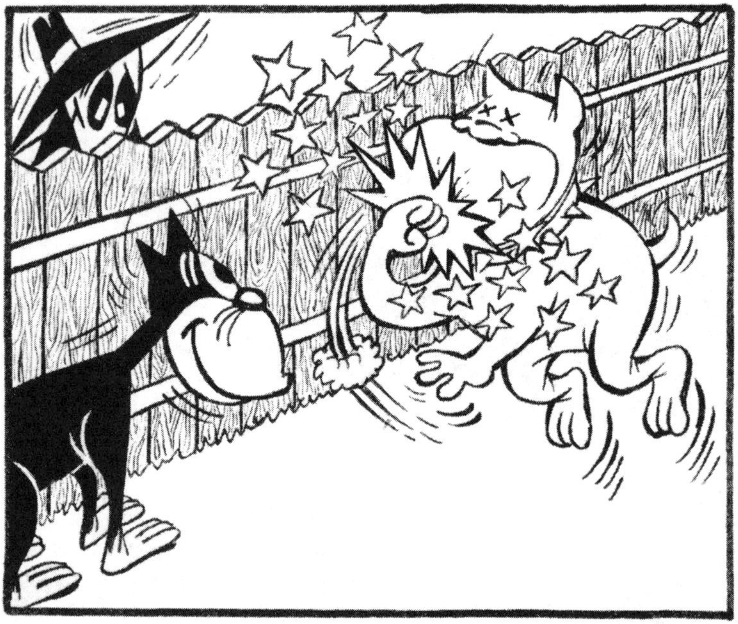

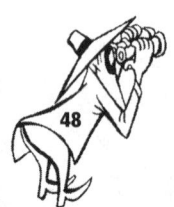

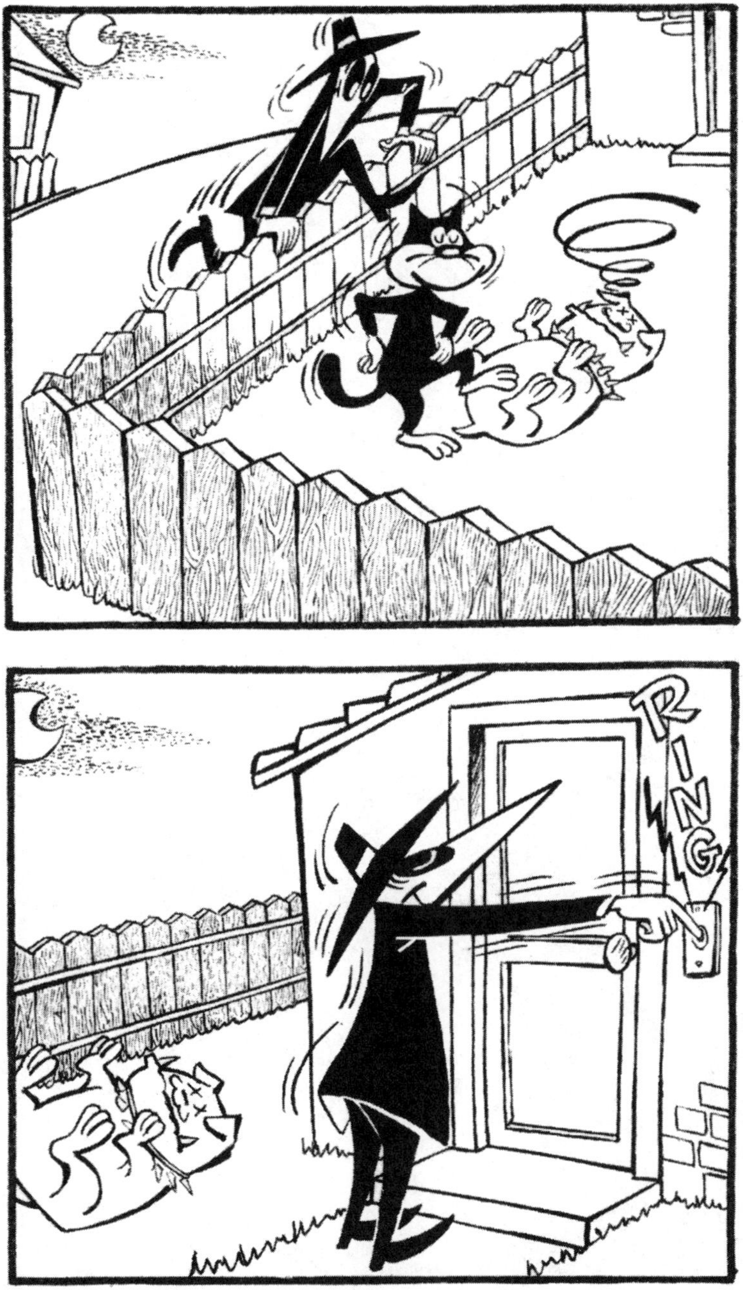
RING

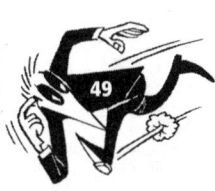

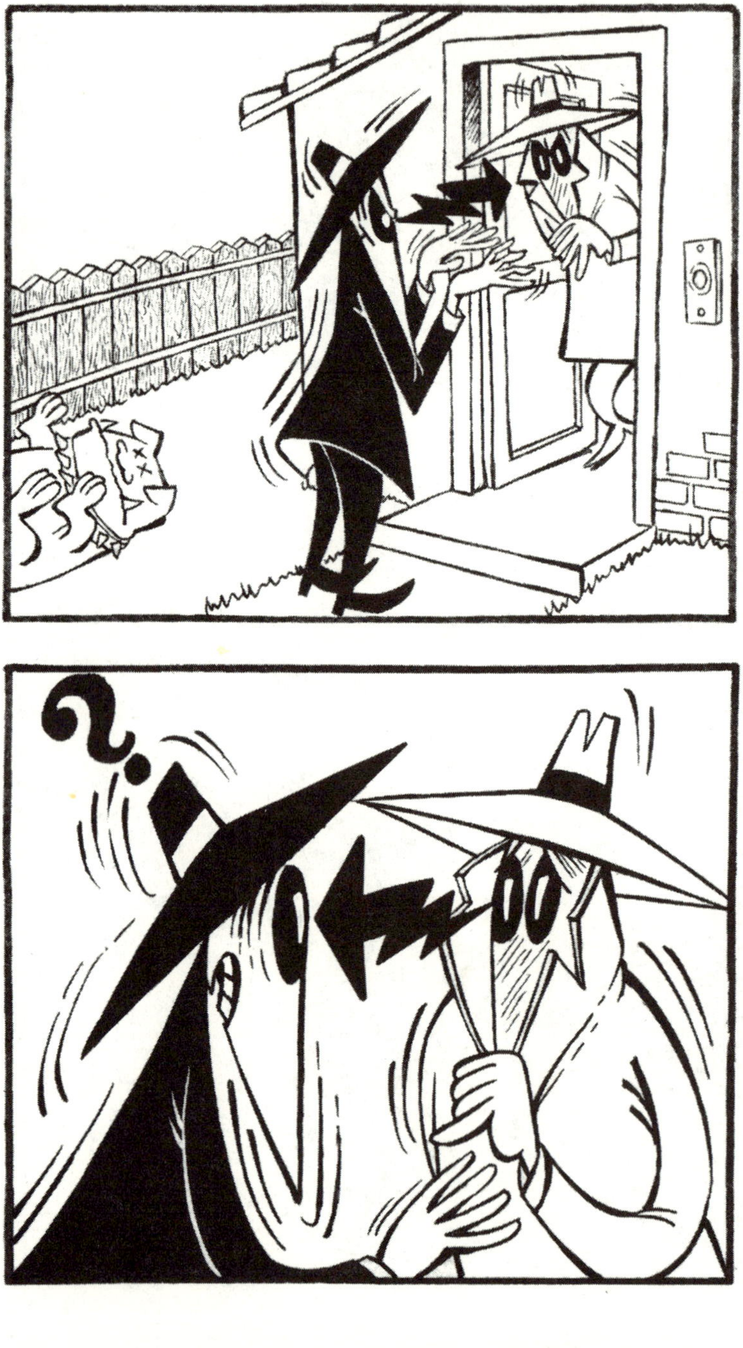

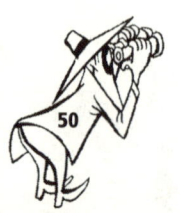

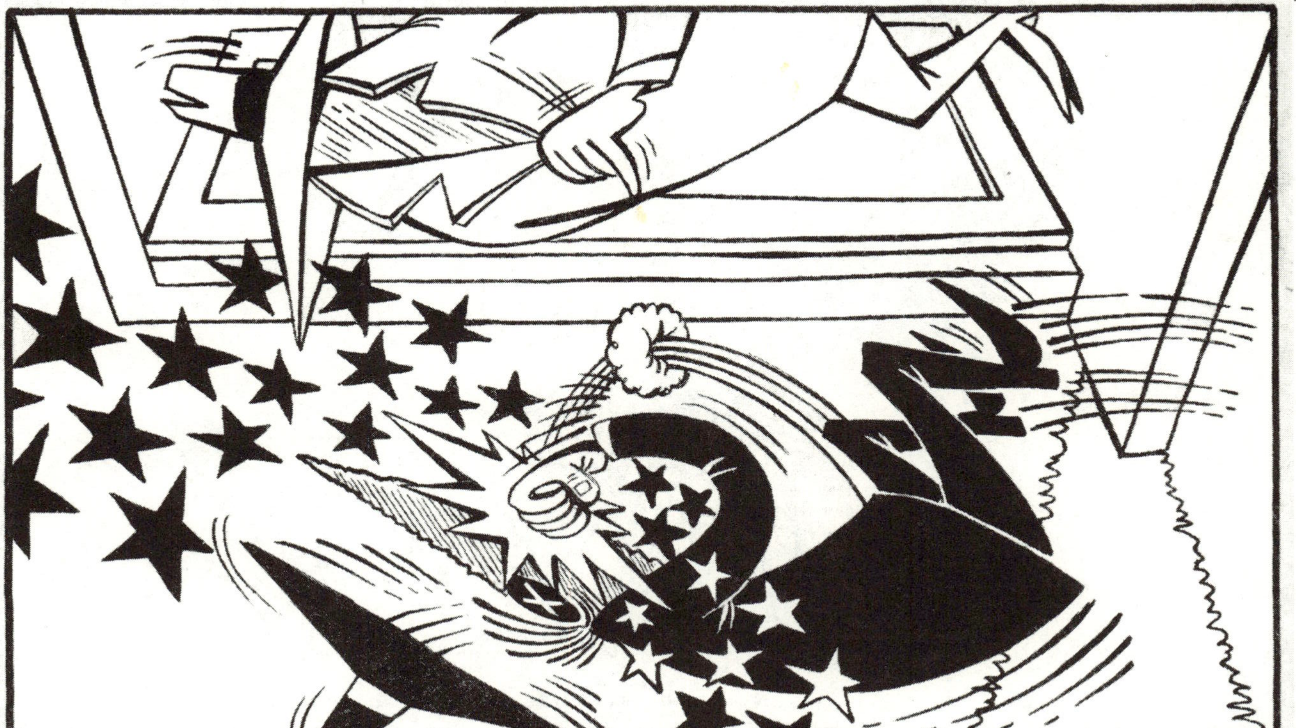

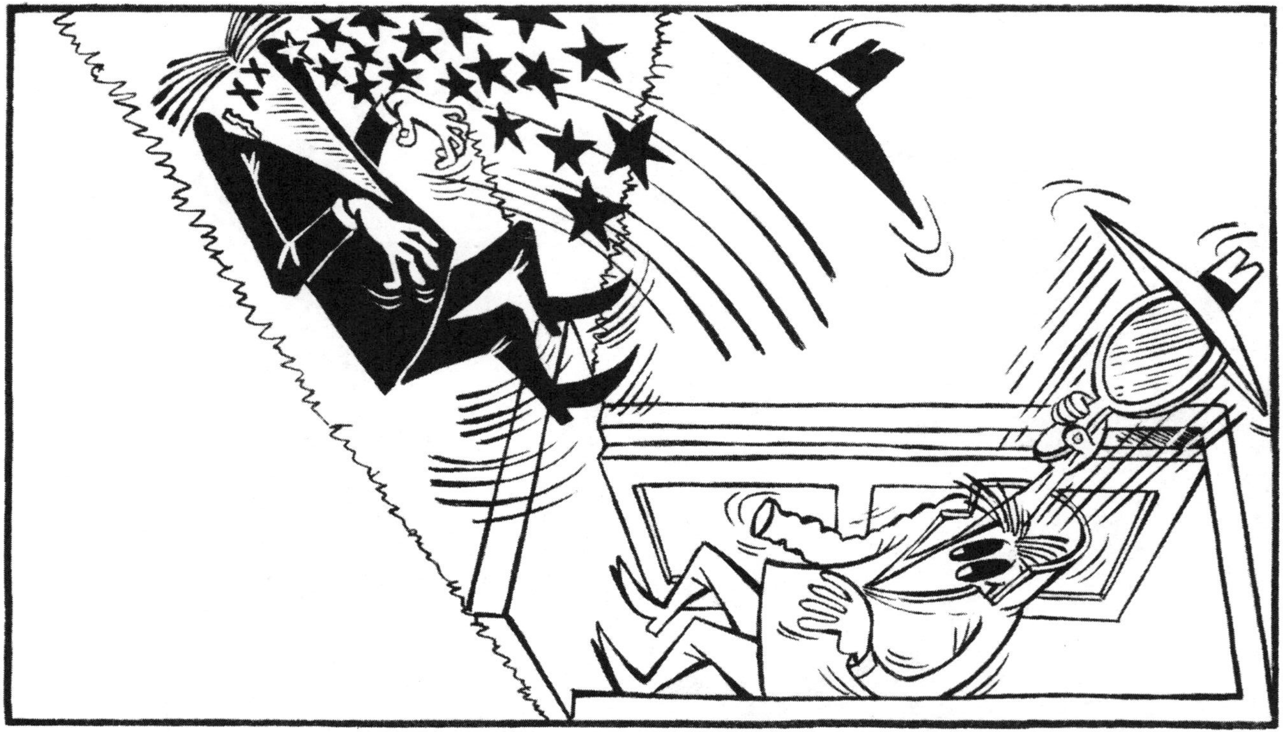

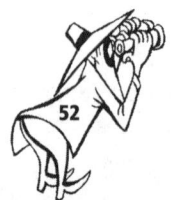

OPERATION: SAFE CONDUCT

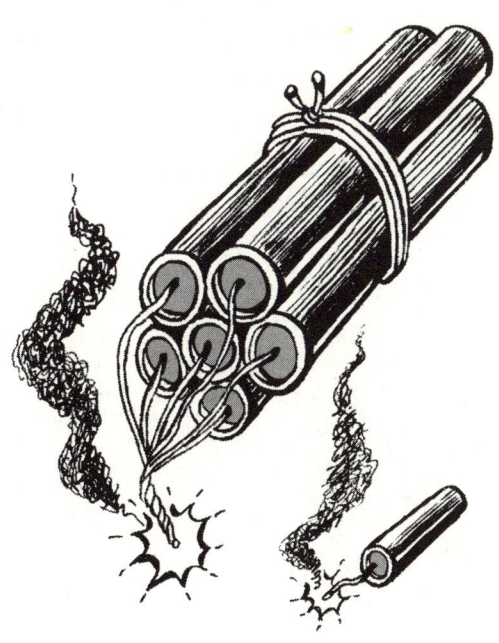

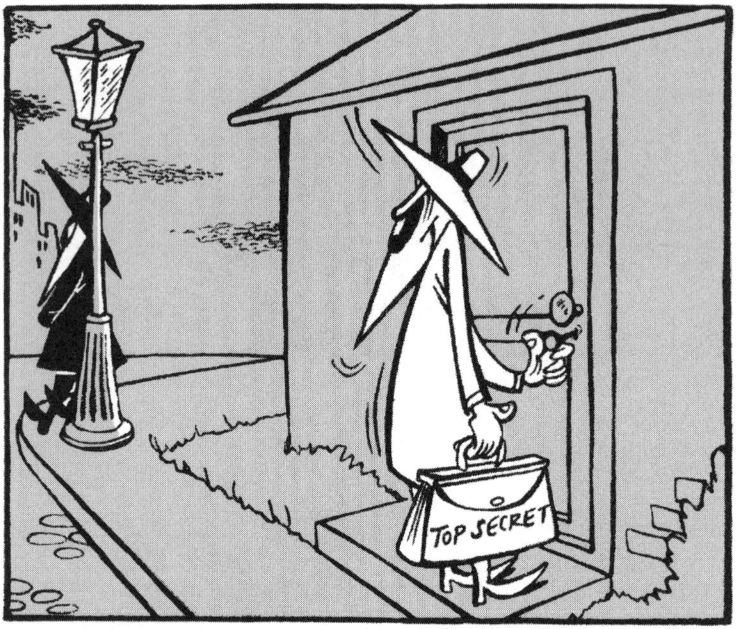
TOP SECRET

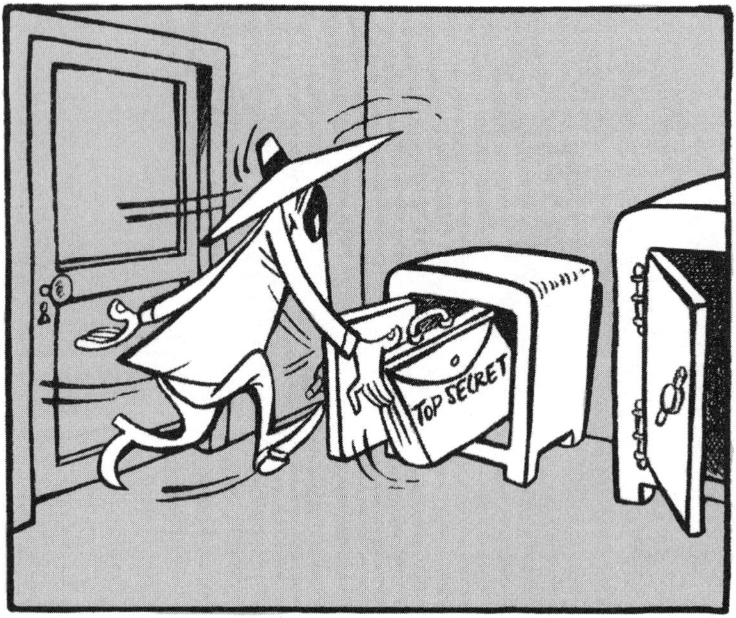
TOP SECRET

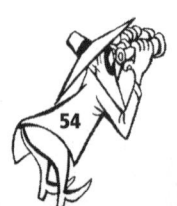

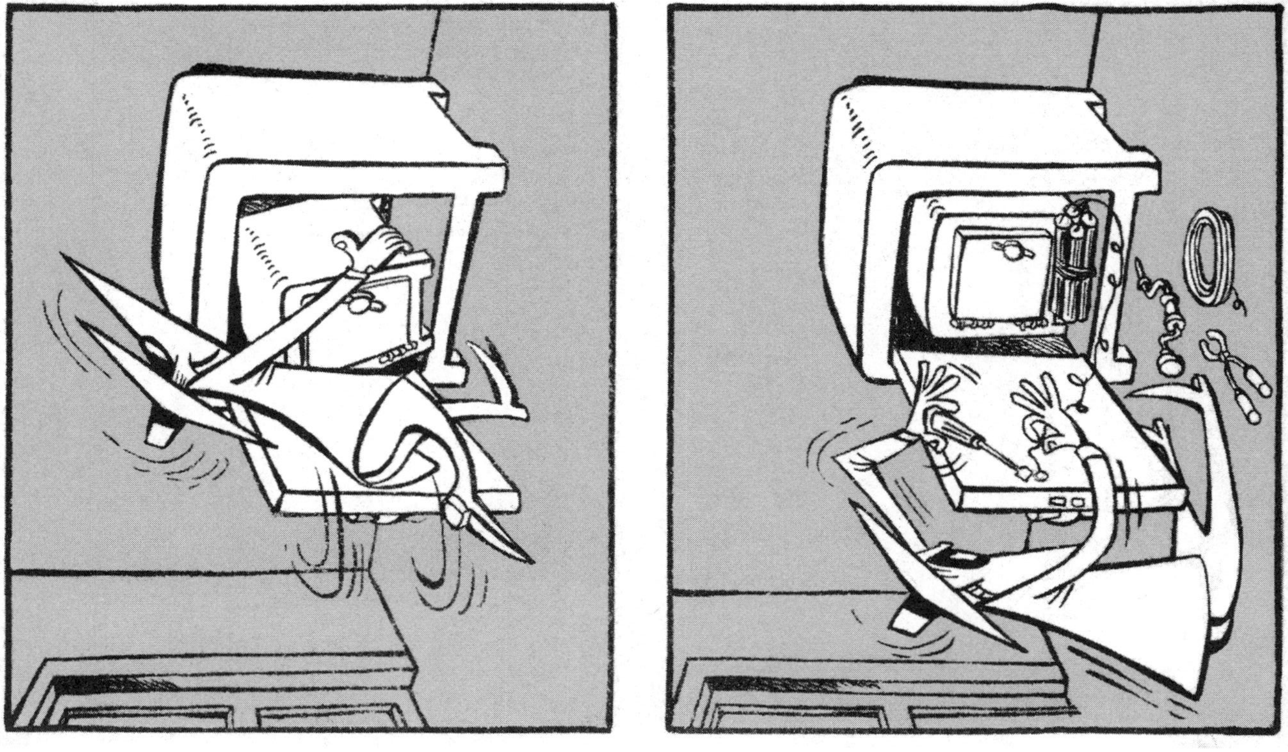

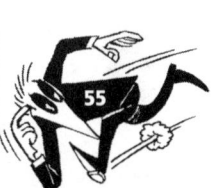

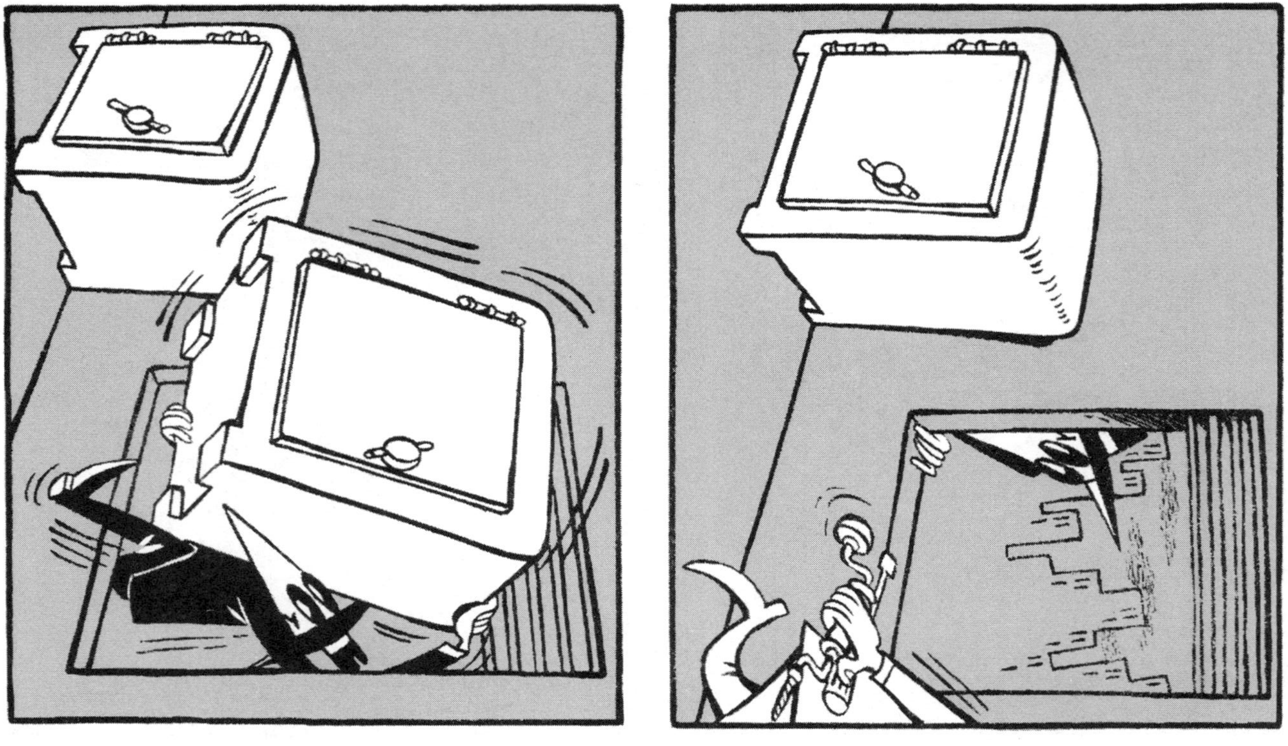

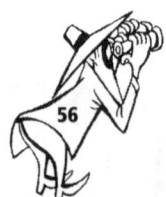

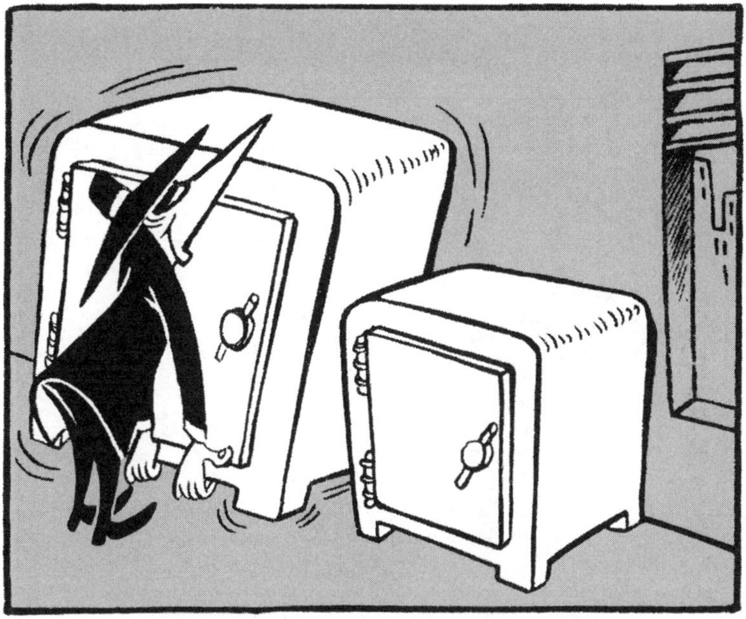

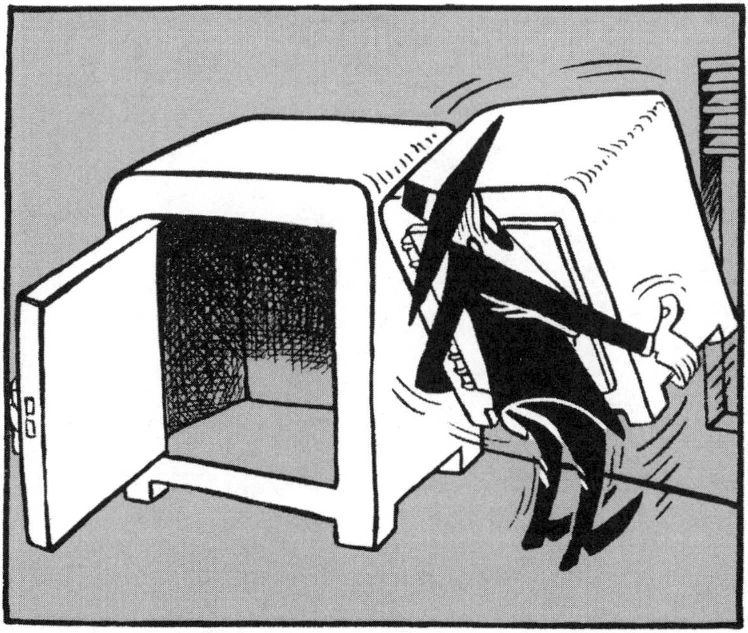

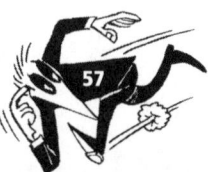

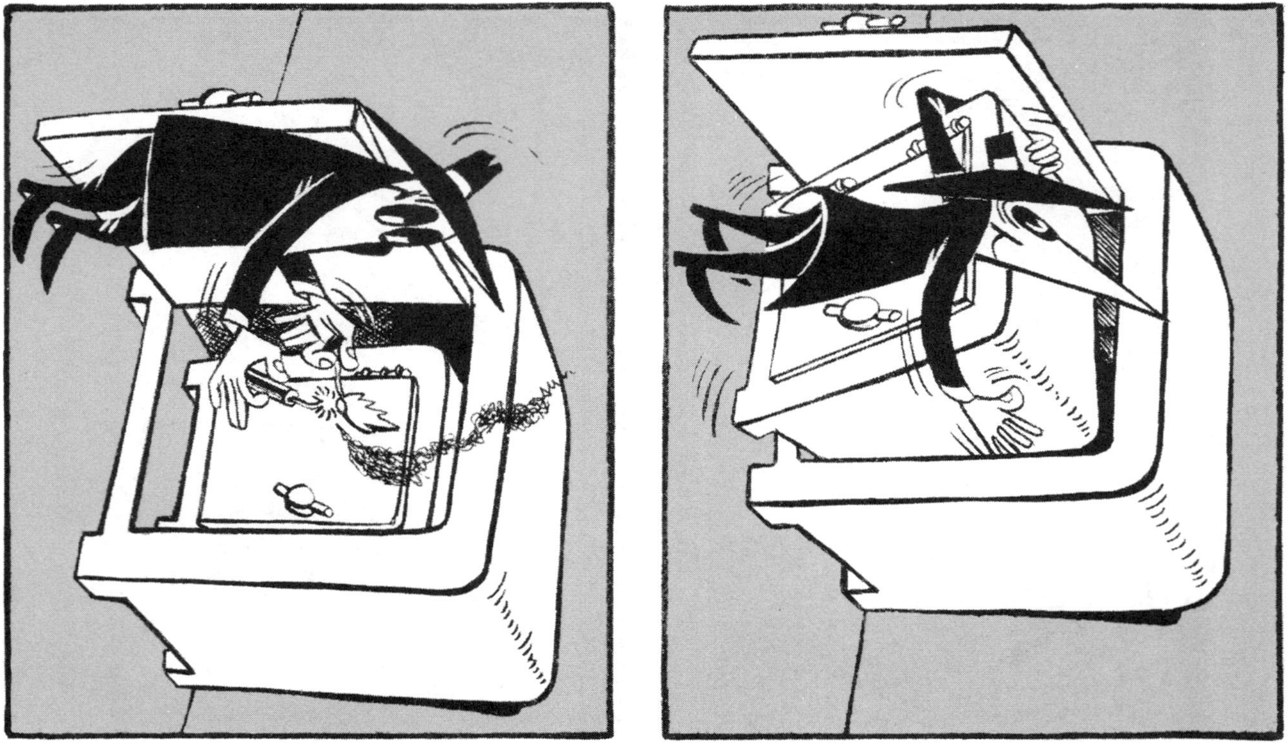

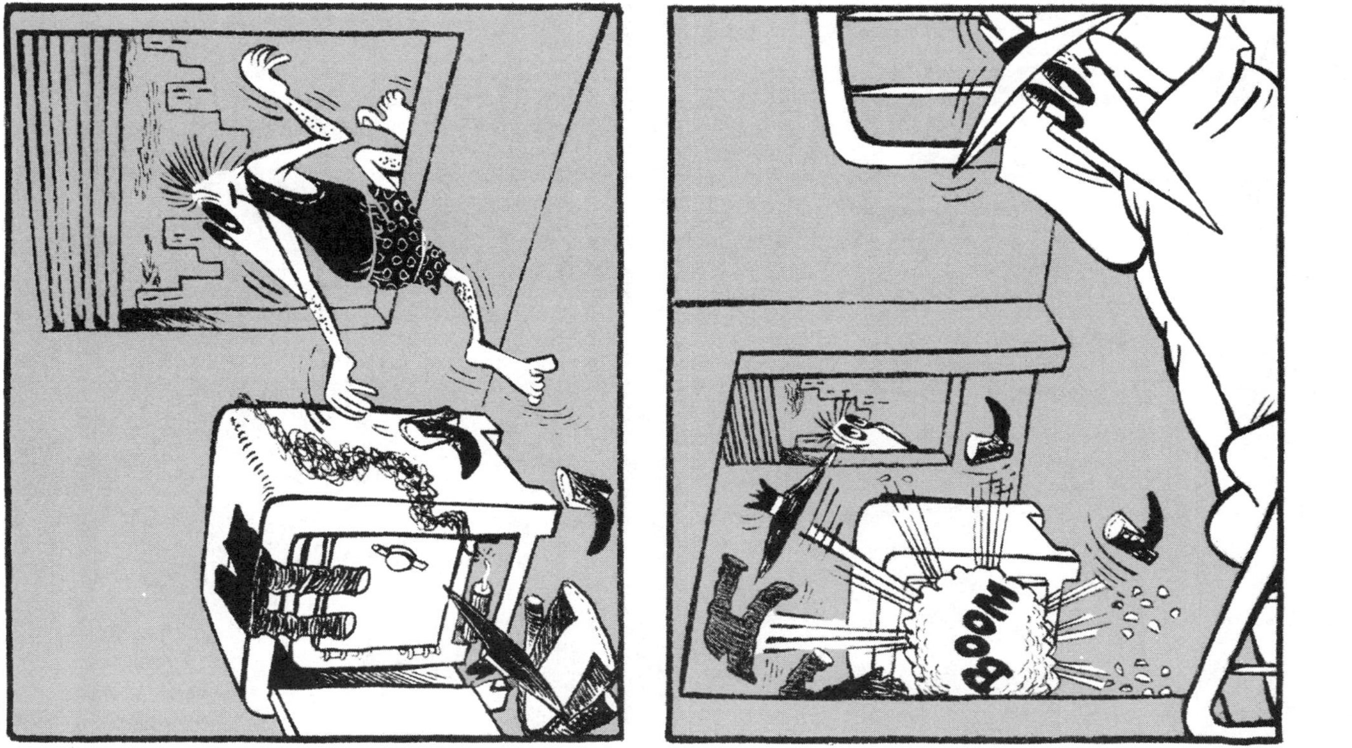
BOOM

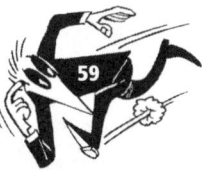

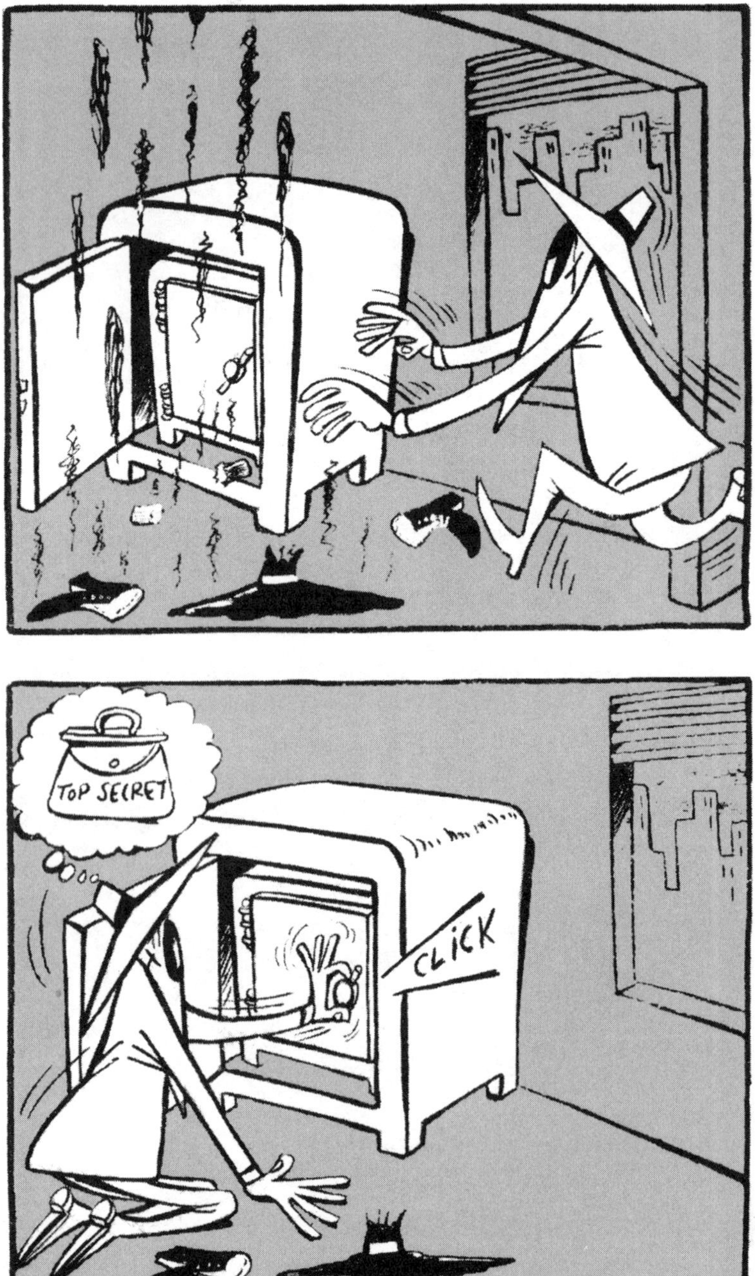
TOP SECRET
CLICK

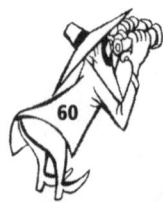

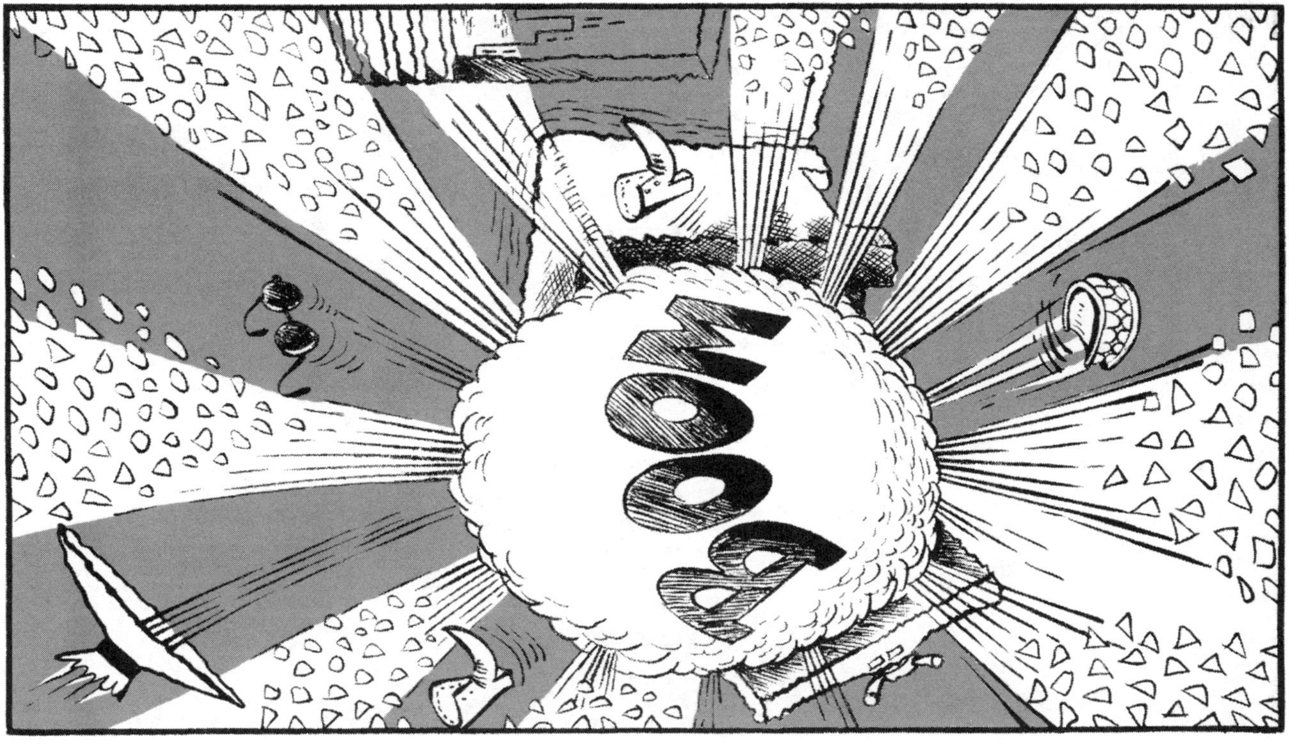
BOOM

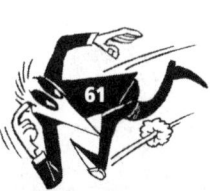

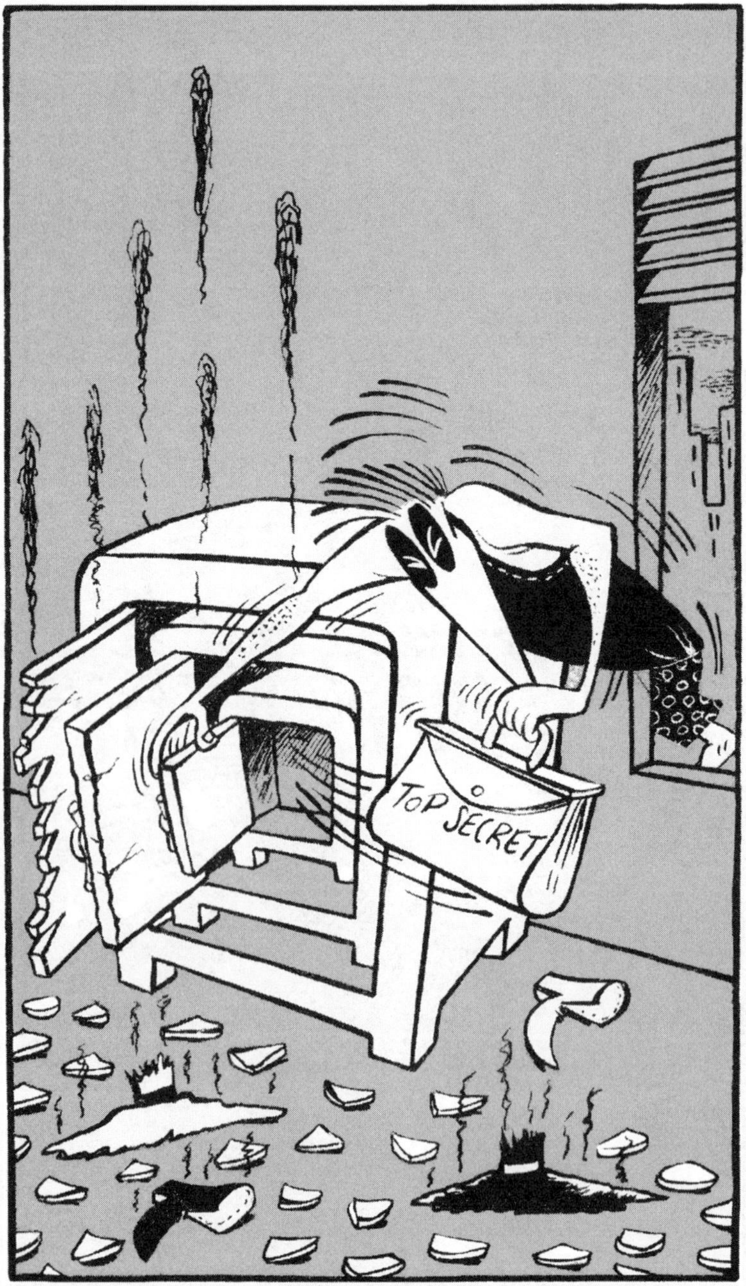
TOP SECRET

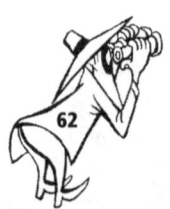

OPERATION: TROJAN HORSEPLAY

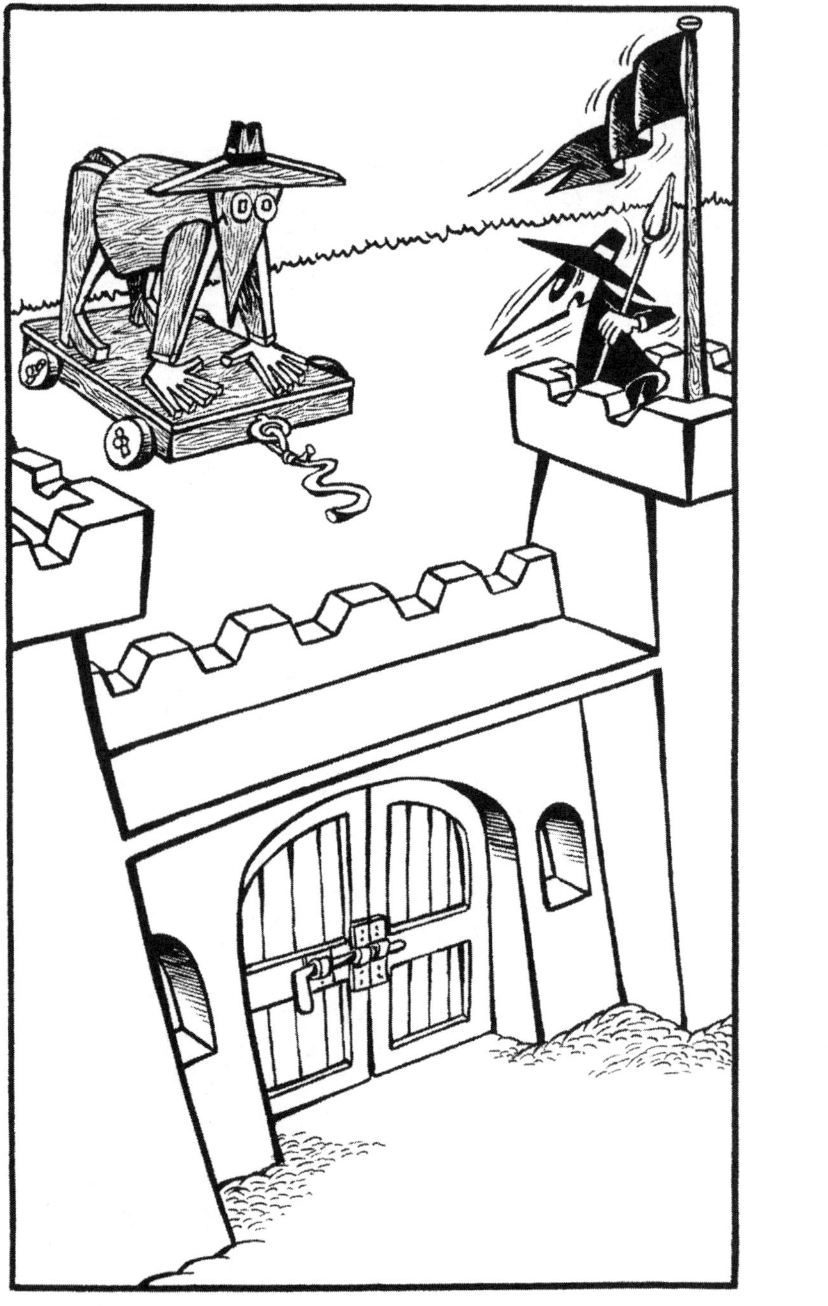

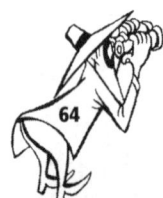

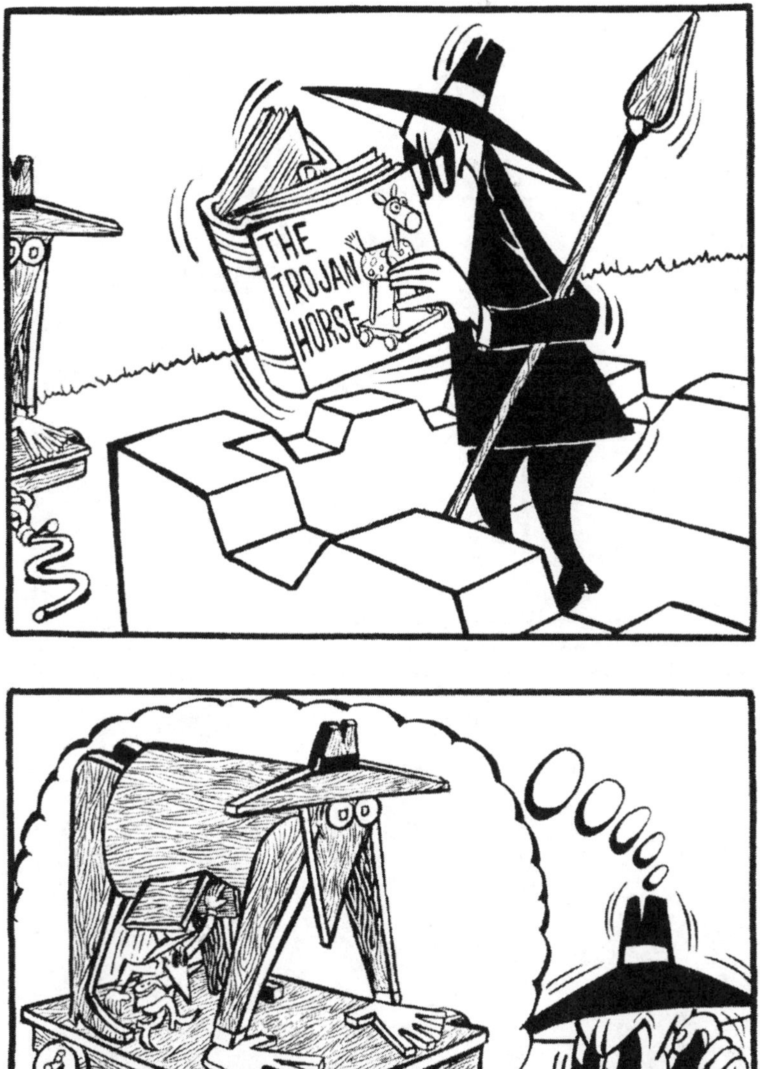
THE TROJAN HORSE

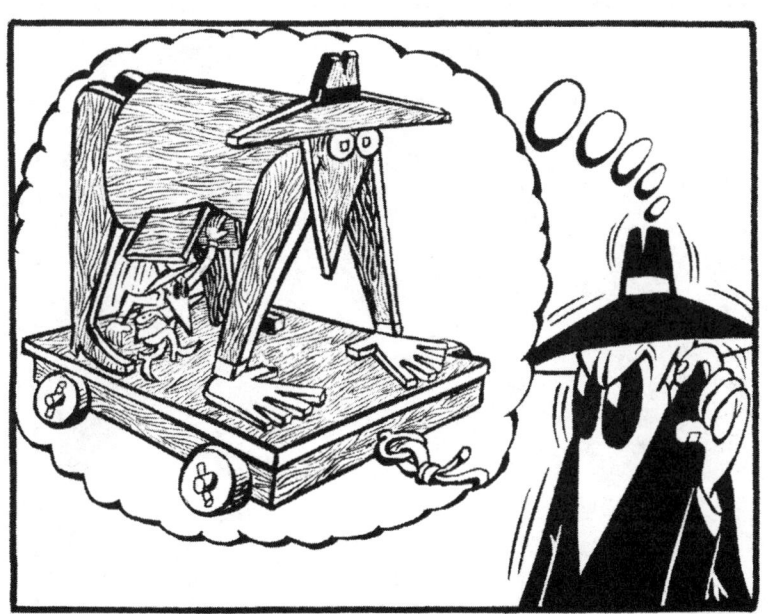

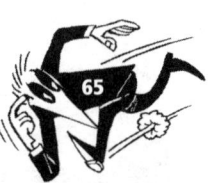

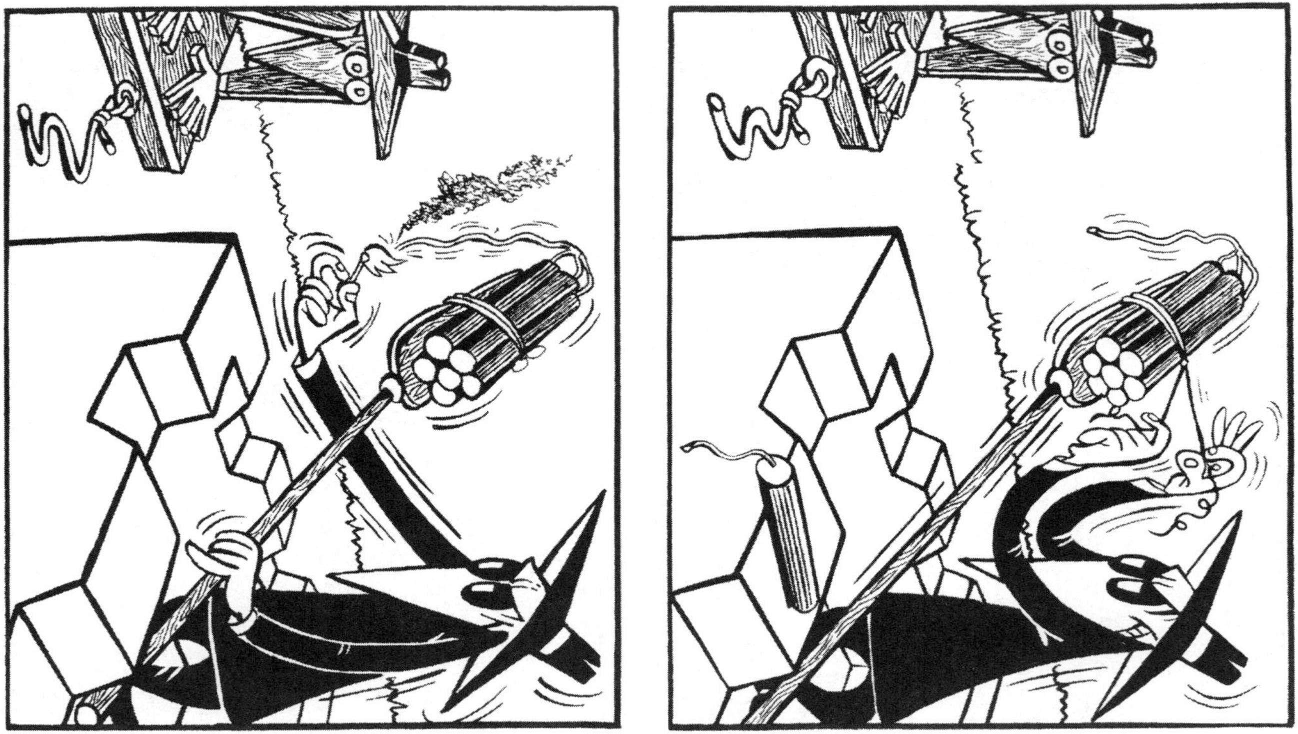

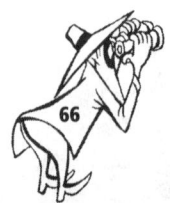

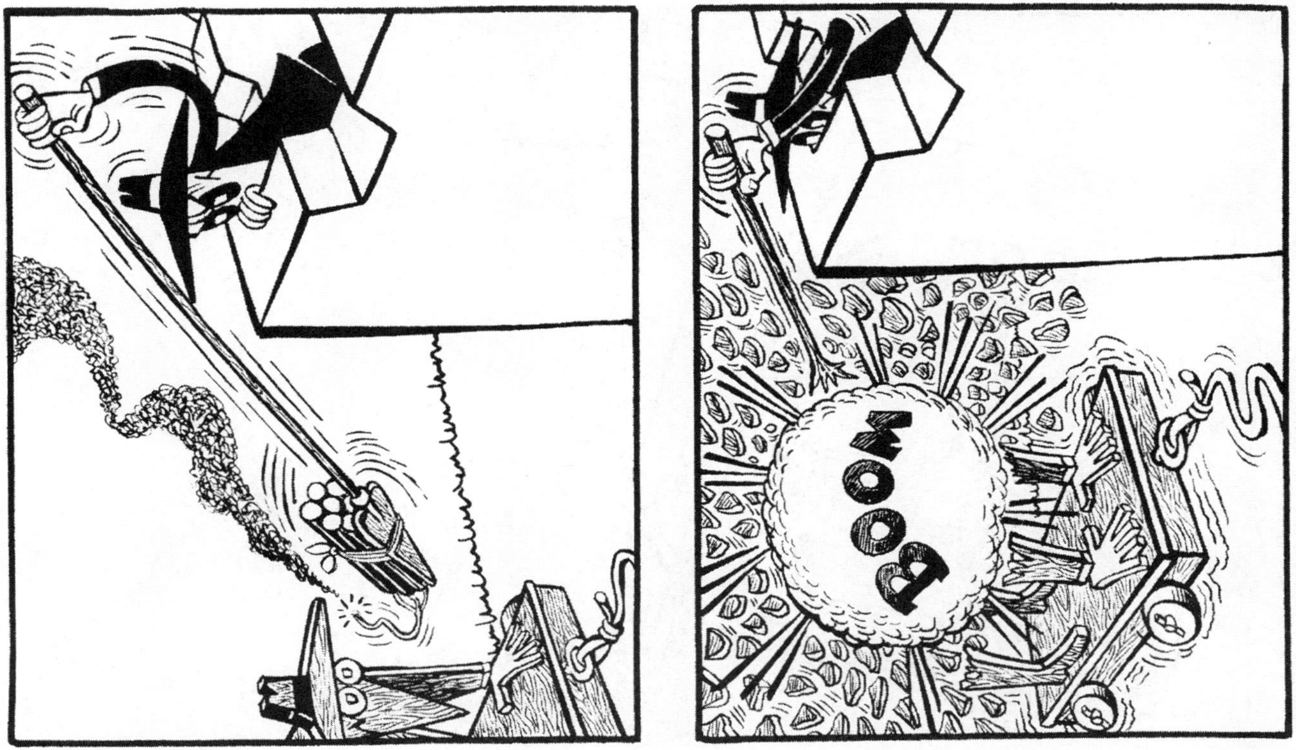
BOOM

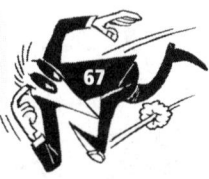

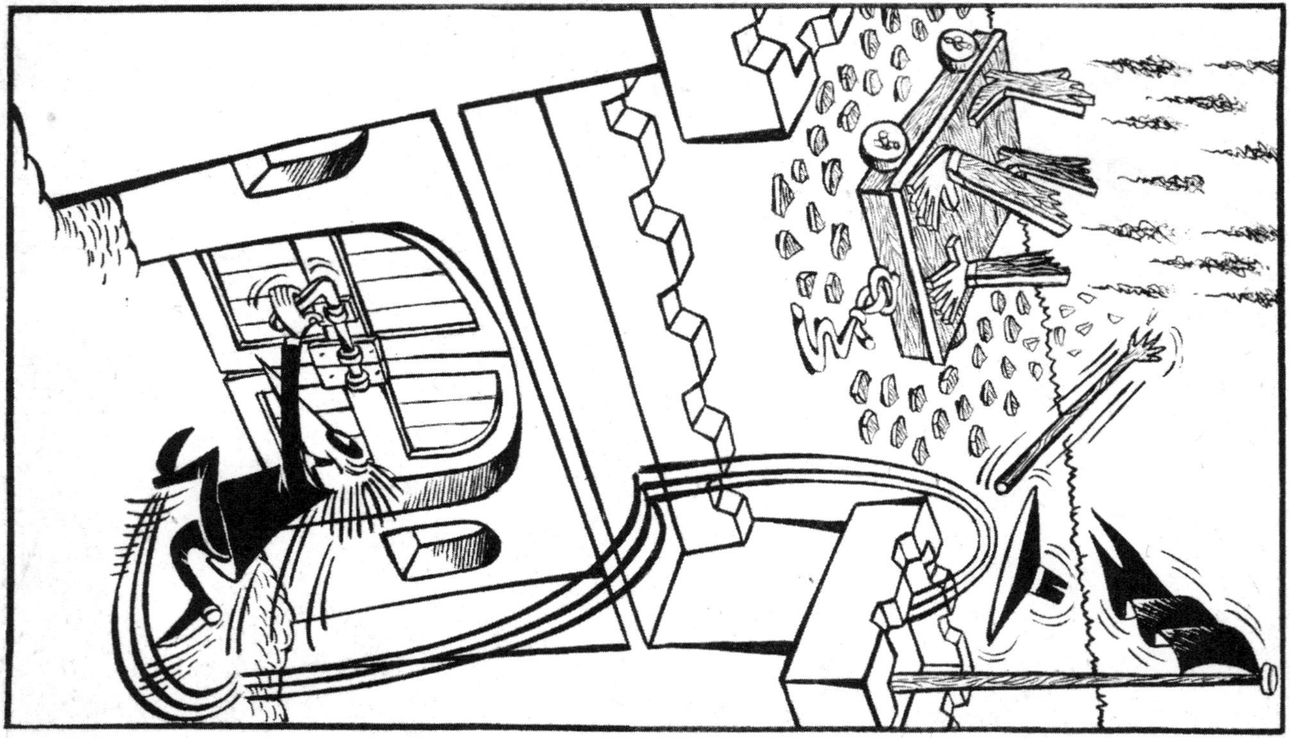

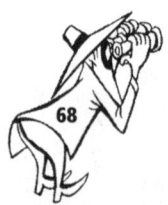

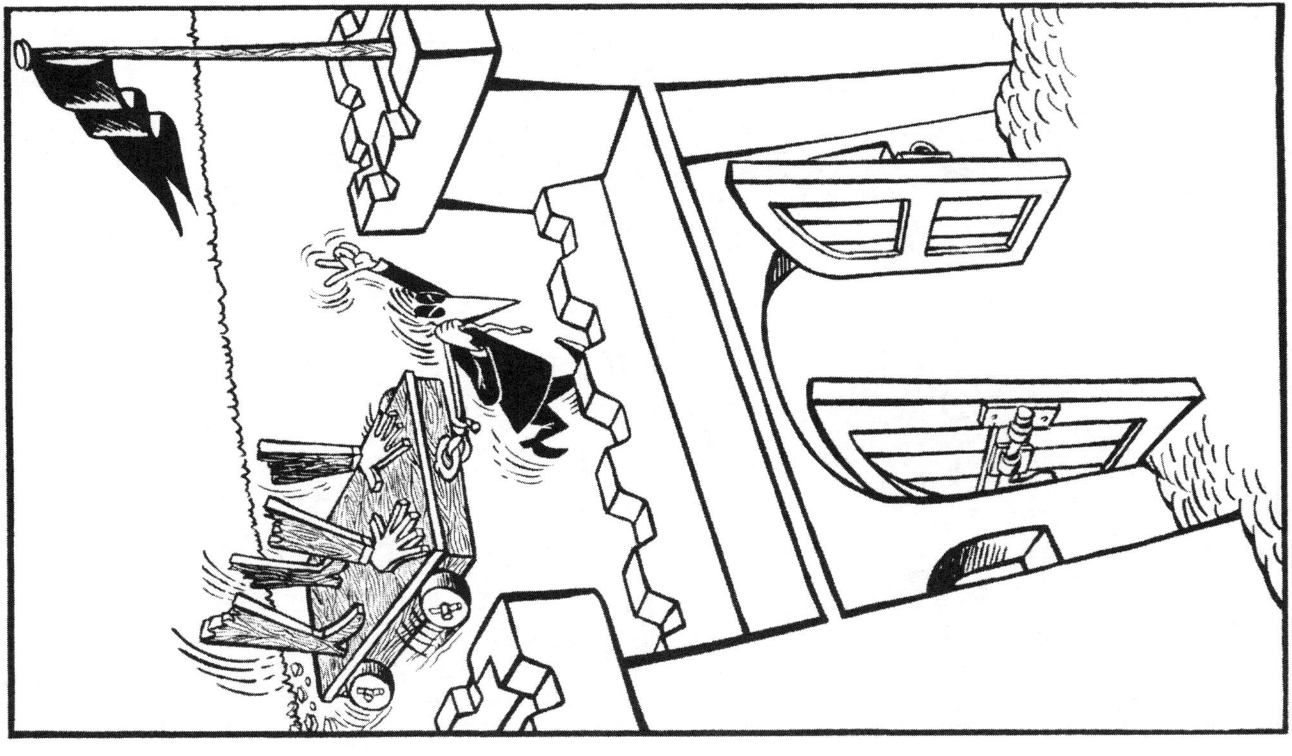

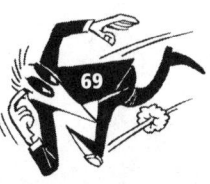

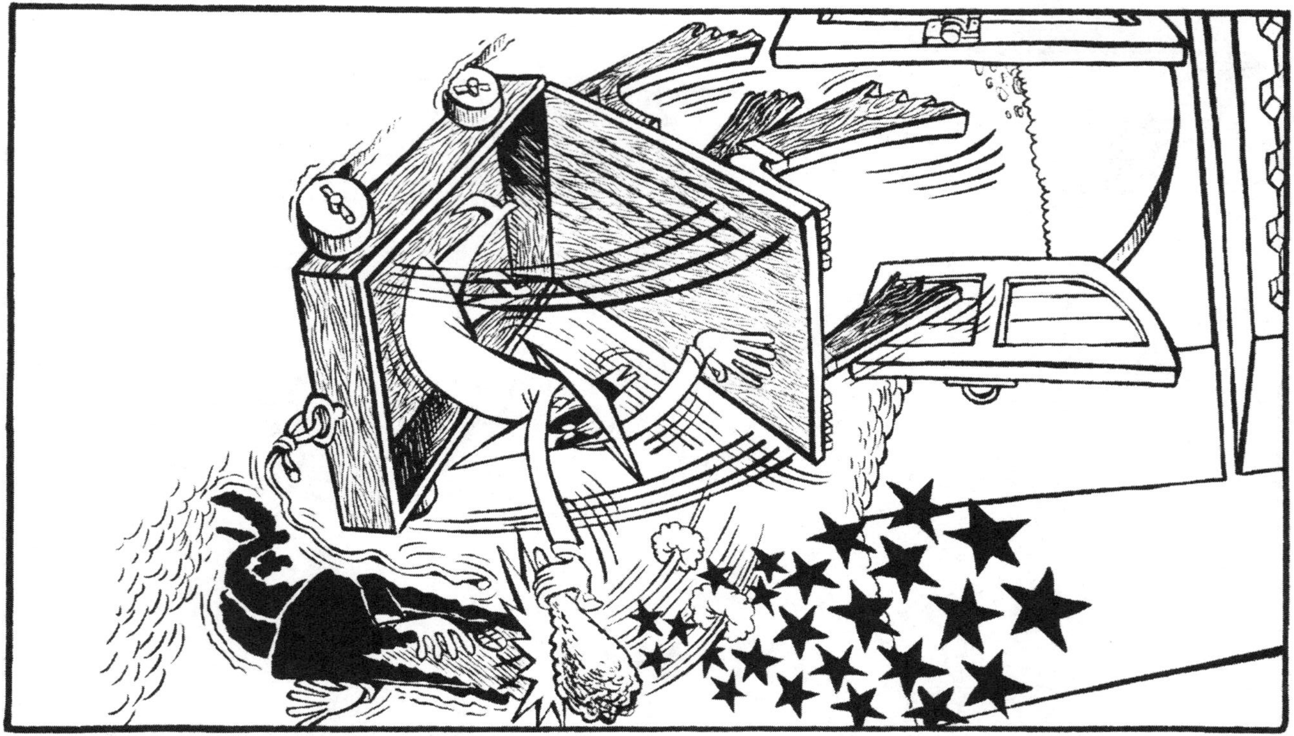

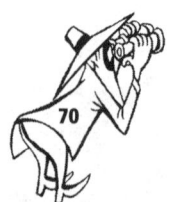

OPERATION: MOUTH TRAP

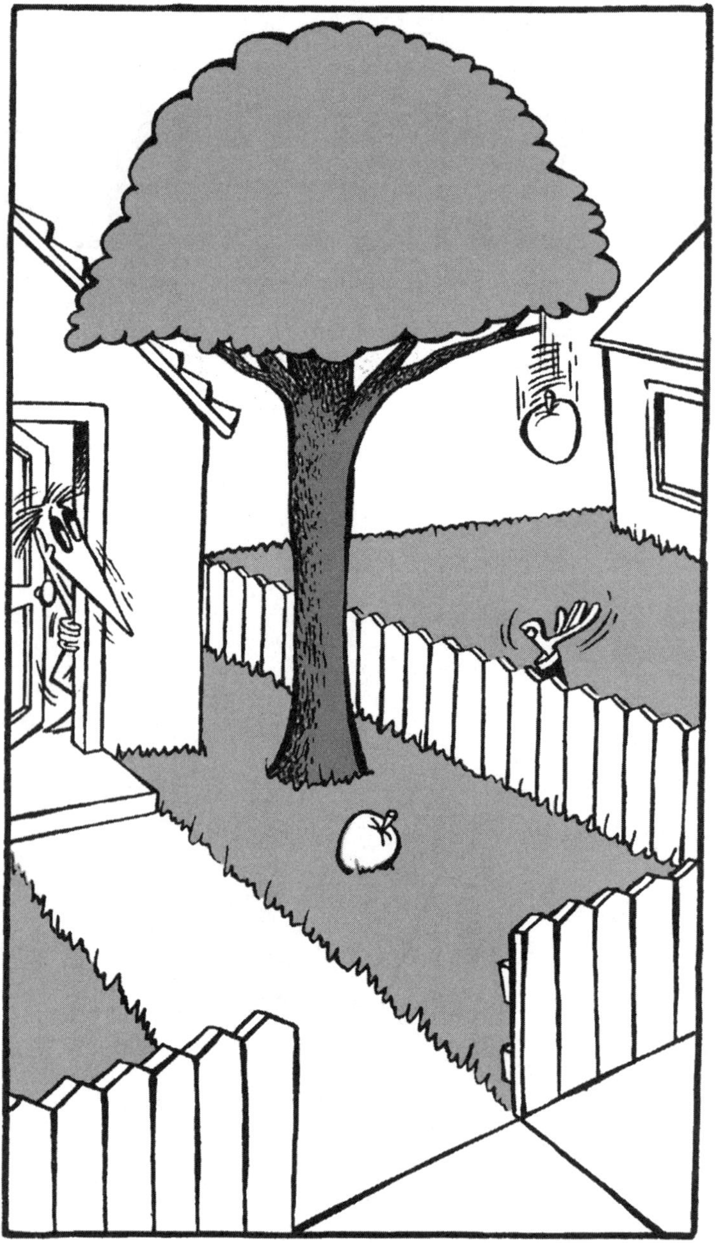

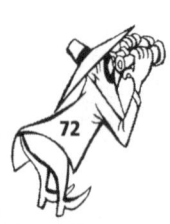

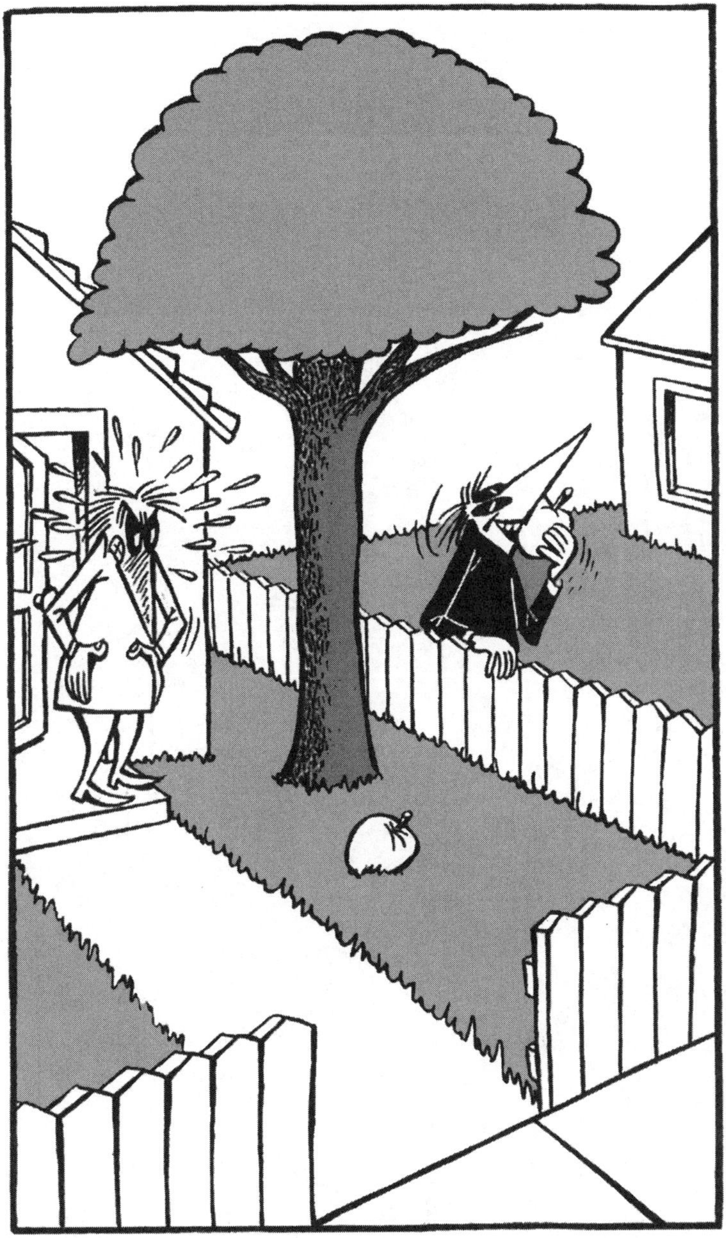

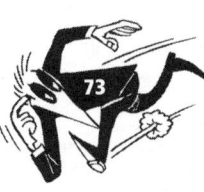

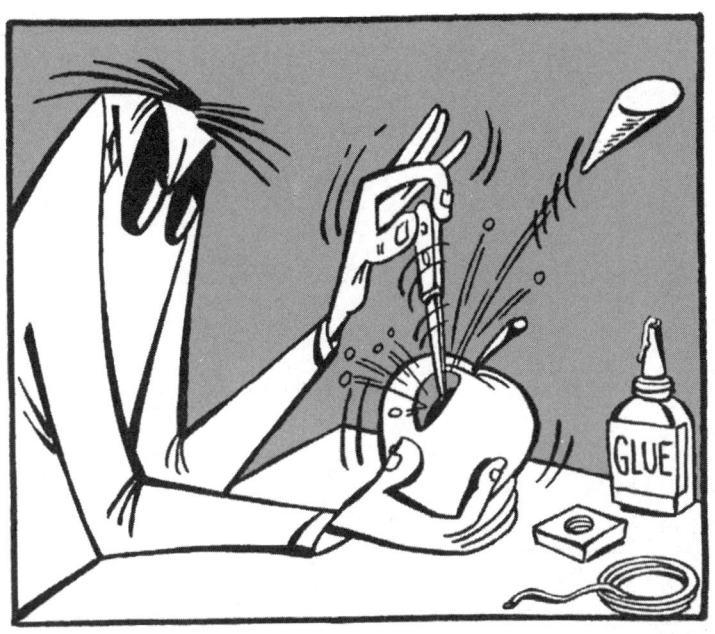
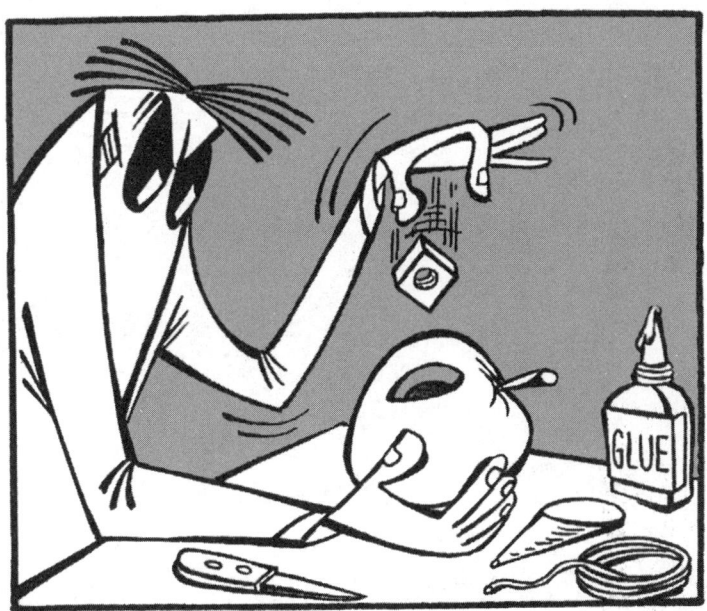

OPERATION: MOUTH TRAP

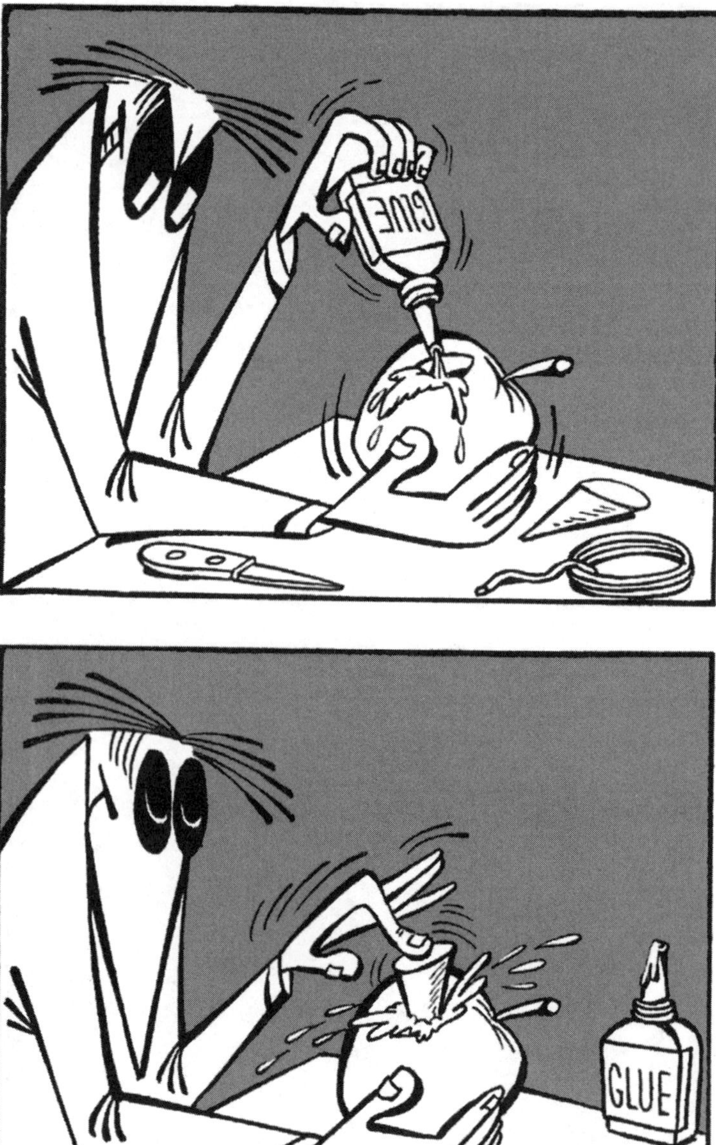
GLUE
GLUE

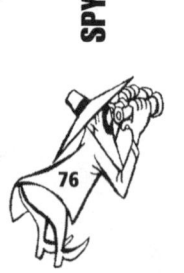

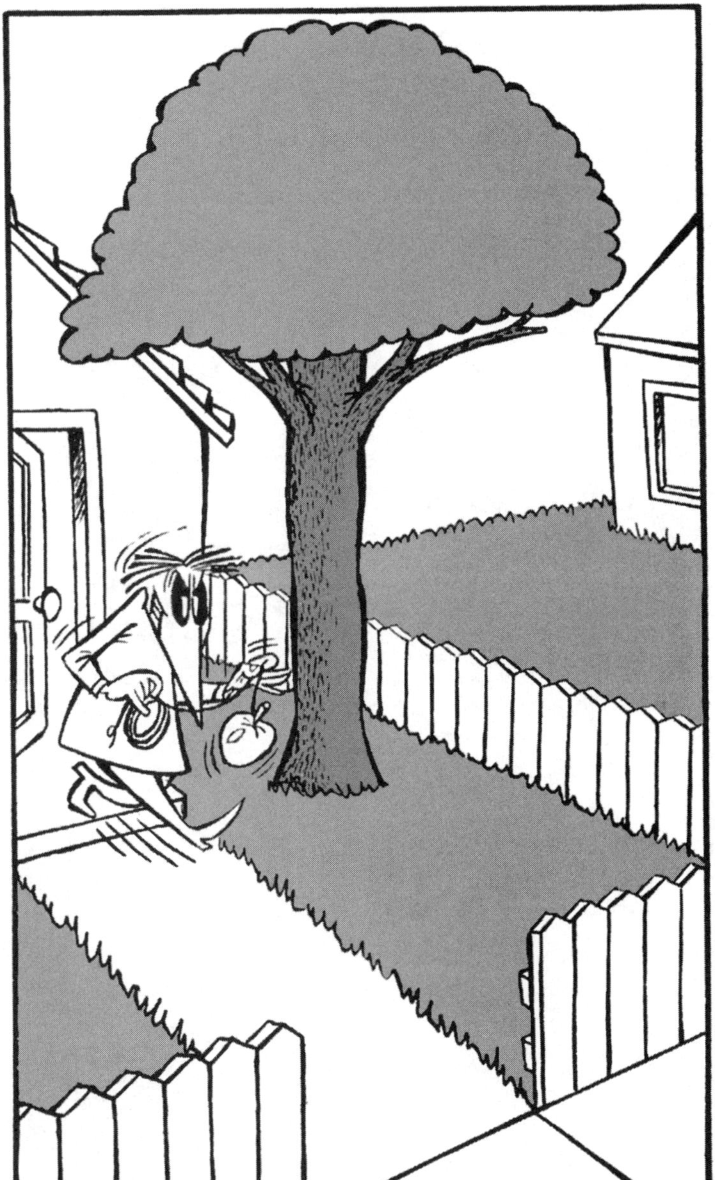

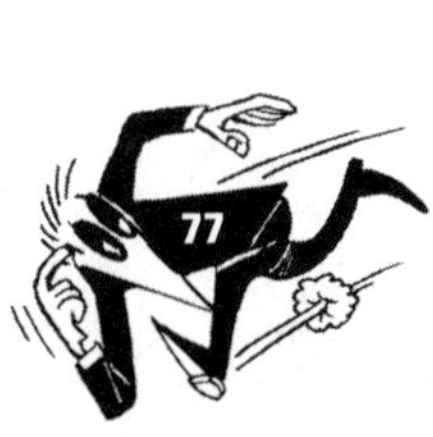

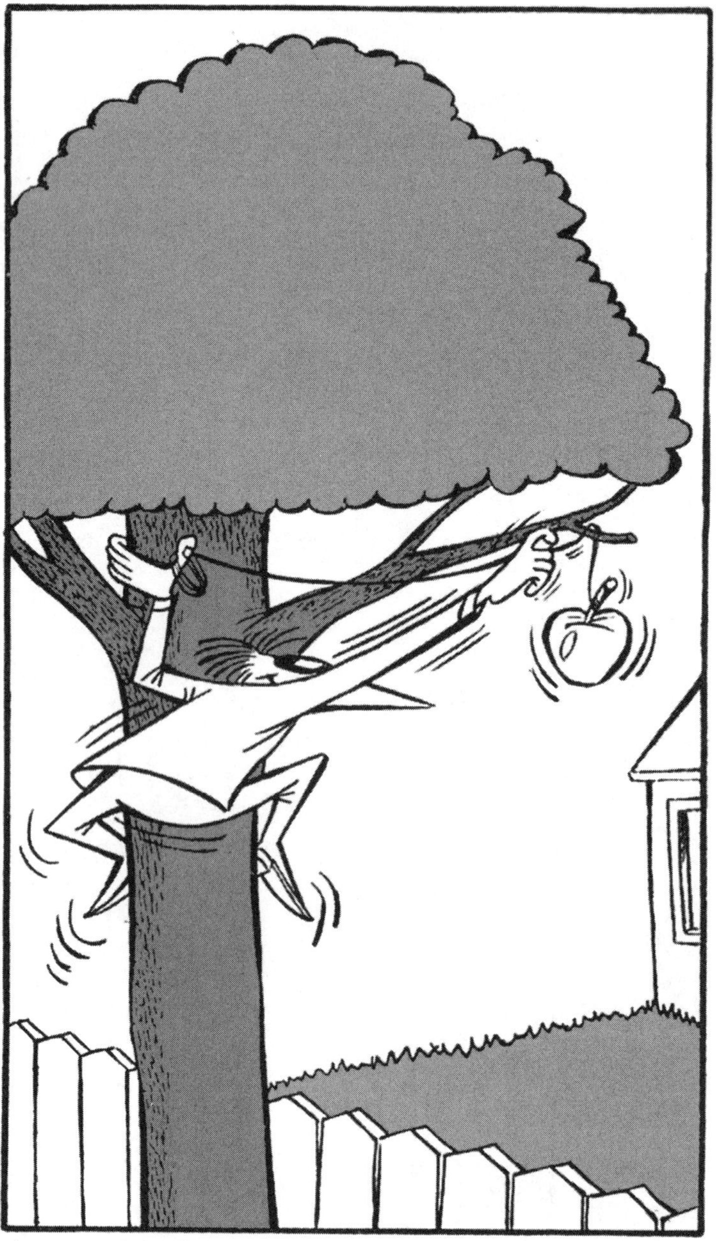

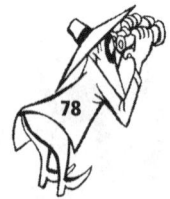

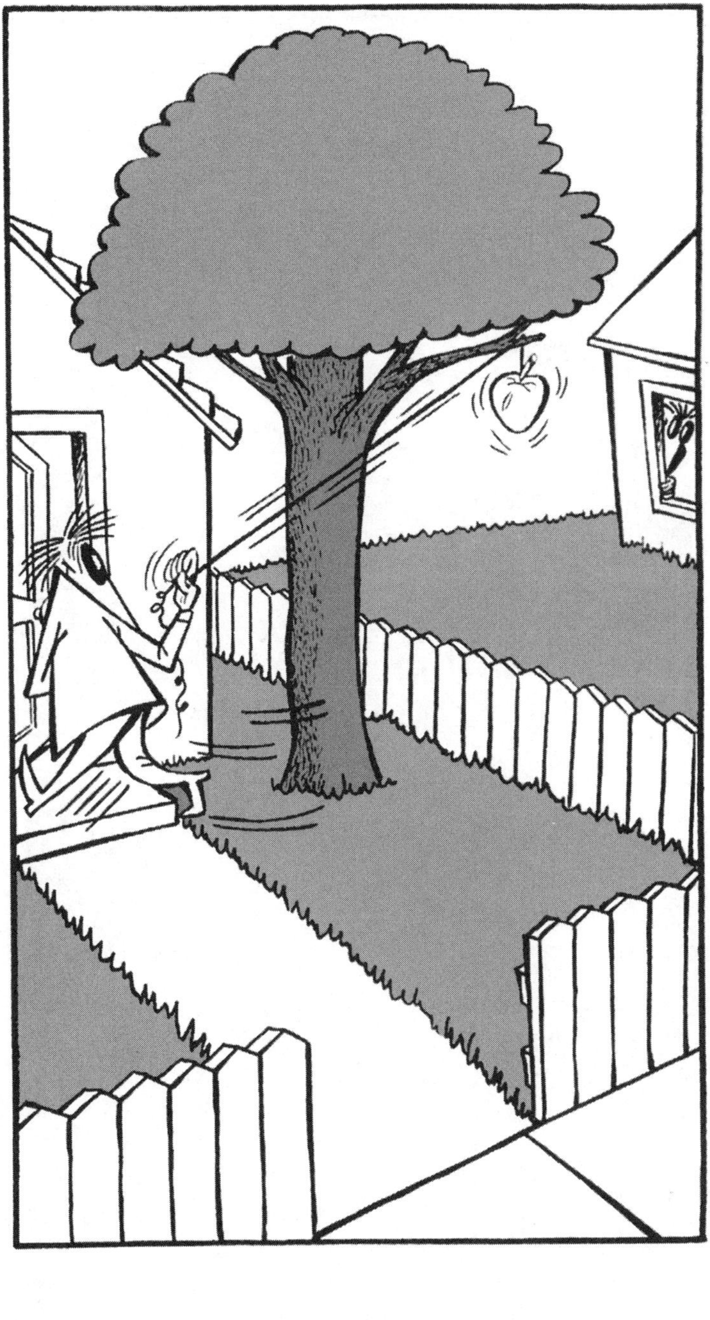

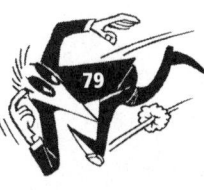

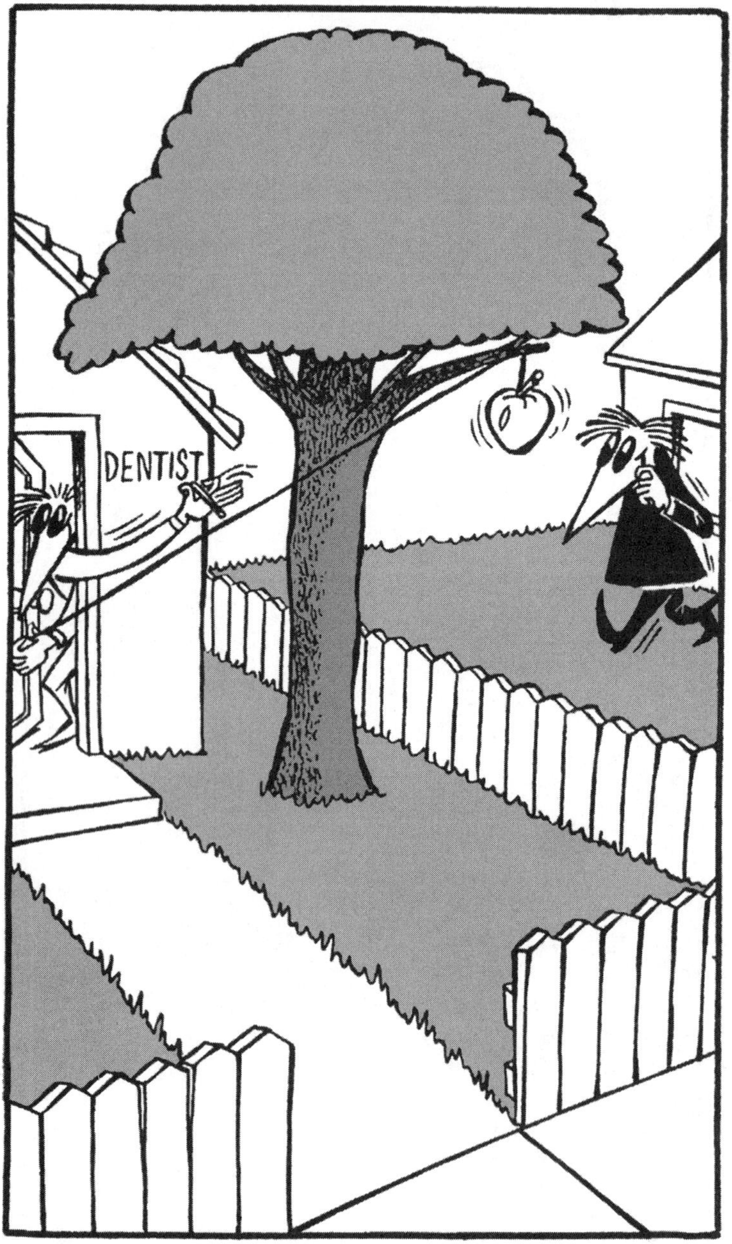
DENTIST

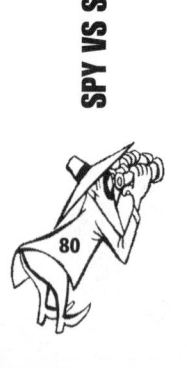

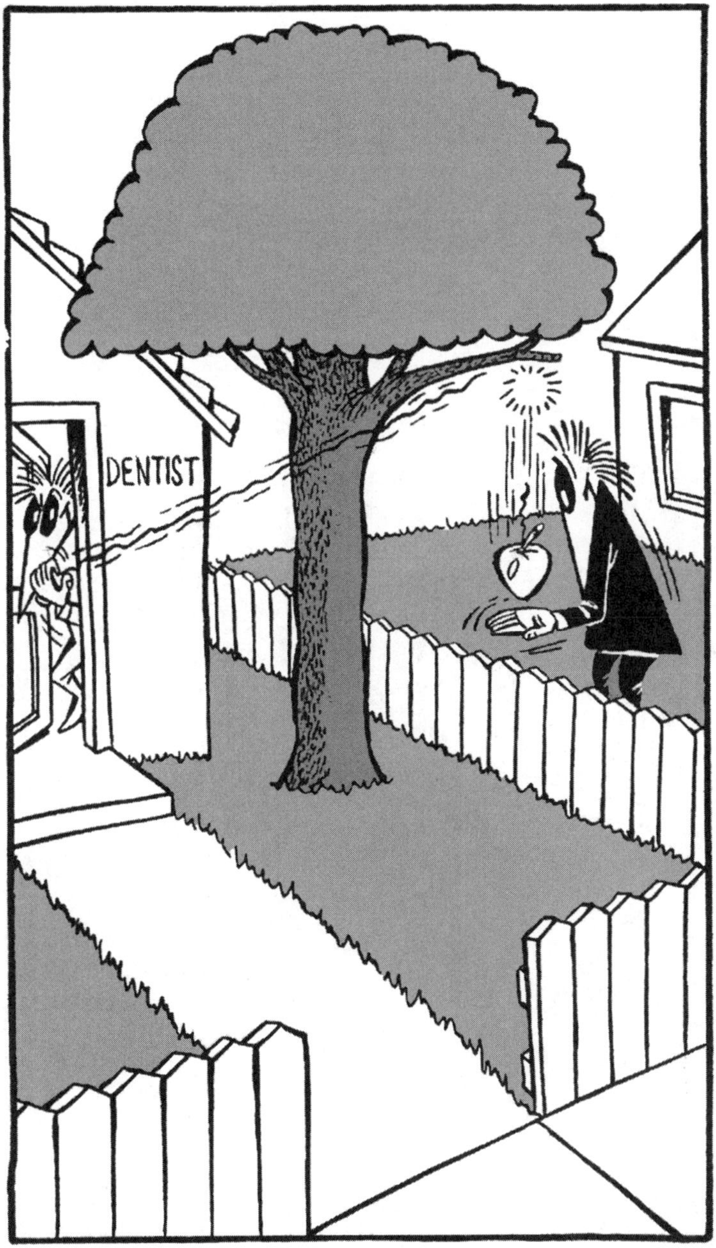
DENTIST

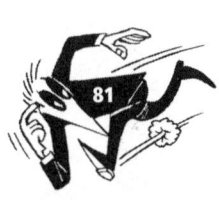

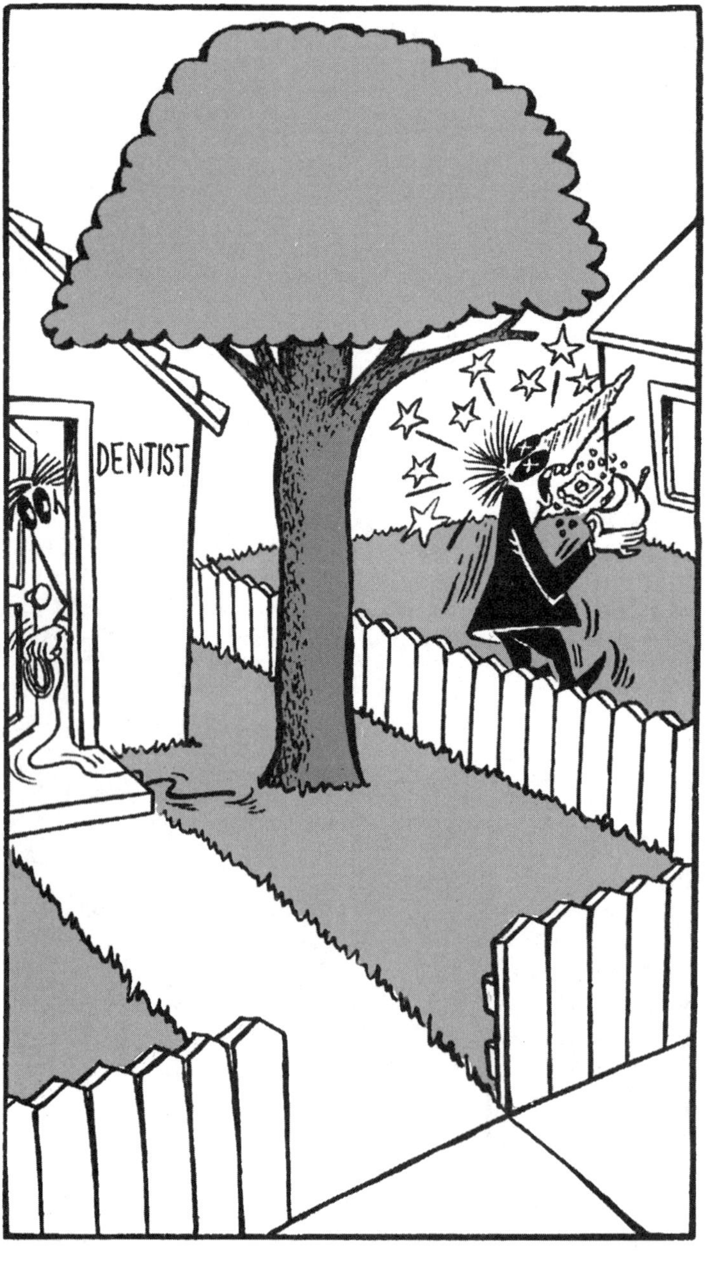
DENTIST

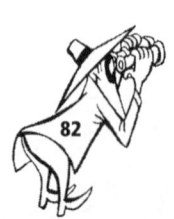

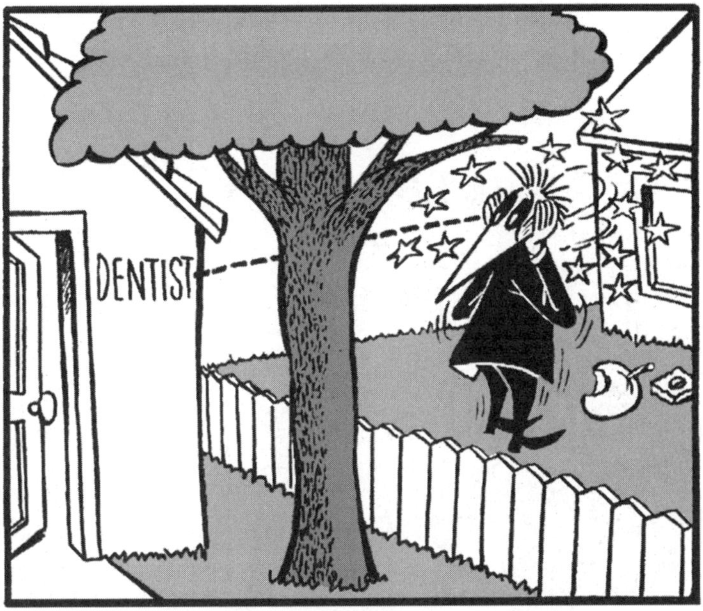
DENTIST

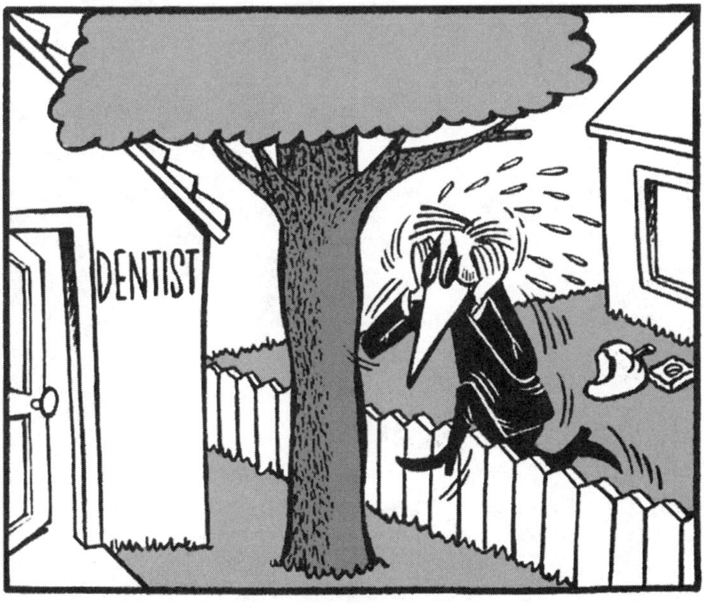
DENTIST

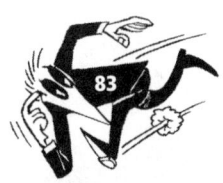

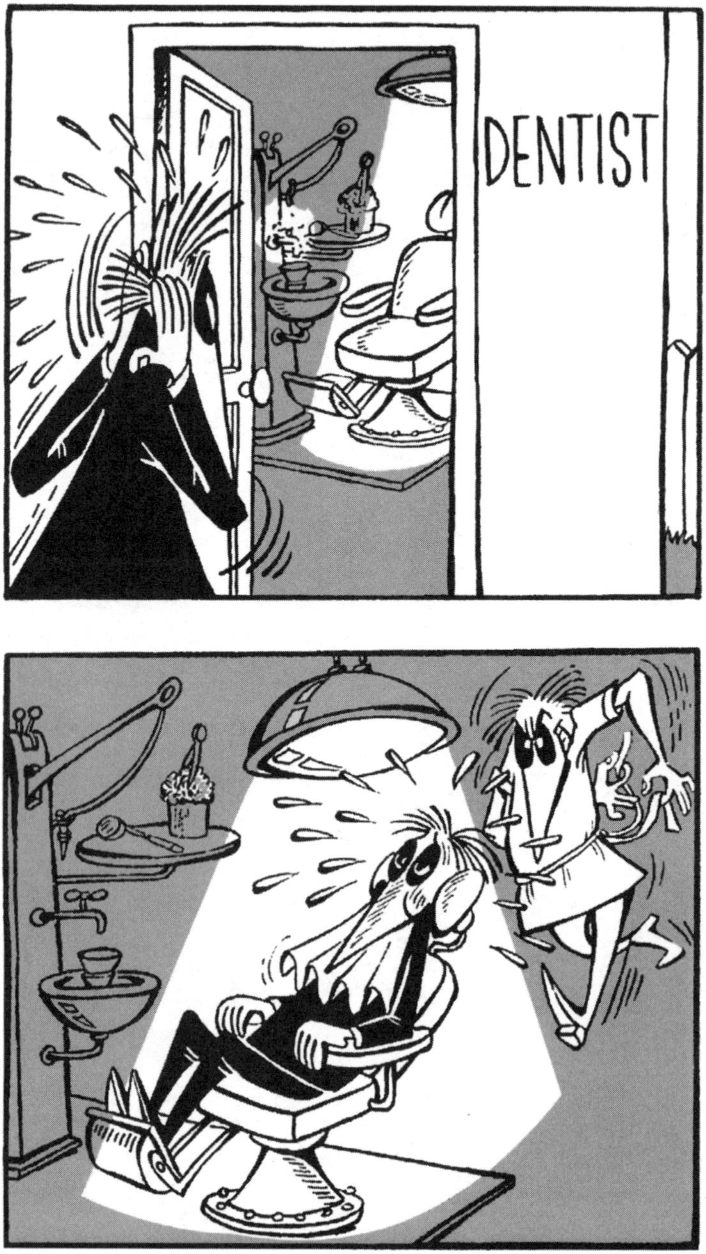
DENTIST

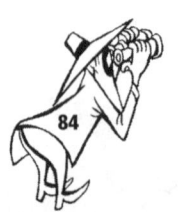

OPERATION: MOUTH TRAP

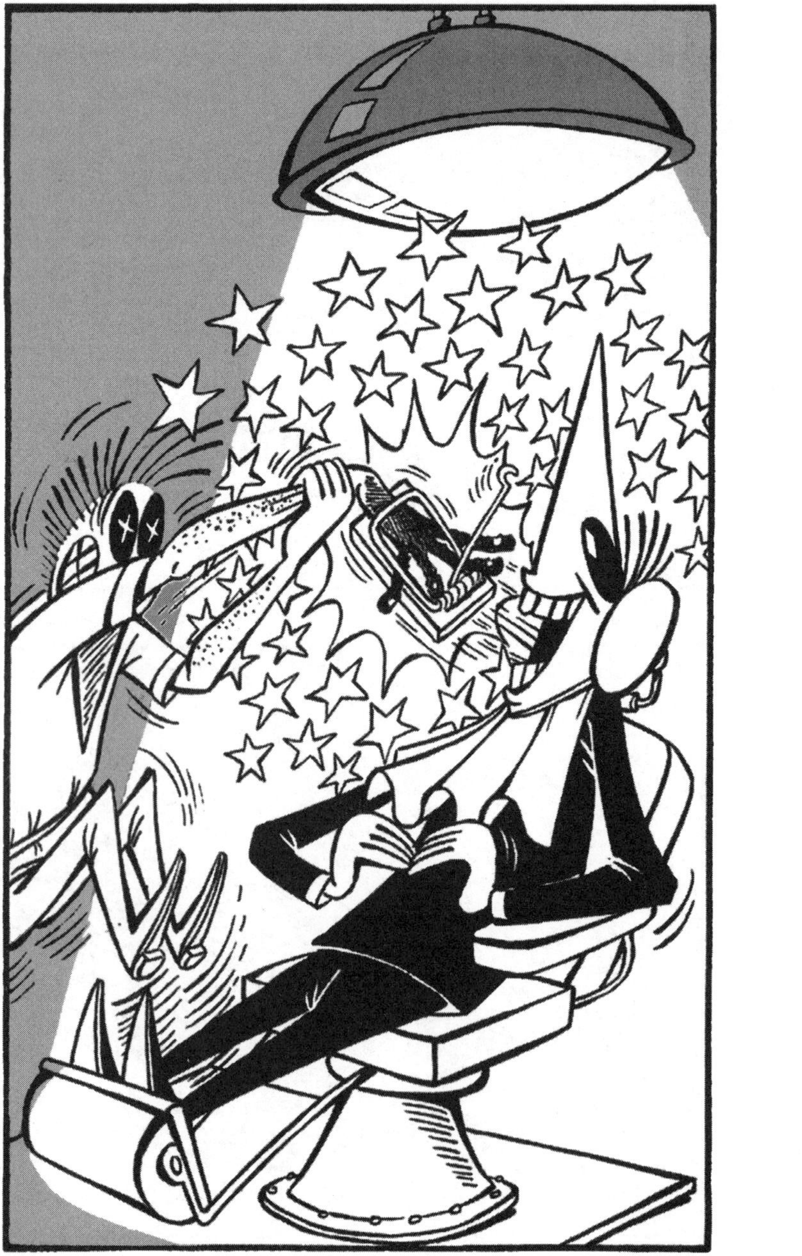

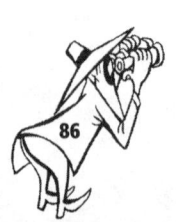

OPERATION: GUIDED MISCHIEF

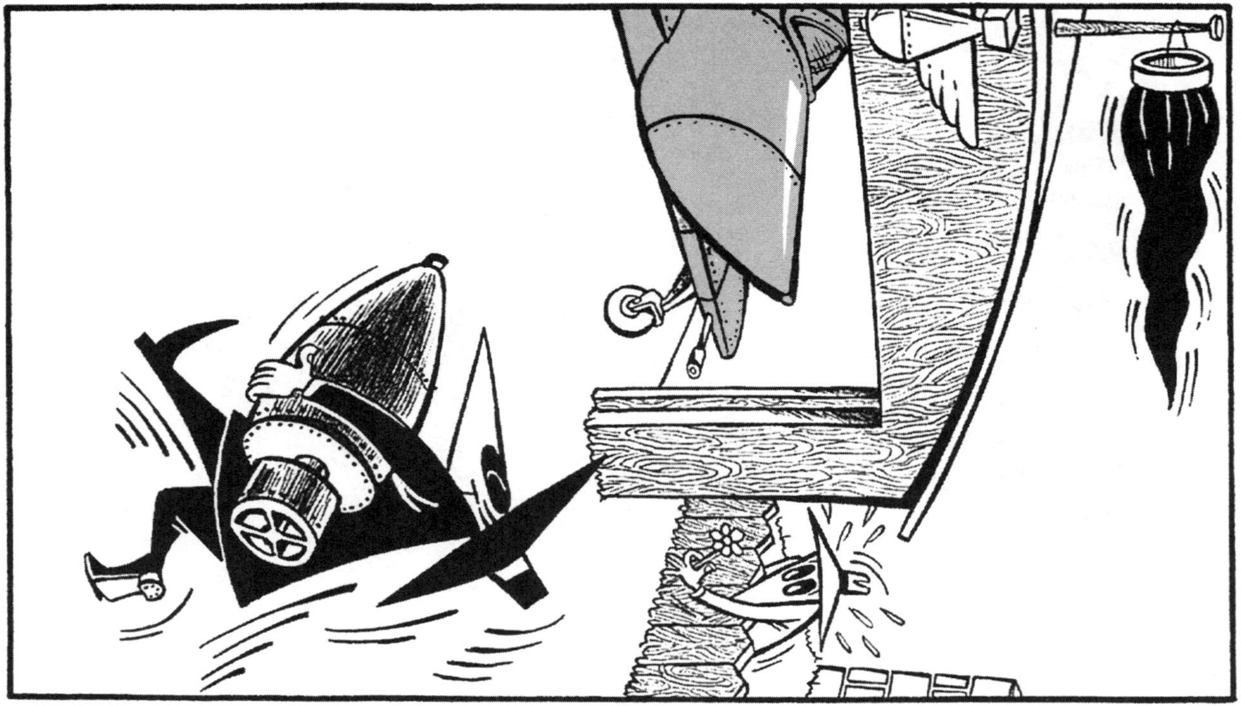

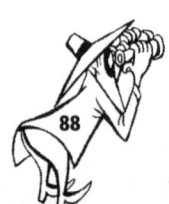

TOP SECRET
SHELTER

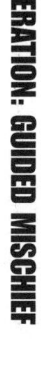

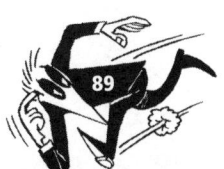

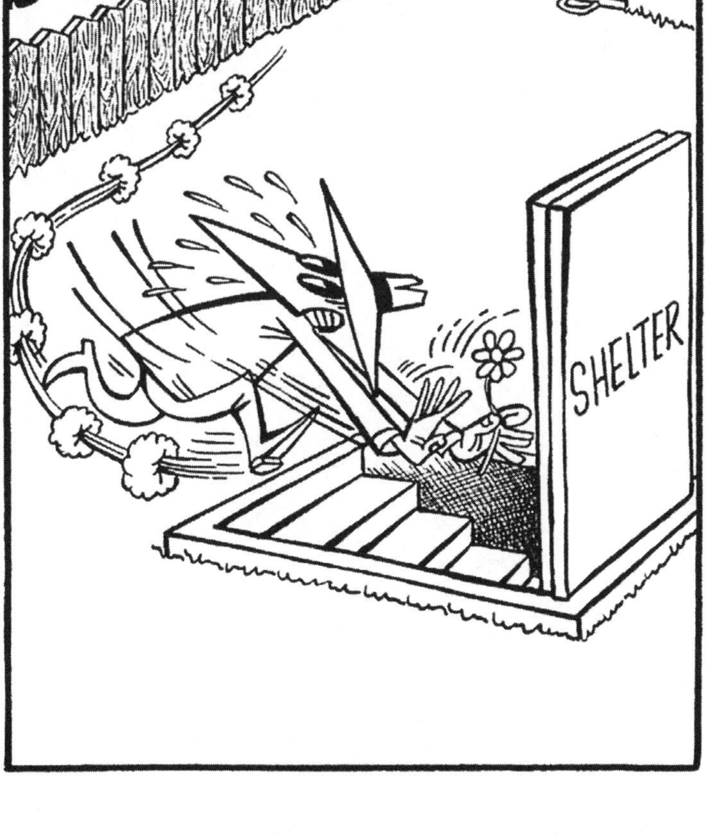

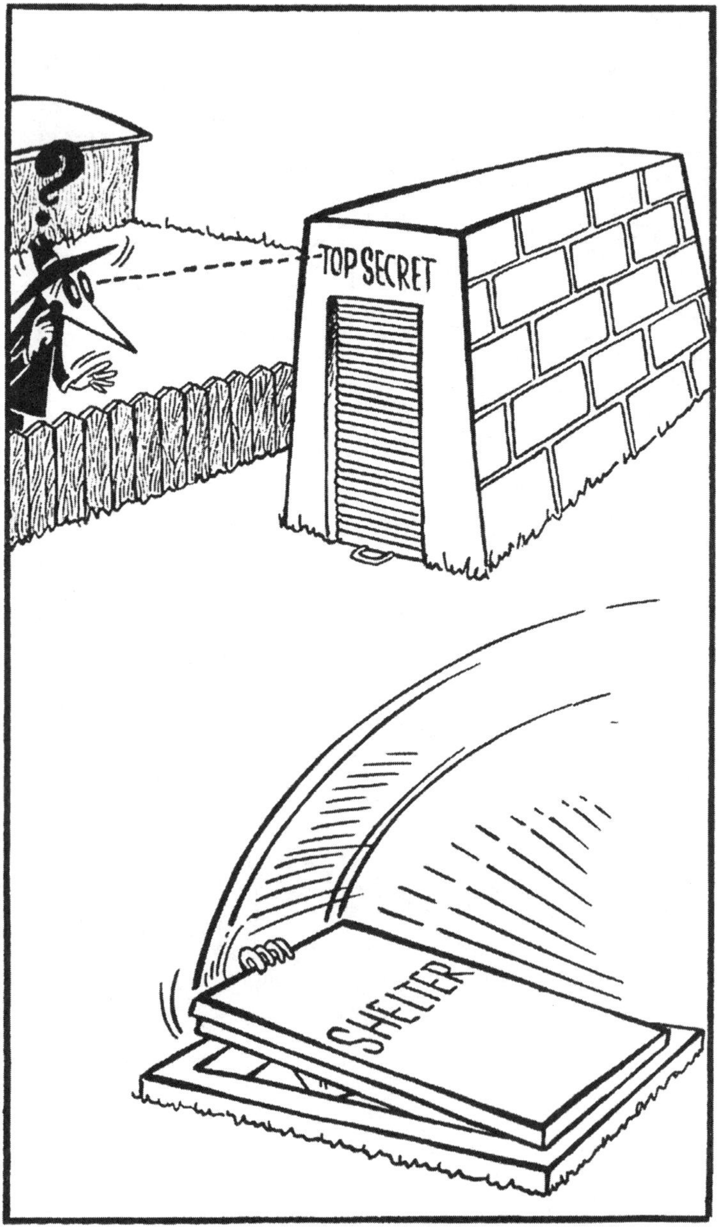
TOP SECRET
SHELTER

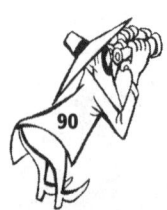

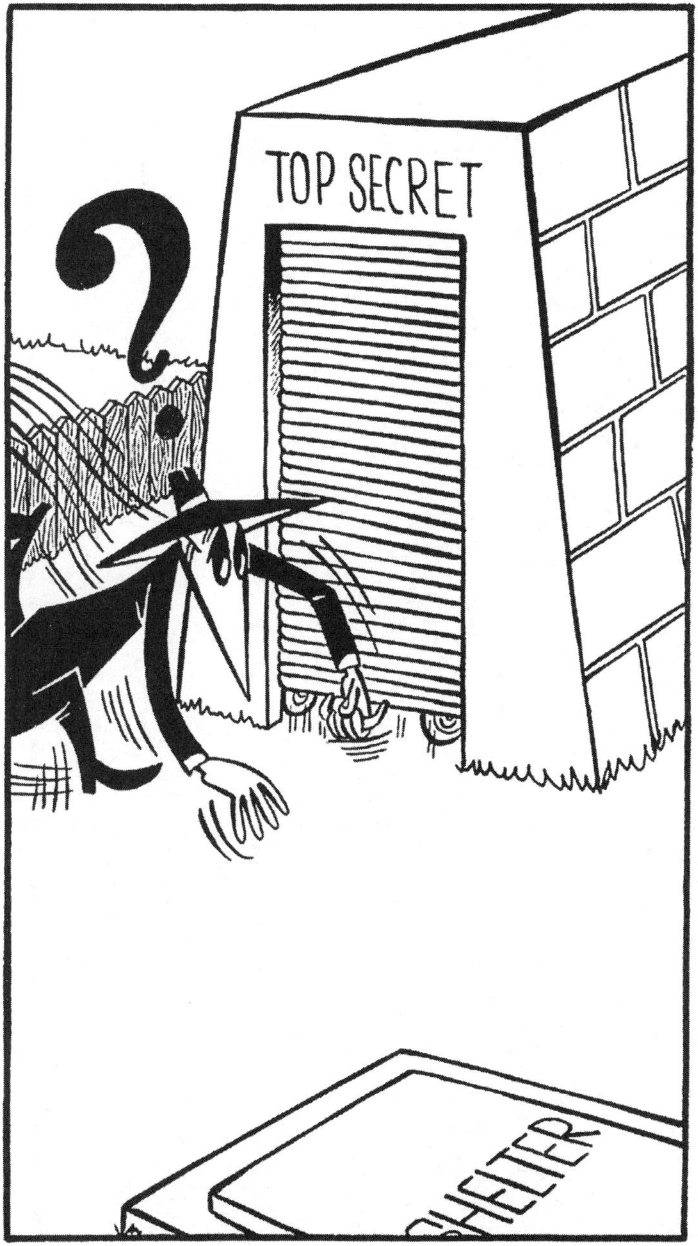
TOP SECRET
HELTER

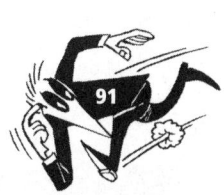

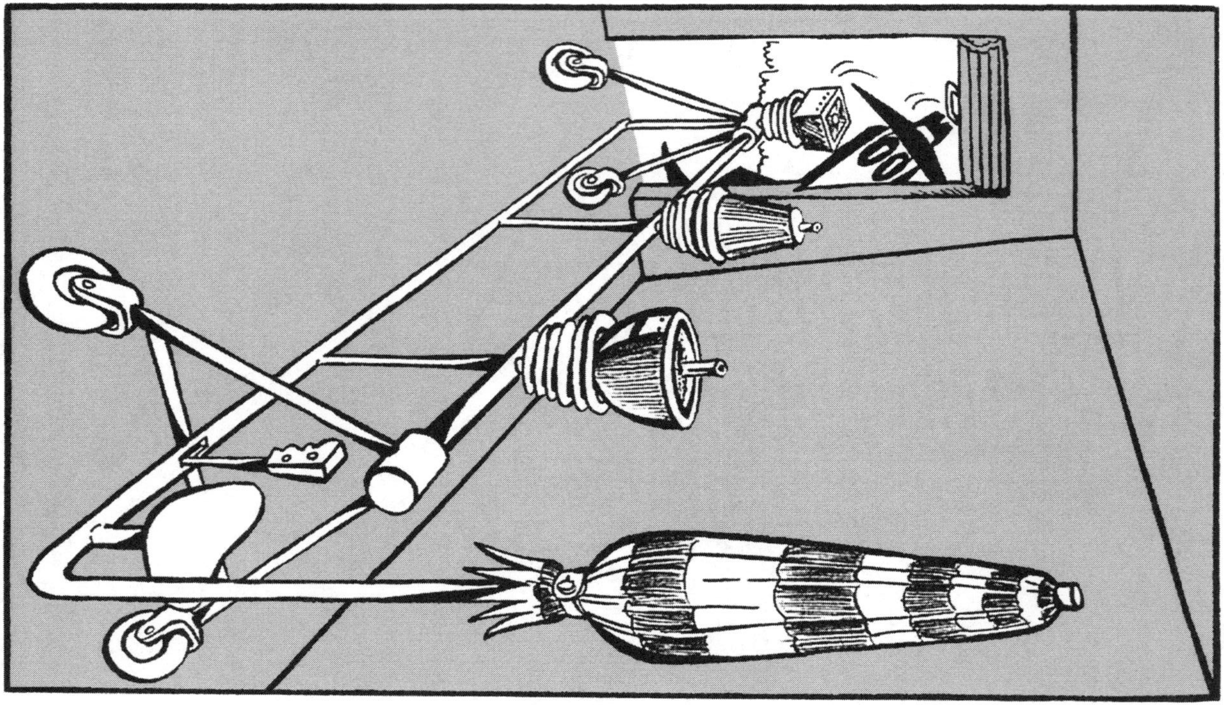

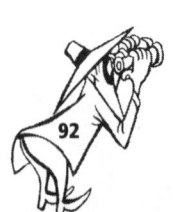

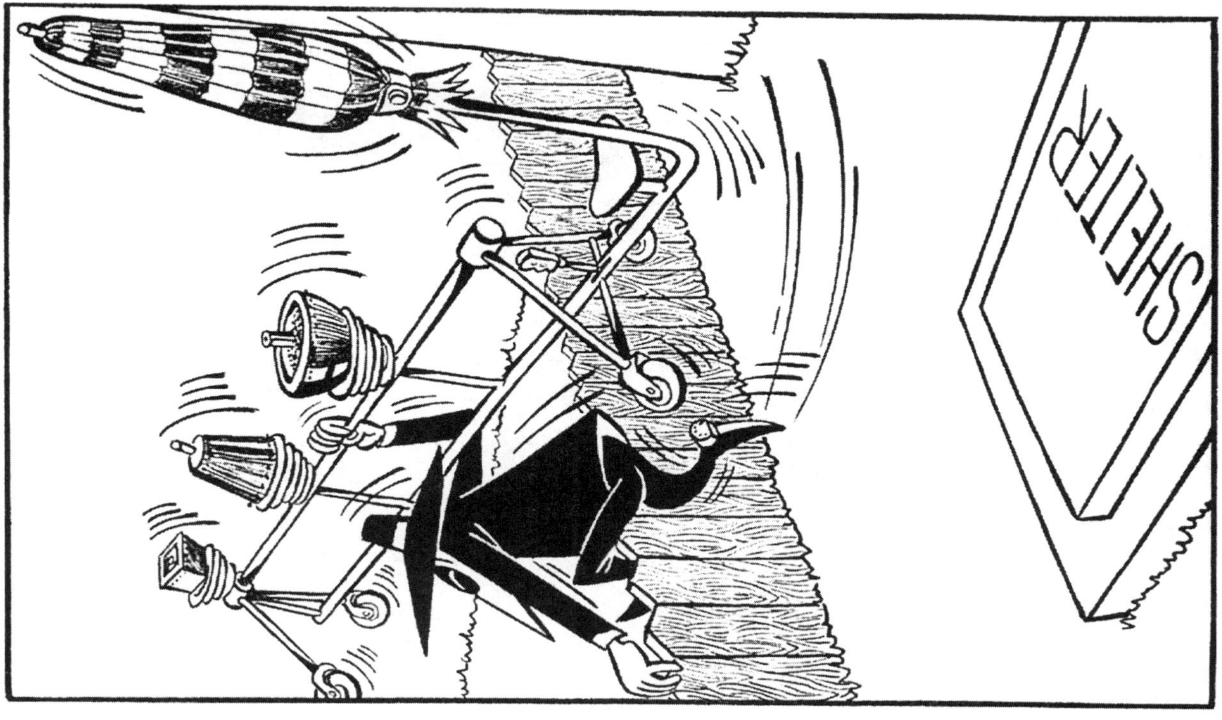
SHELTER

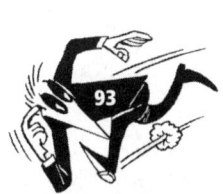

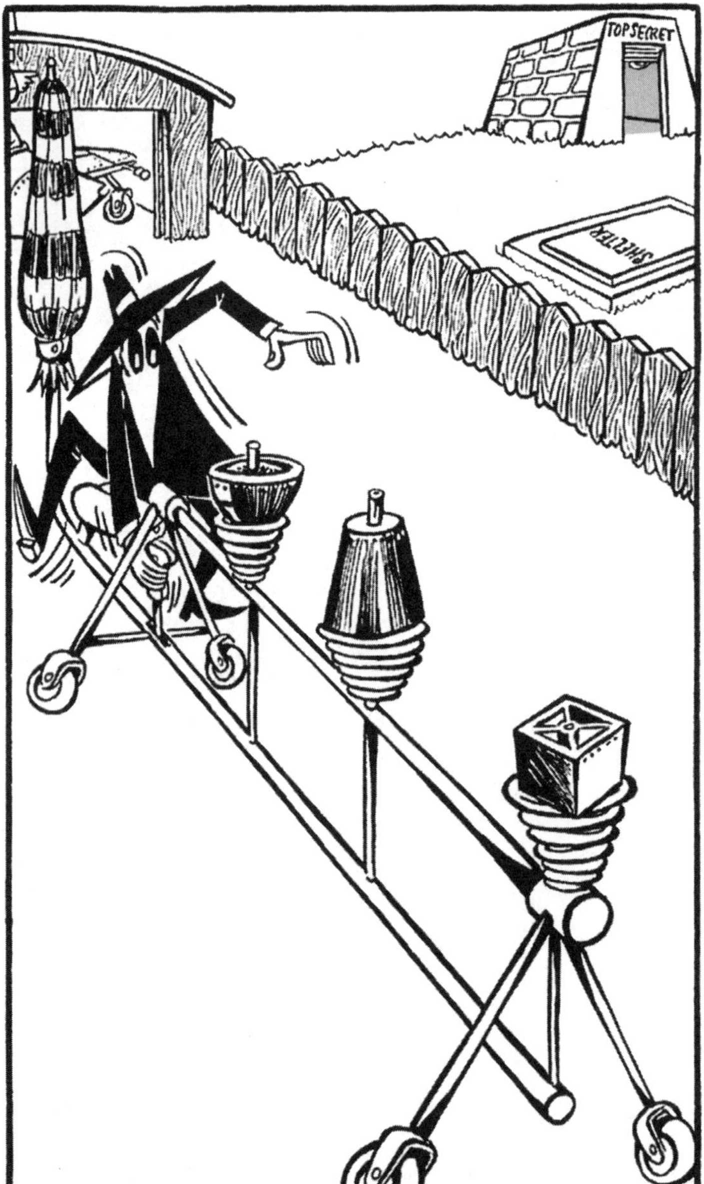
TOP SECRET
SHELTER

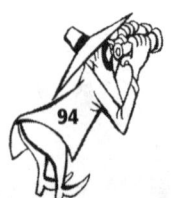

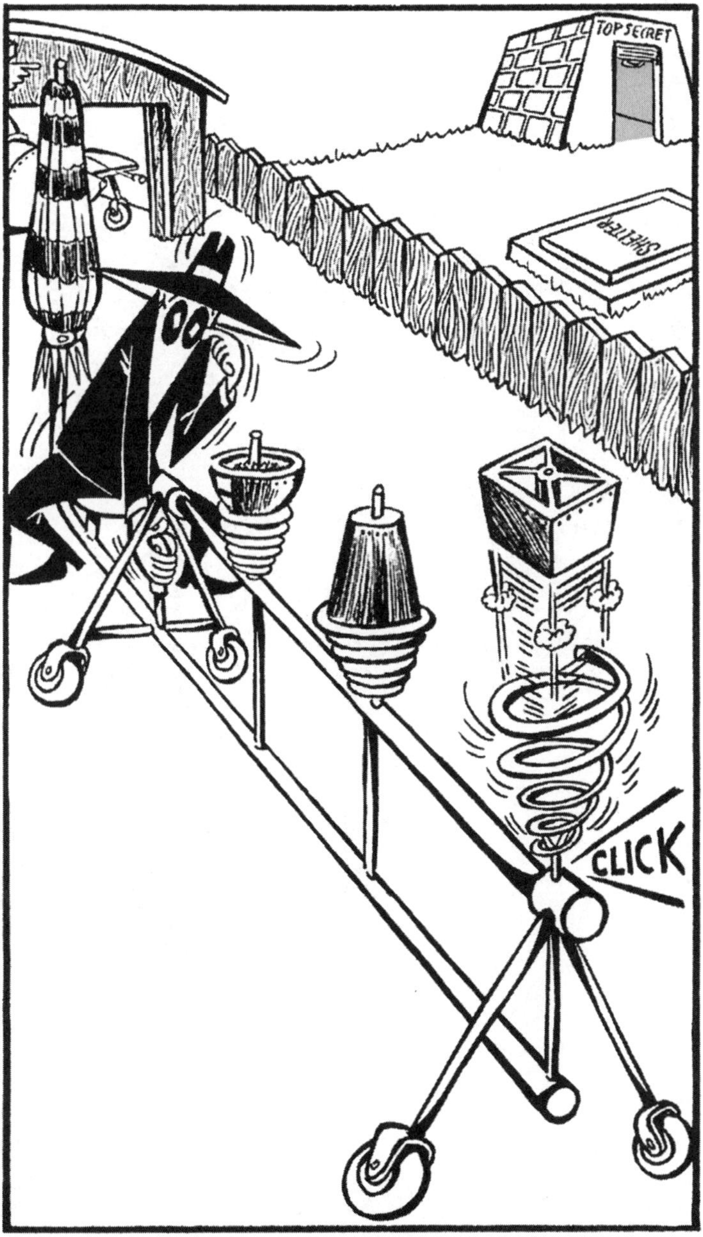
TOP SECRET
SHELTER
CLICK

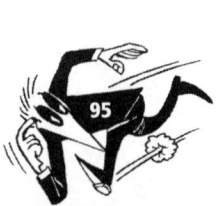

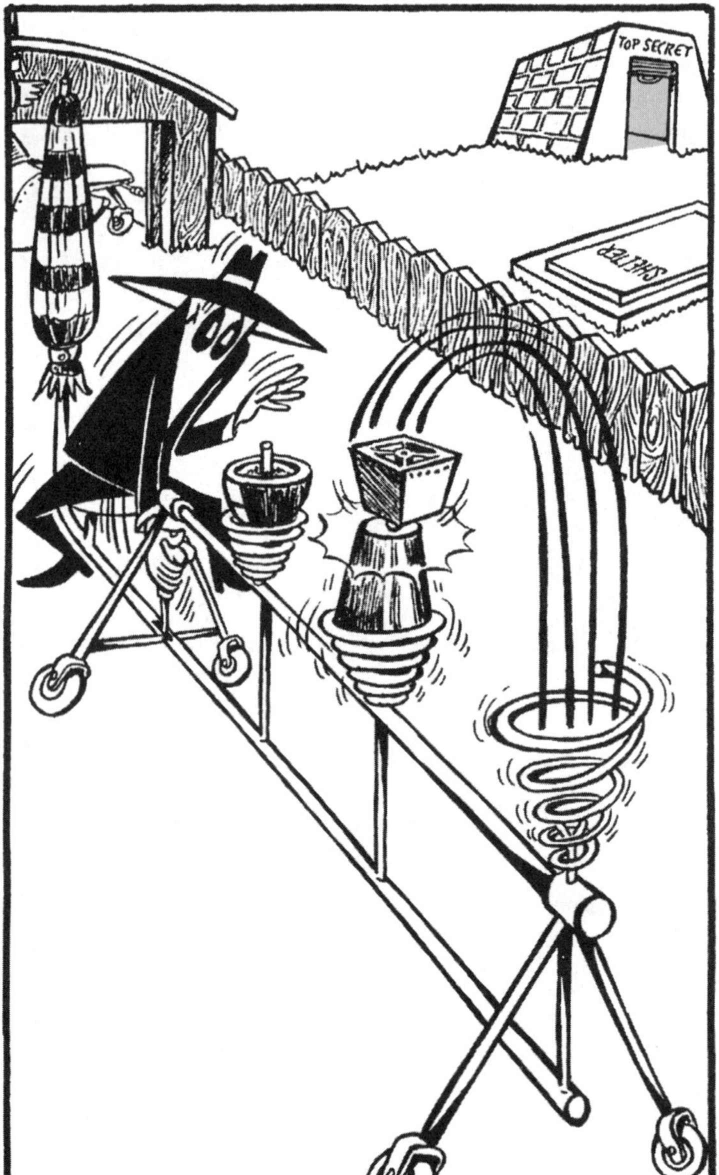
TOP SECRET
SHELTER

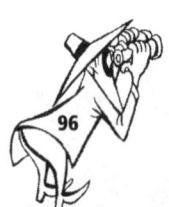

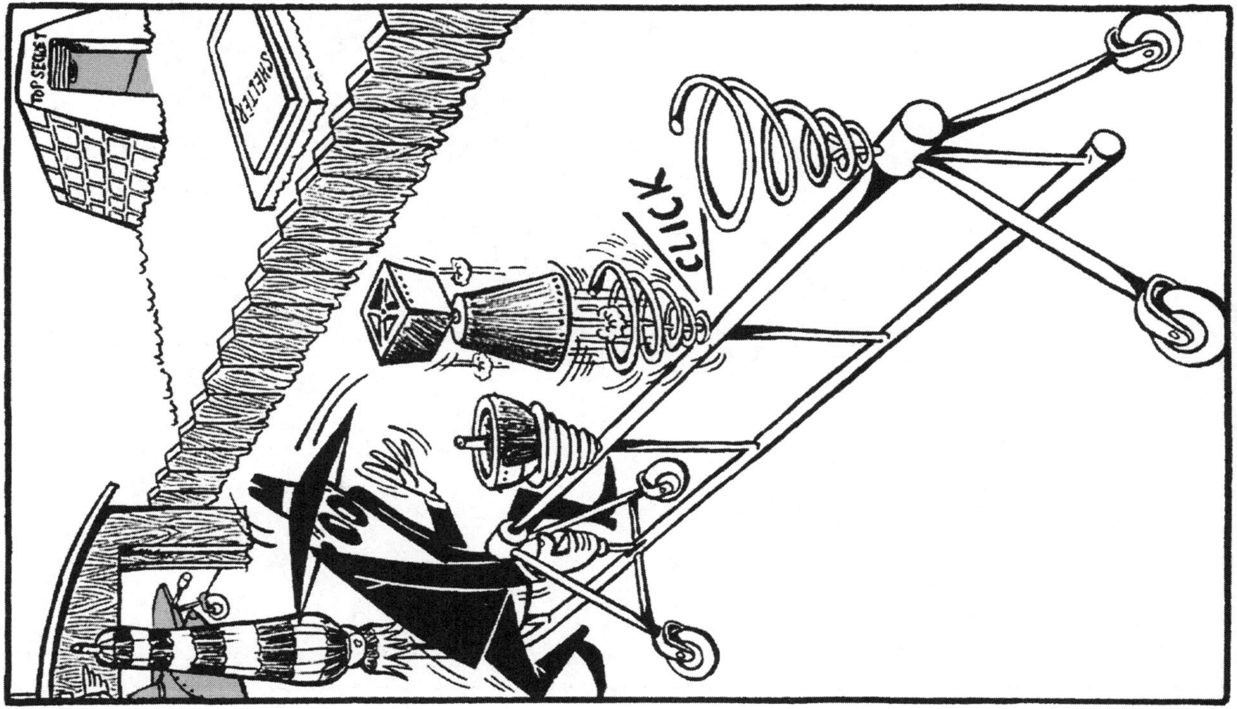
TOP SECRET
SHELTER
CLICK

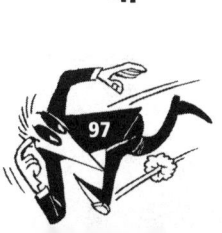

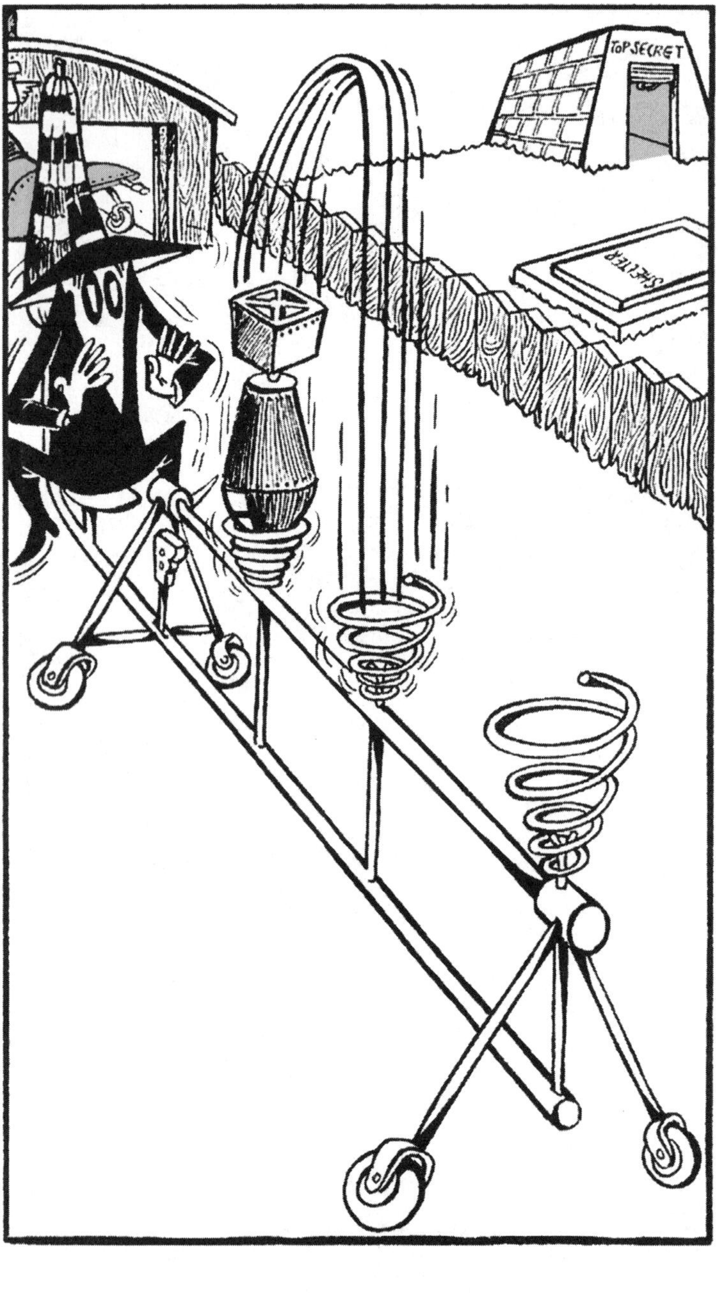
TOP SECRET
SHELTER

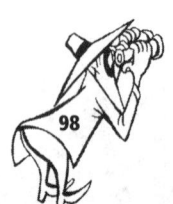

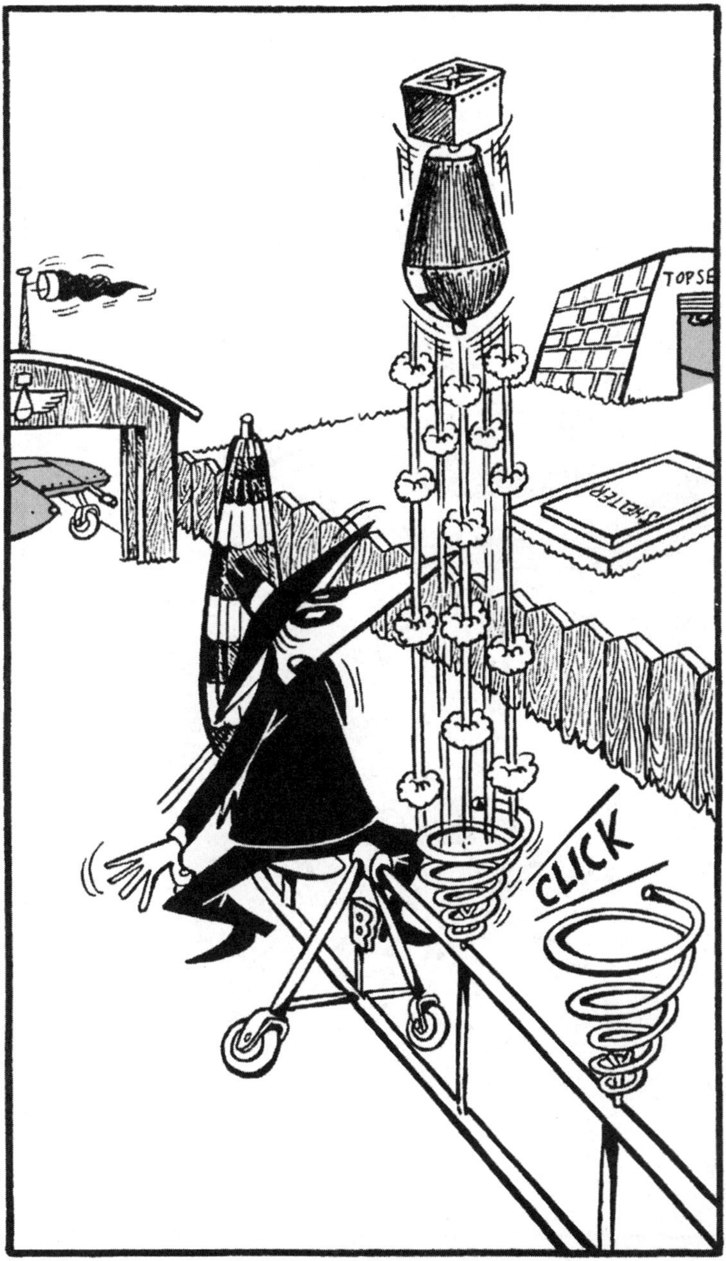
TOPSE
SHELTER
CLICK

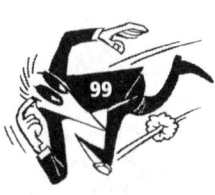

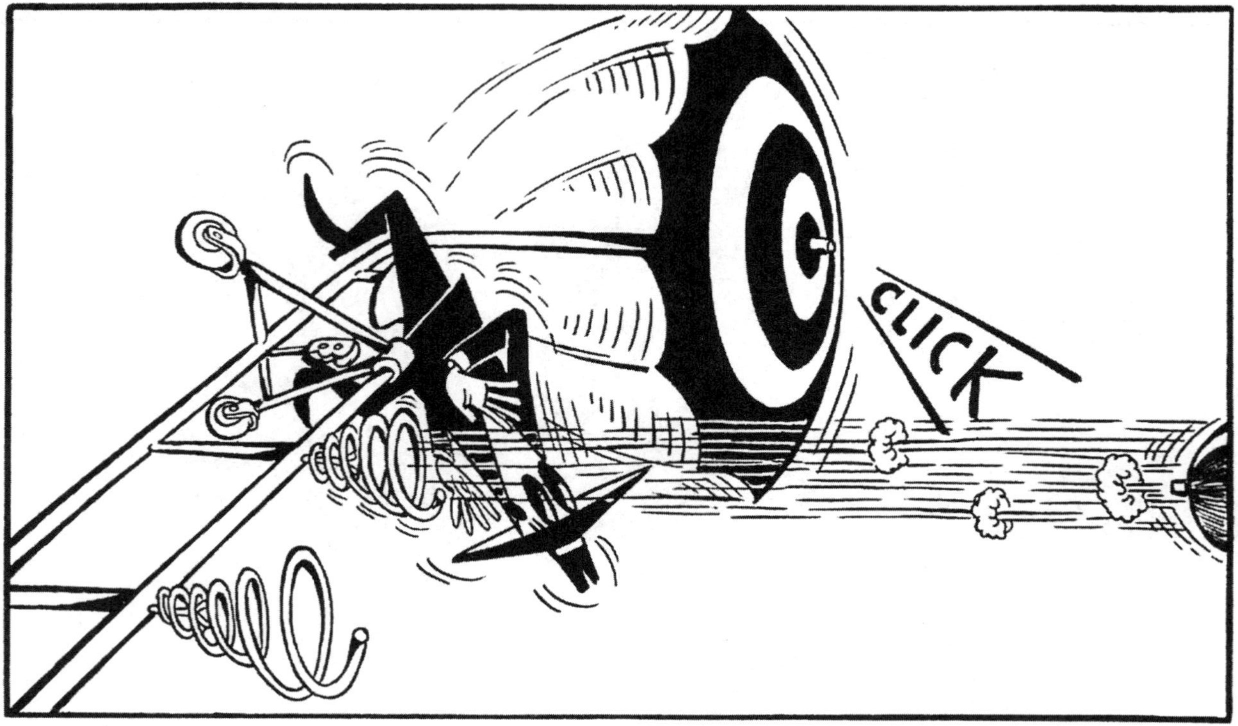
CLICK

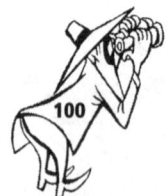

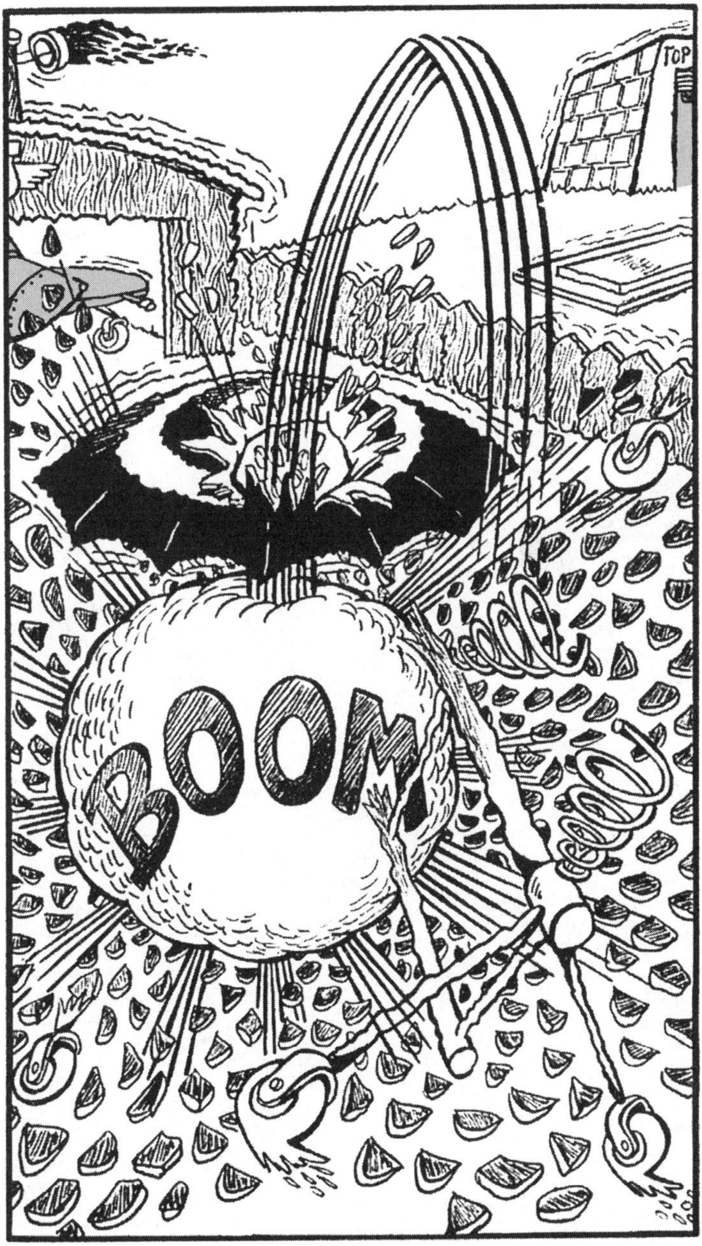
TOP
BOOM

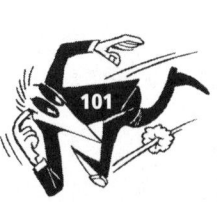

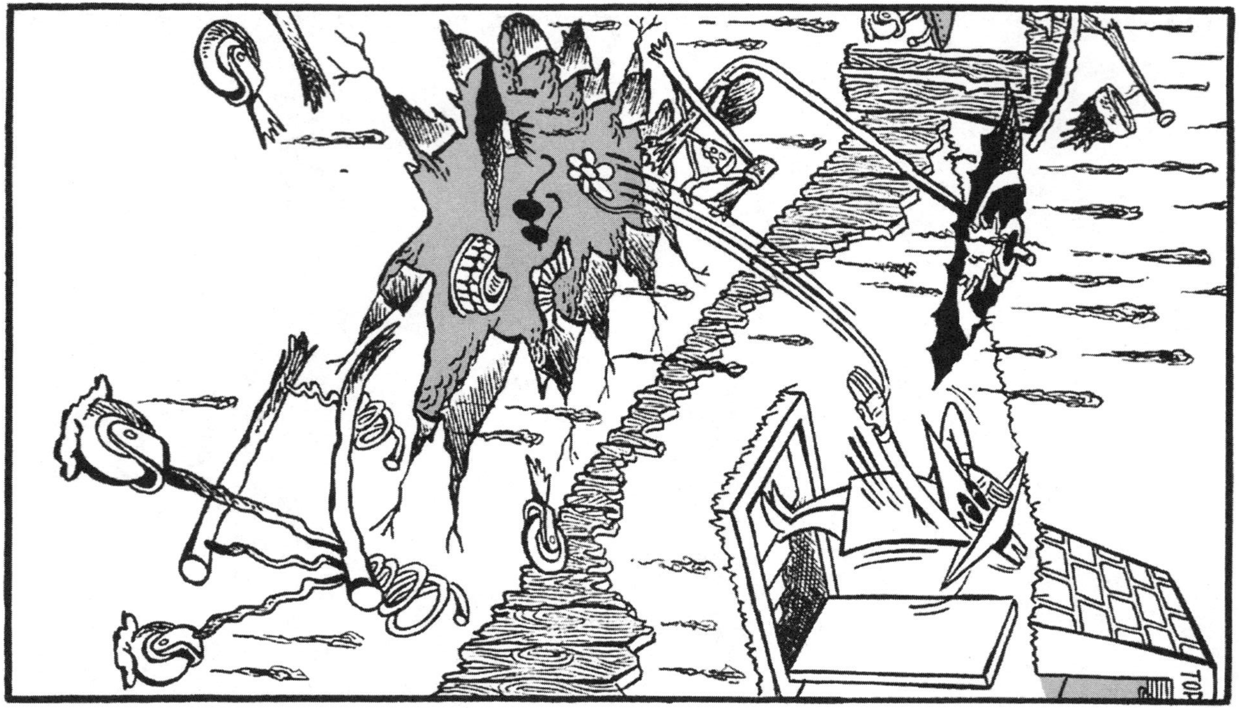
TOP

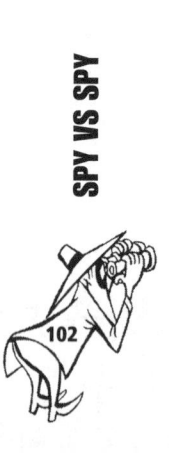

OPERATION: SHOE-IN

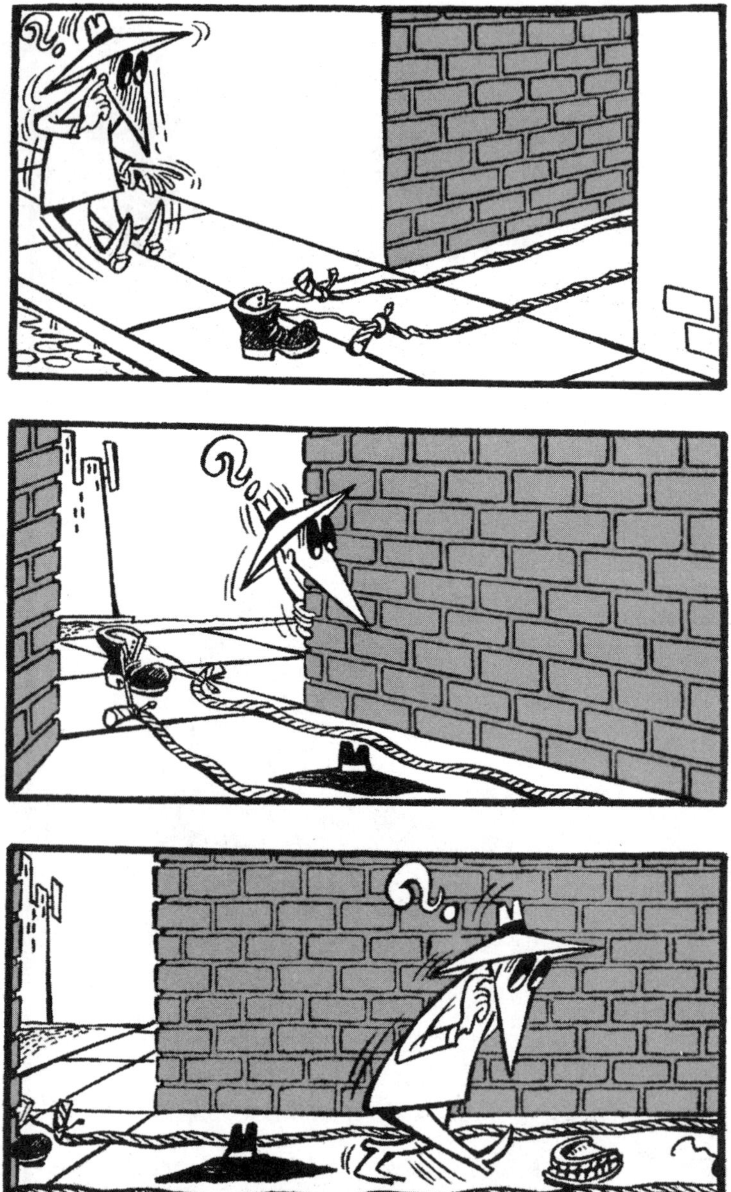

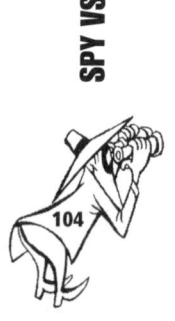

OPERATION: SHOE-IN

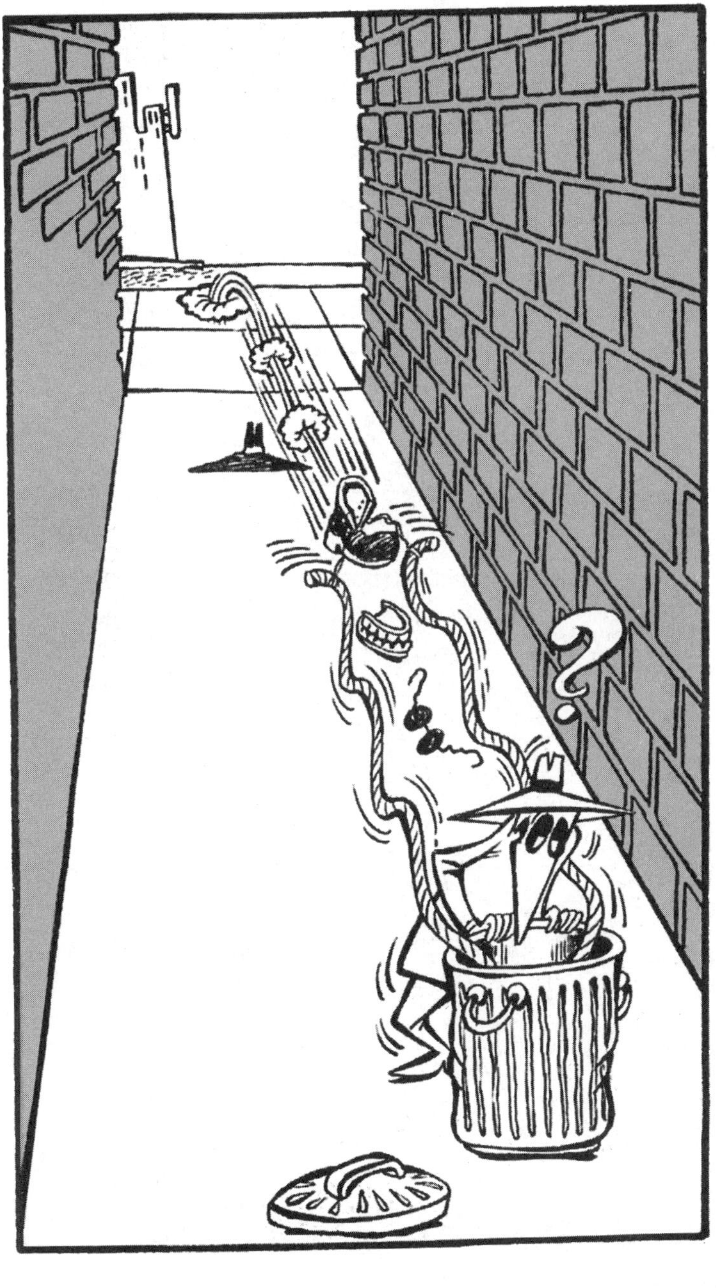

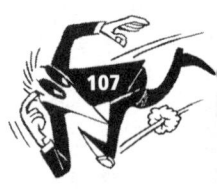

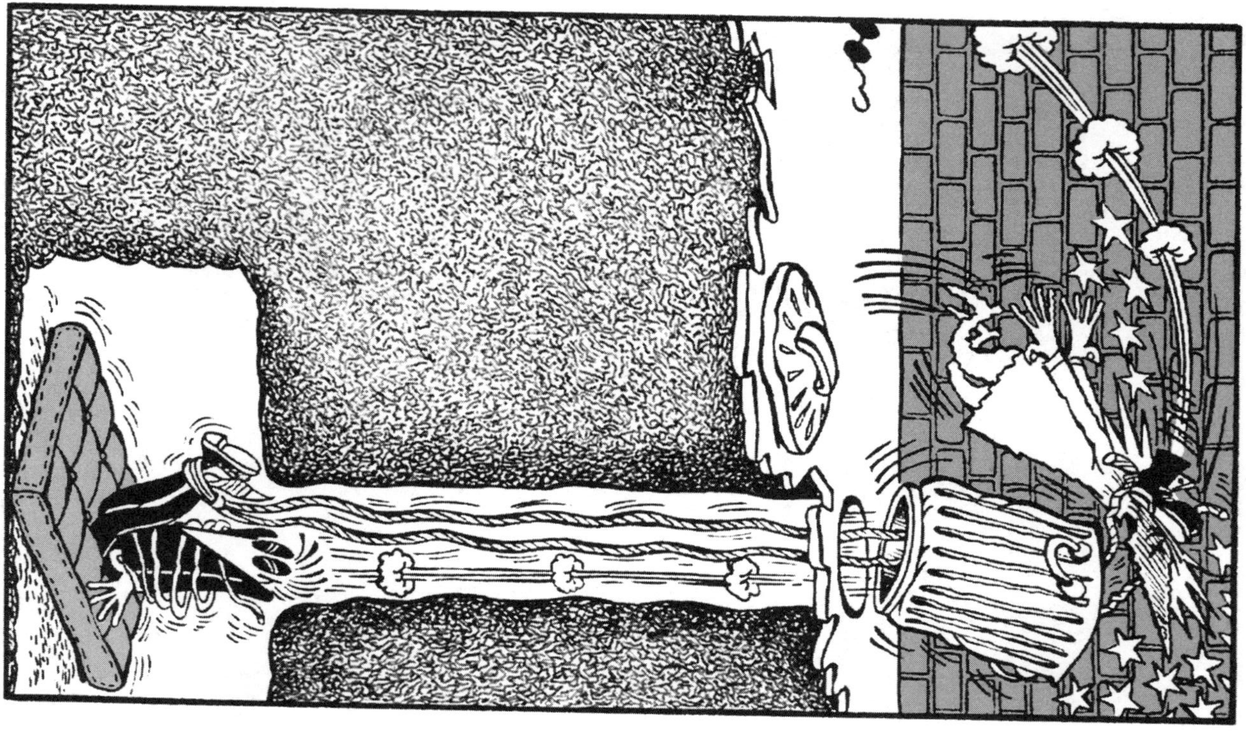

OPERATION: SUBVERSUS

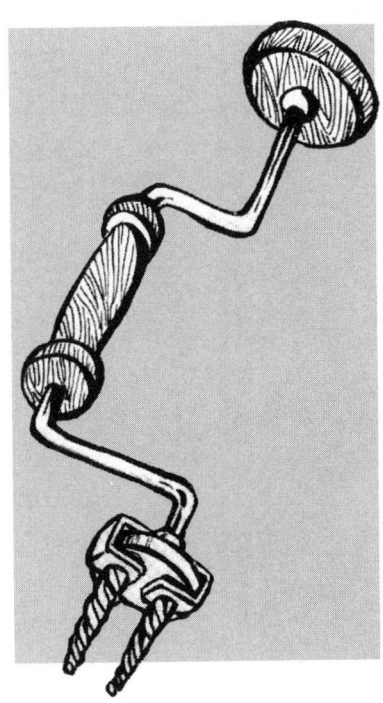

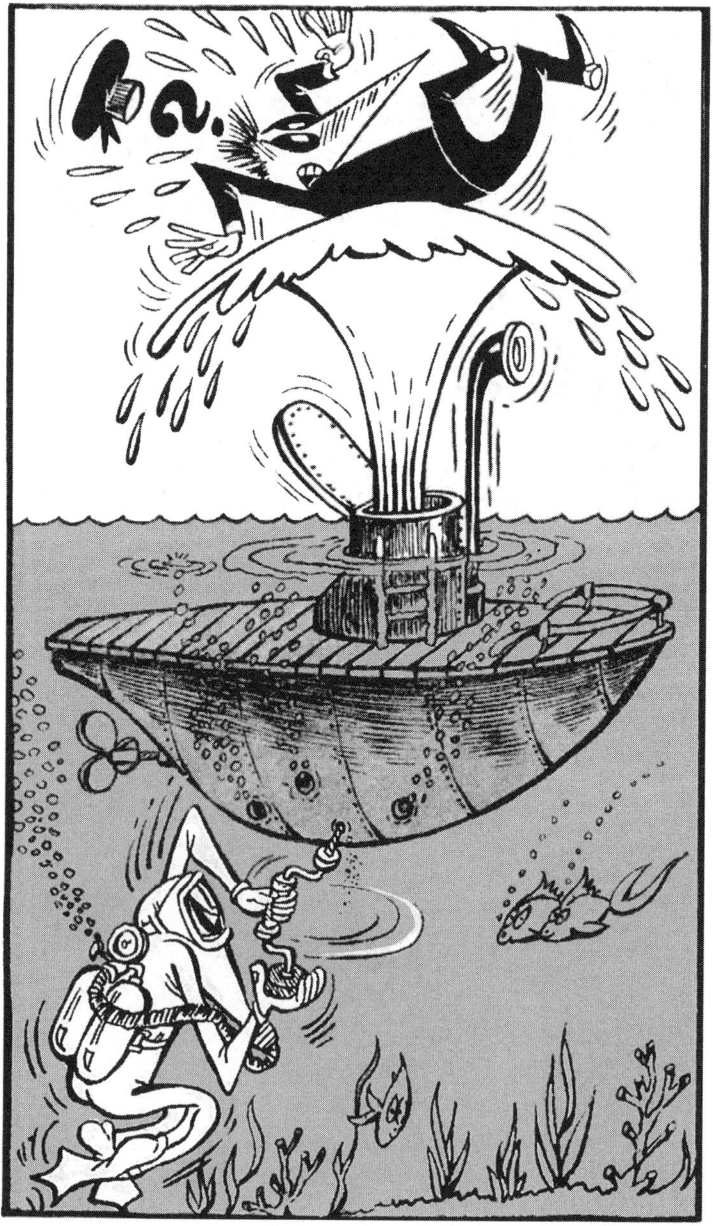

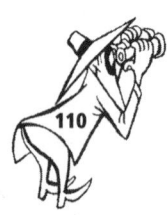

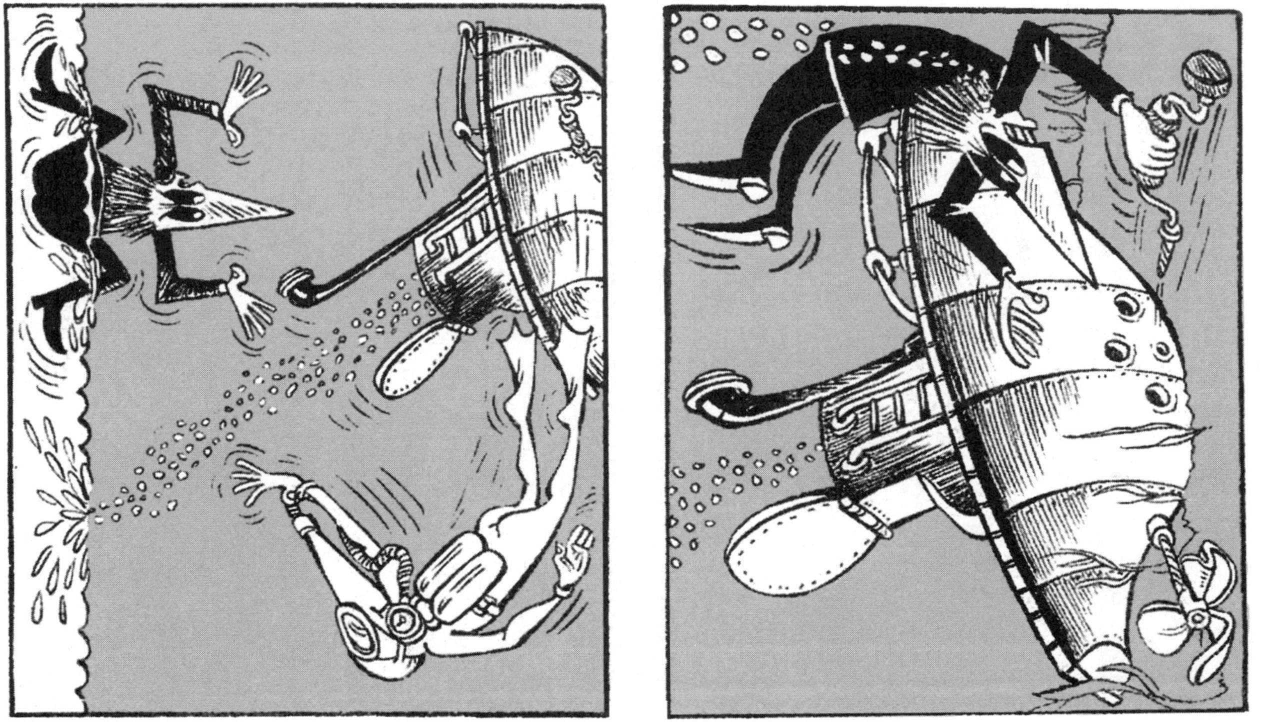

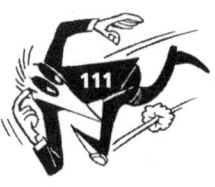

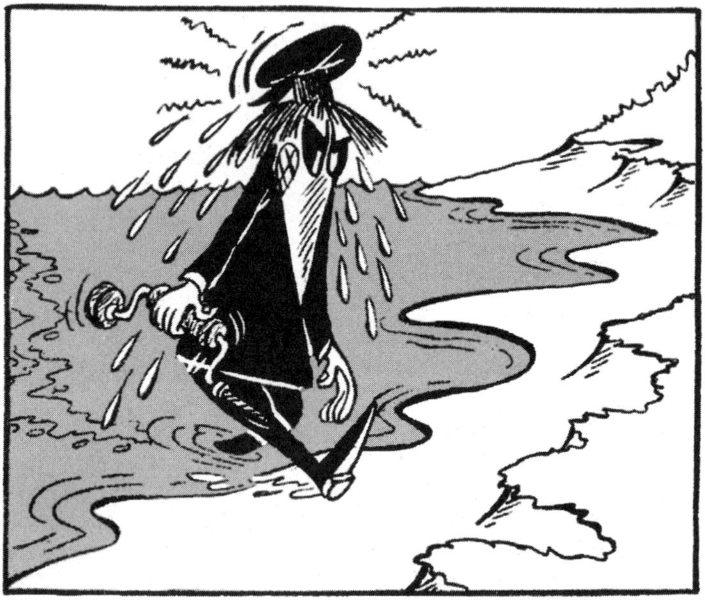

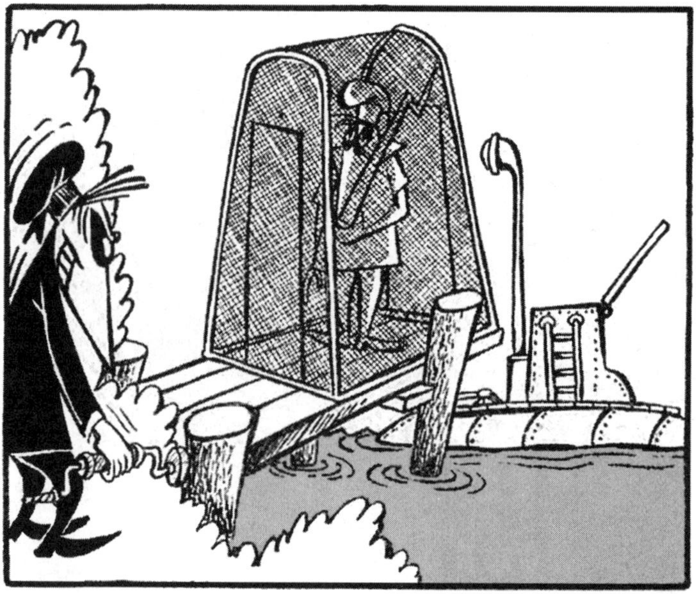

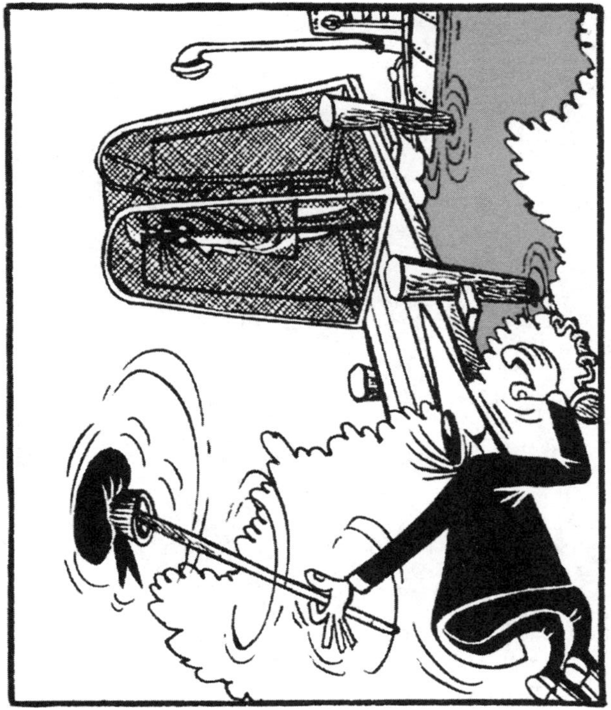

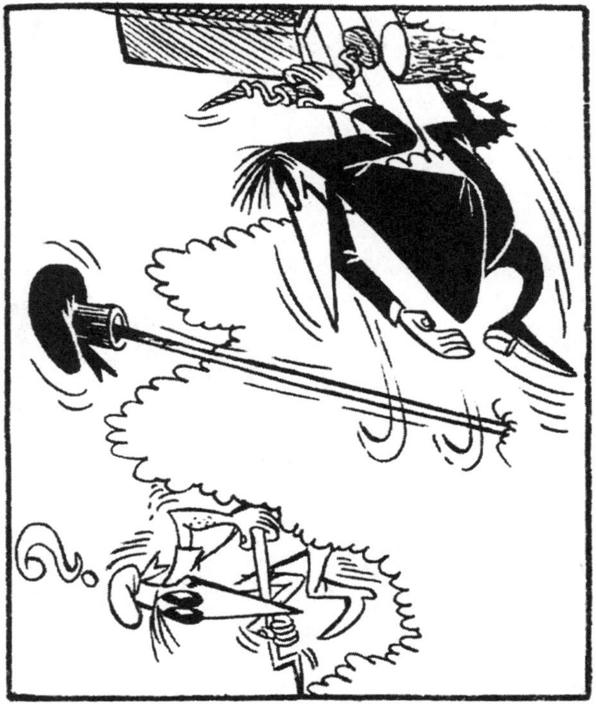

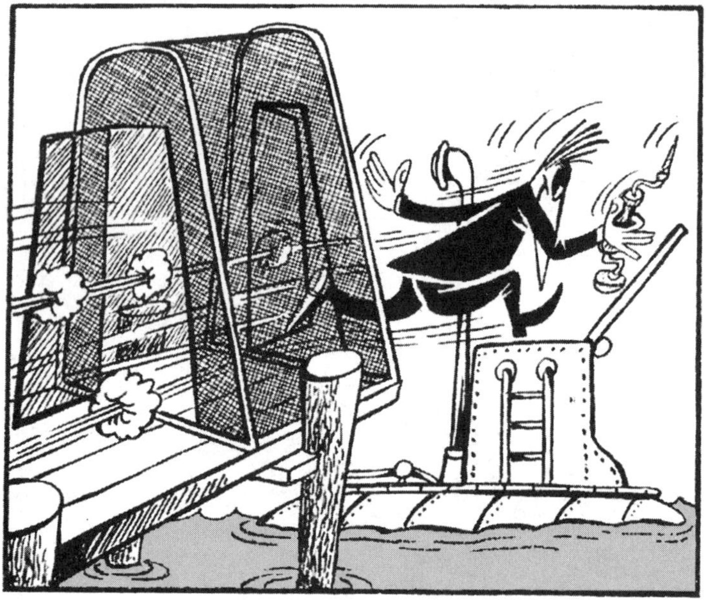

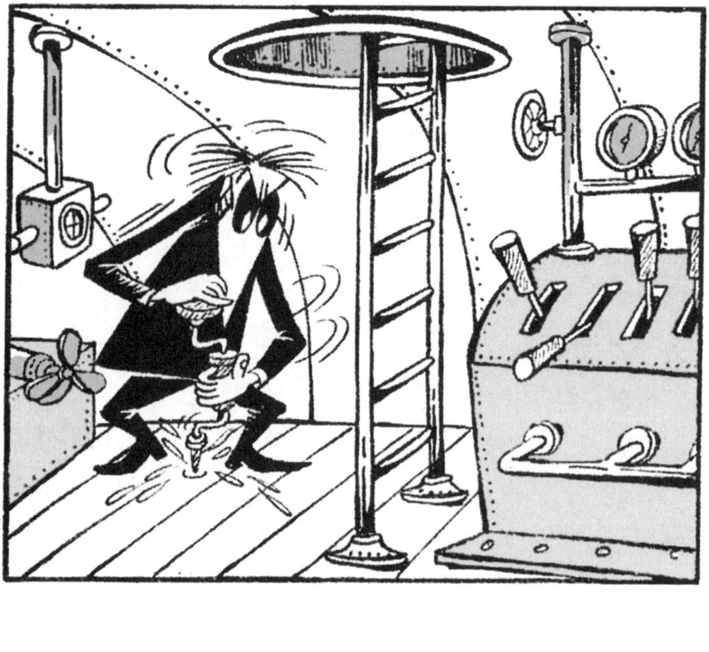

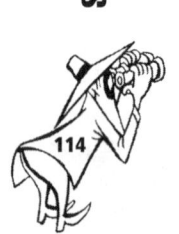

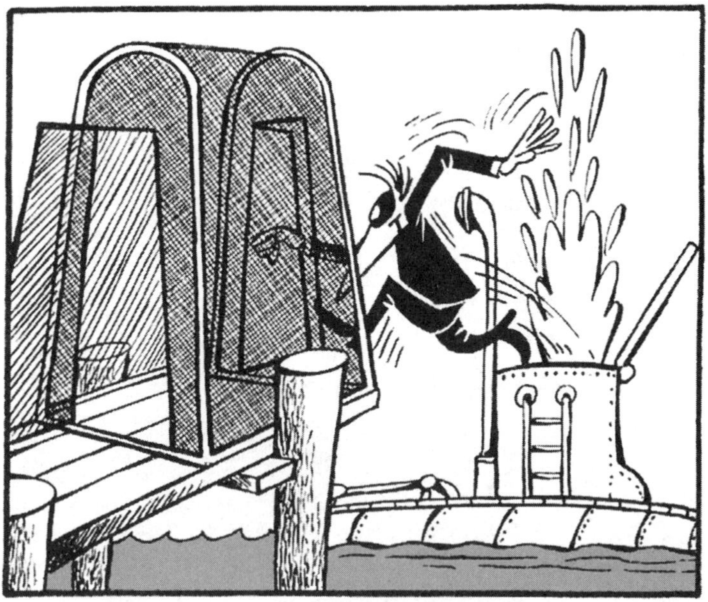

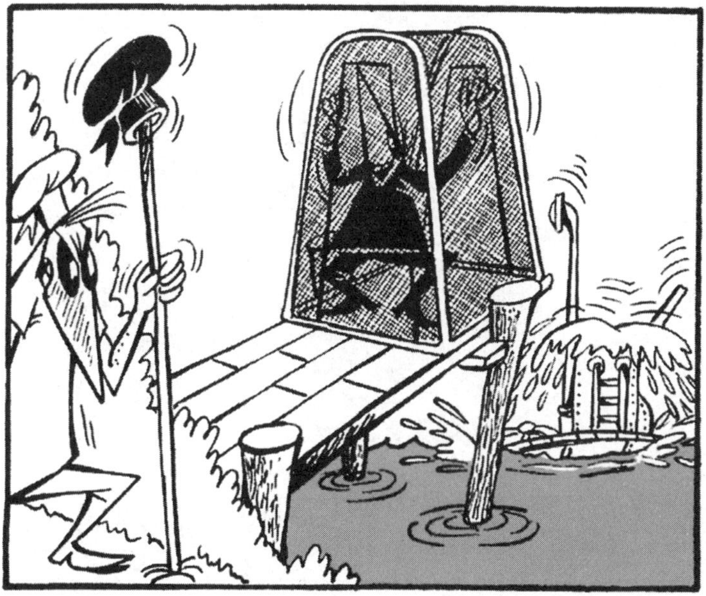

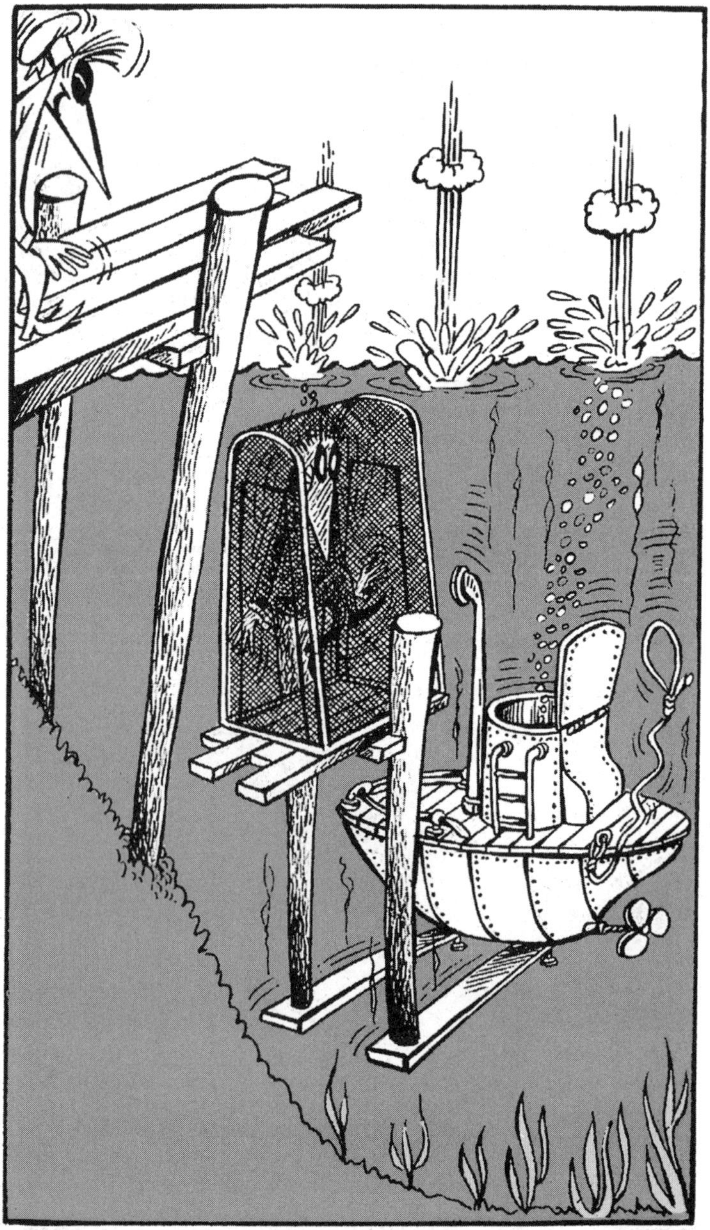

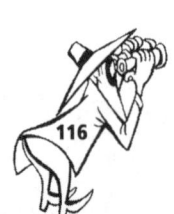

OPERATION: PORTAL TO PORTAL PLAY

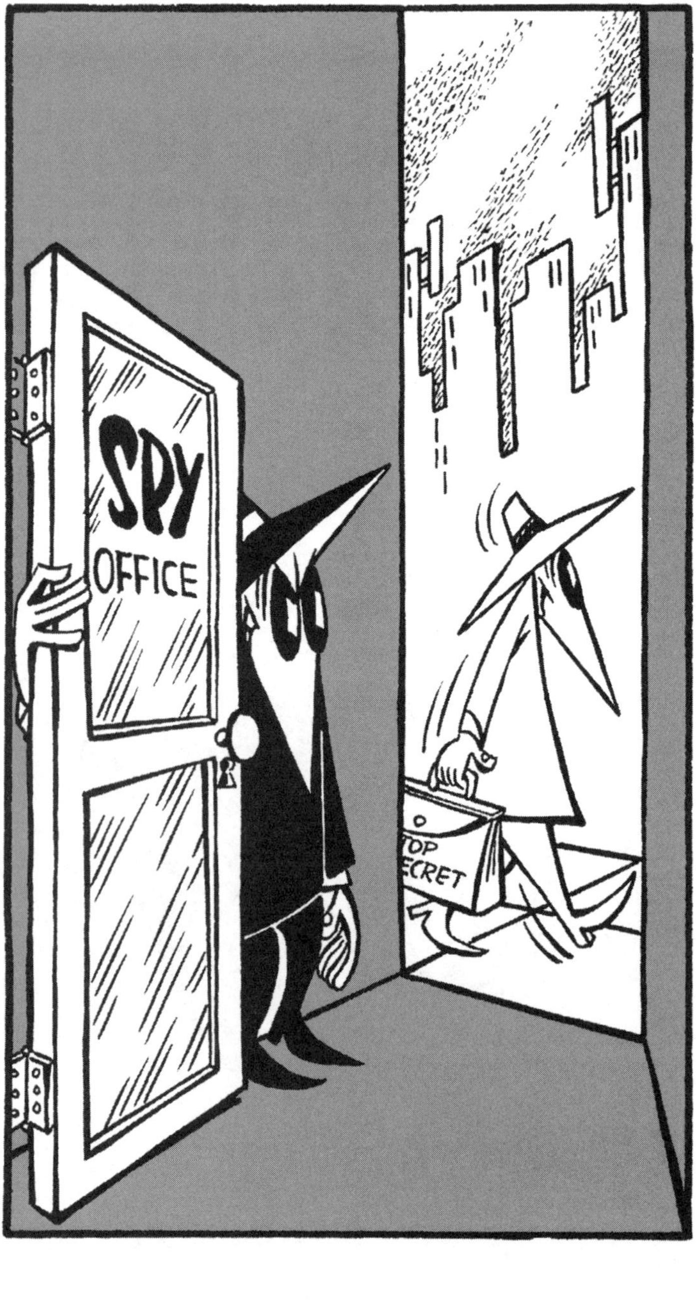
SPY
OFFICE

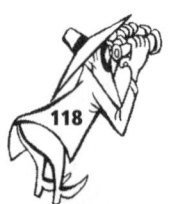

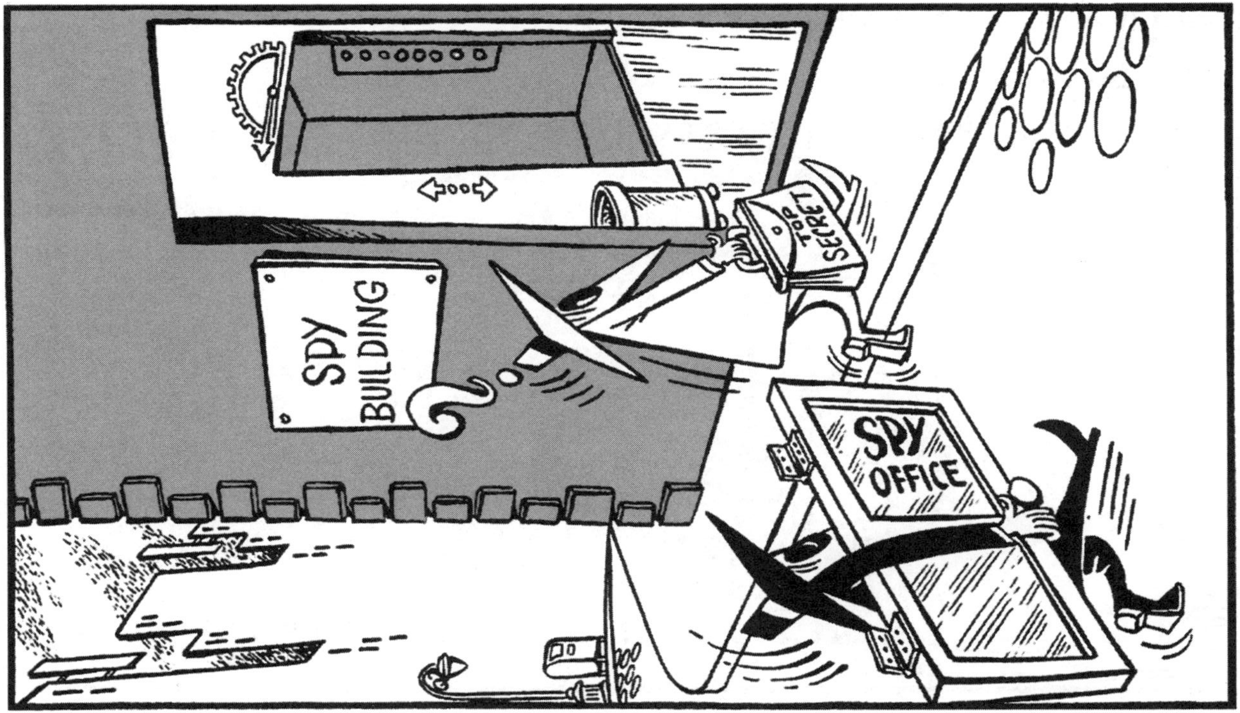
SPY BUILDING
TOP SECRET
SPY OFFICE

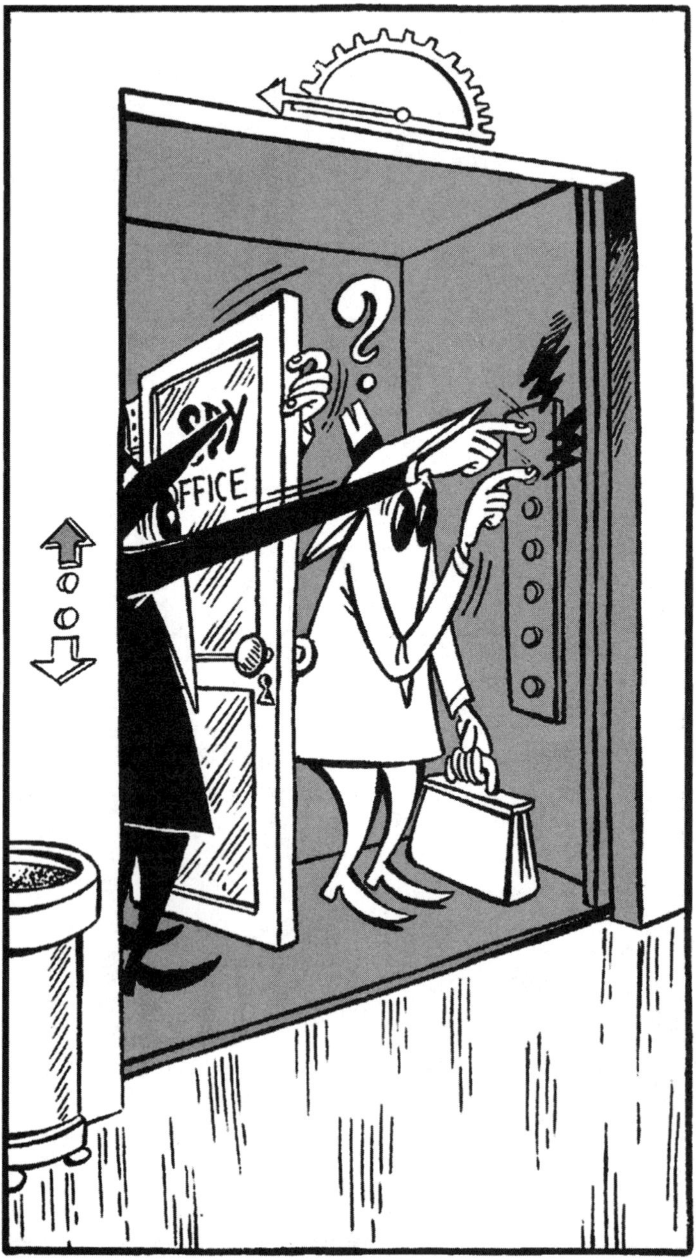
SPY
FFICE

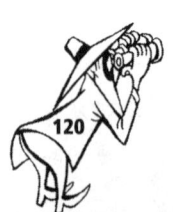

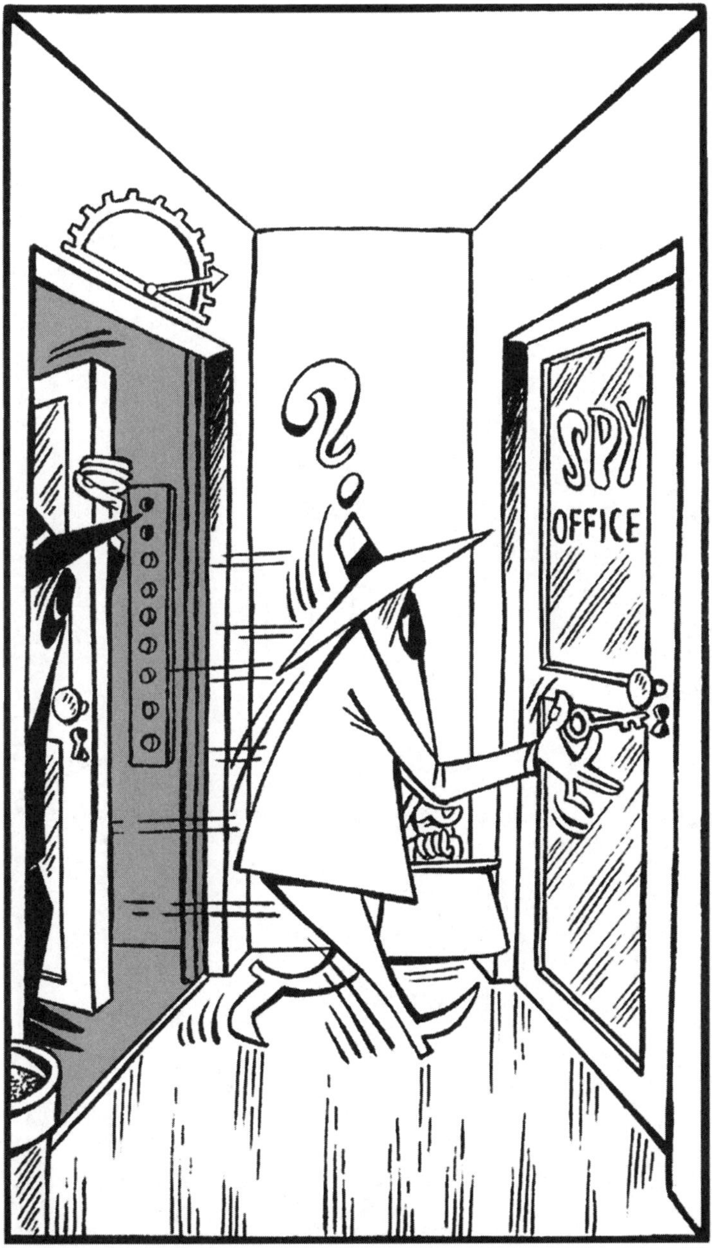
SPY
OFFICE

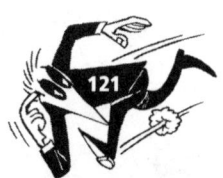

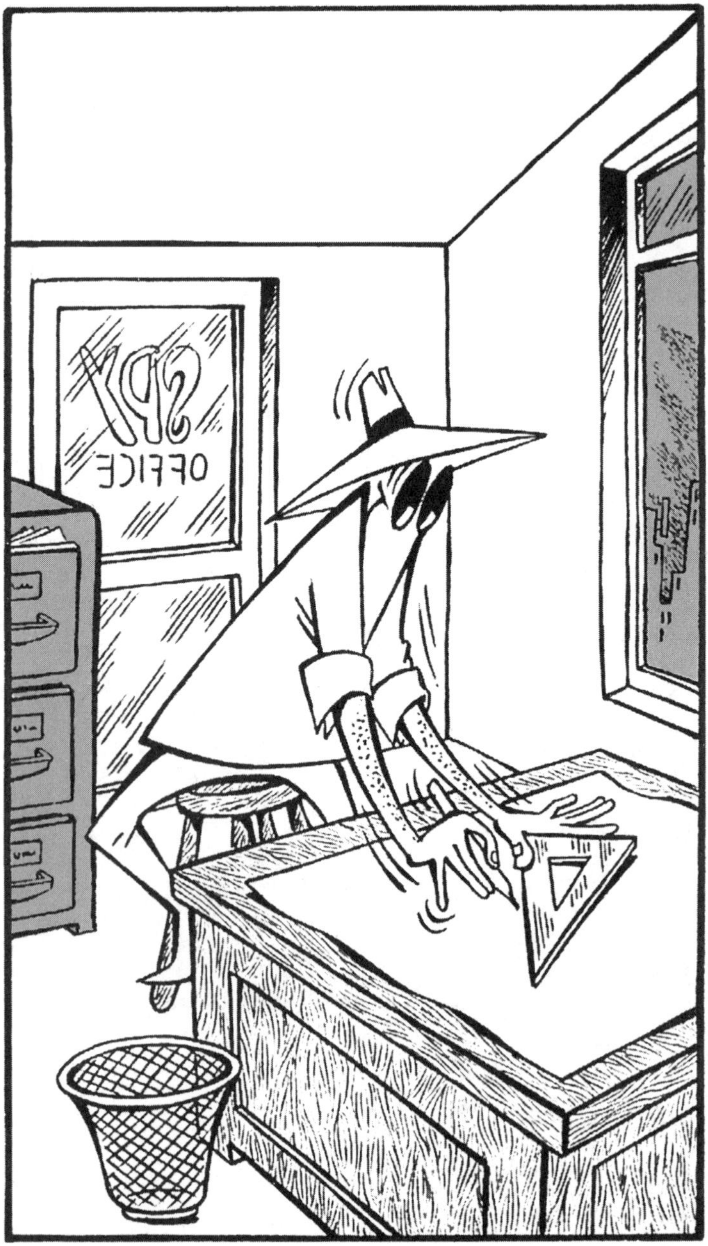
SPY
OFFICE

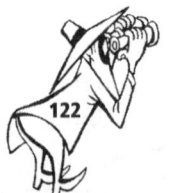

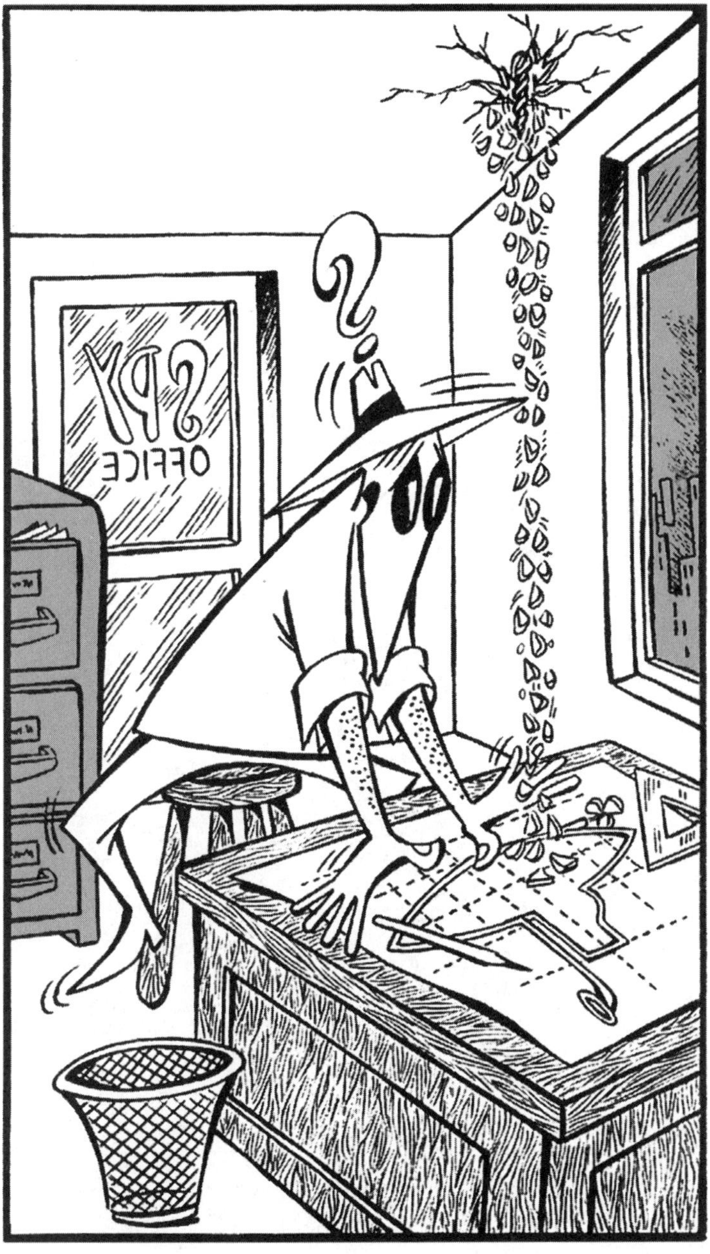
SPY
OFFICE

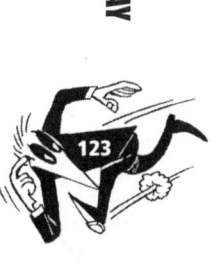

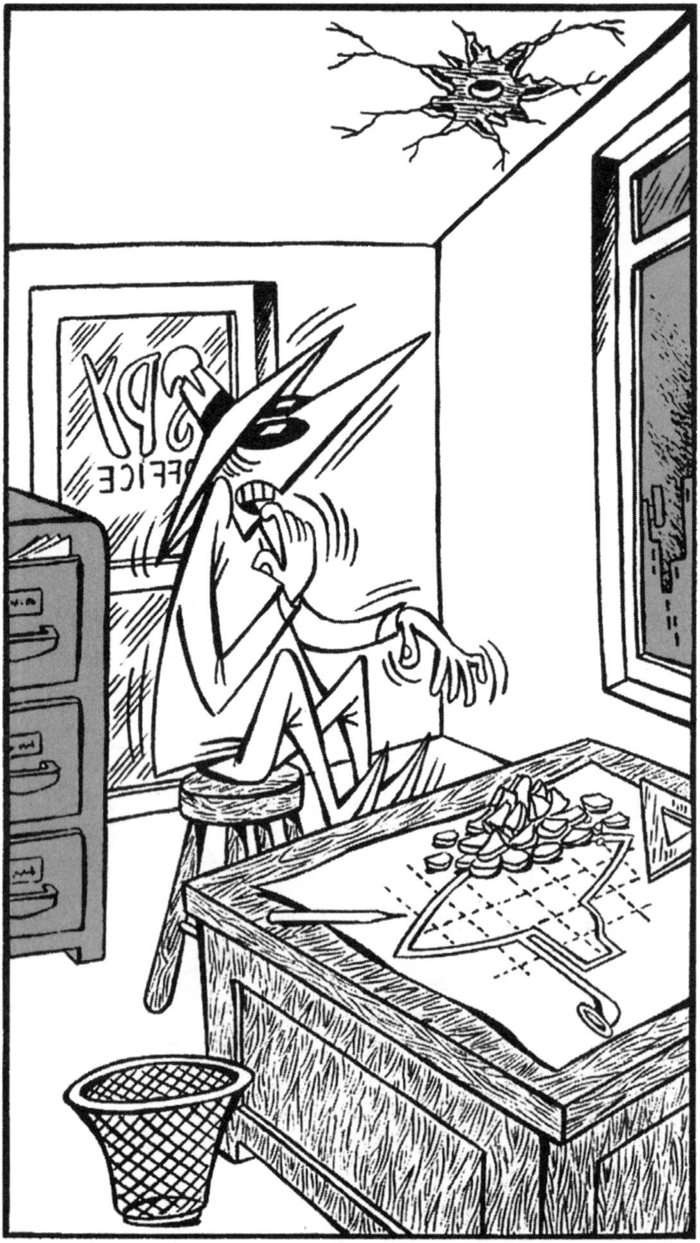

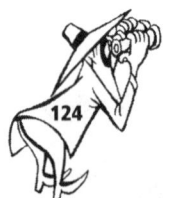

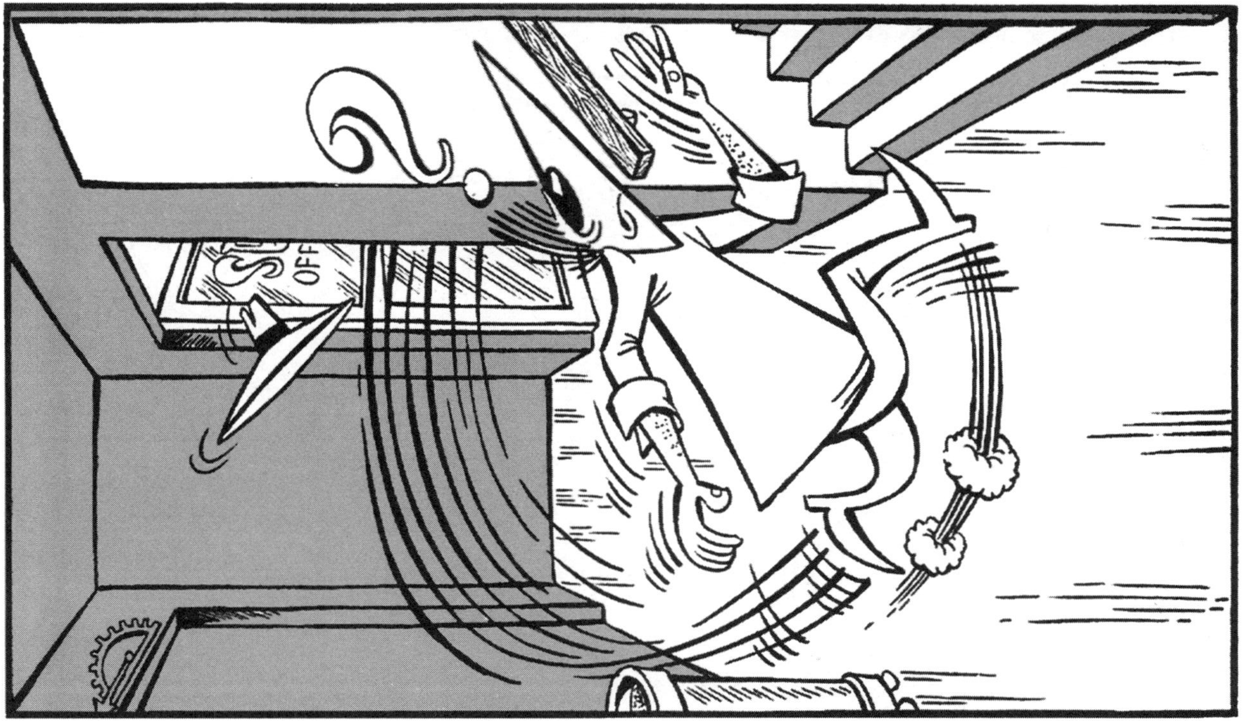

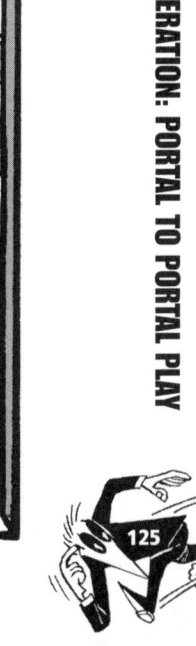

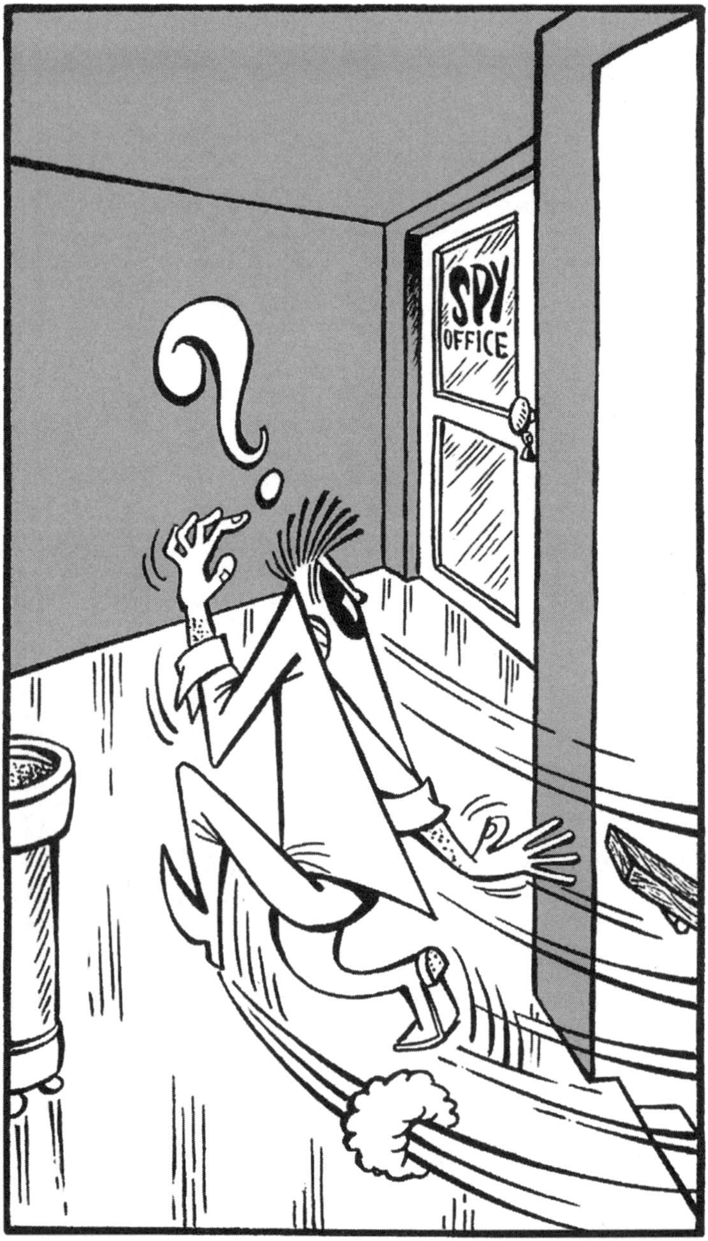
SPY
OFFICE

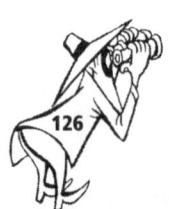

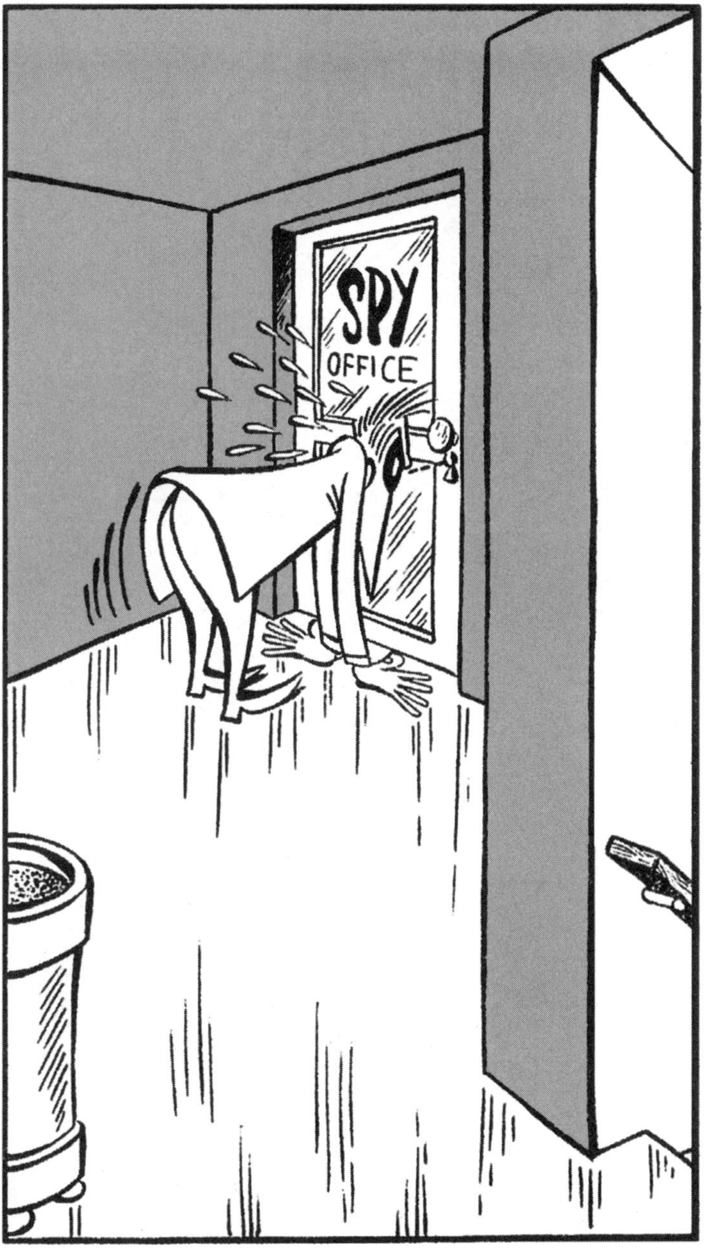
SPY
OFFICE

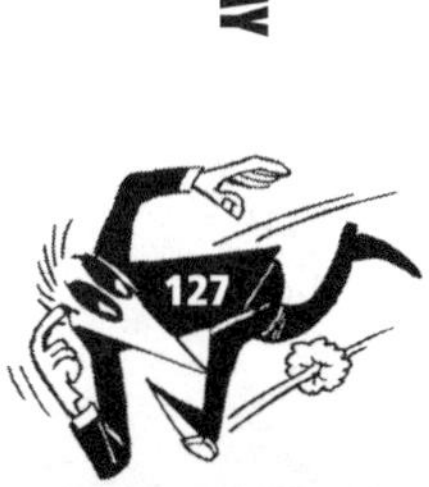

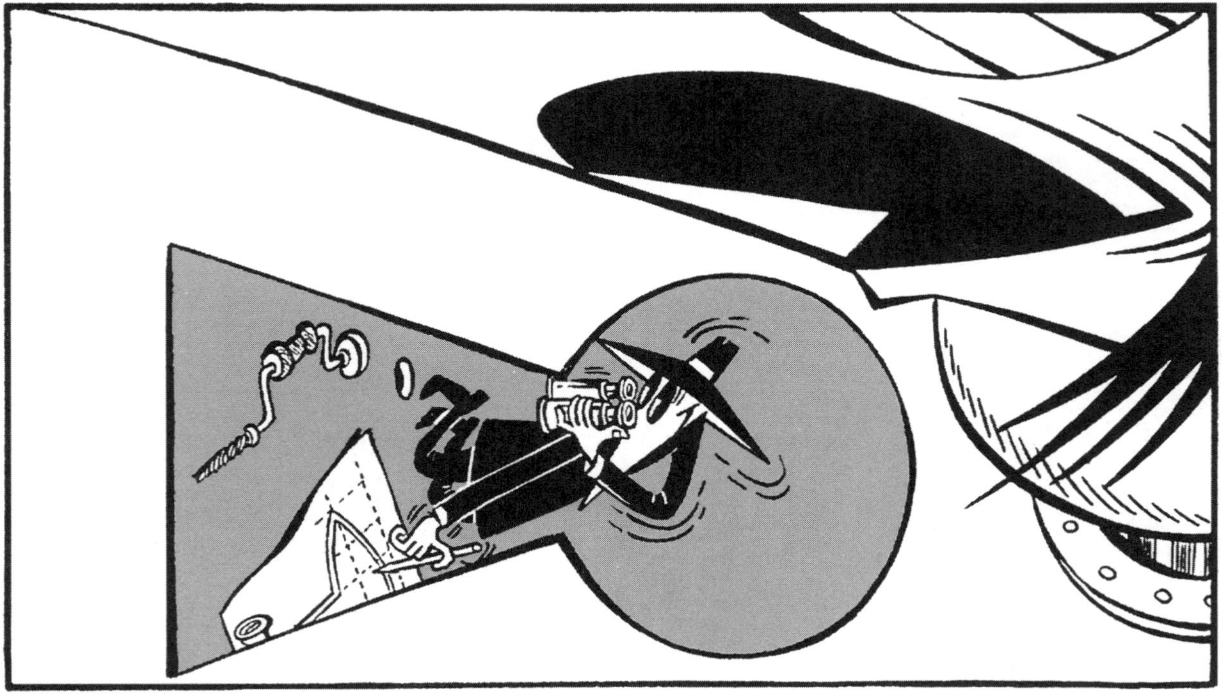

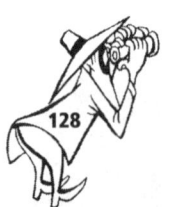

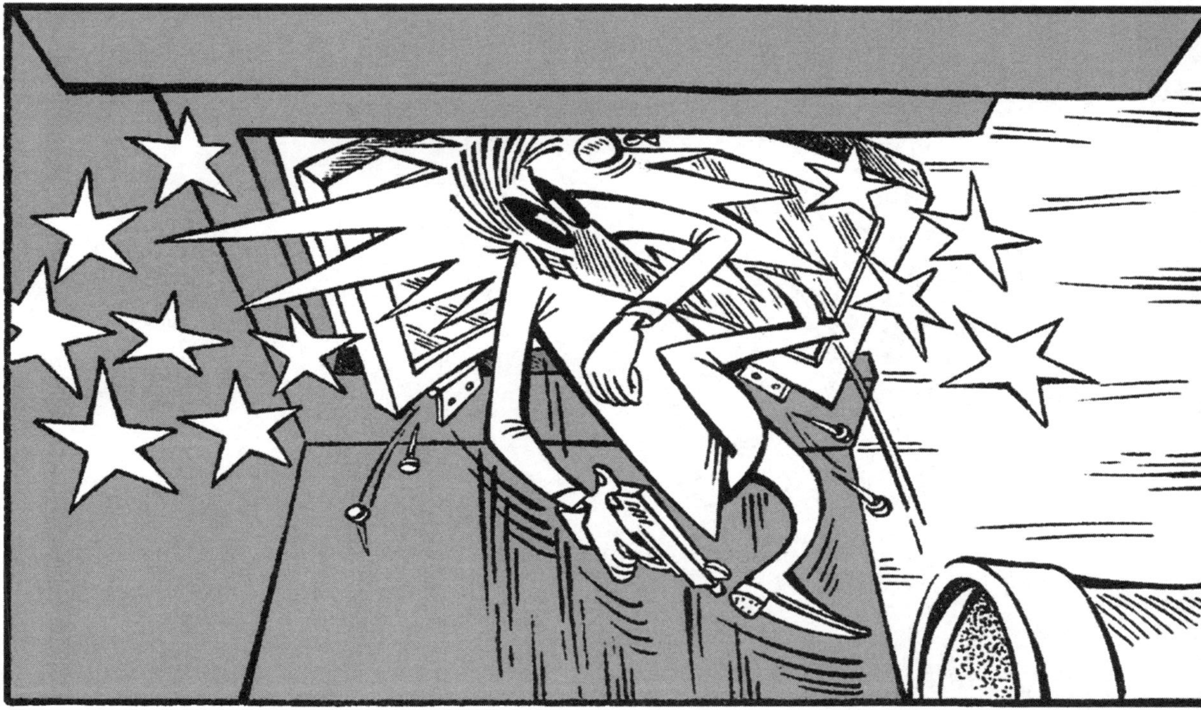

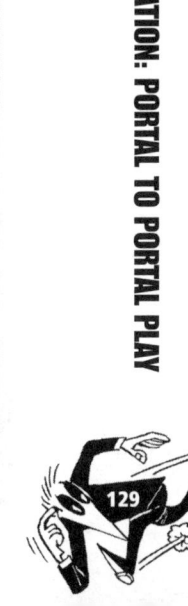

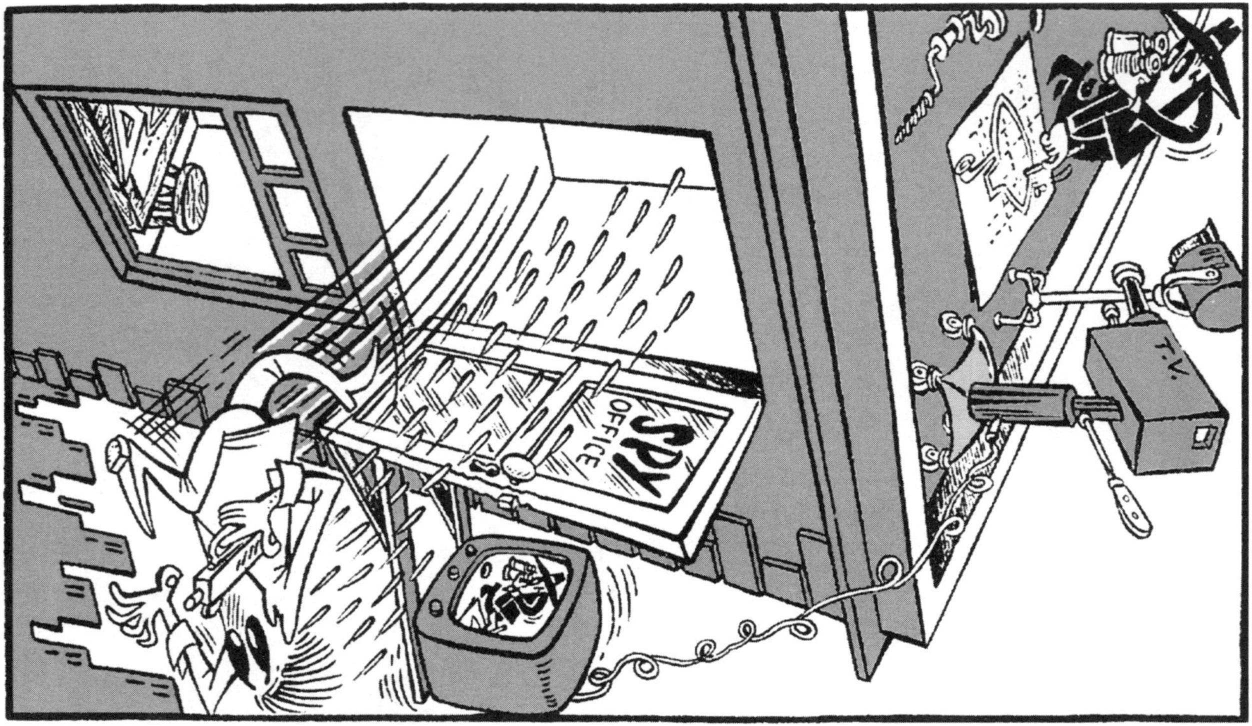
T.V.
SPY
OFFICE

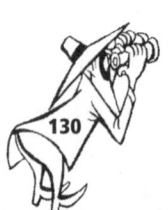

OPERATION: BIG TOW

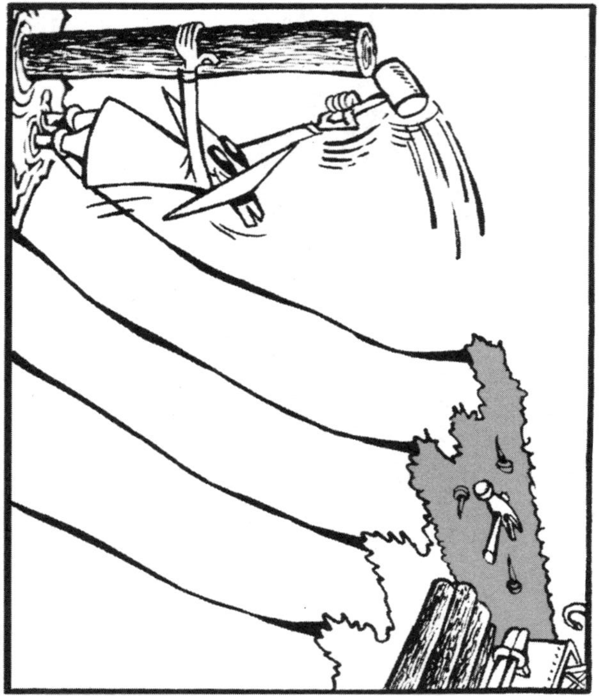

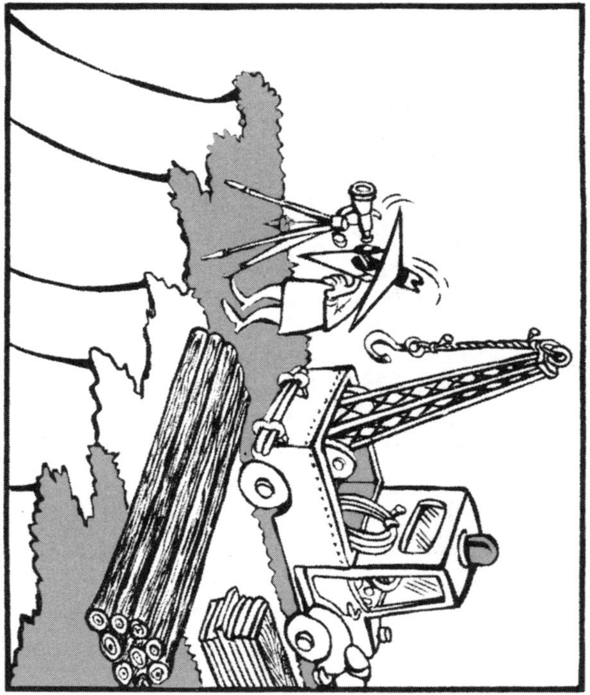

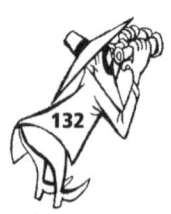

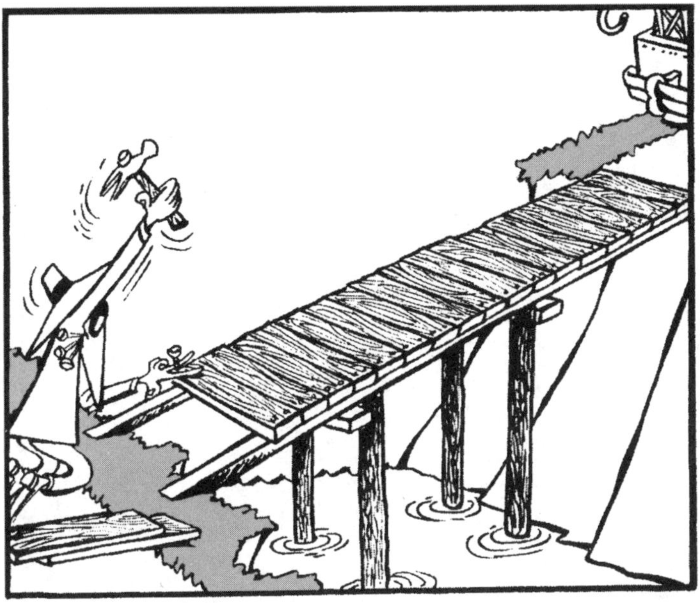

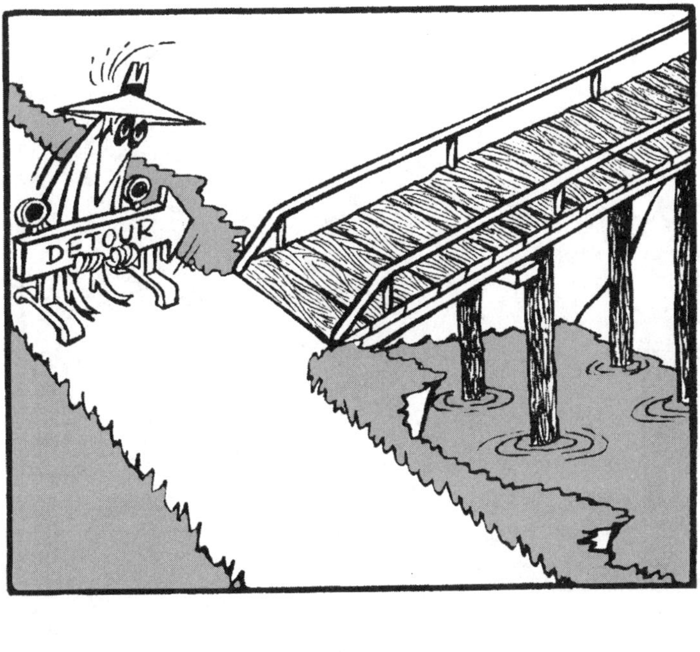
DETOUR

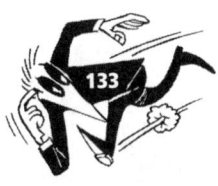

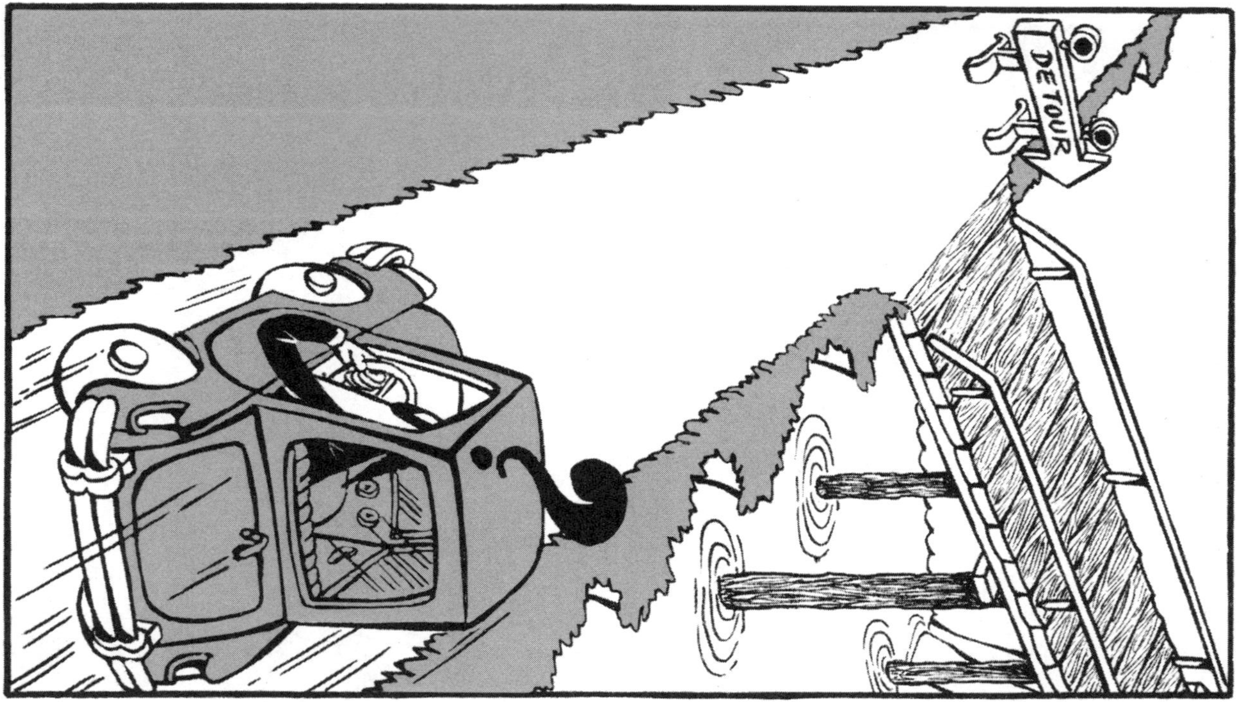
DETOUR

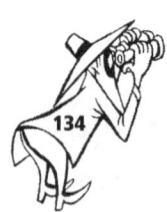

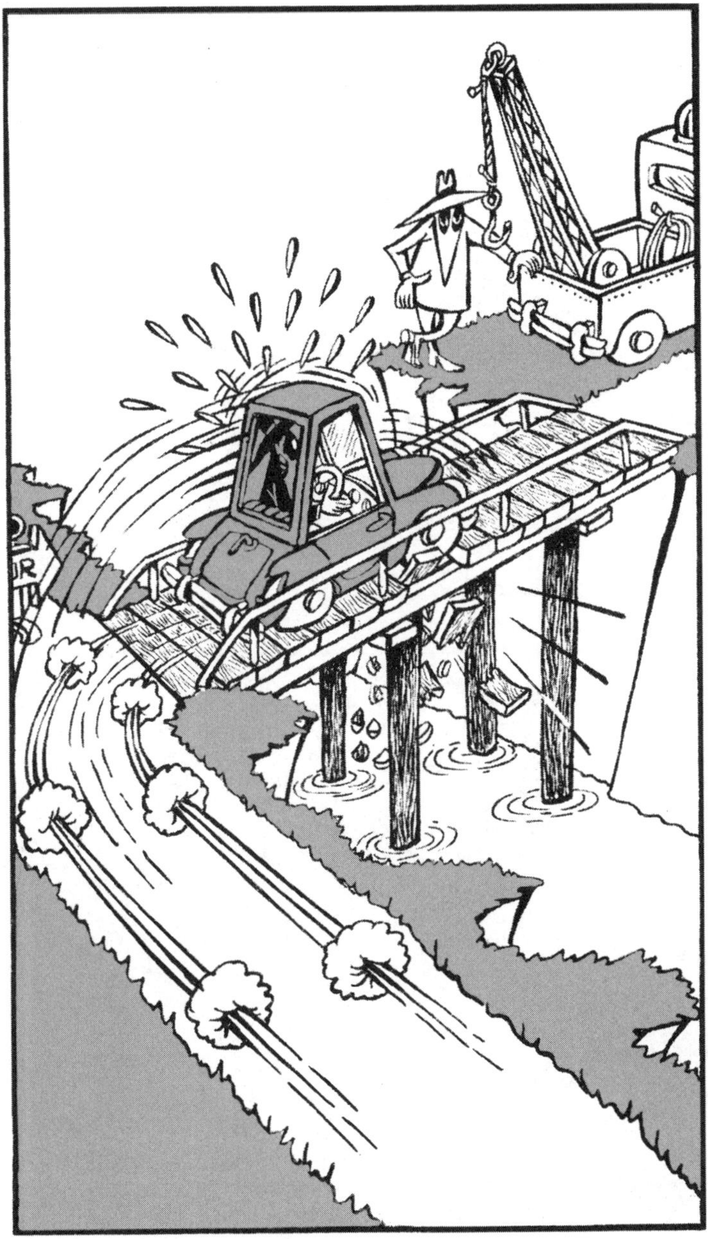

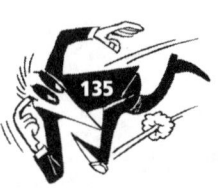

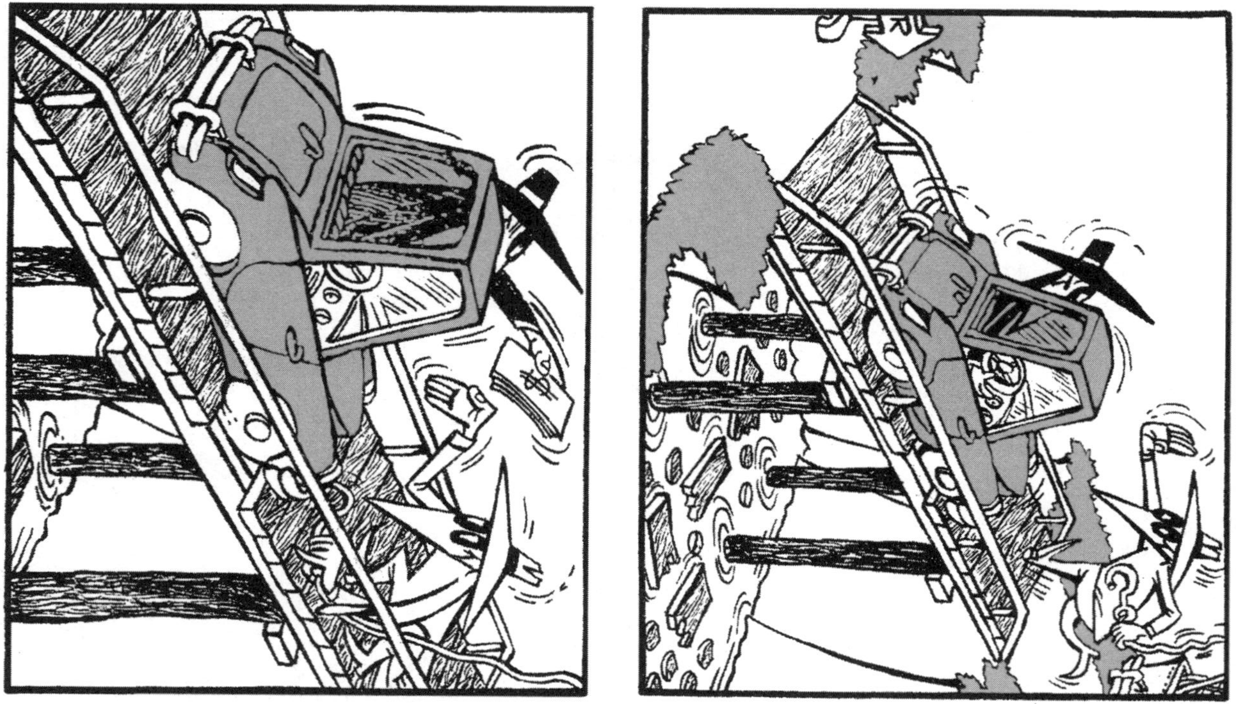

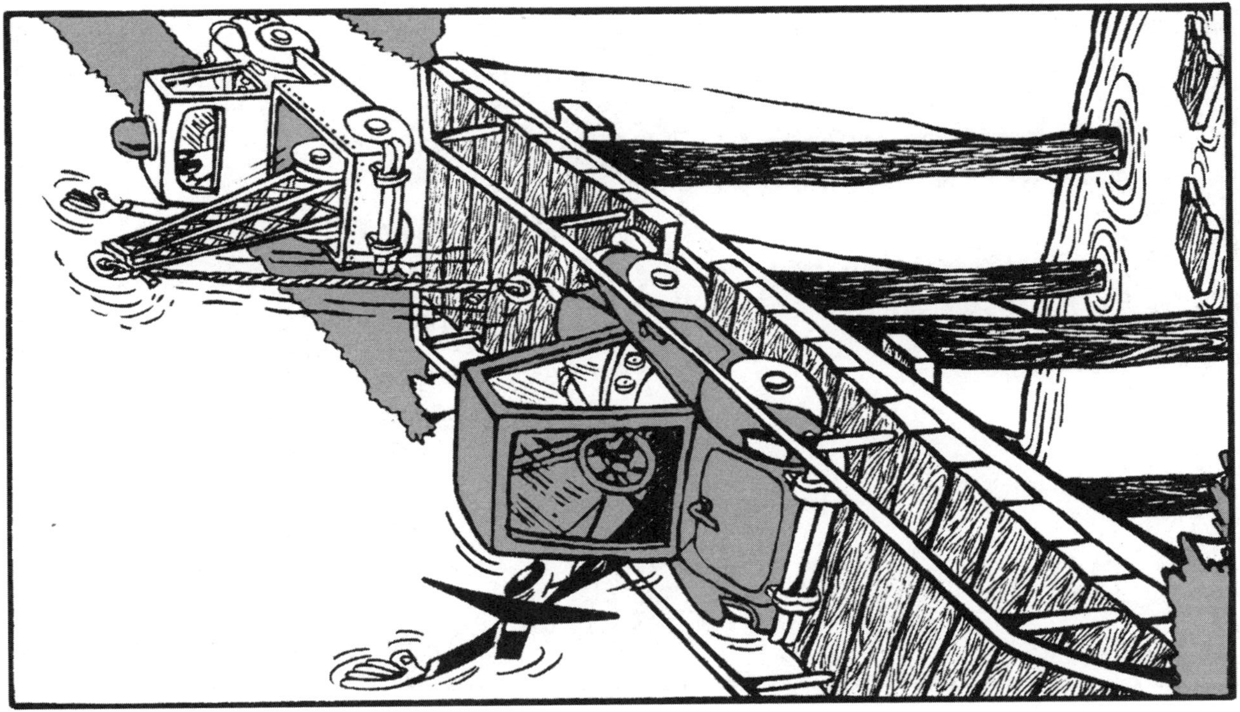

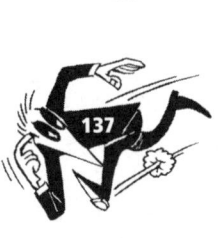

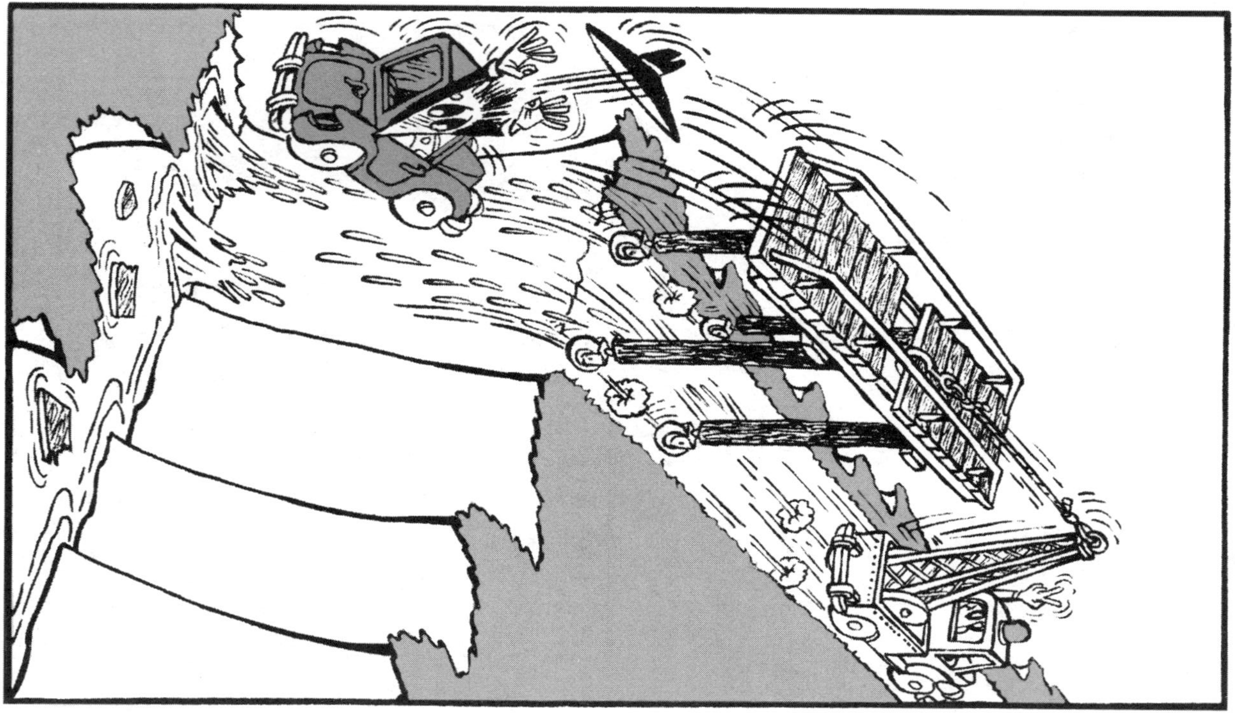

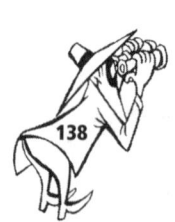

OPERATION: CIGAR STORE

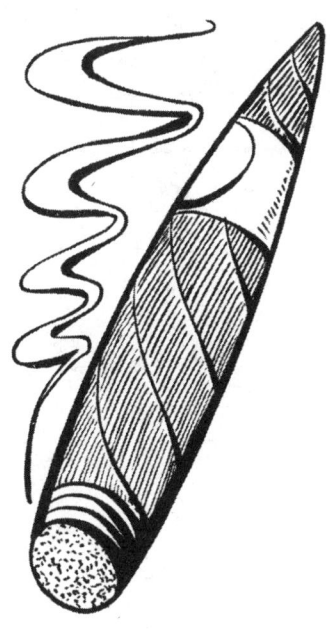

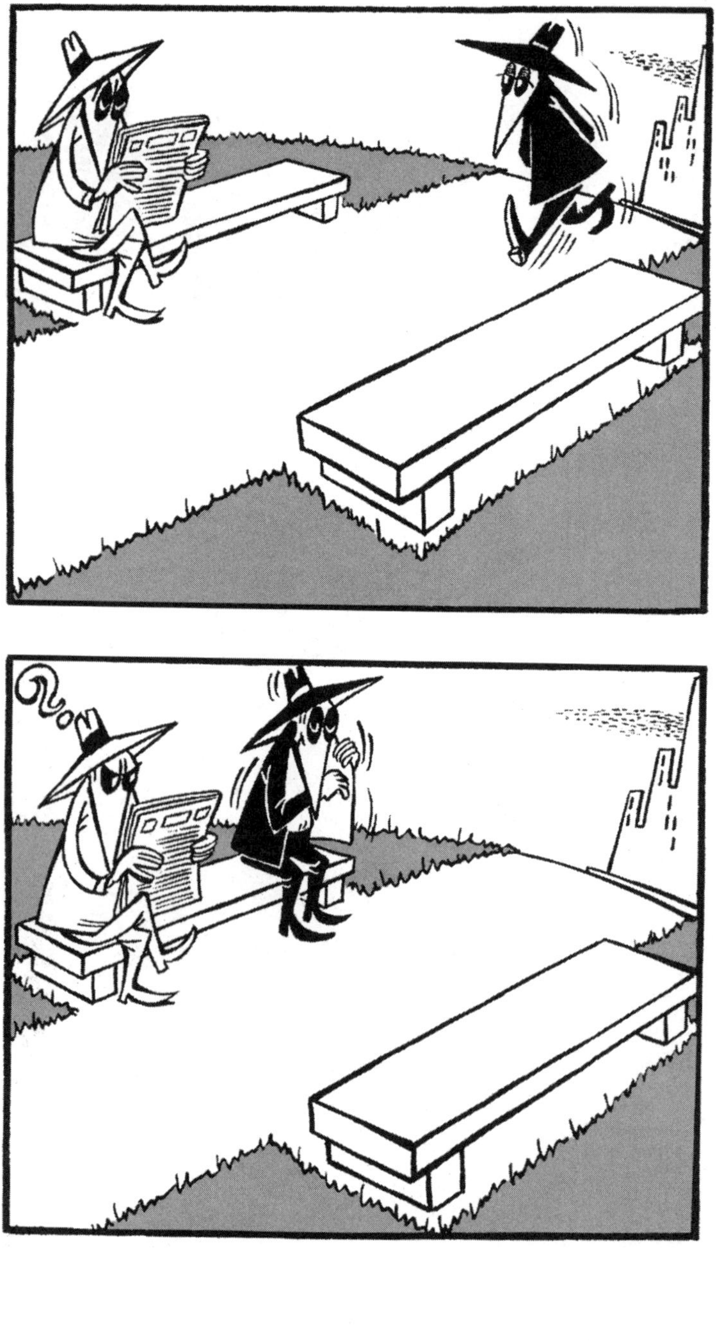

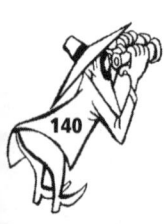

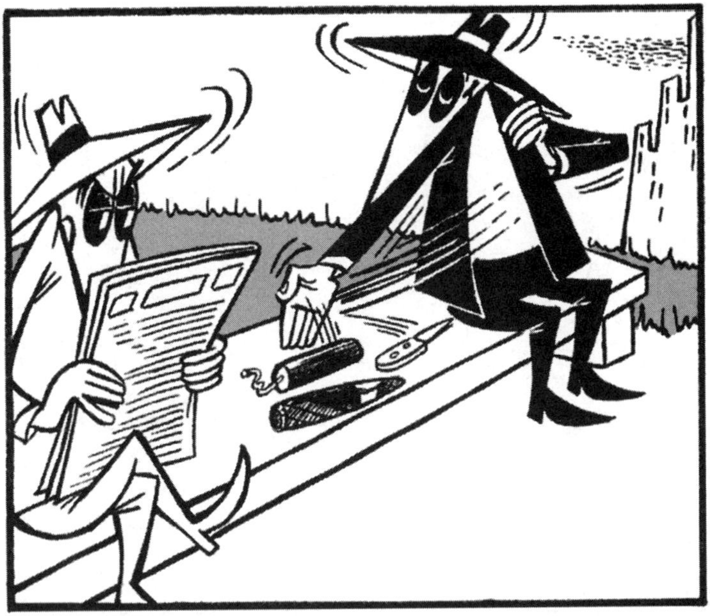

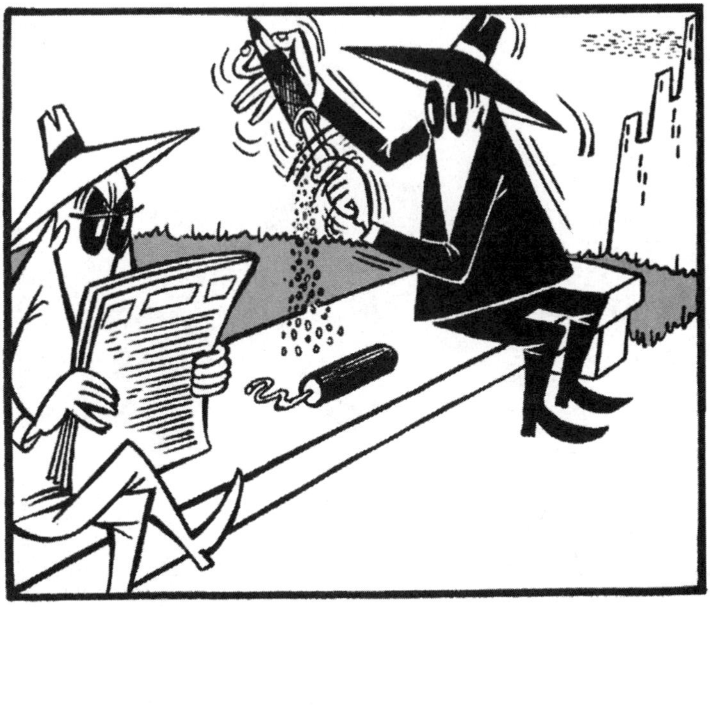

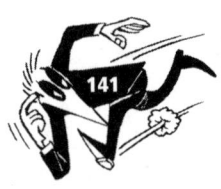

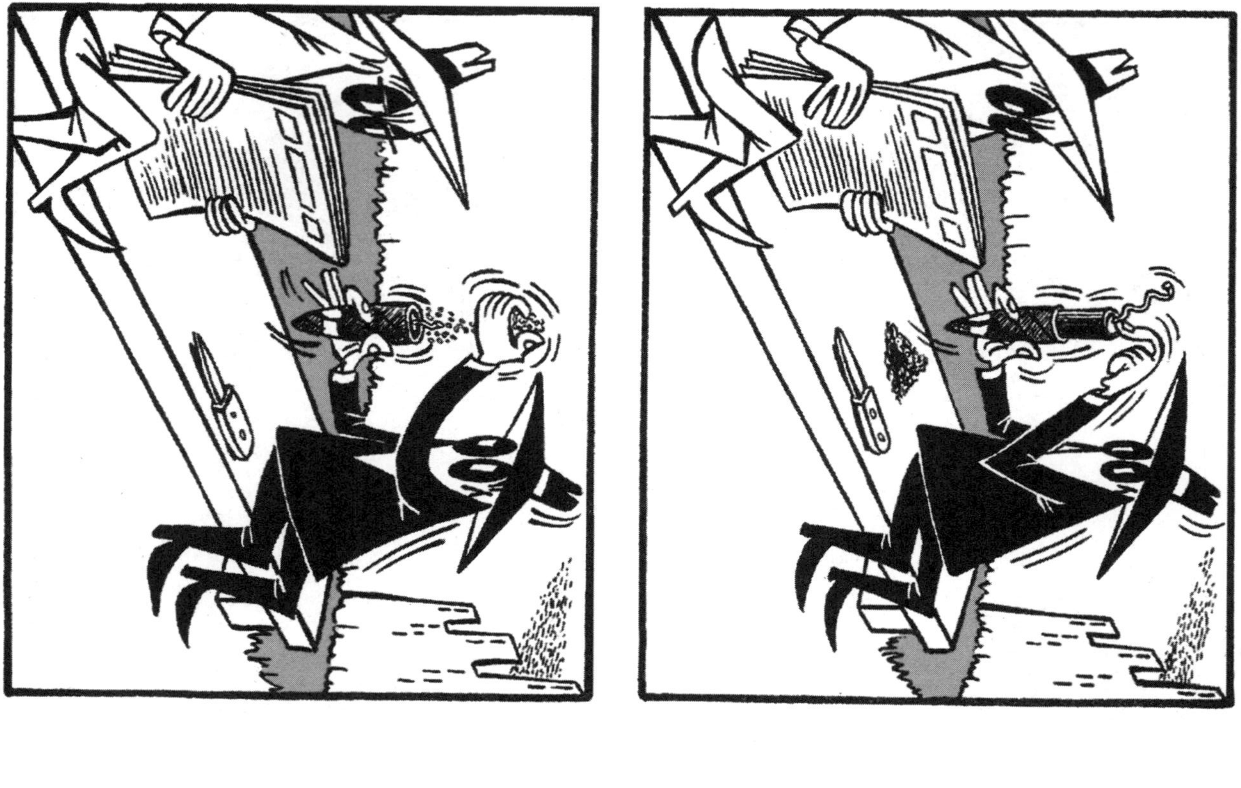

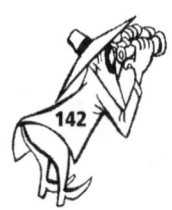

OPERATION: CIGAR STORE

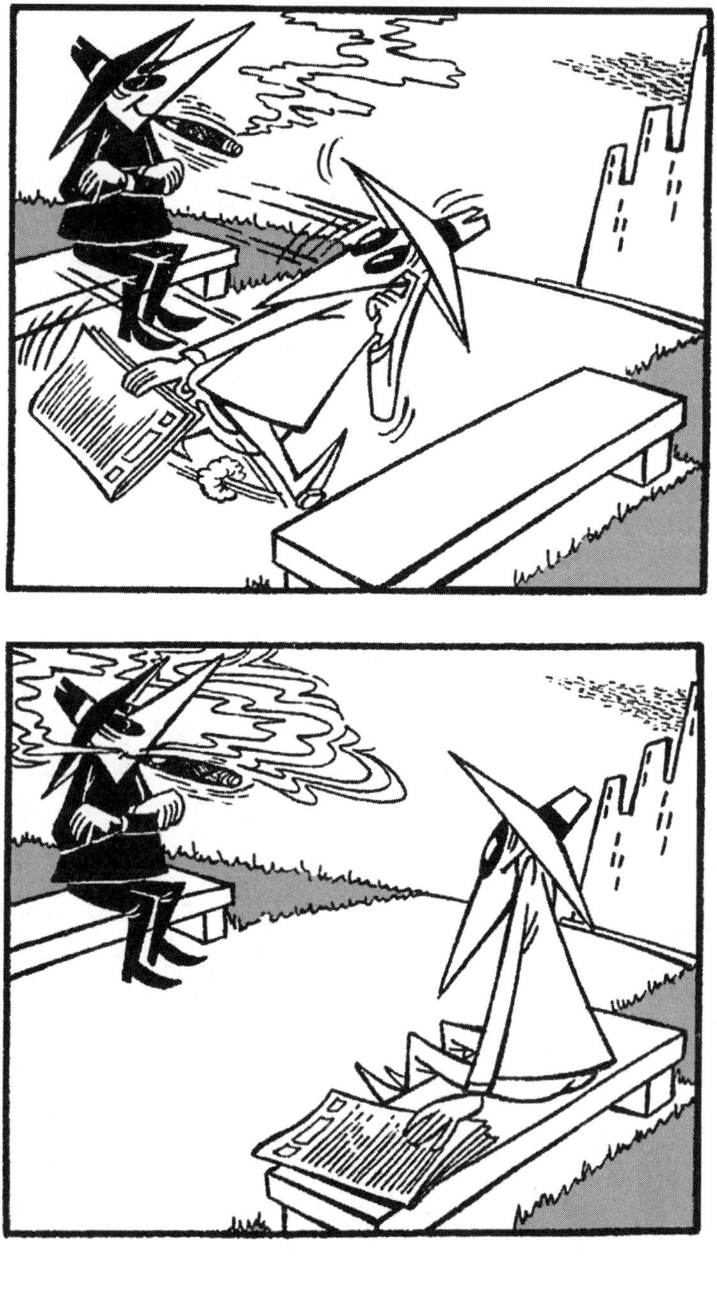

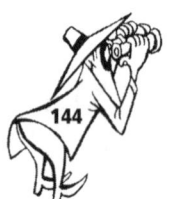

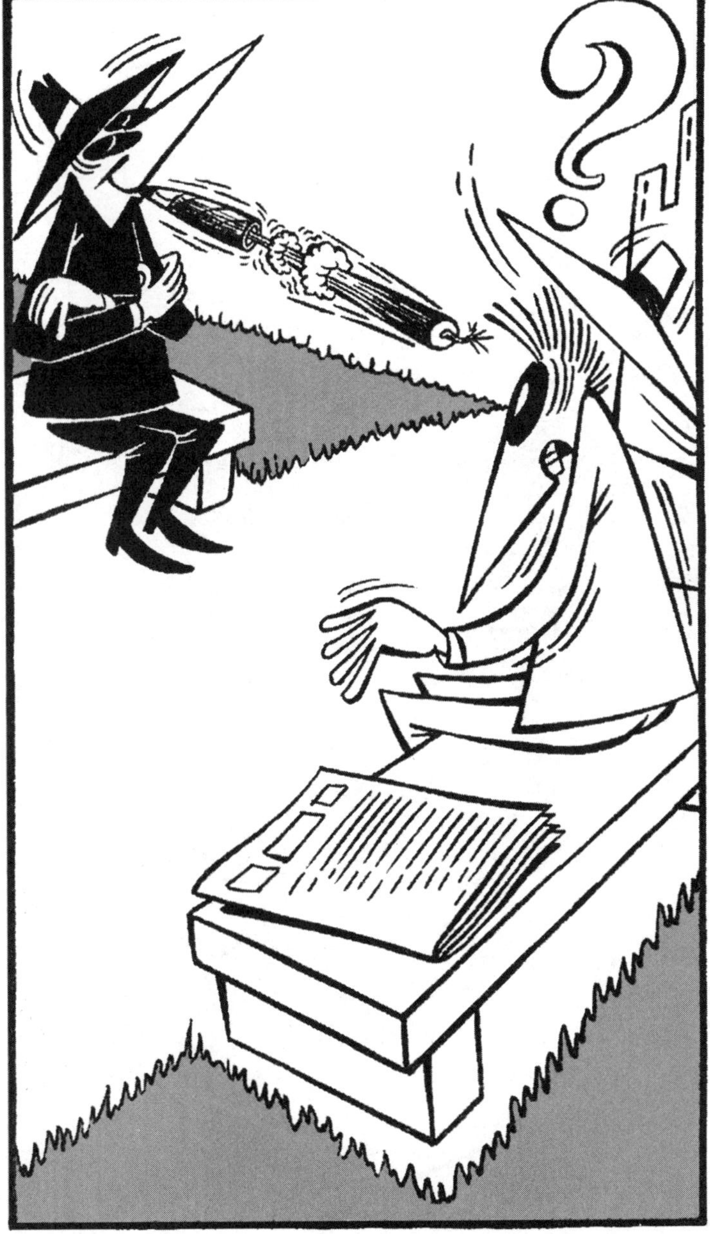

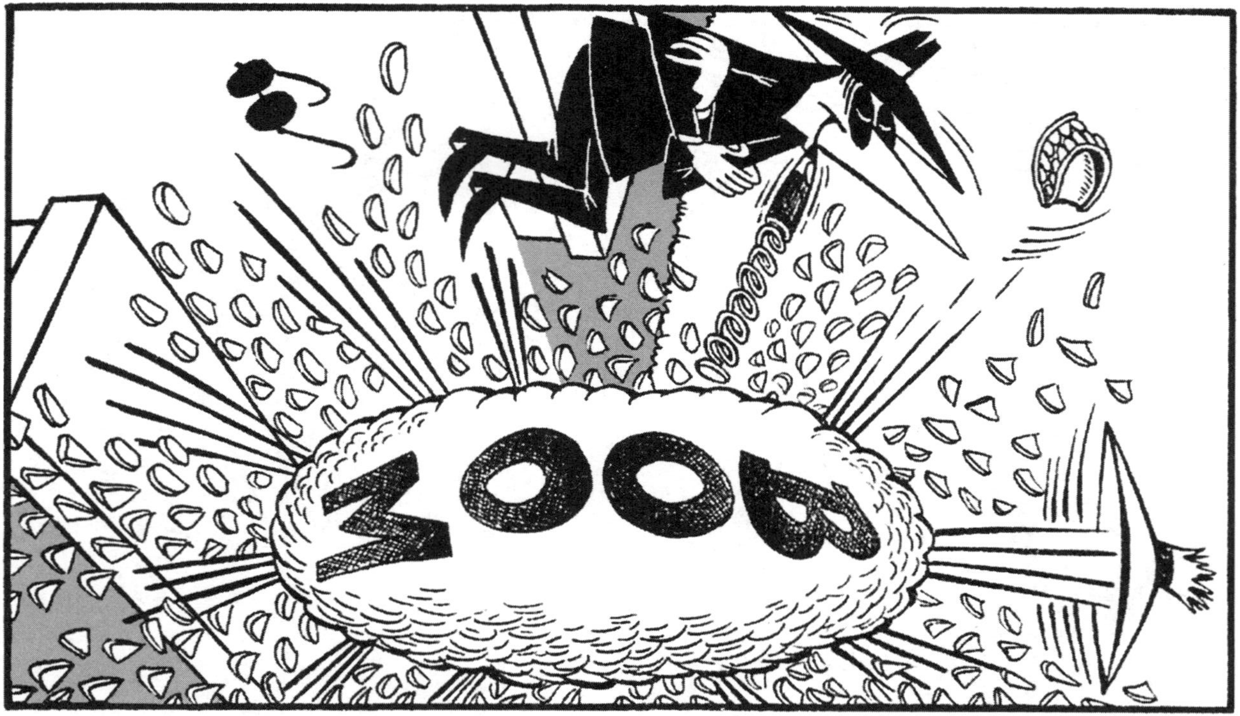
BOOM

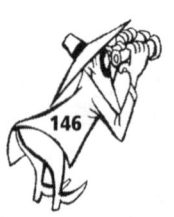

OPERATION: OPERATION

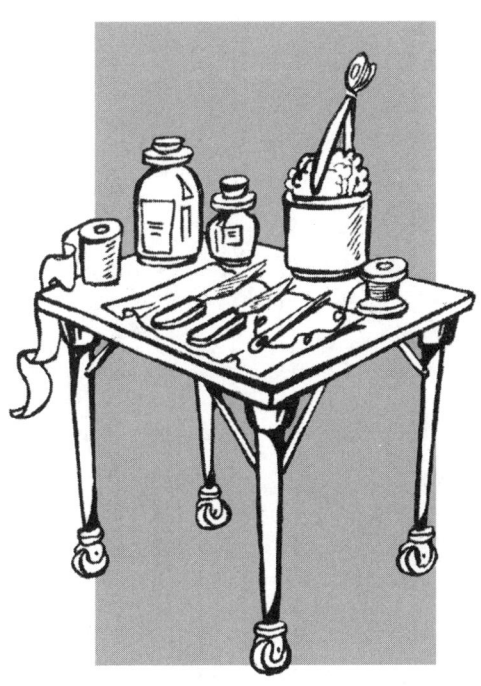

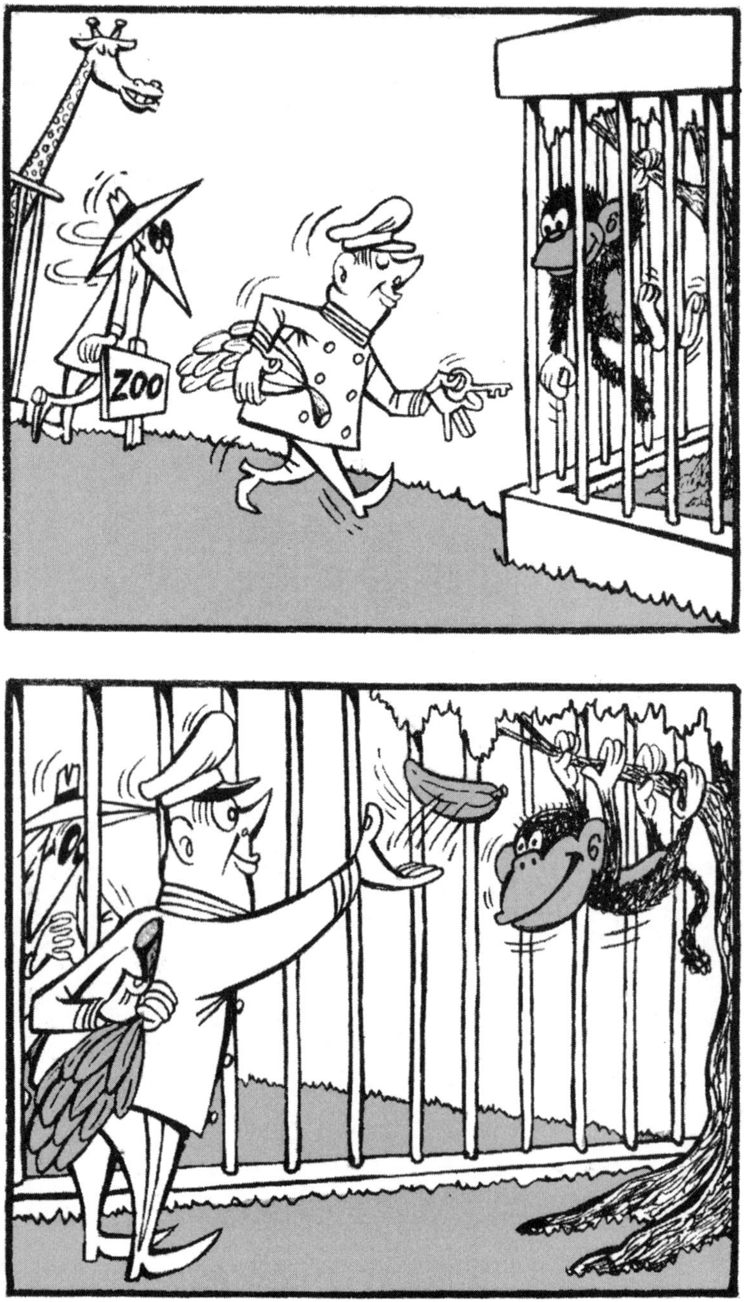
ZOO

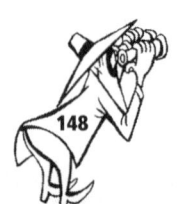

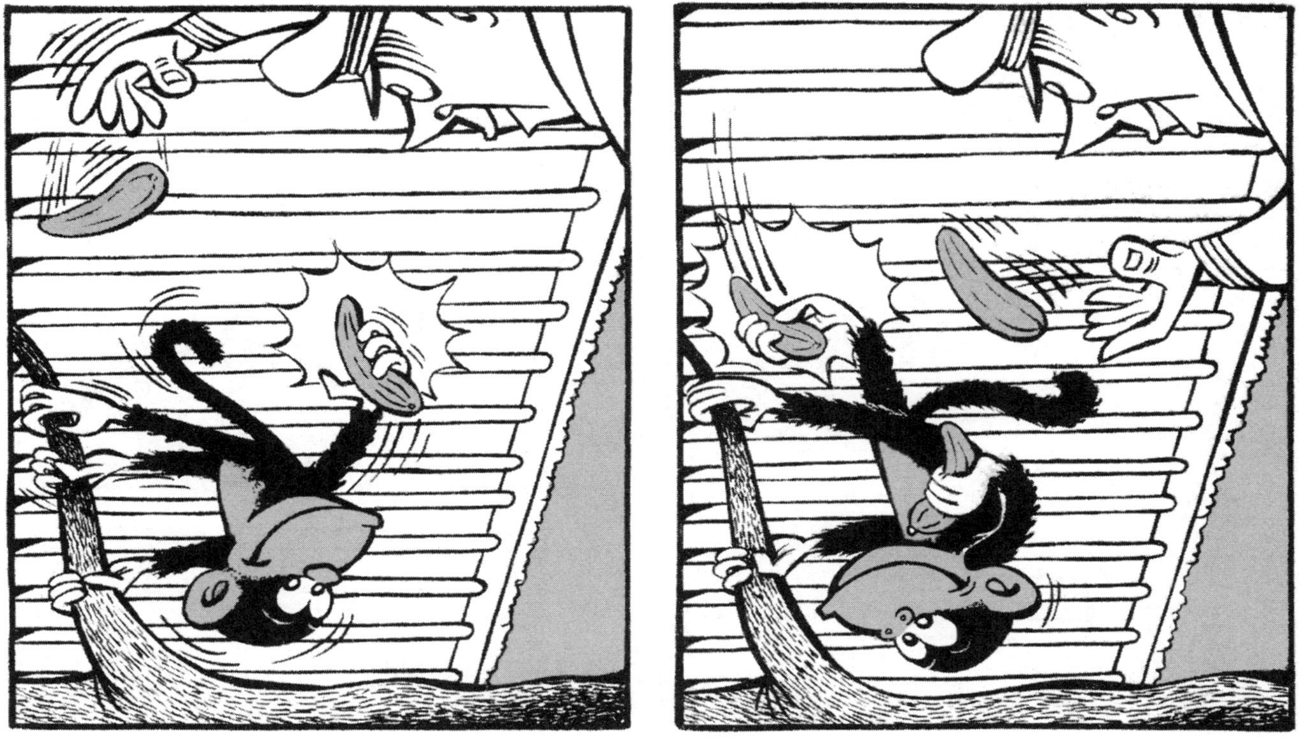

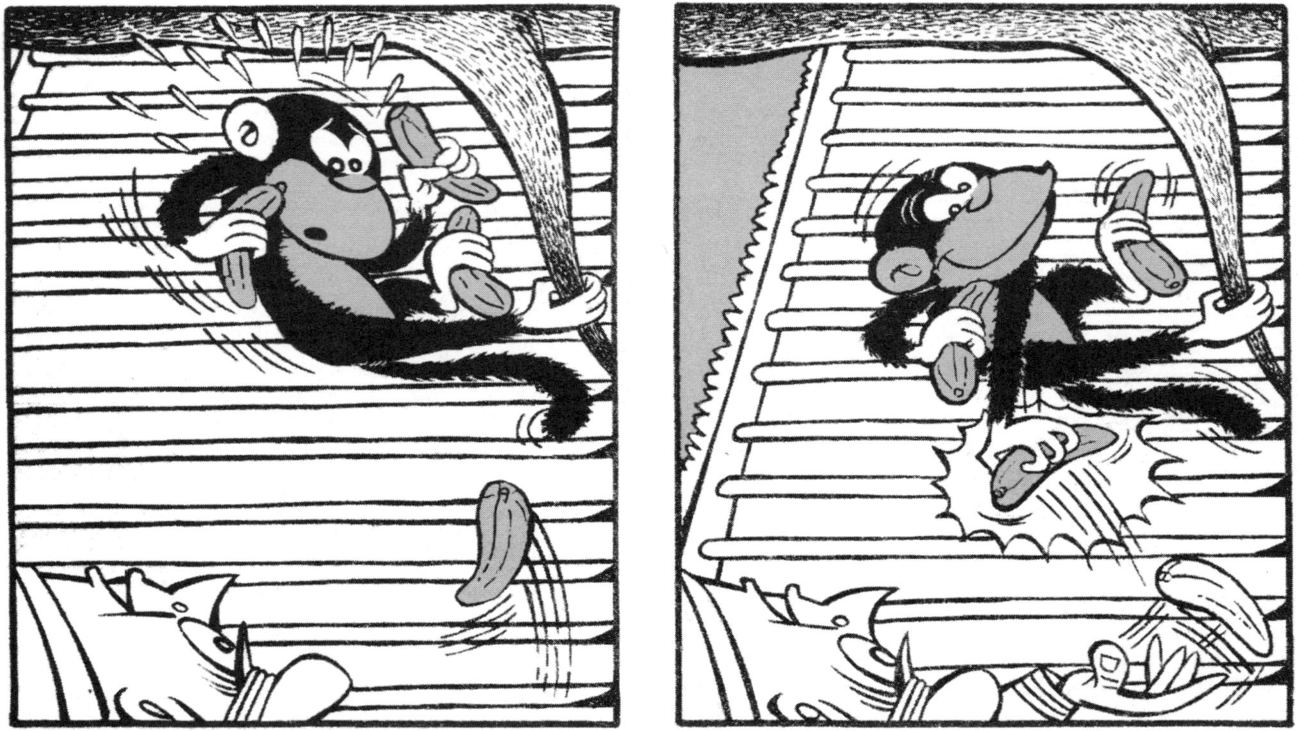

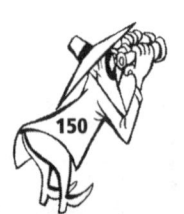

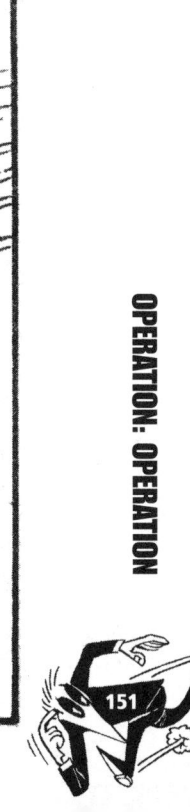

OPERATION: OPERATION

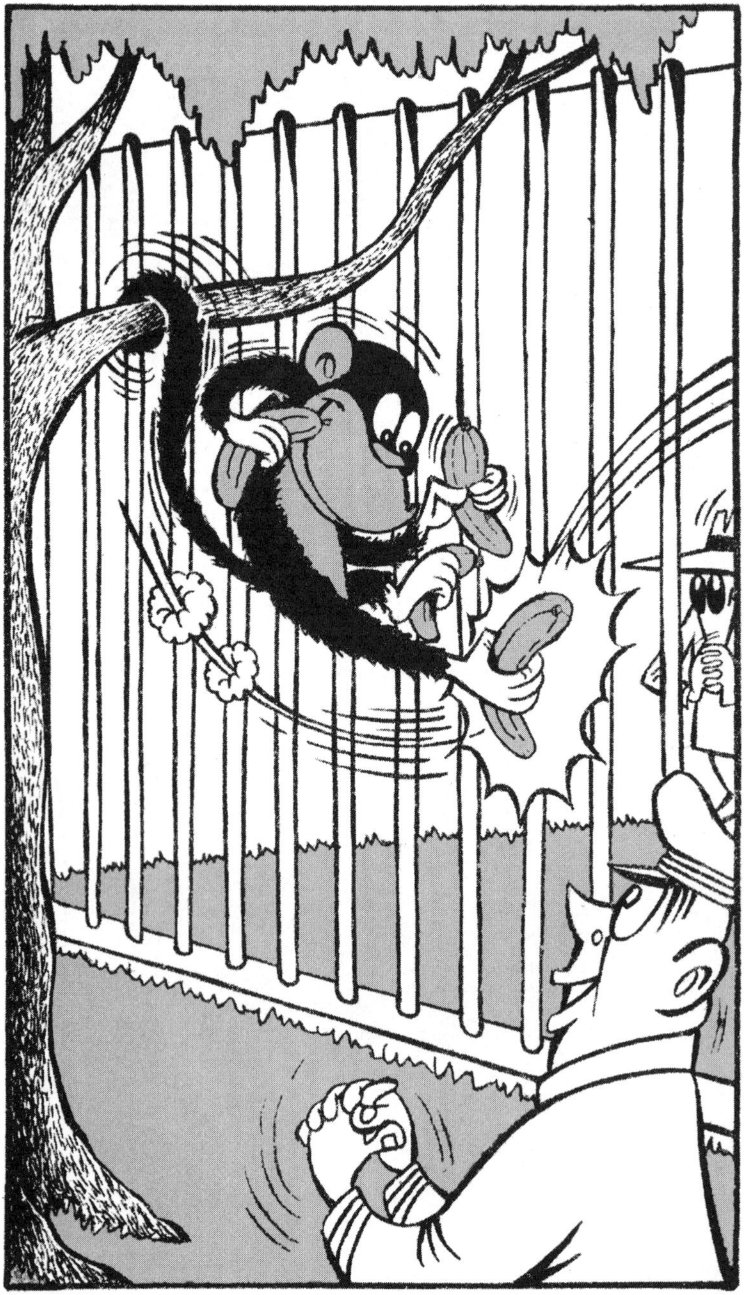

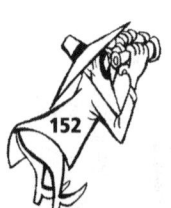

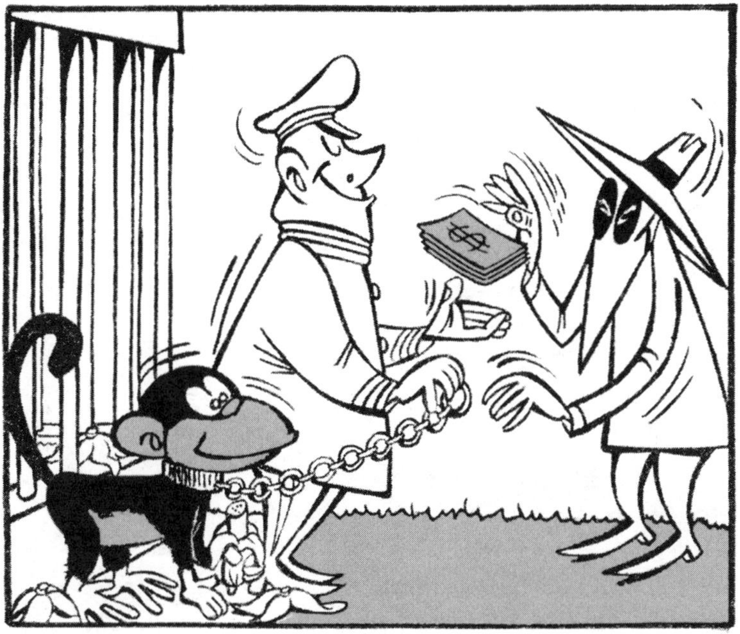

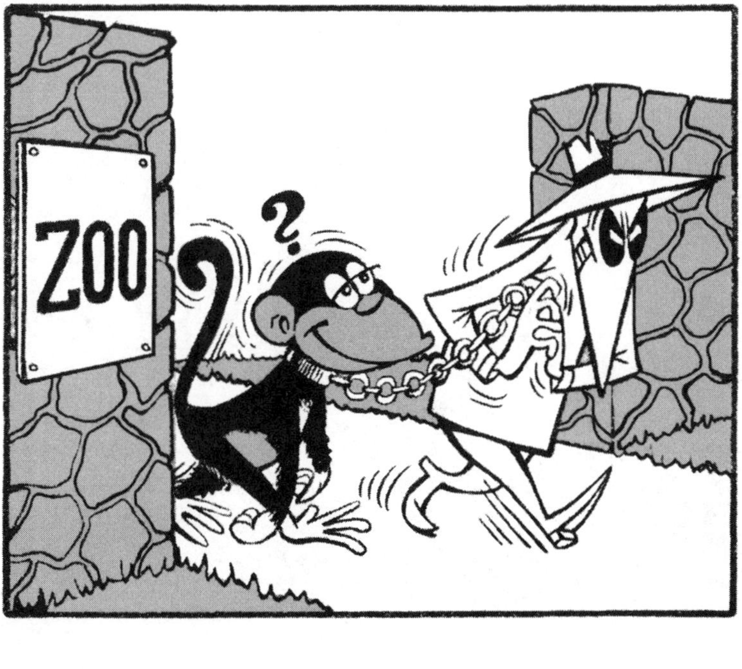
ZOO

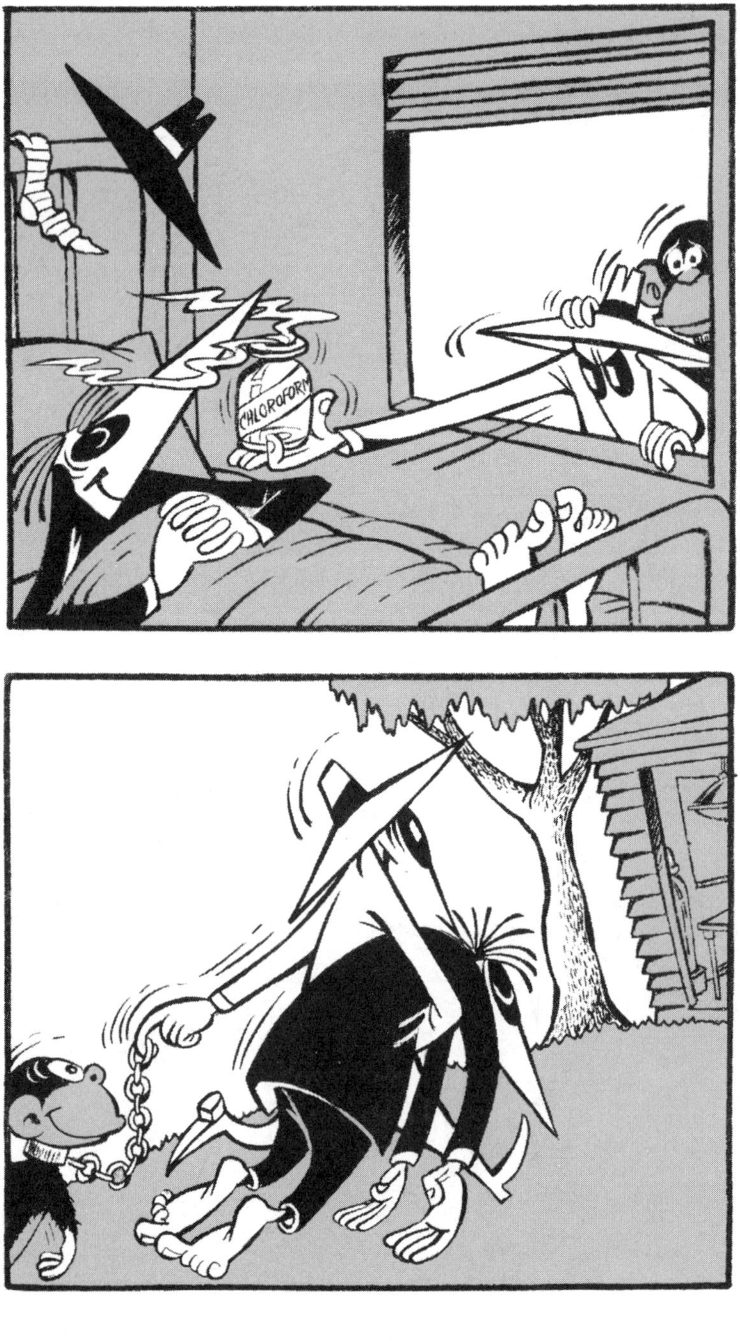
CHLOROFORM

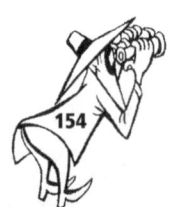

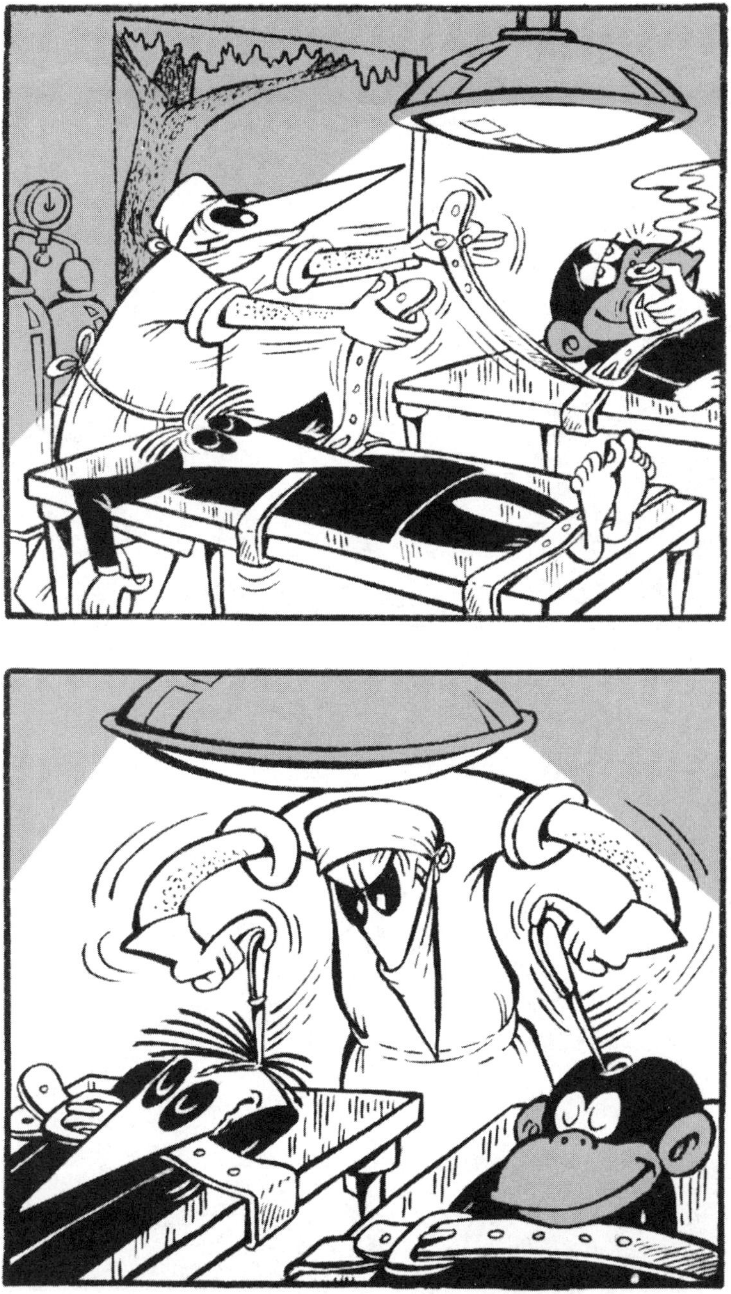

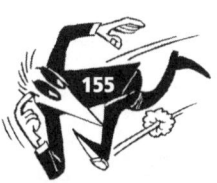

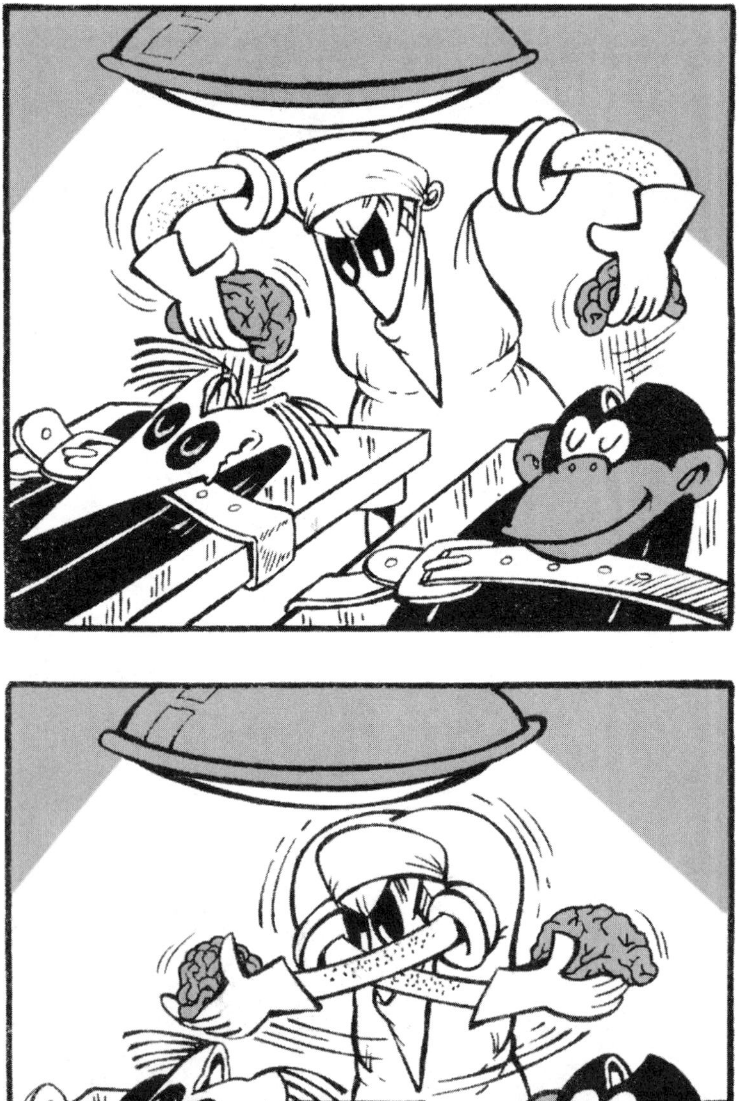

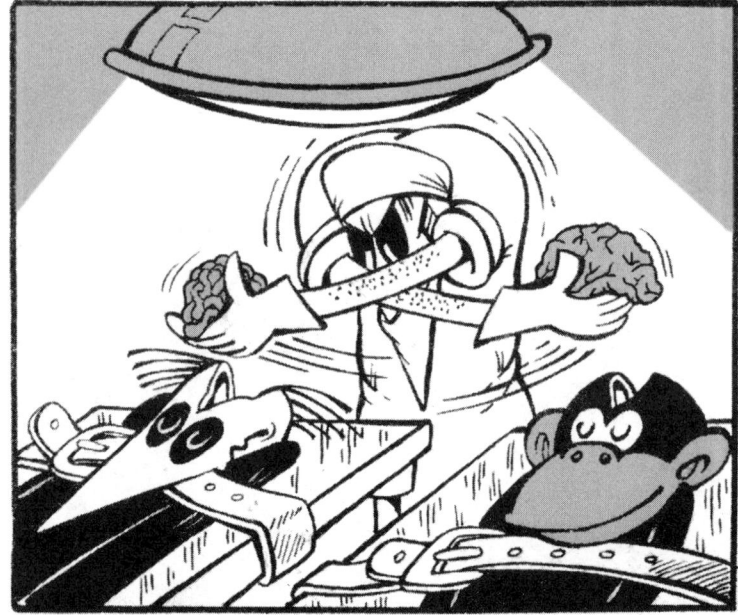

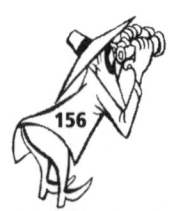

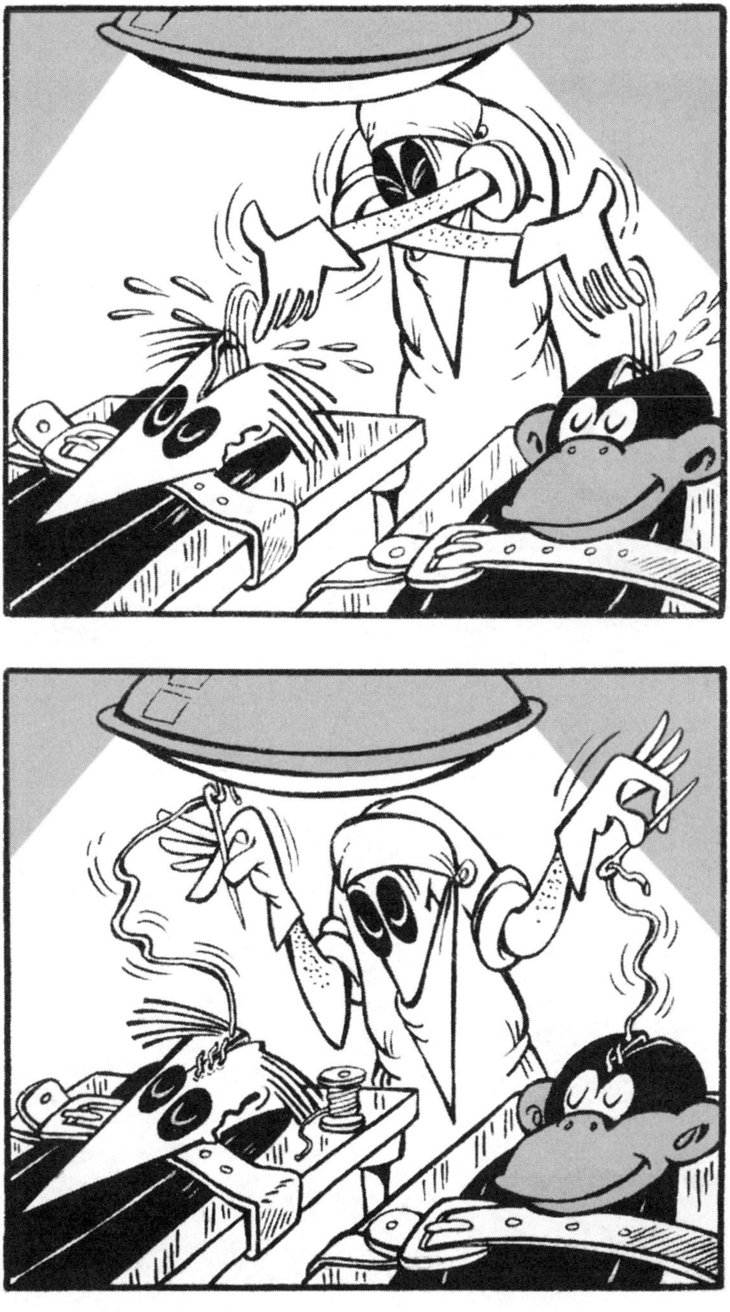

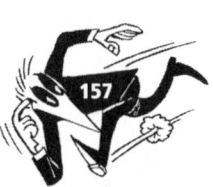

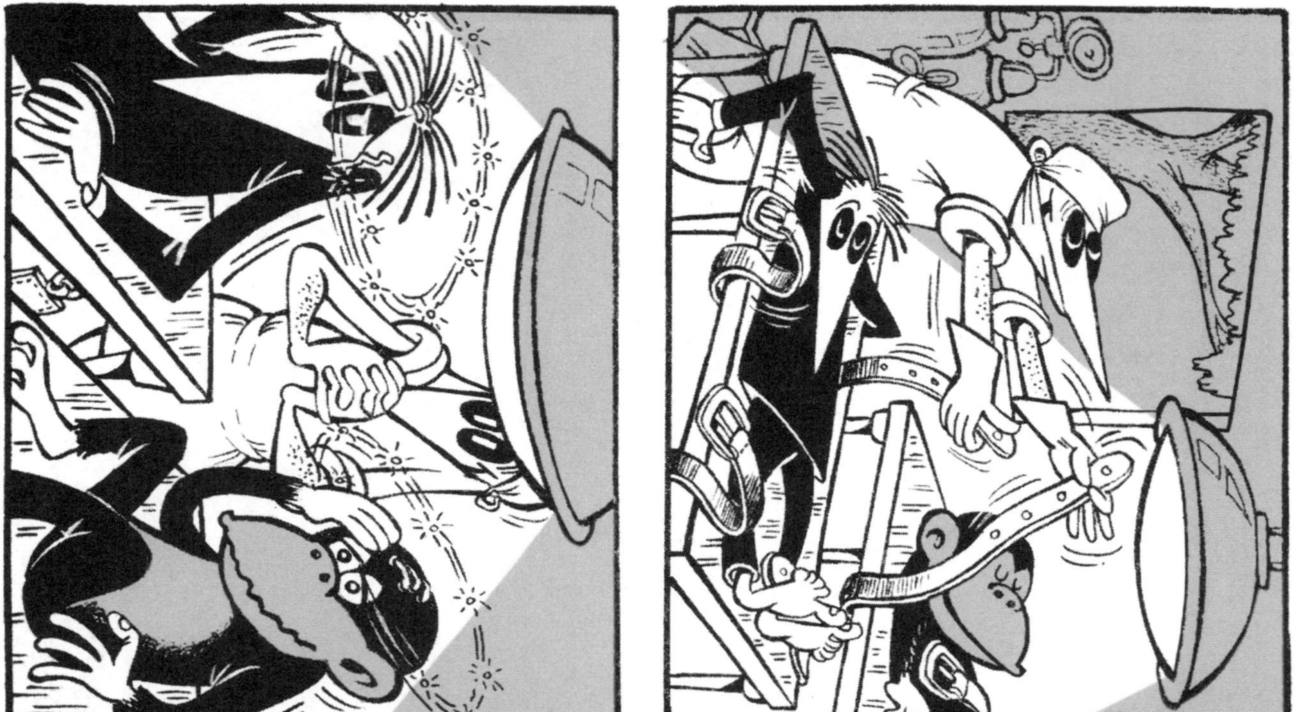

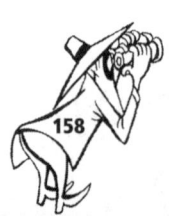

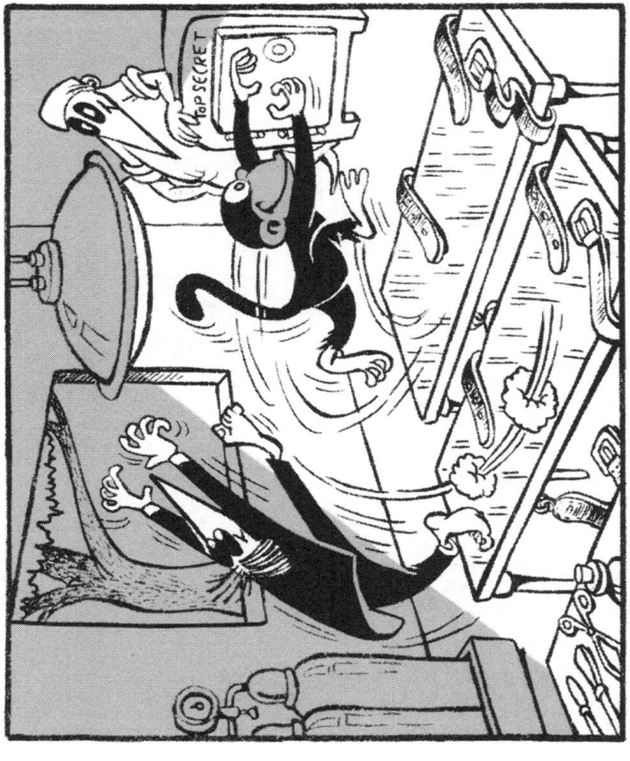
TOP SECRET

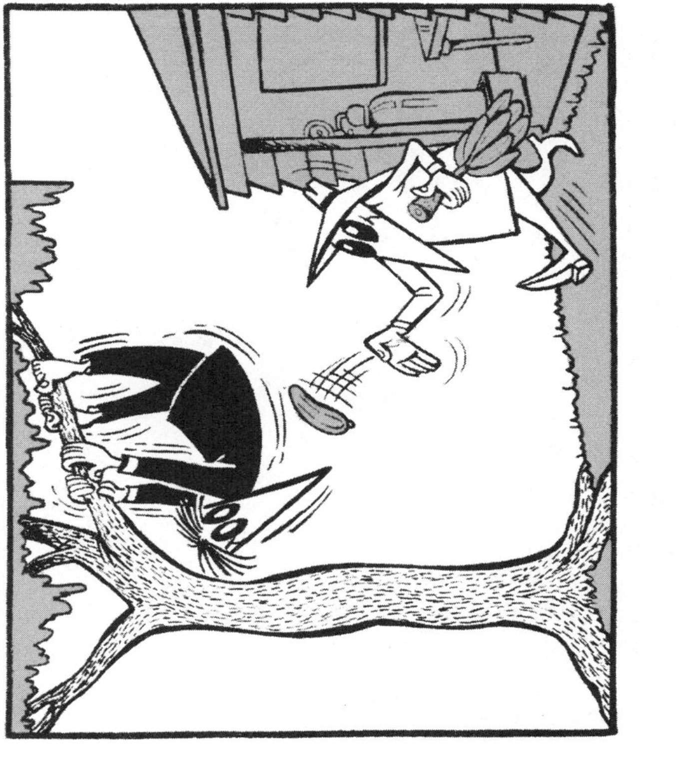

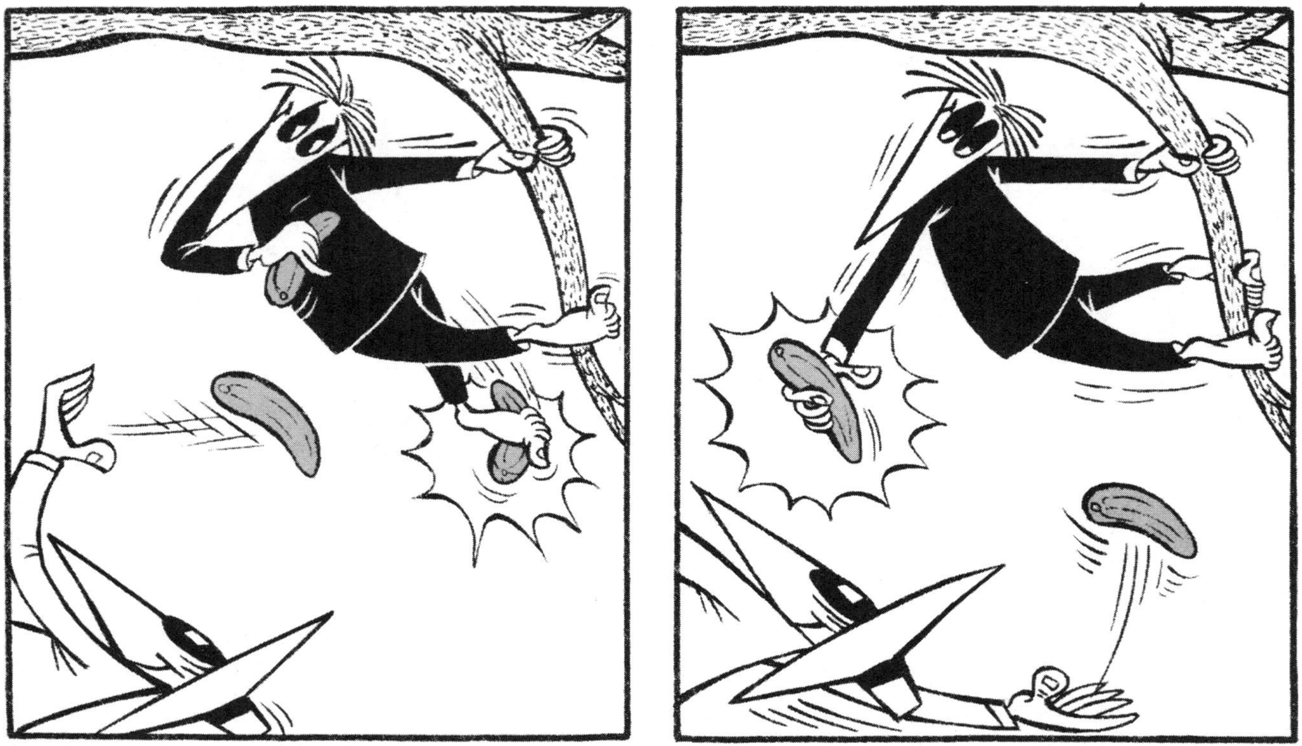

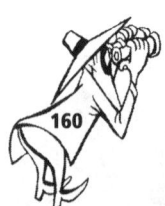

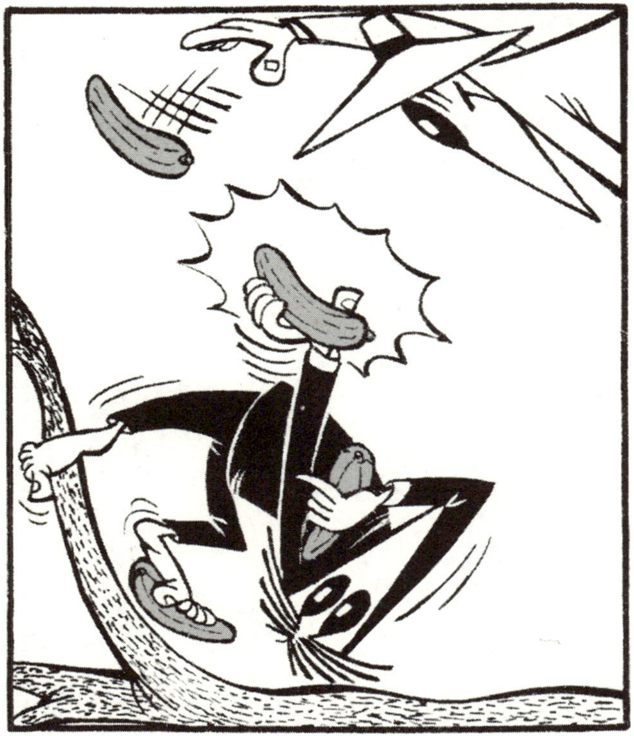

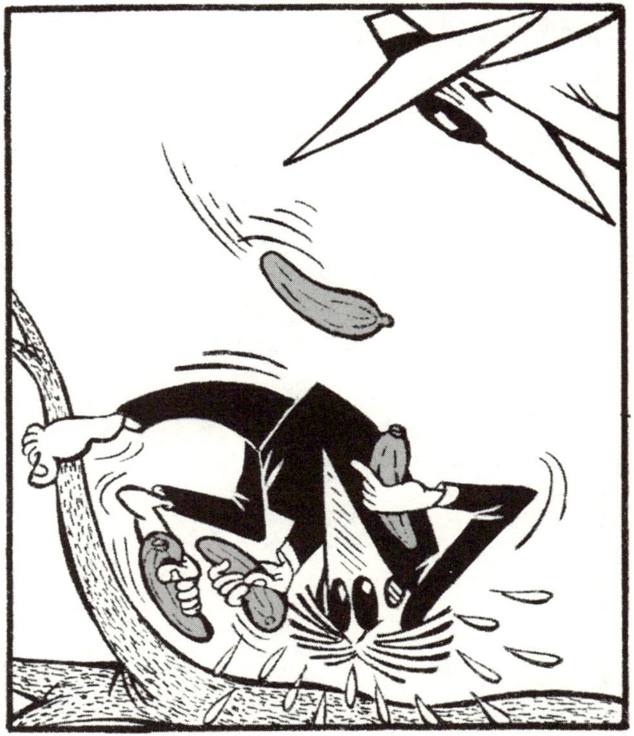

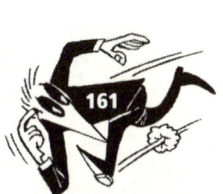

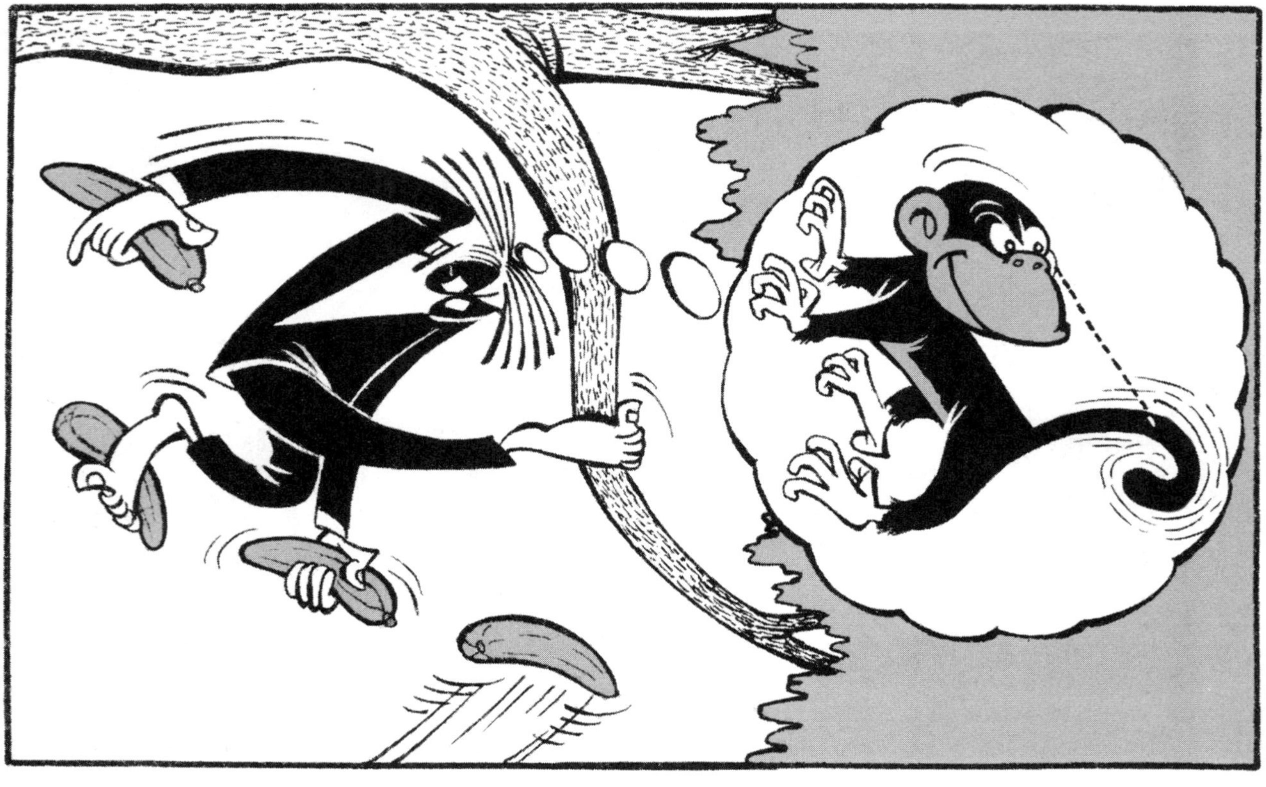

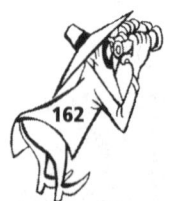

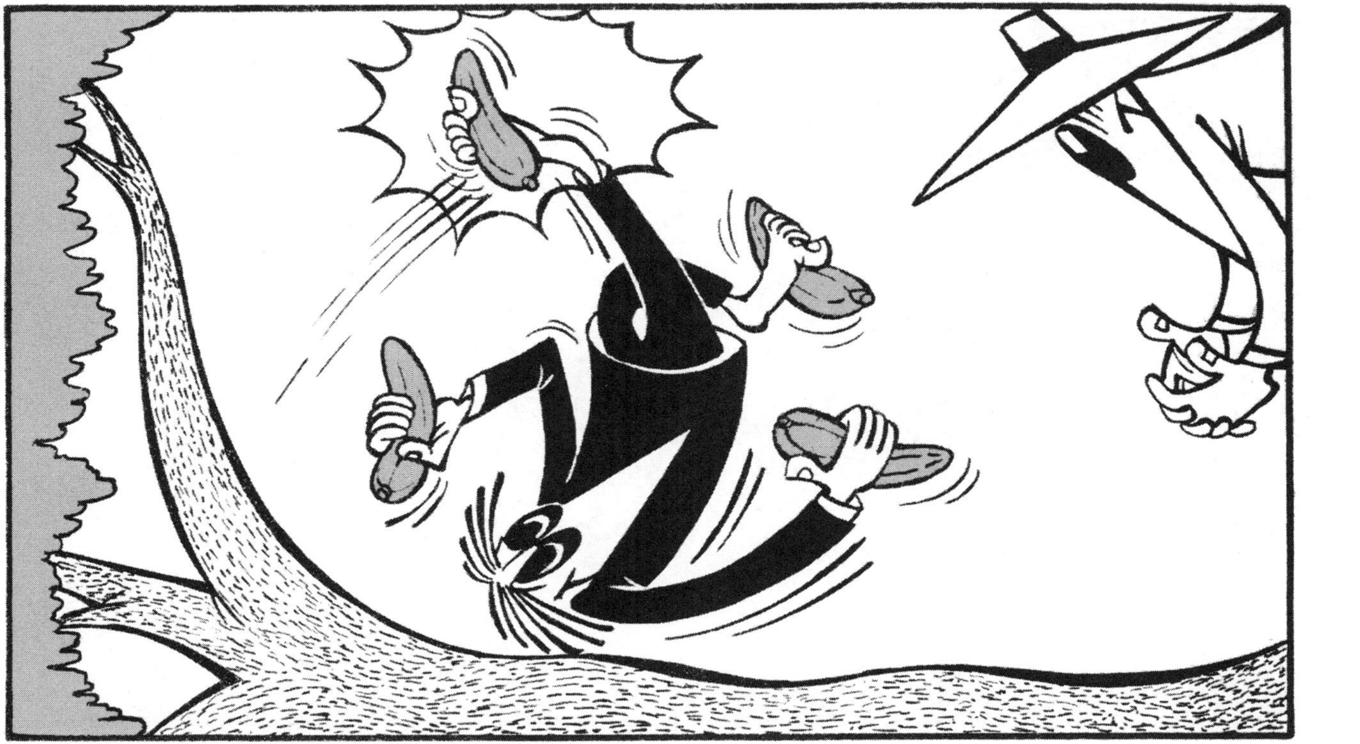

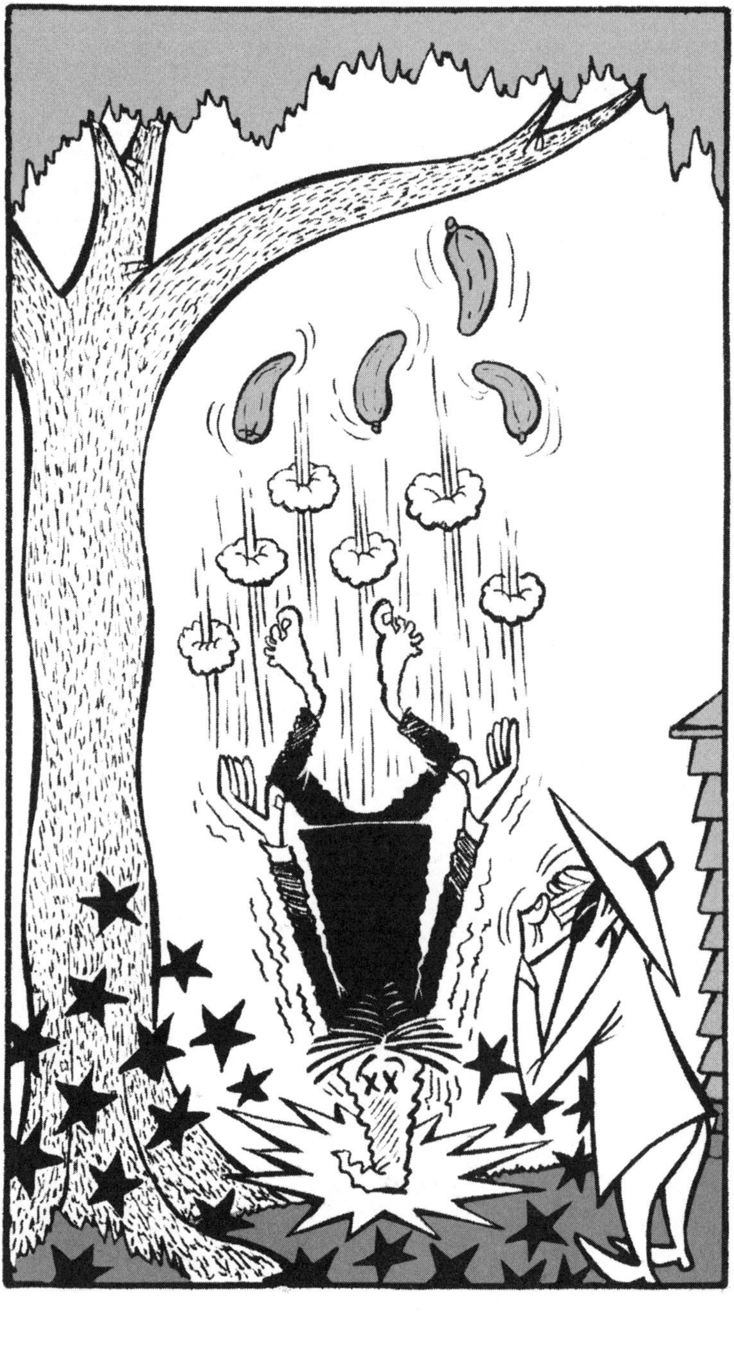

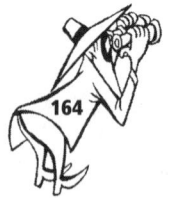

OPERATION: ONE-WAY TRICK

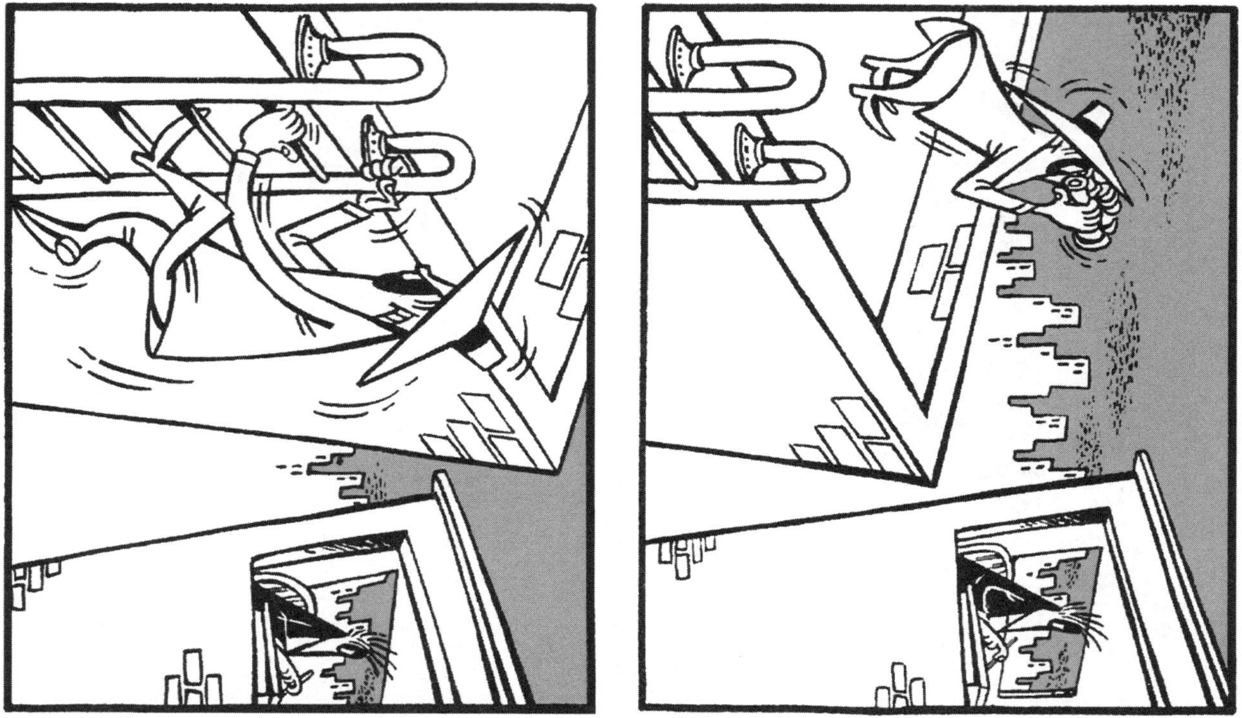

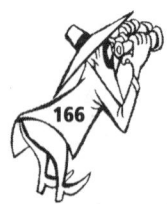

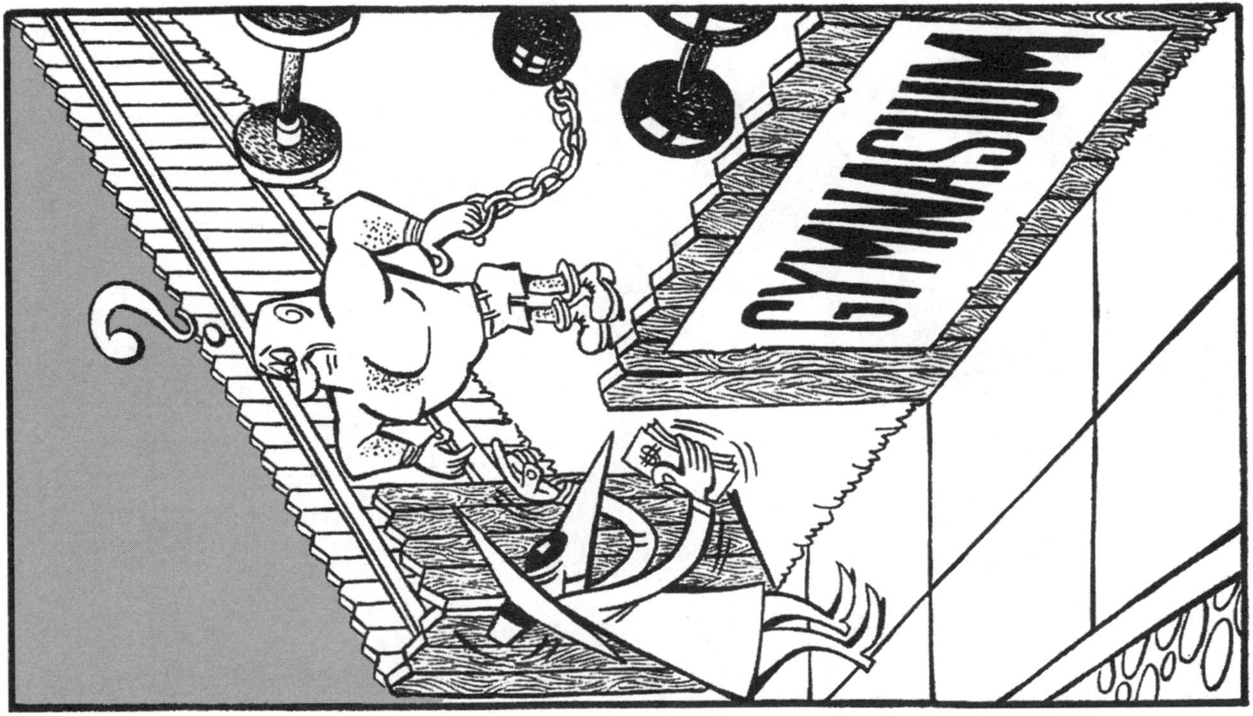
GYMNASIUM

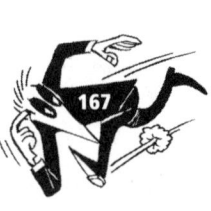

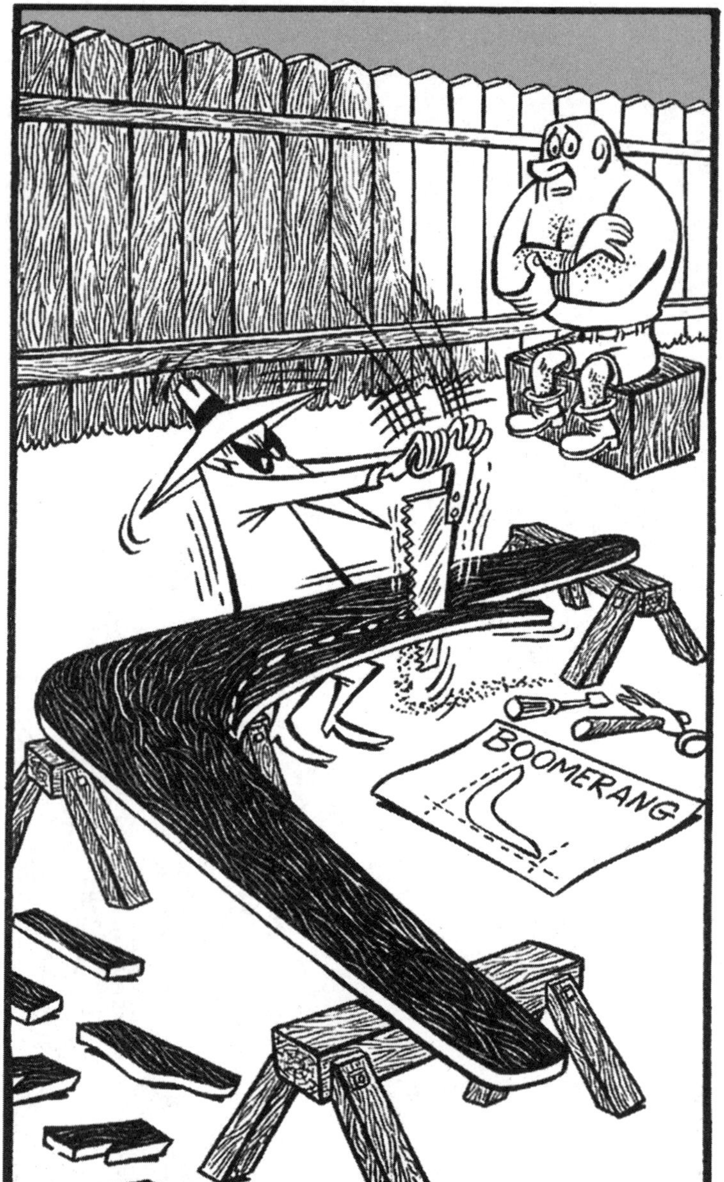
BOOMERANG

OPERATION: ONE-WAY TRICK

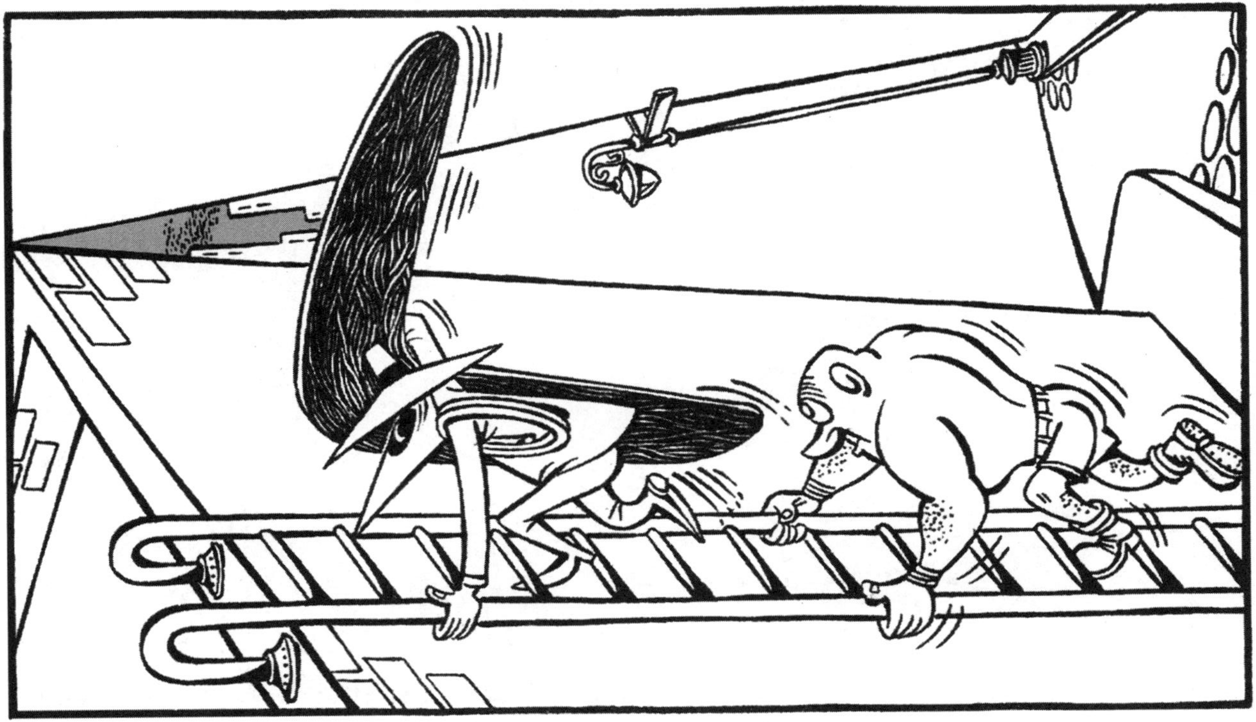

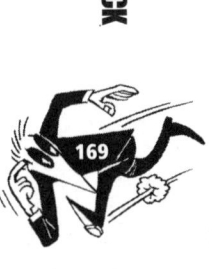

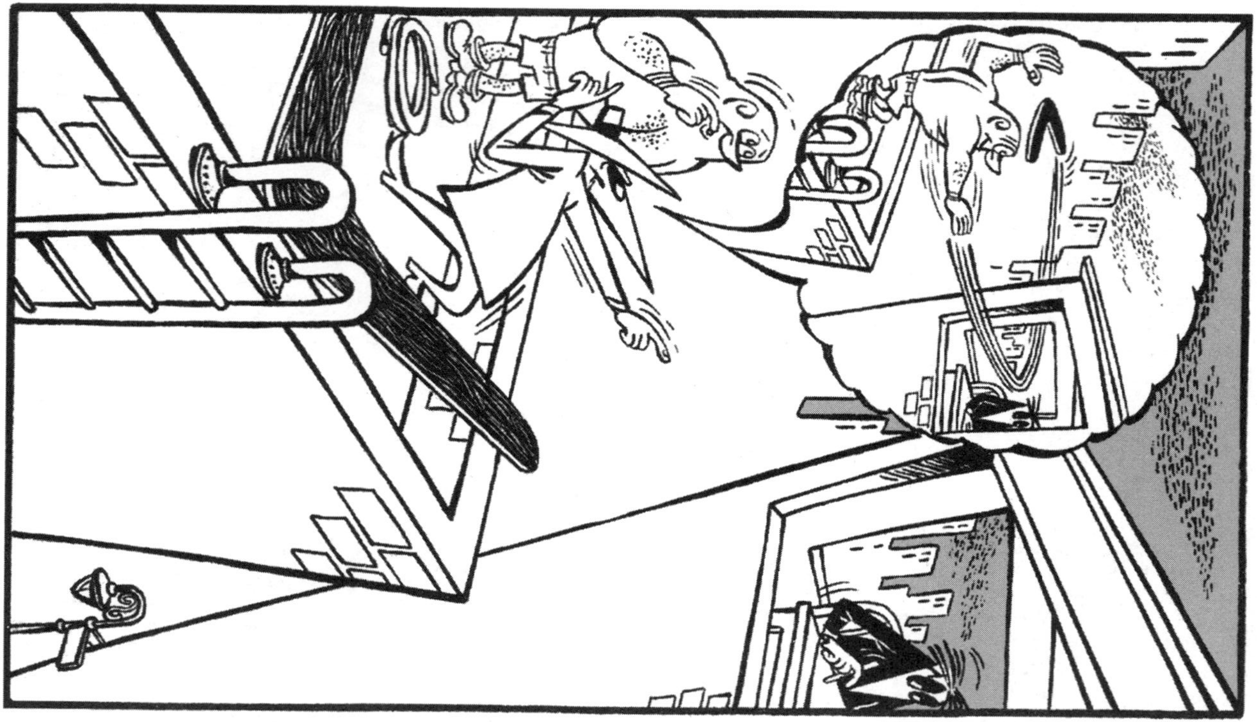

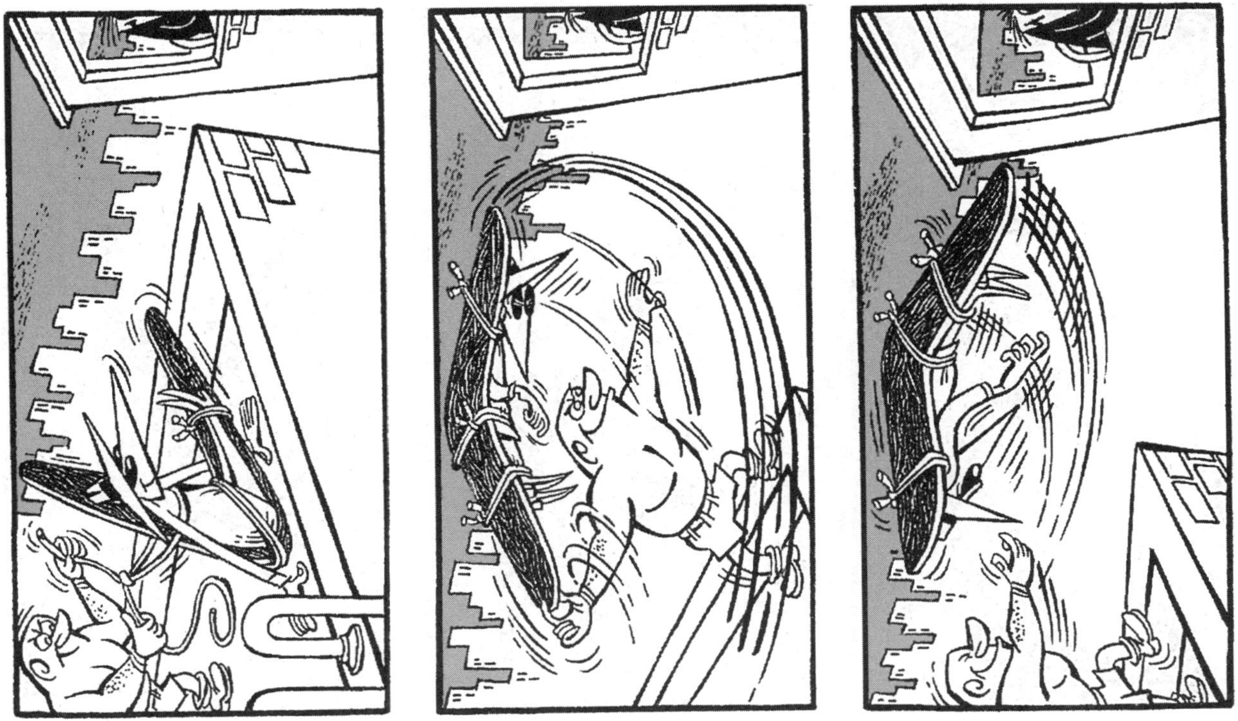

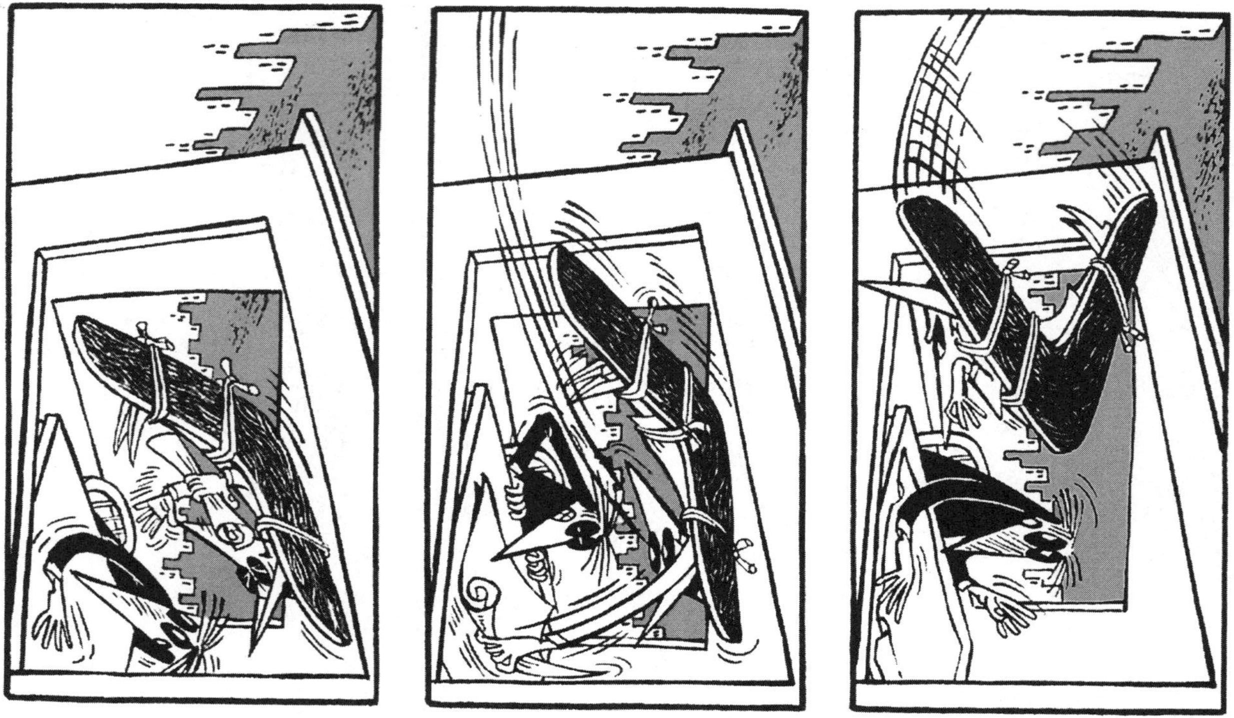

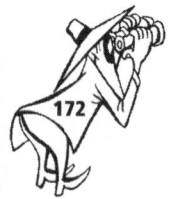

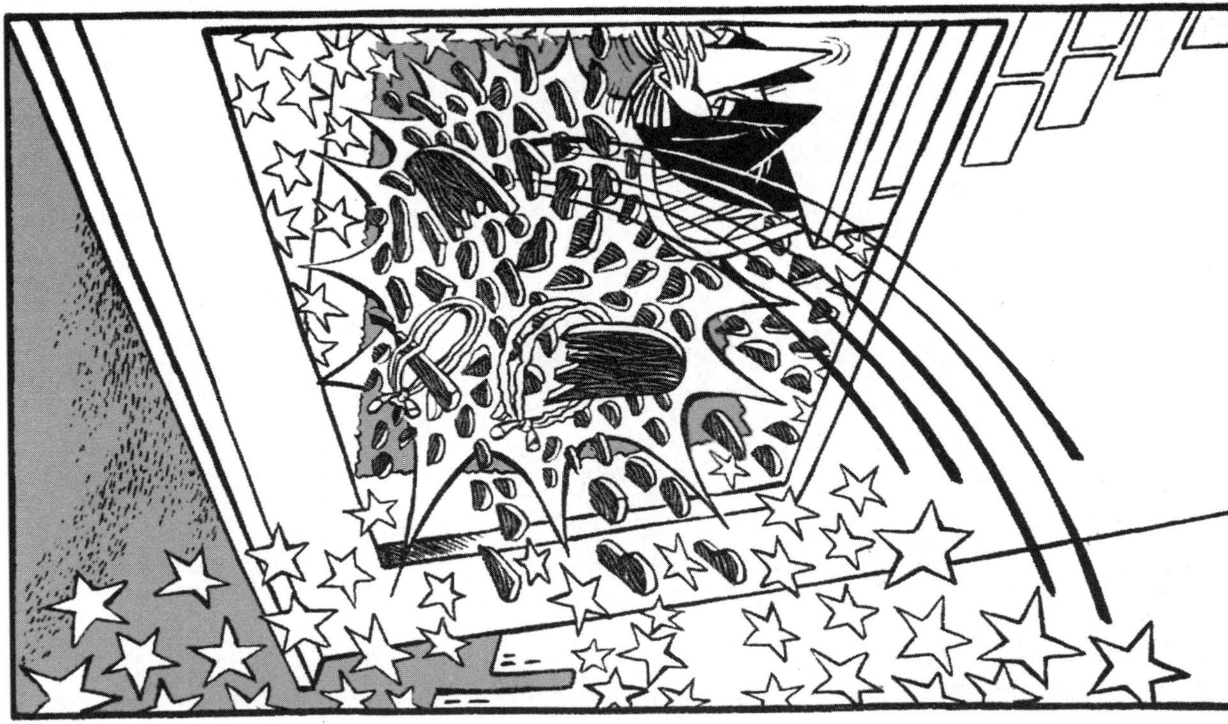

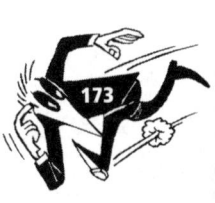

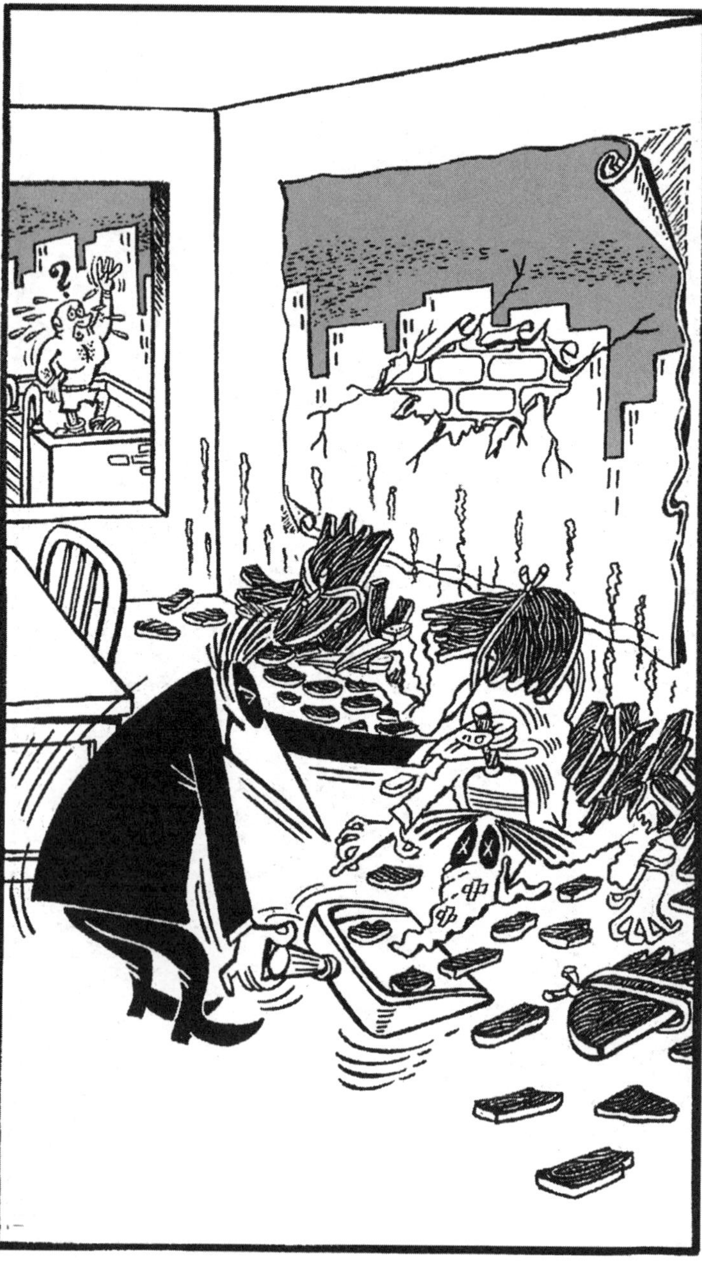

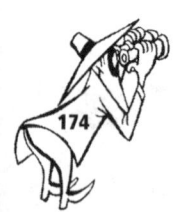

OPERATION: MAID OF STEEL

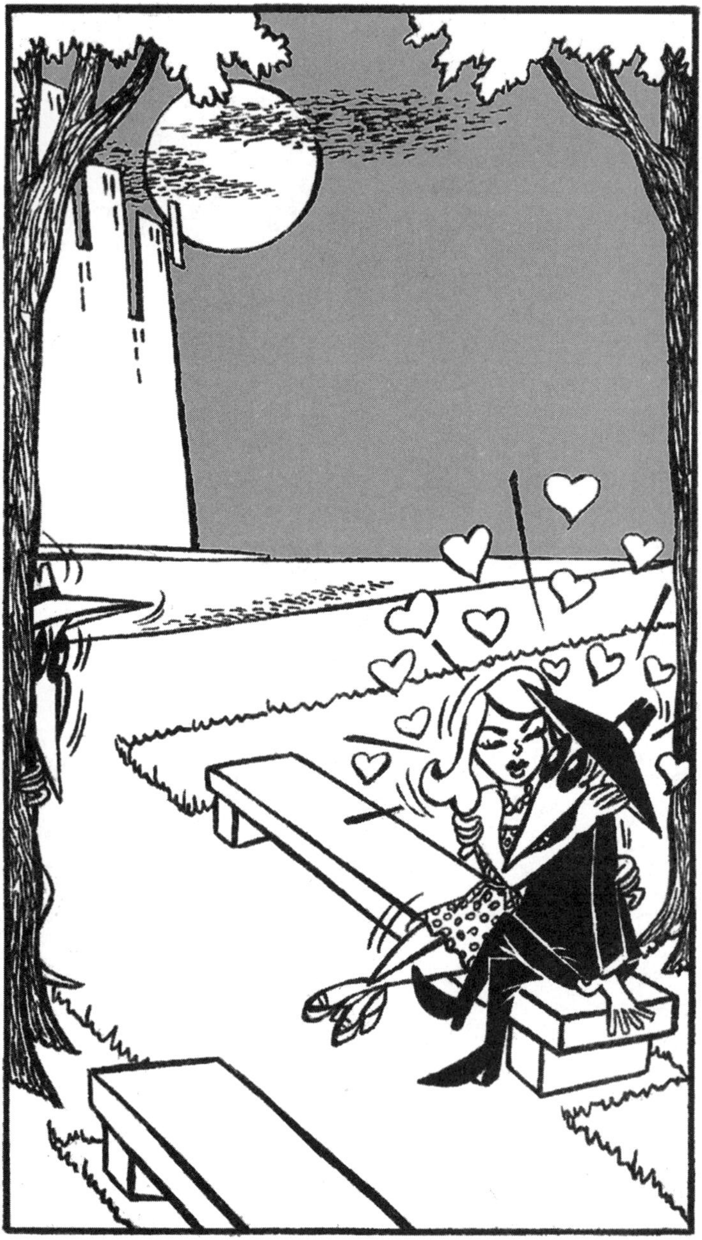

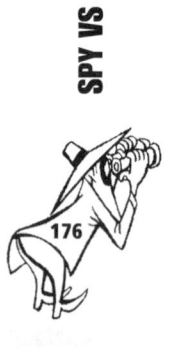

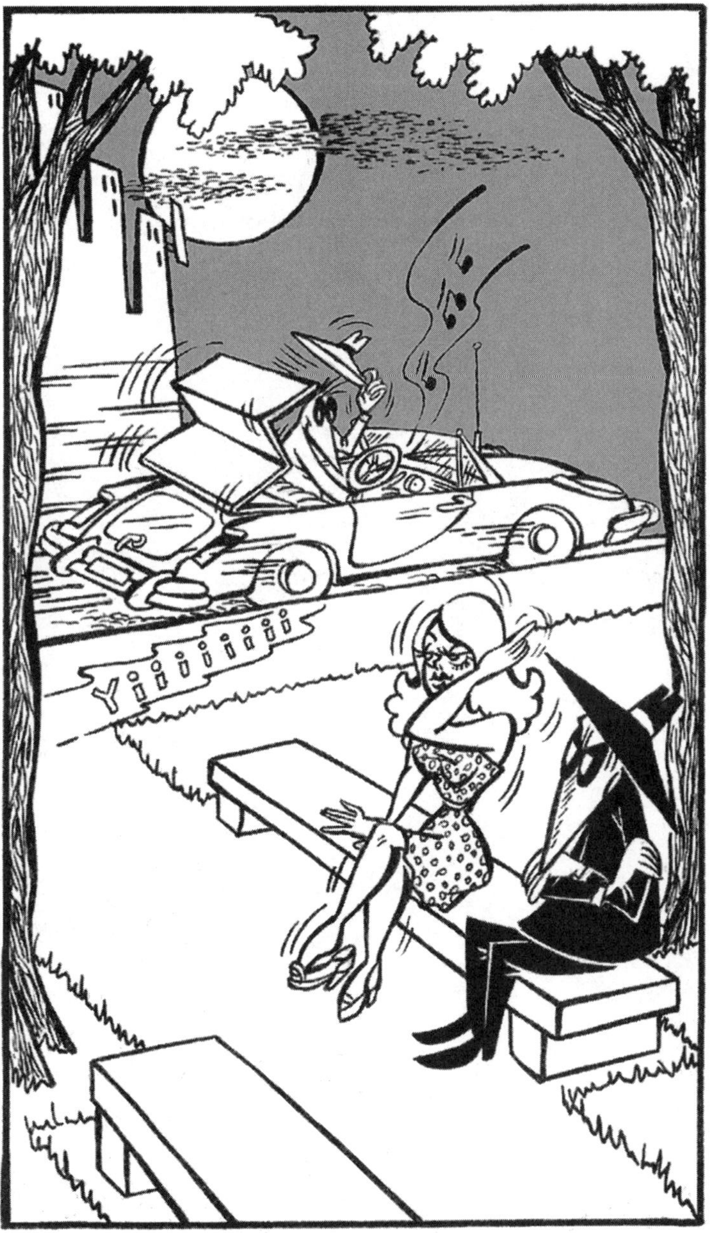
Yiiiiiiii

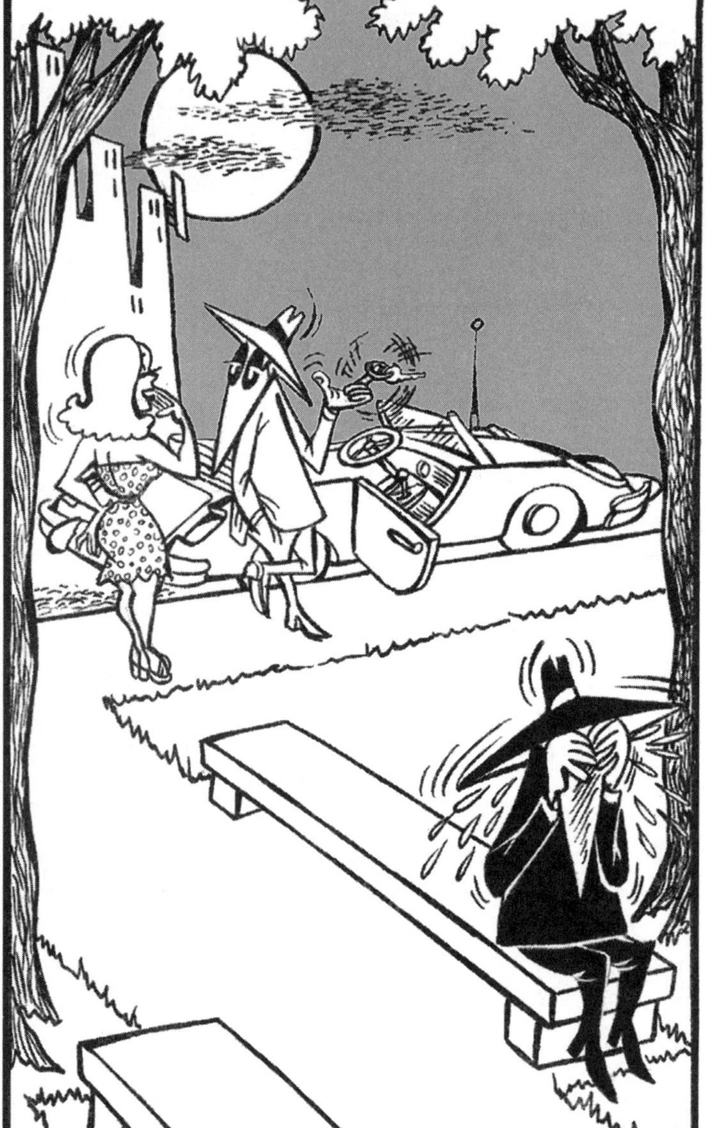

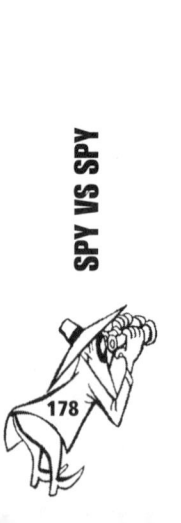

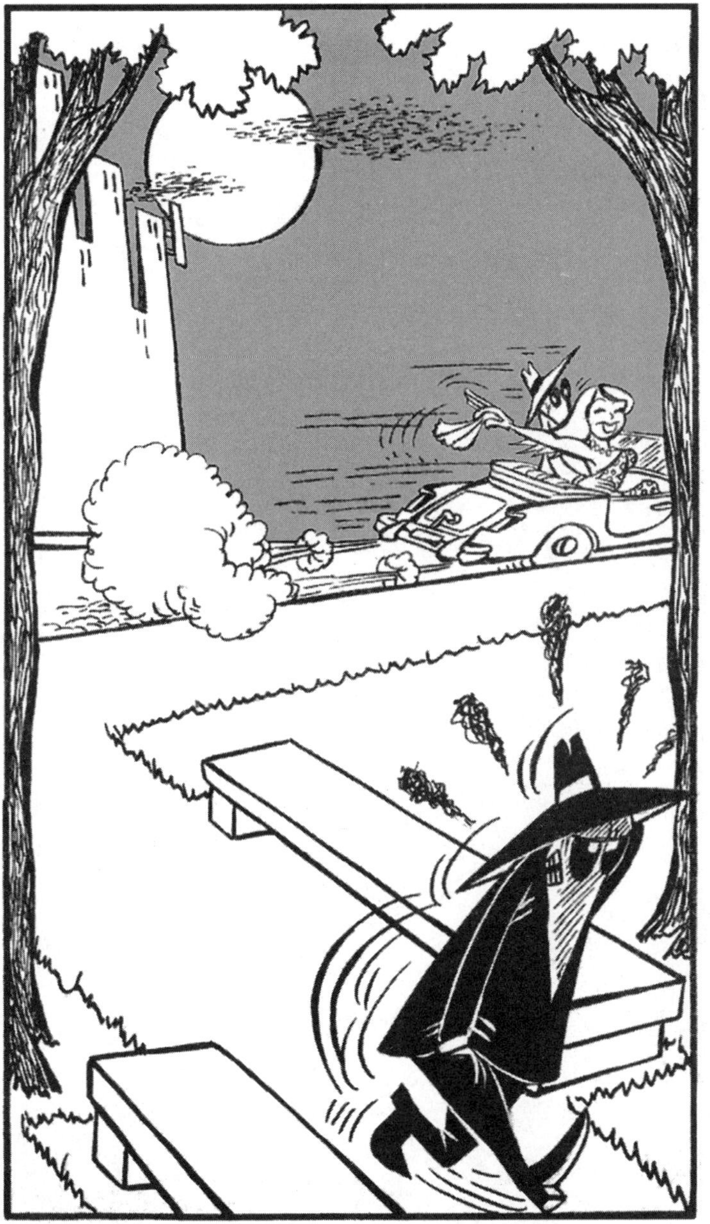

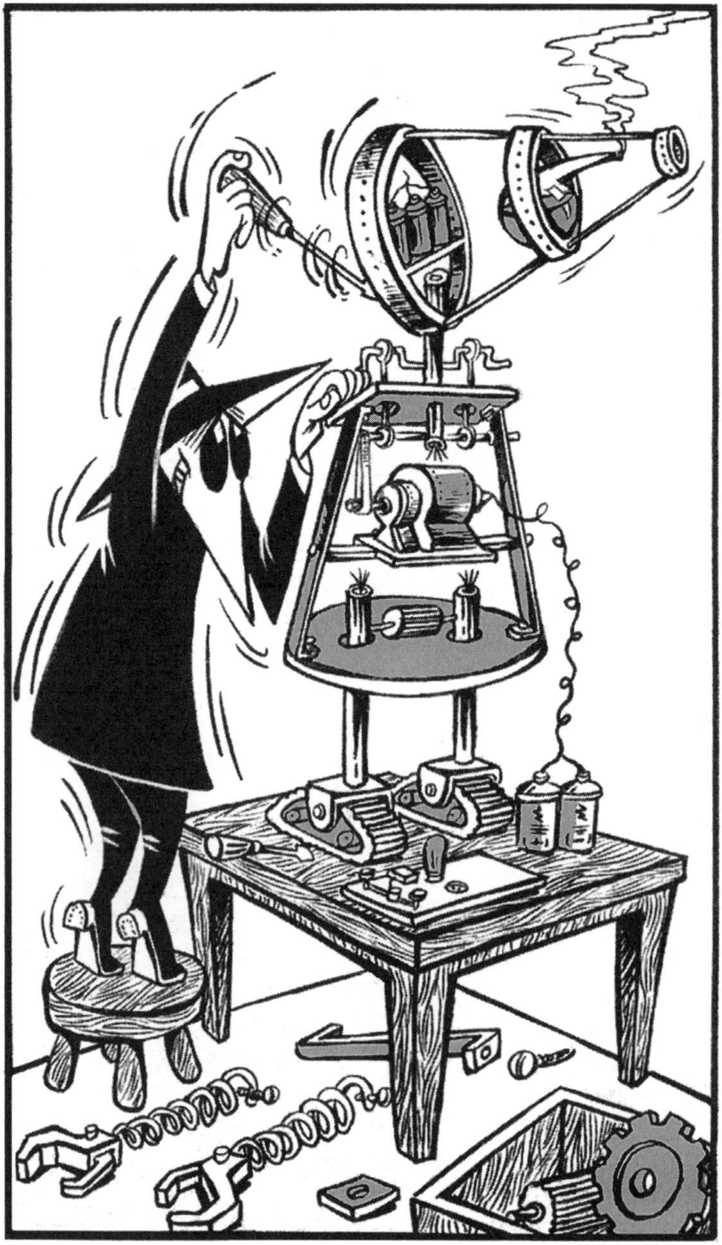

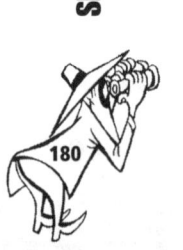

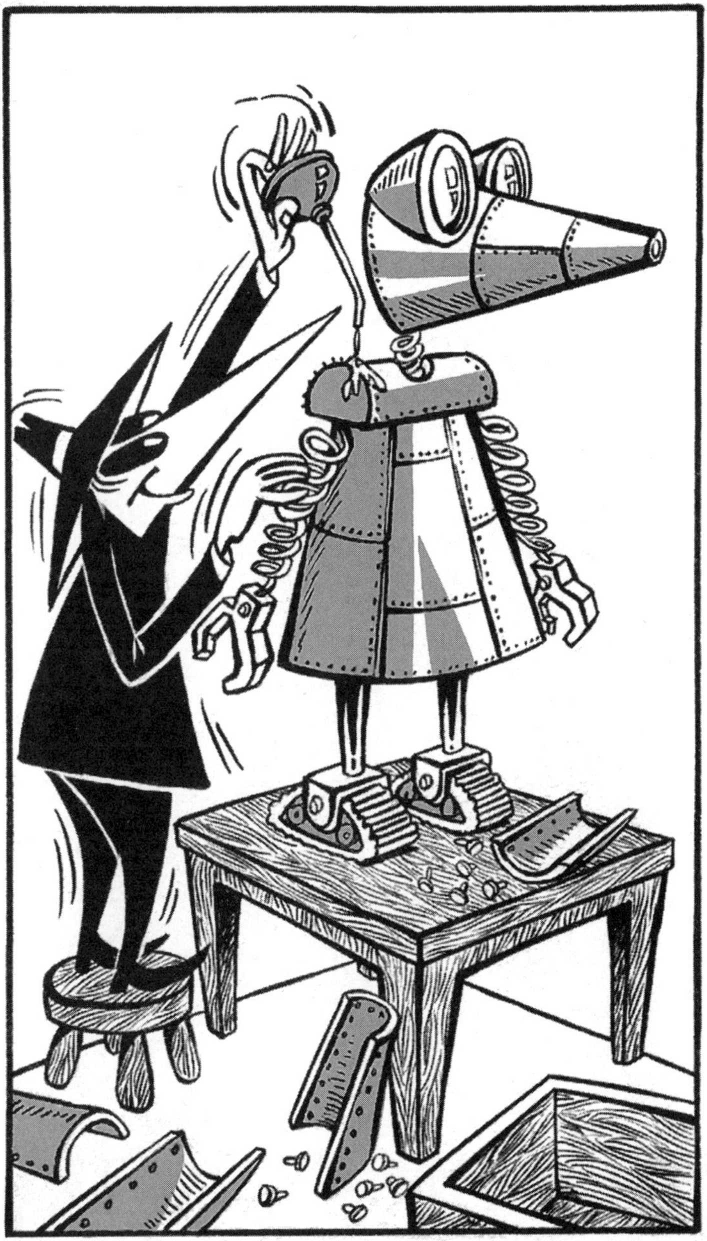

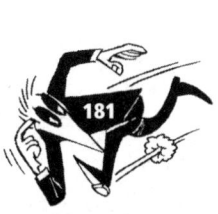

OPERATION: MAID OF STEEL

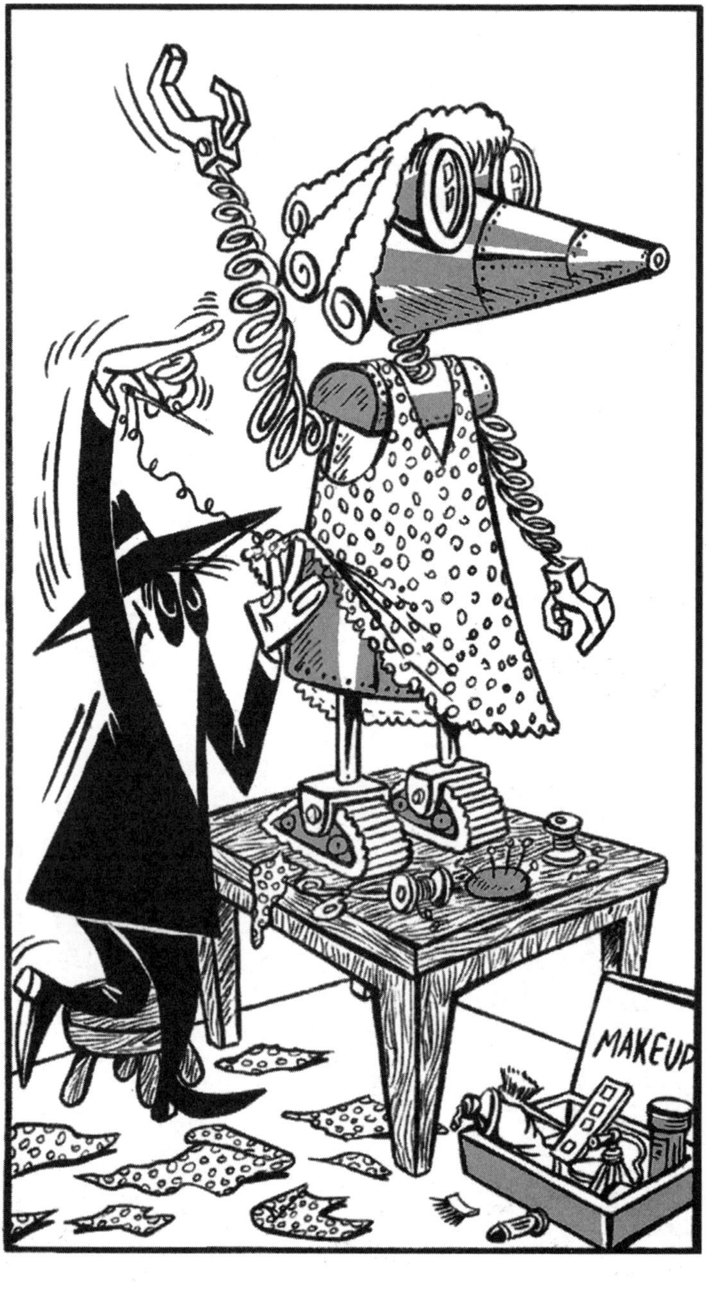
MAKEUP

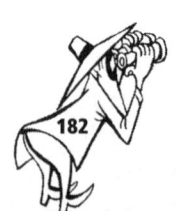

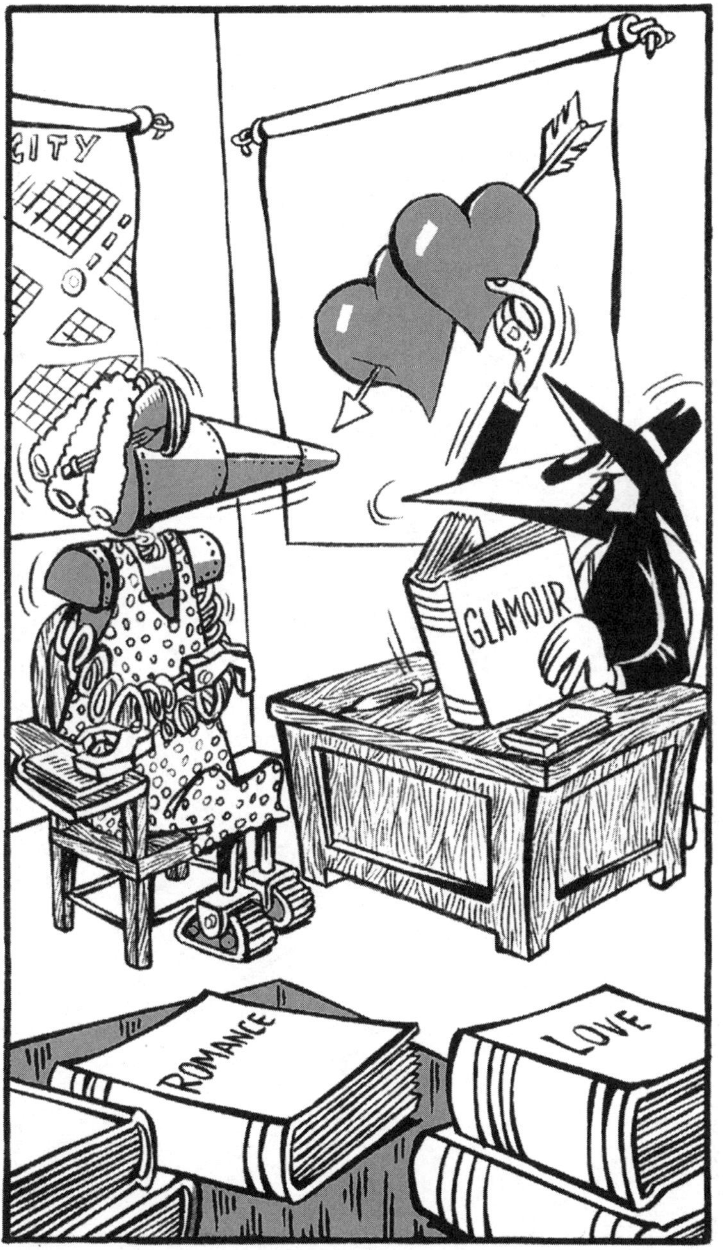
CITY
GLAMOUR
ROMANCE
LOVE

OPERATION: MAID OF STEEL

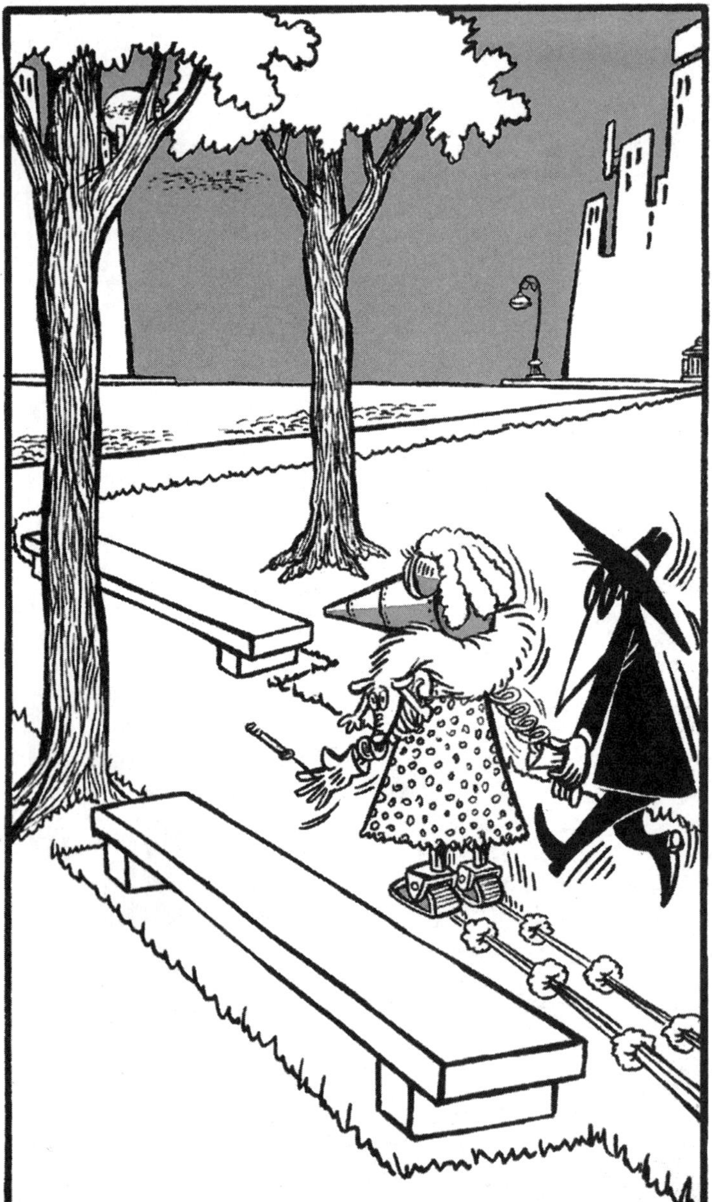

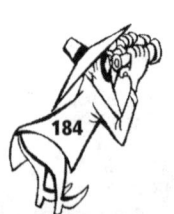

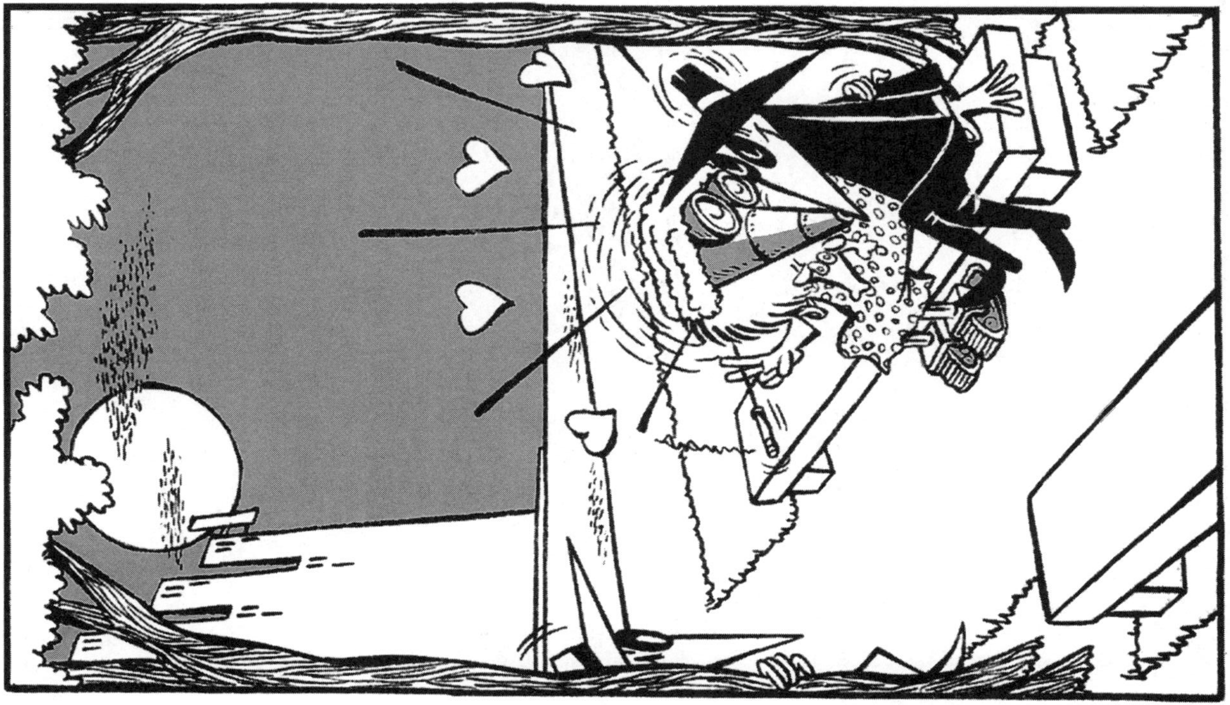

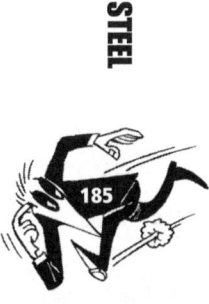

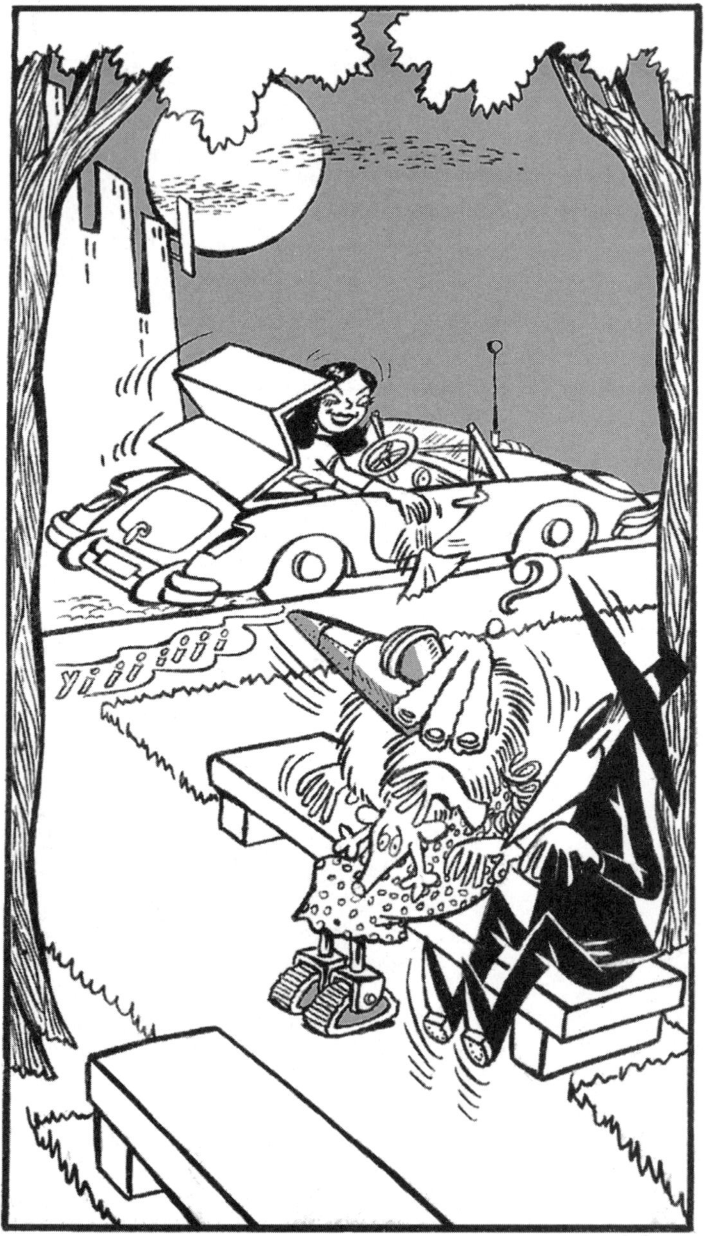
yiiiiiii

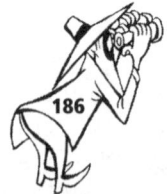

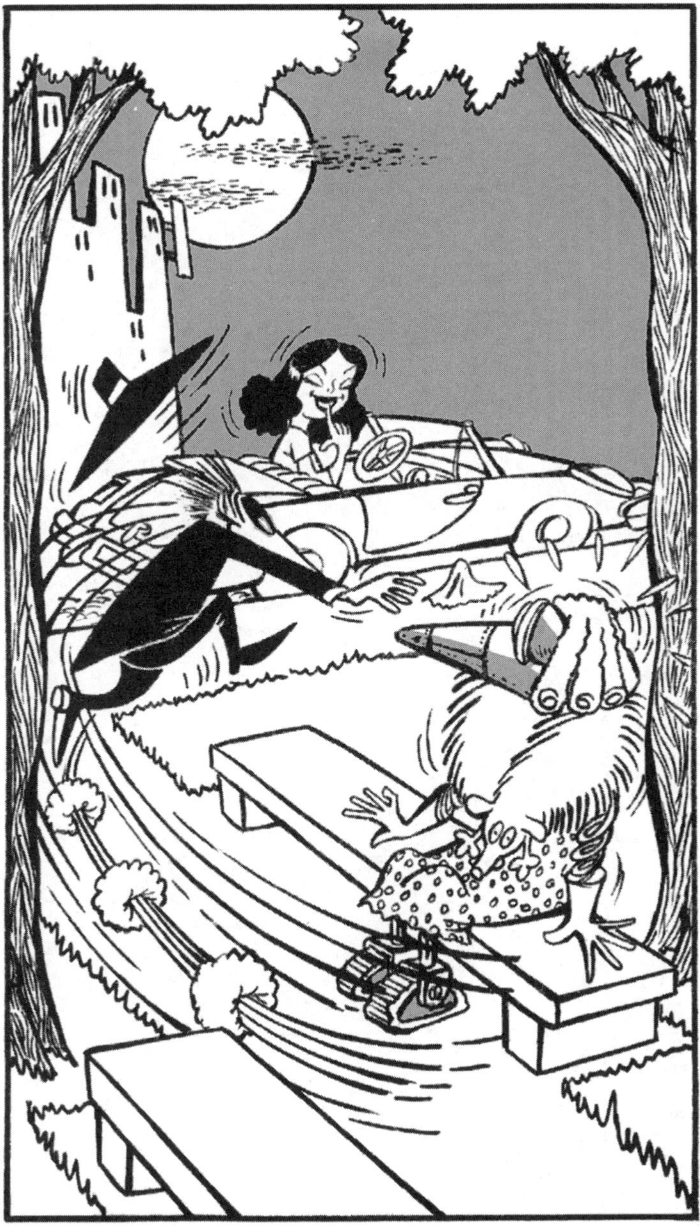

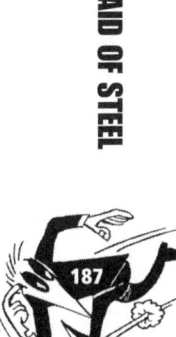

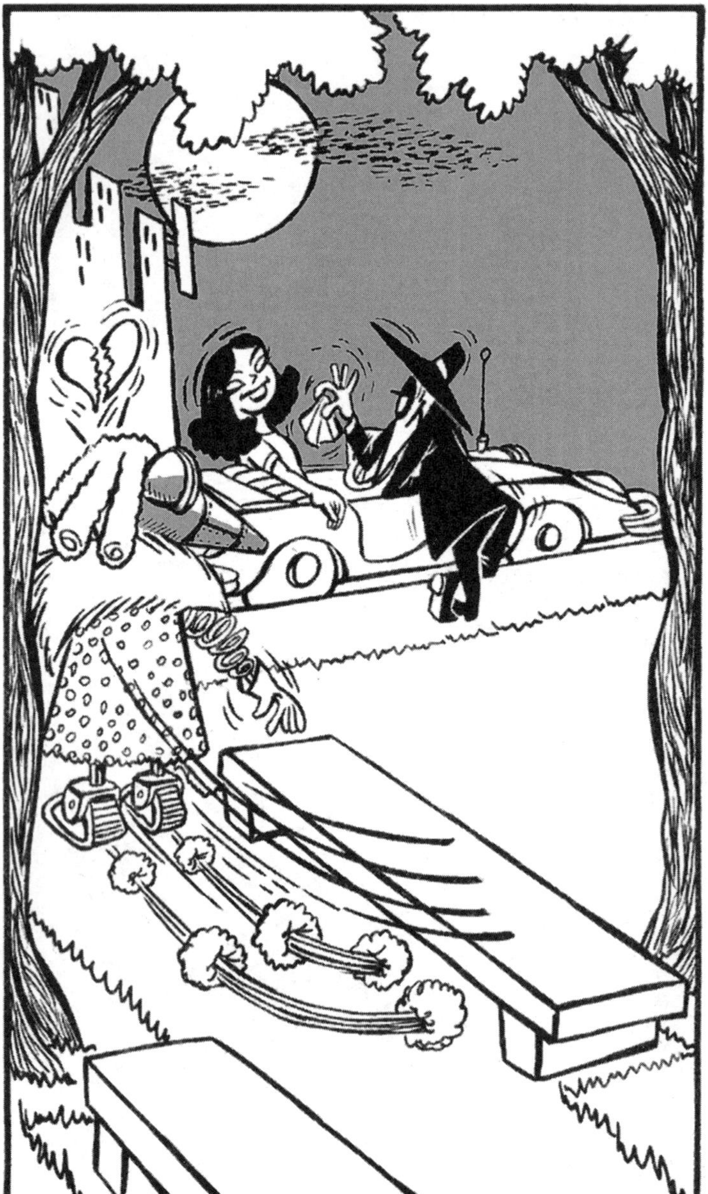

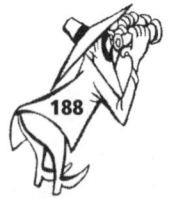

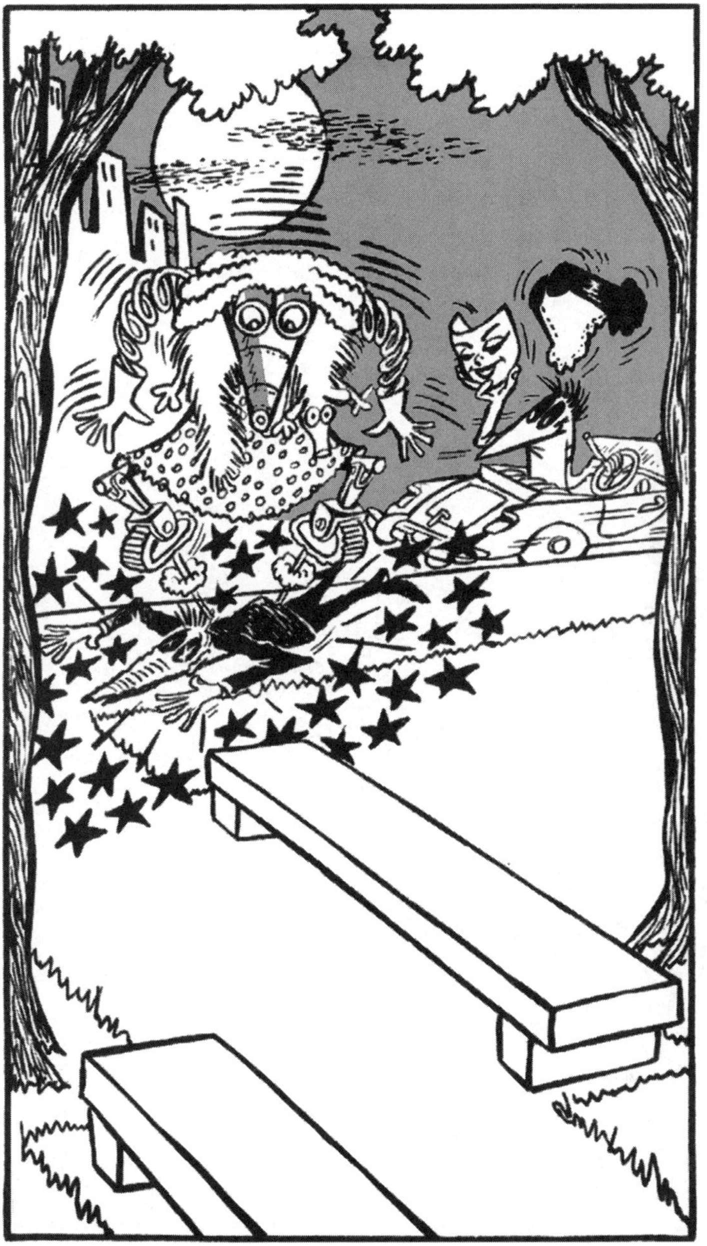

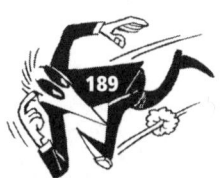

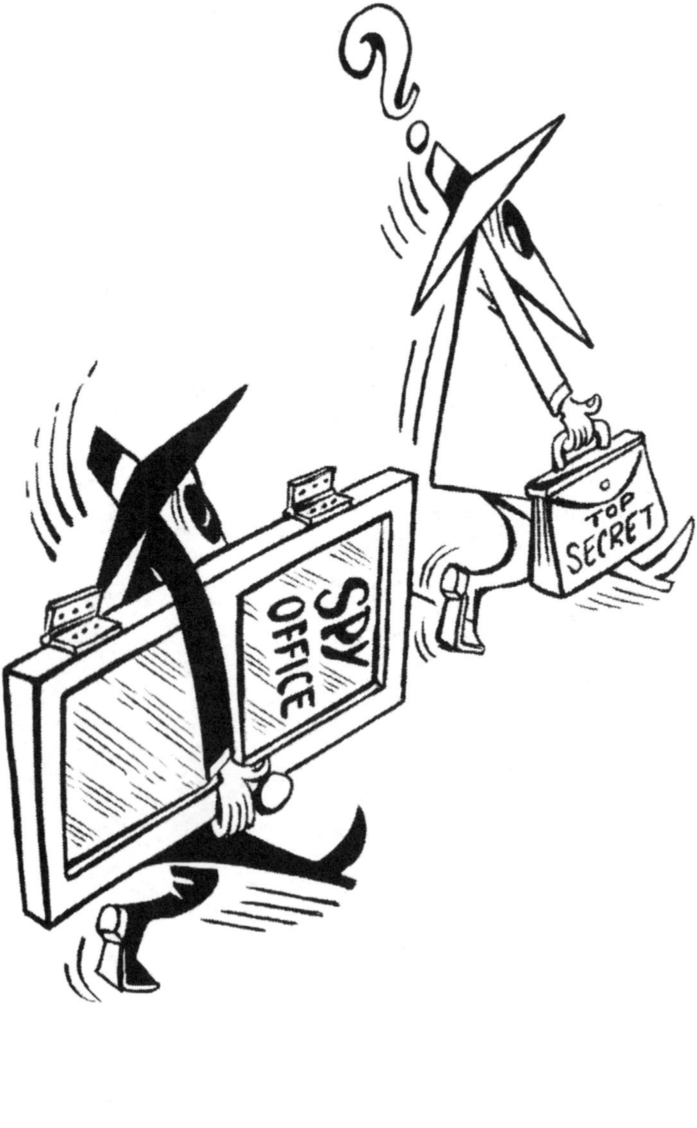
SPY OFFICE
TOP SECRET

THE FATAL FILES

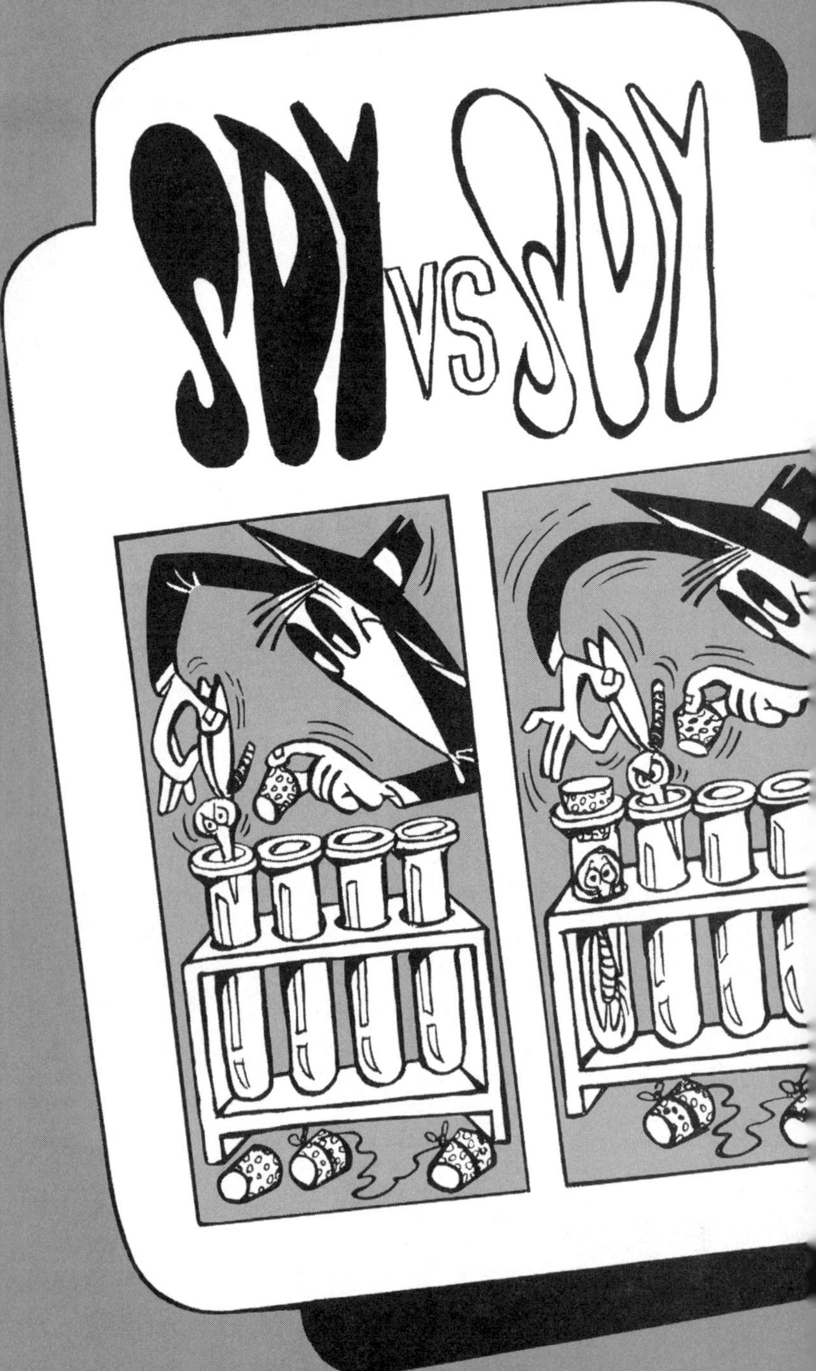
SPY VS SPY

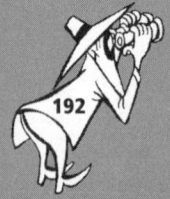

the BUGGING INCIDENT

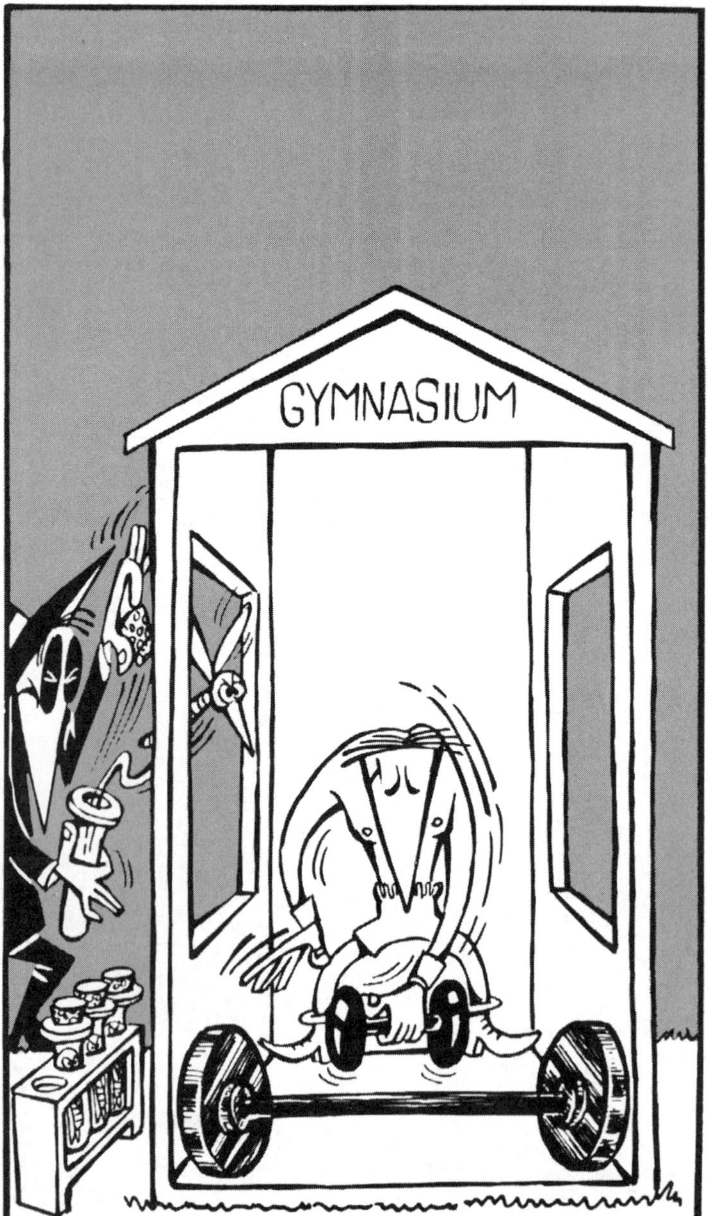
GYMNASIUM

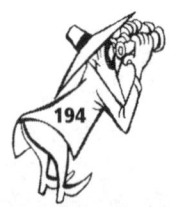

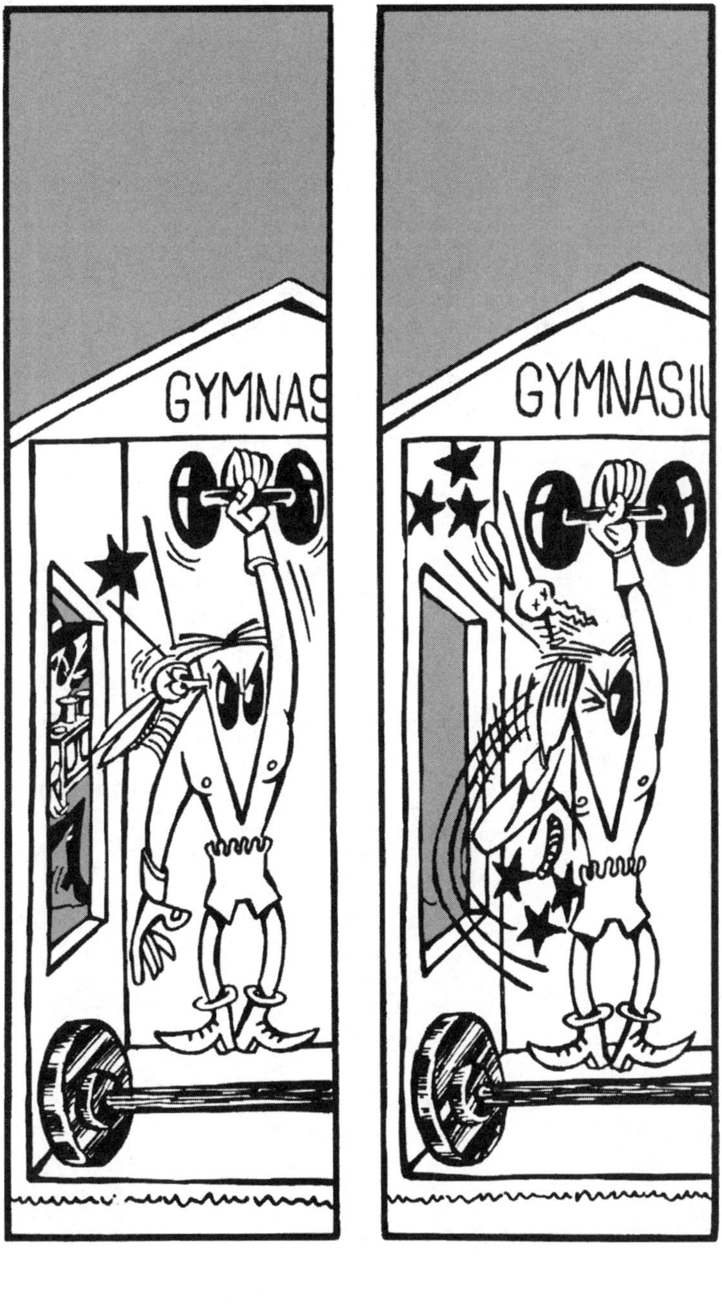
GYMNAS
GYMNASIU

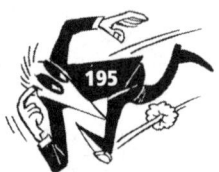

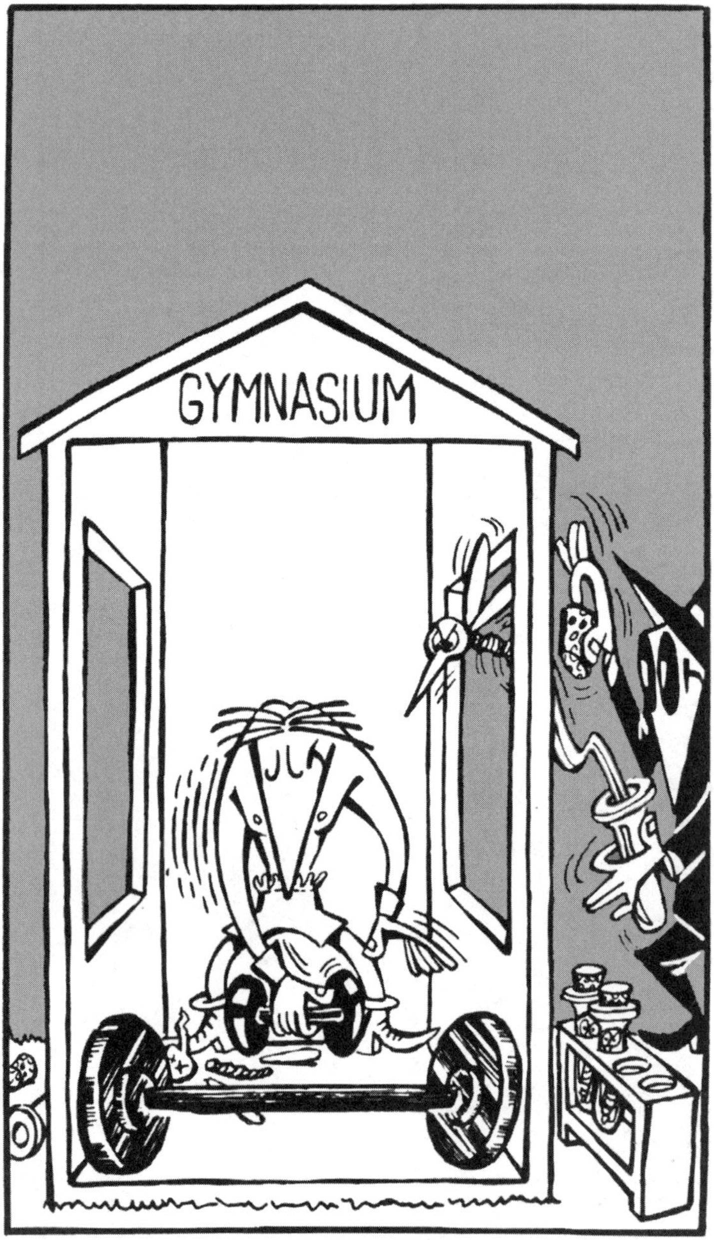
GYMNASIUM
JLH

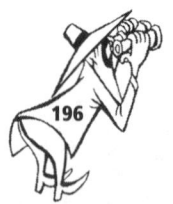

THE BUGGING INCIDENT

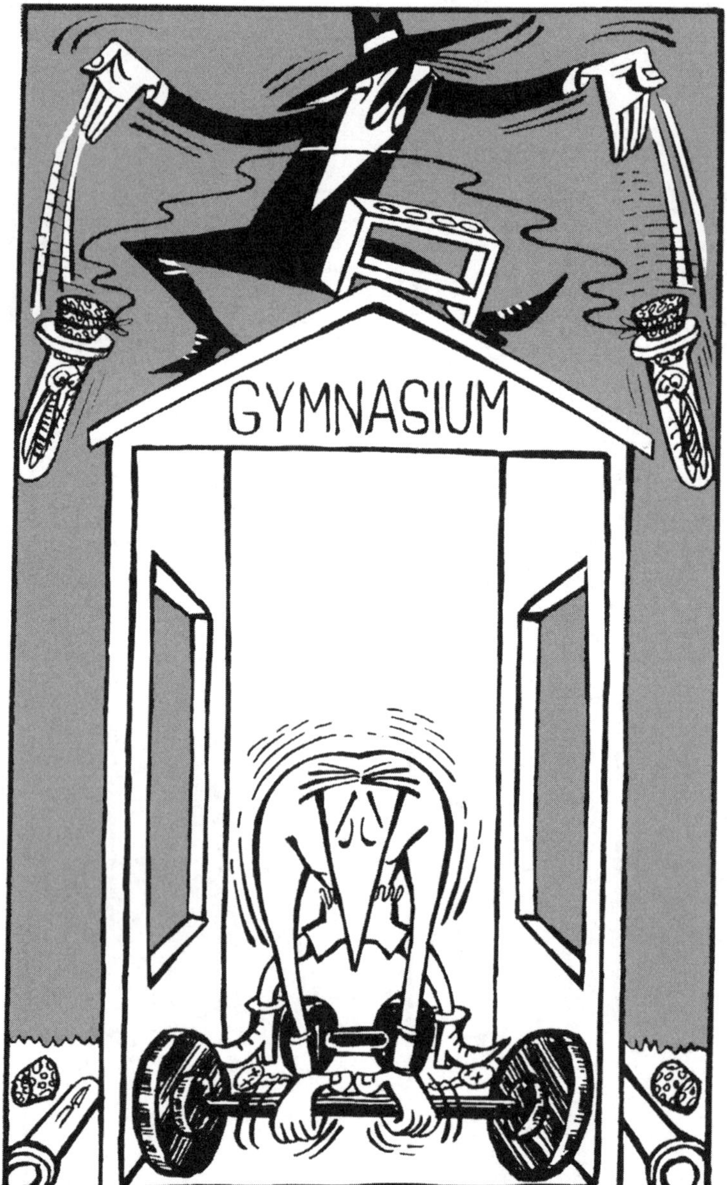
GYMNASIUM

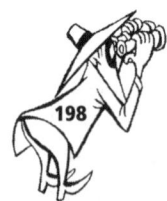

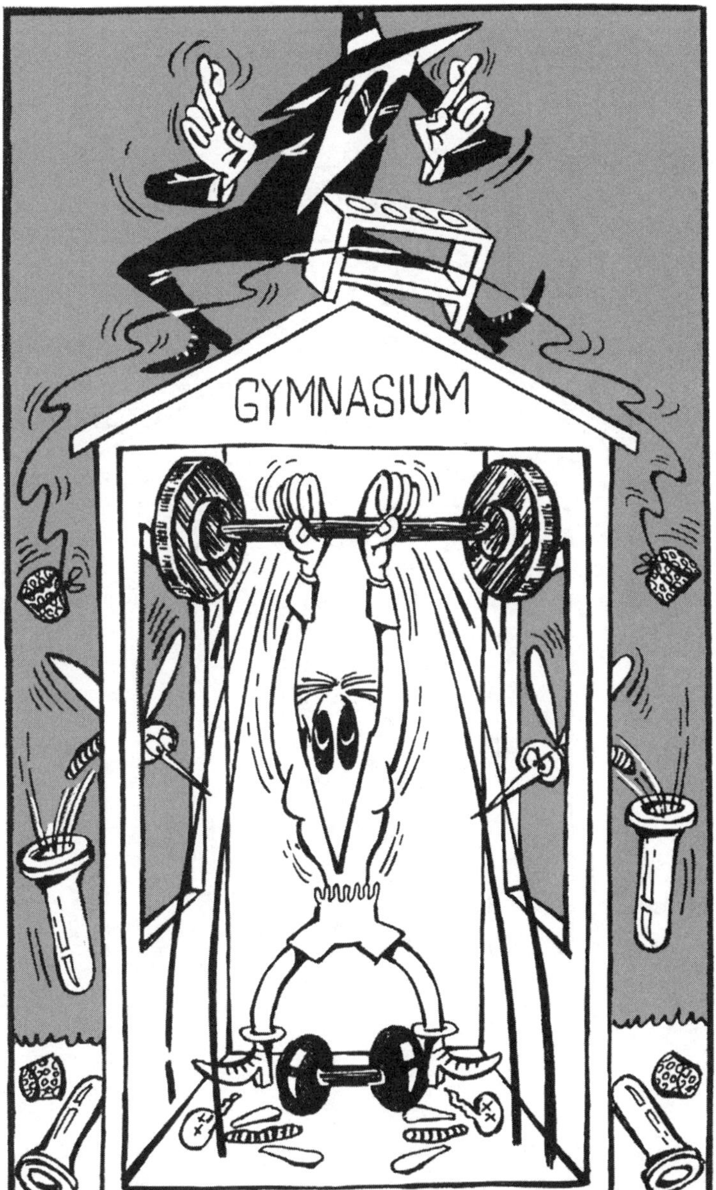
GYMNASIUM

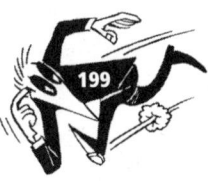

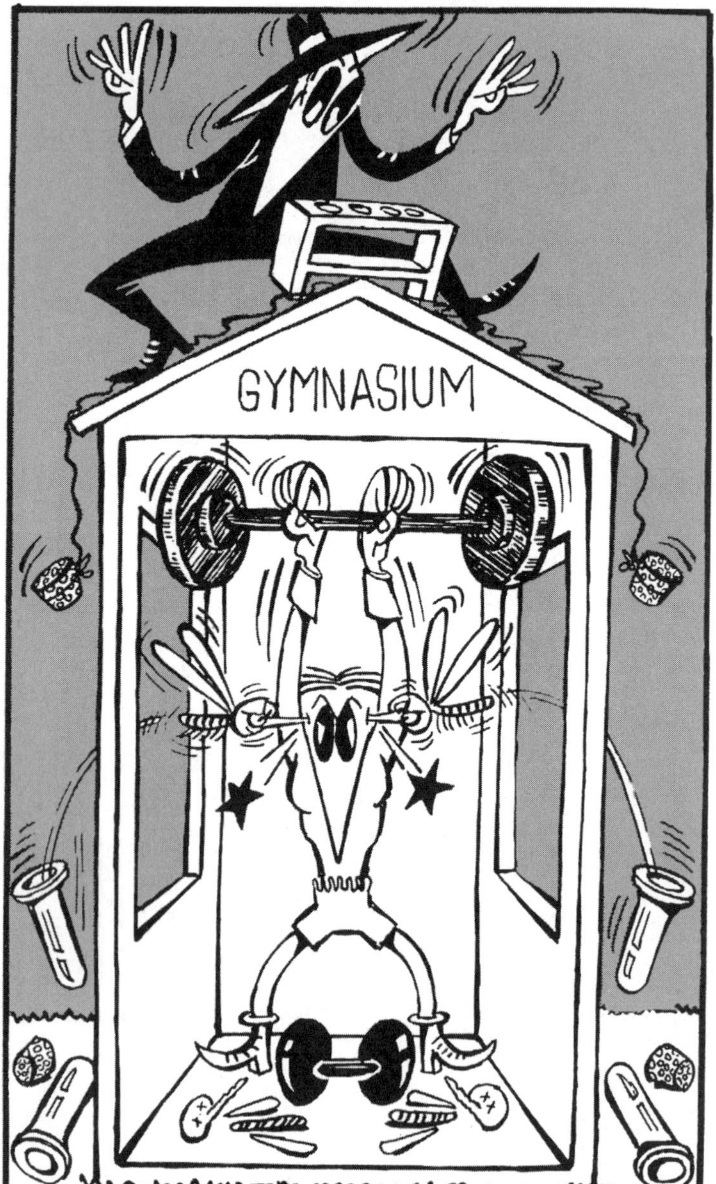
GYMNASIUM

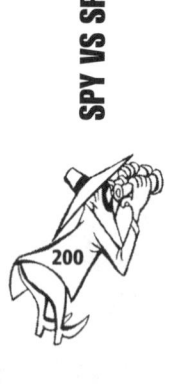

THE BUGGING INCIDENT

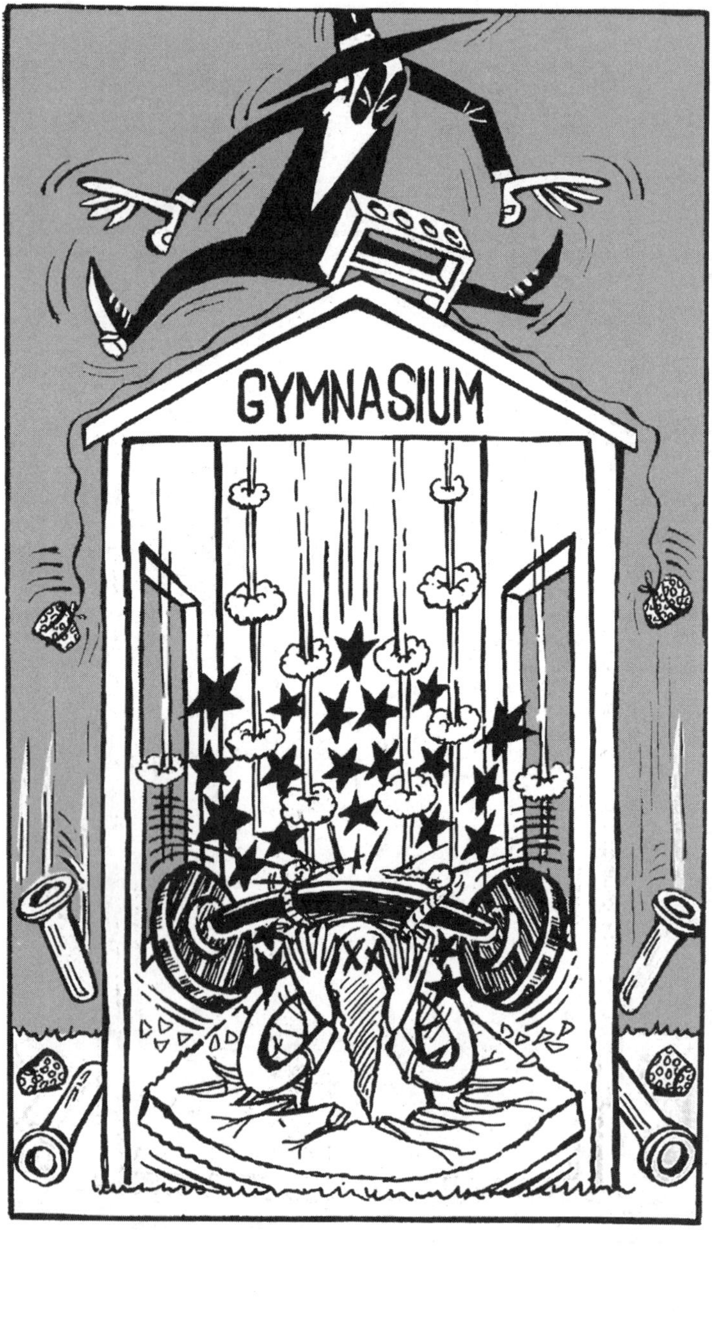
GYMNASIUM

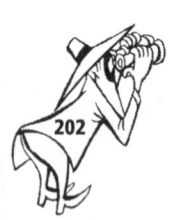

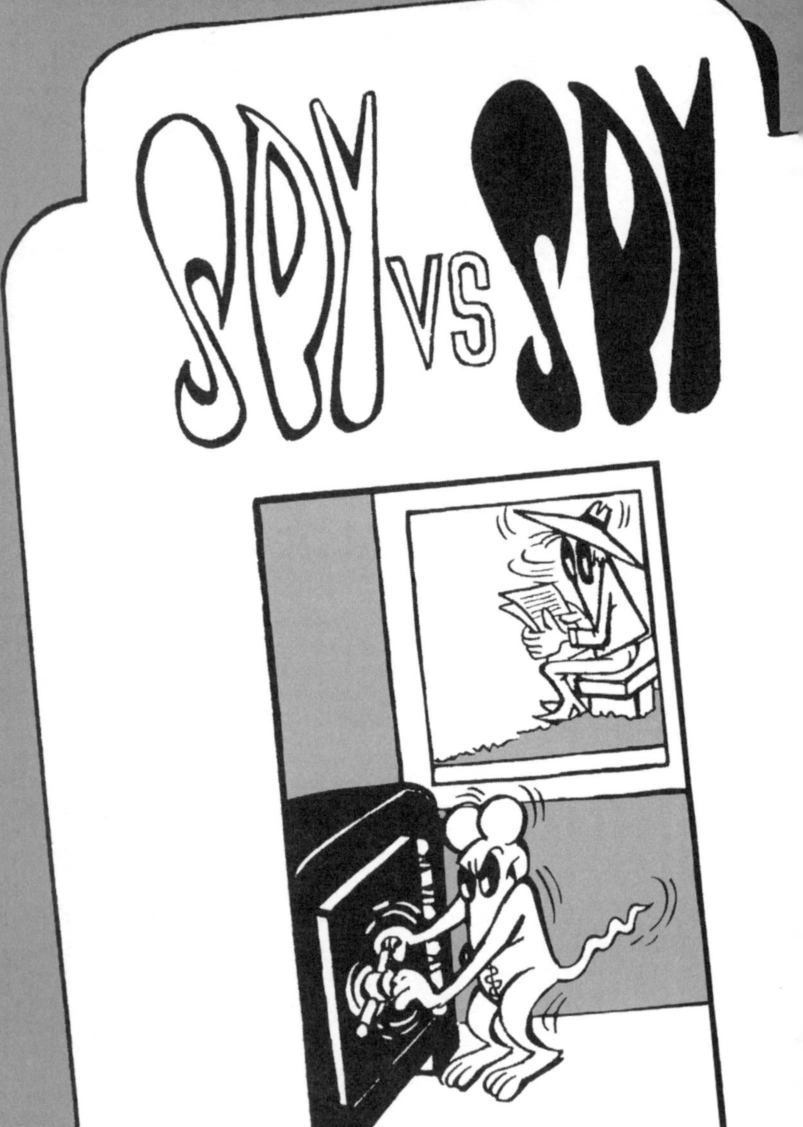
SPY vs SPY

THE RAT-FINK CASE

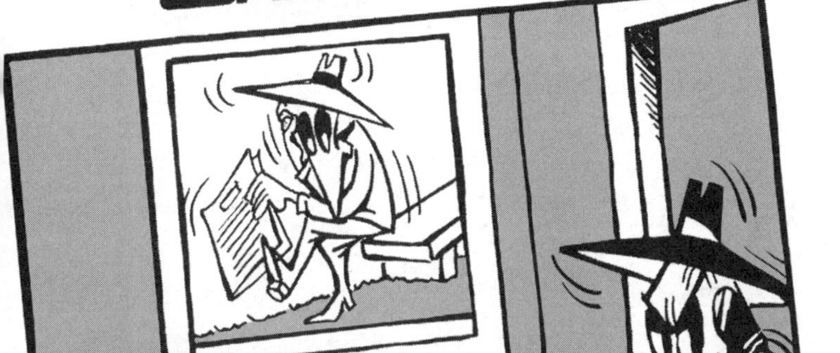
TOP SECRET

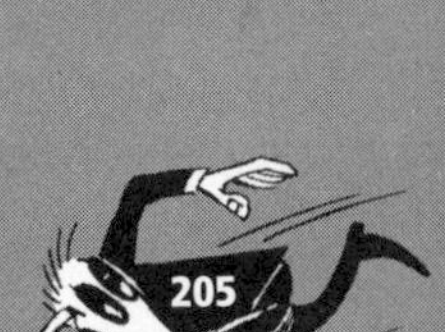

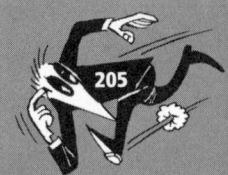

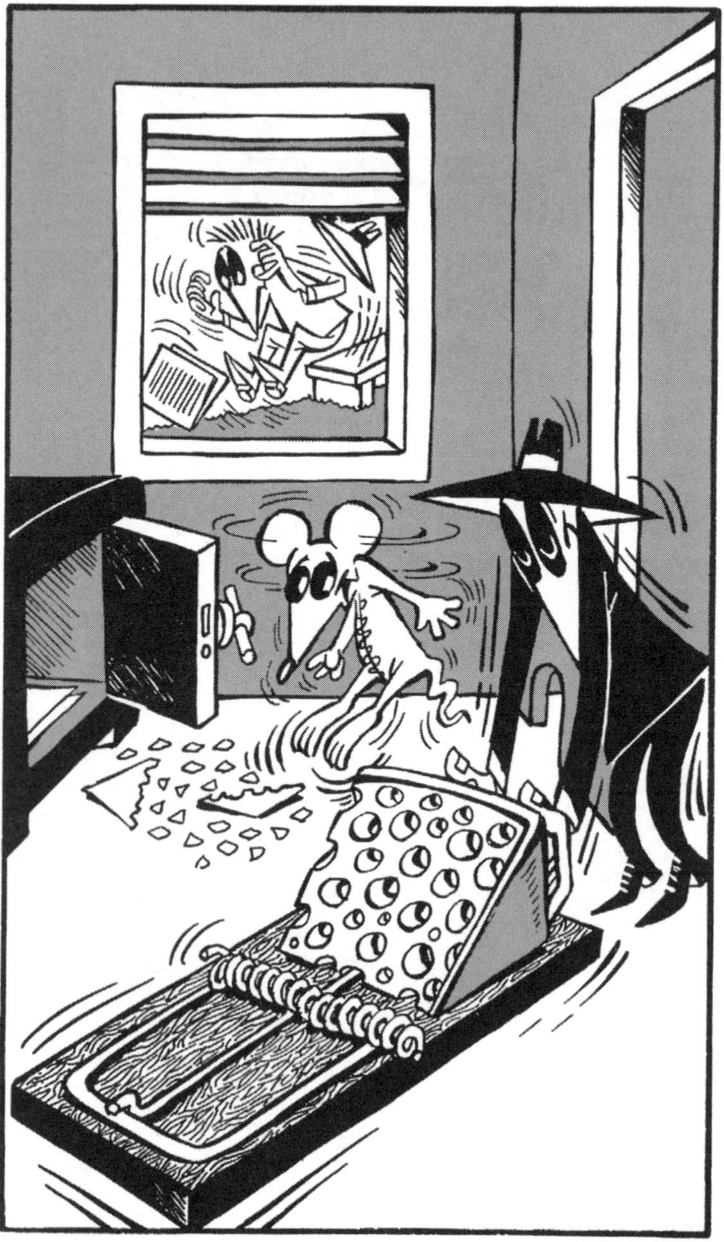

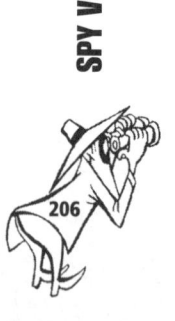

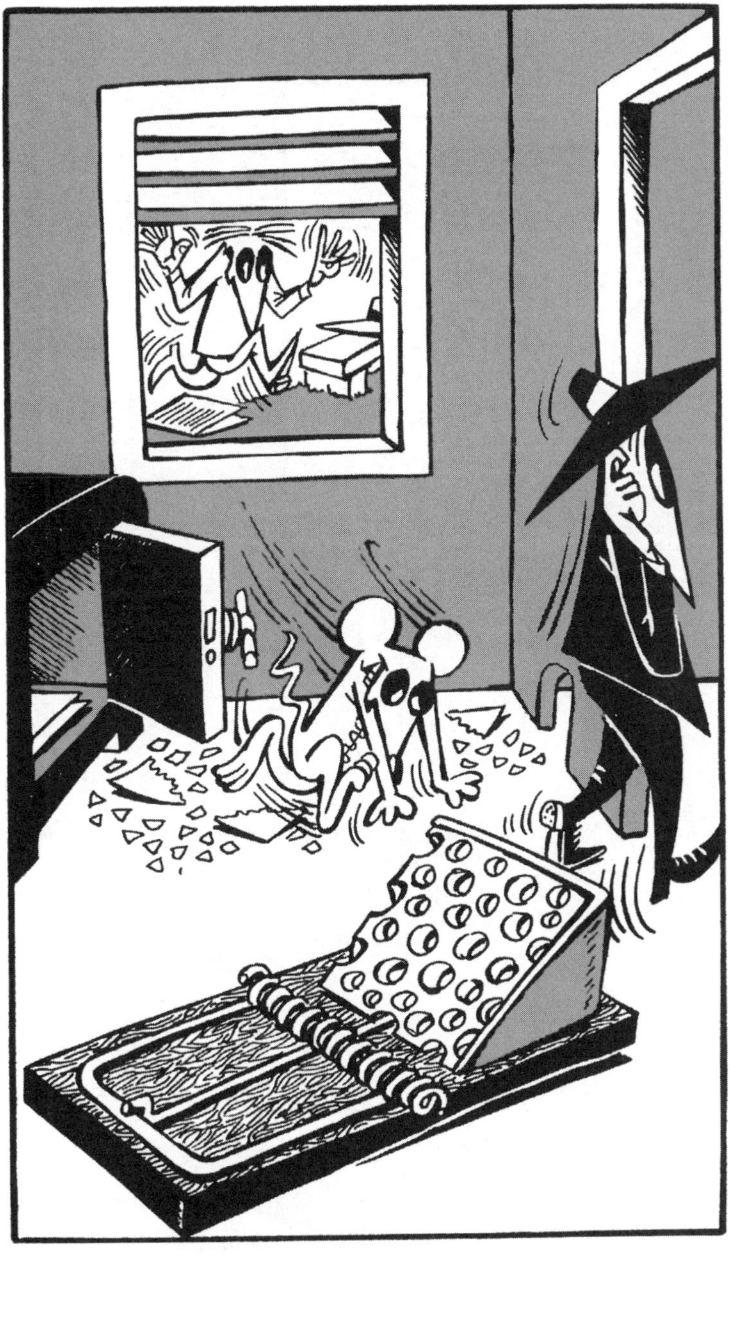

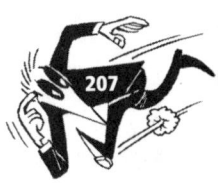

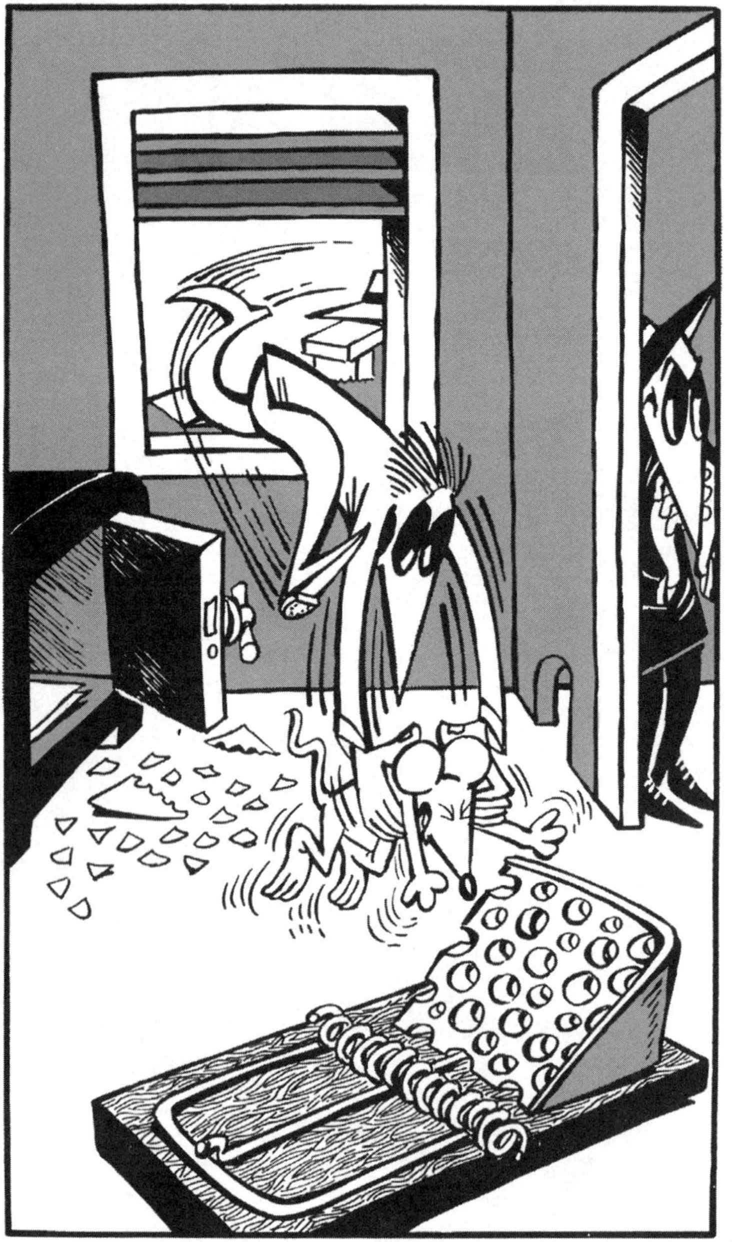

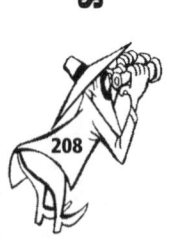

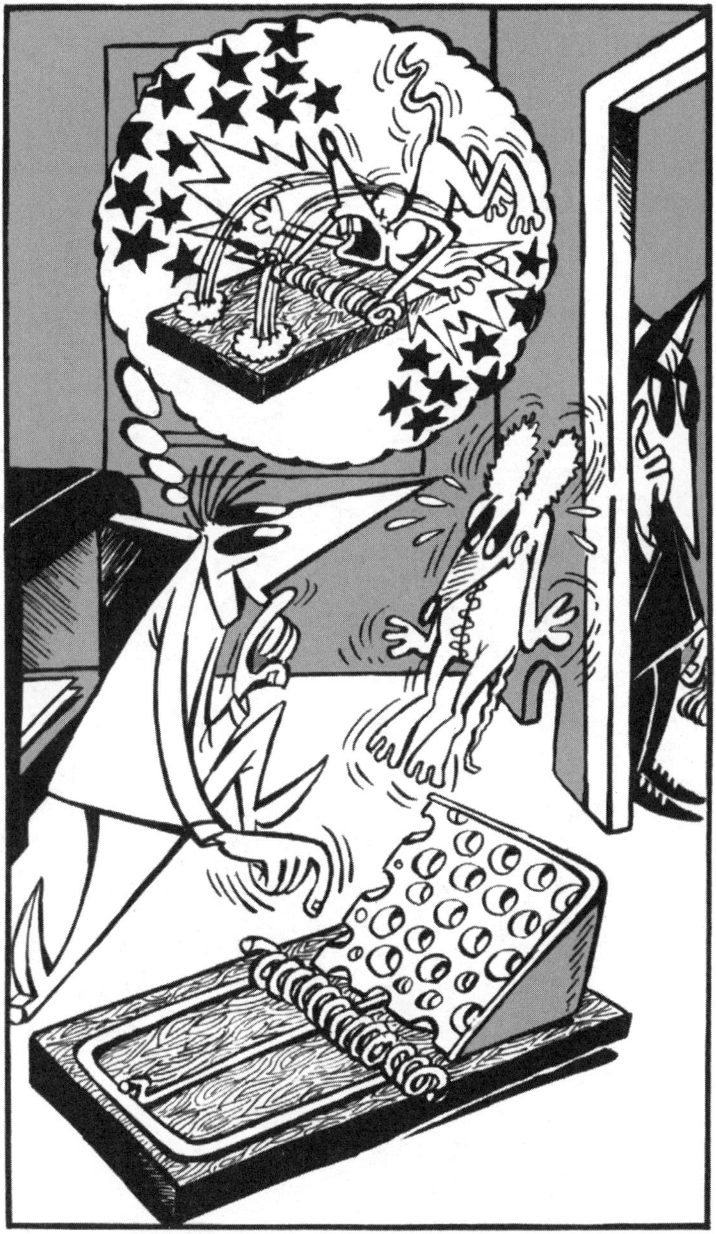

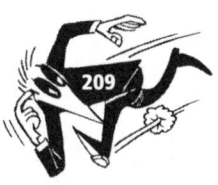

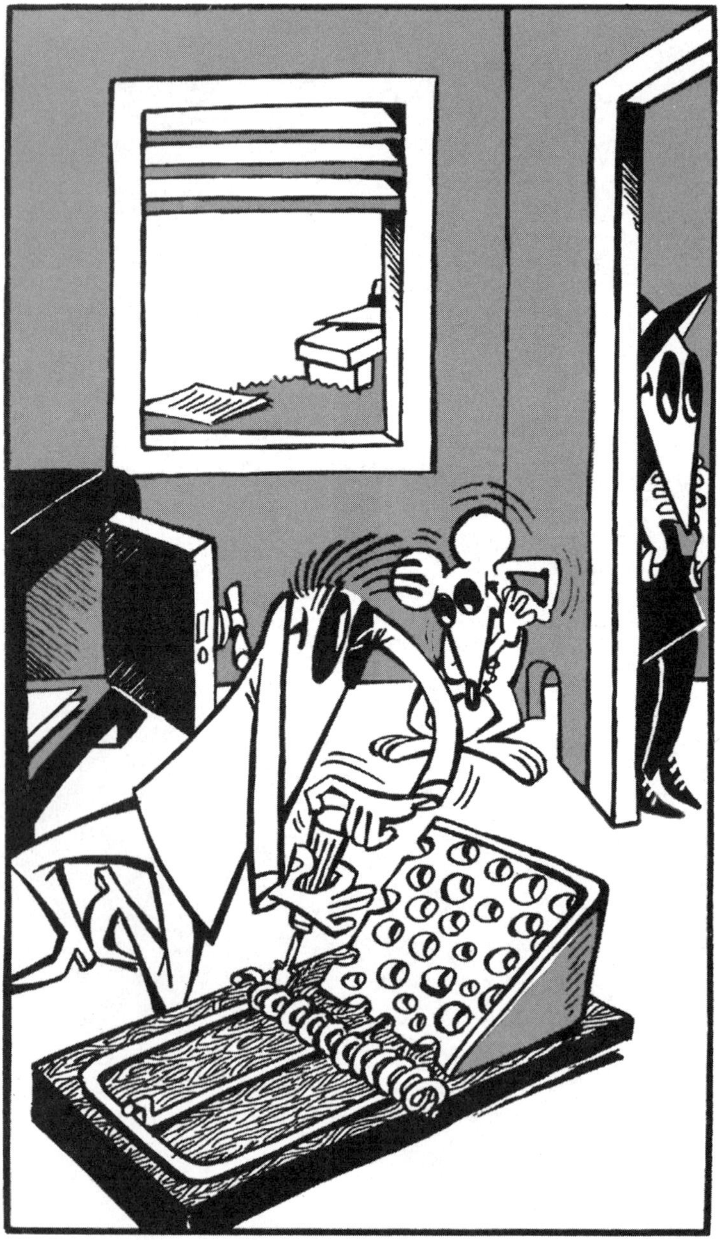

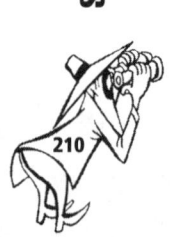

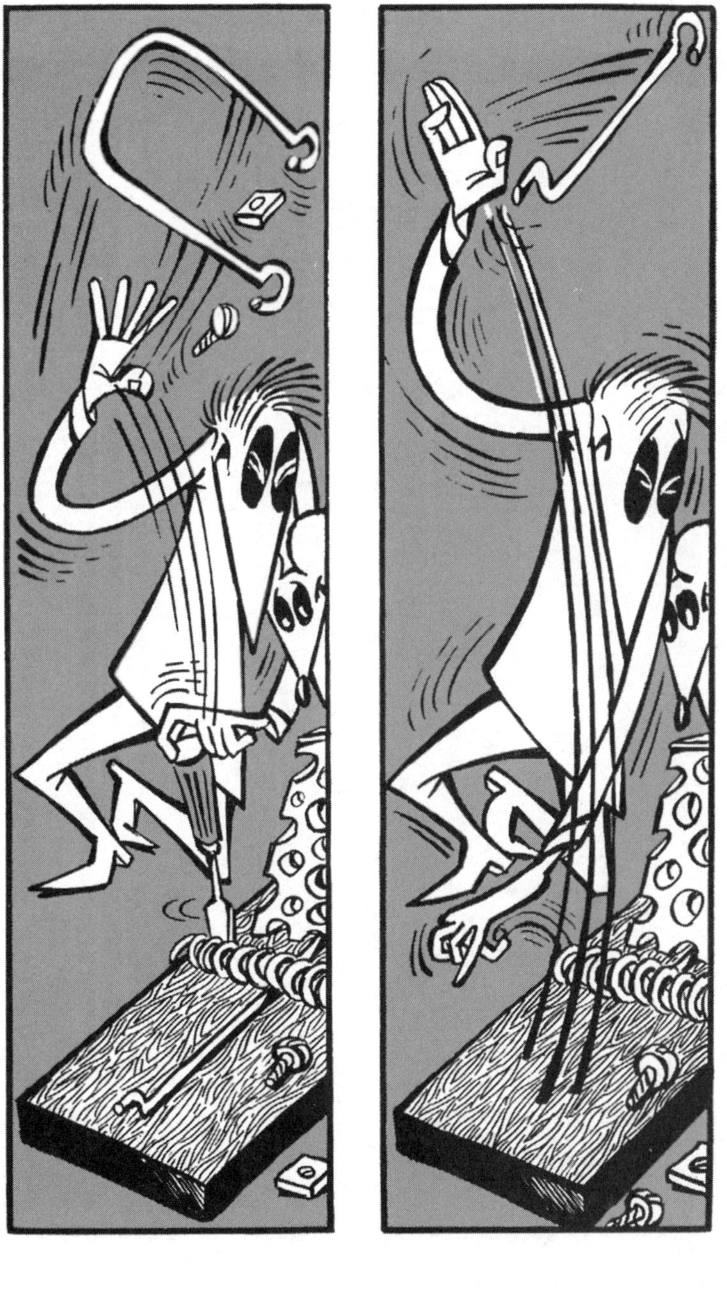

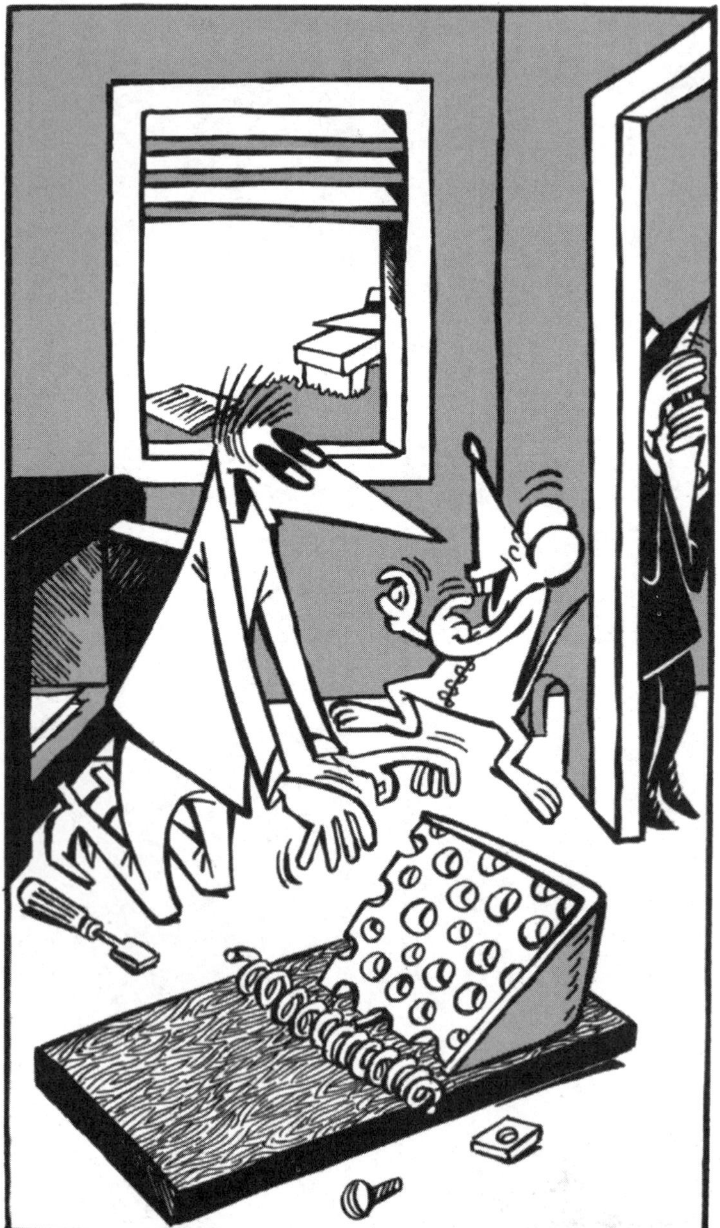

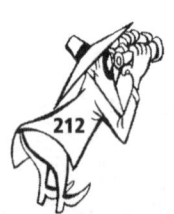

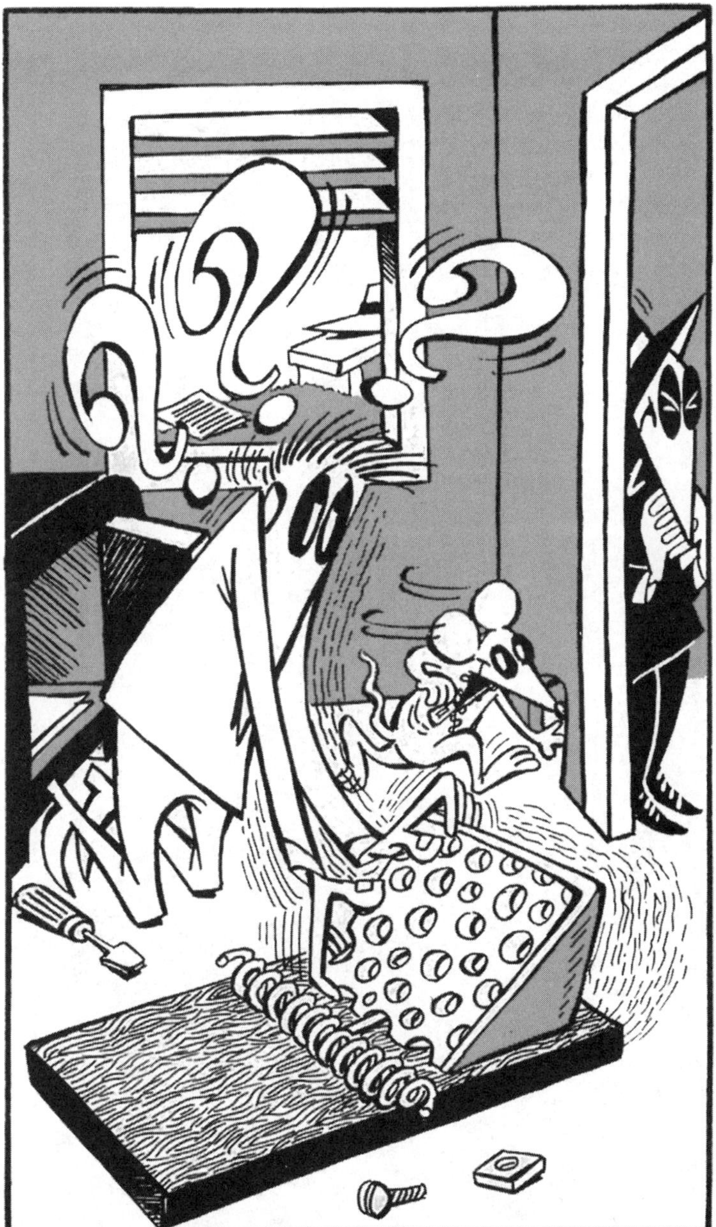

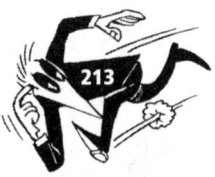

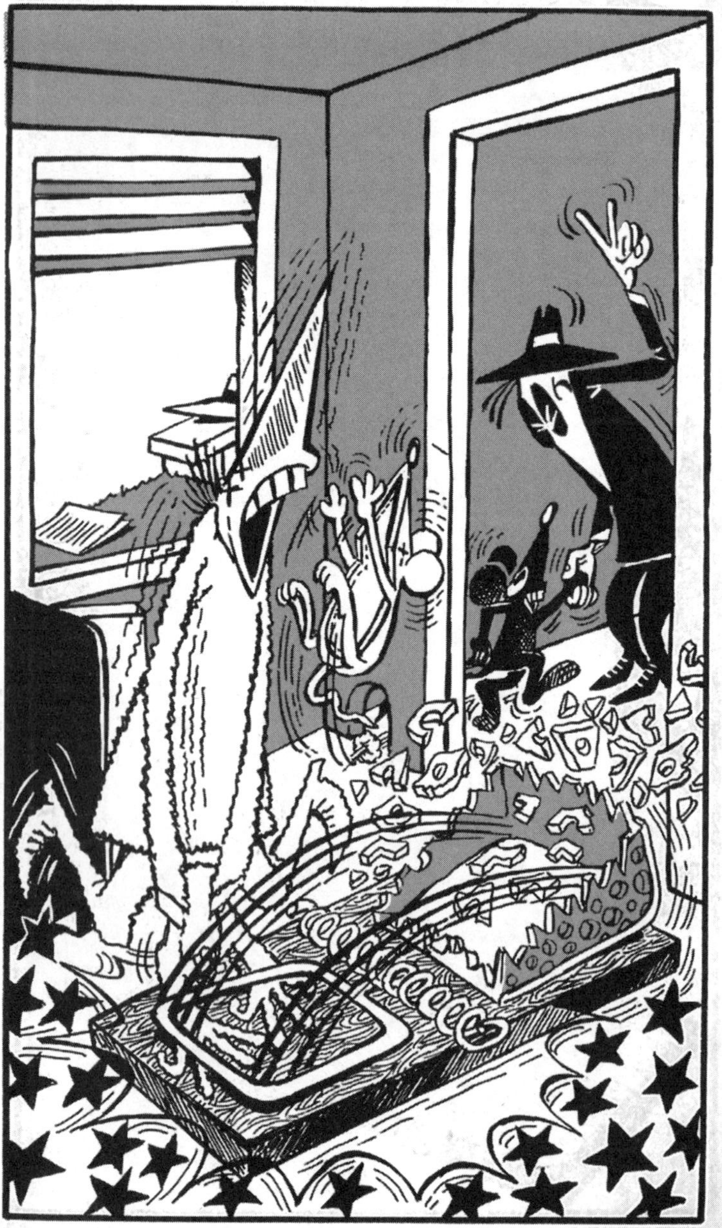

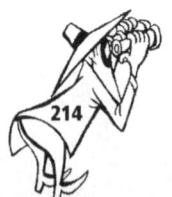

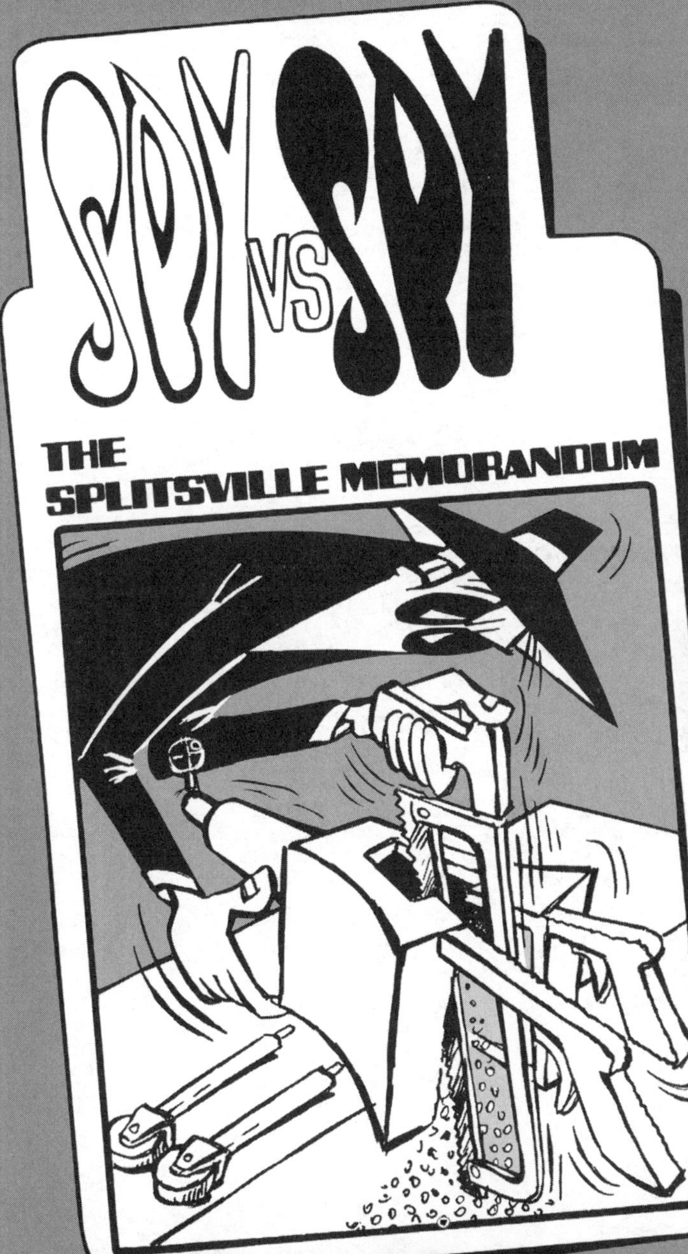
SPY vs SPY
THE SPLITSVILLE MEMORANDUM

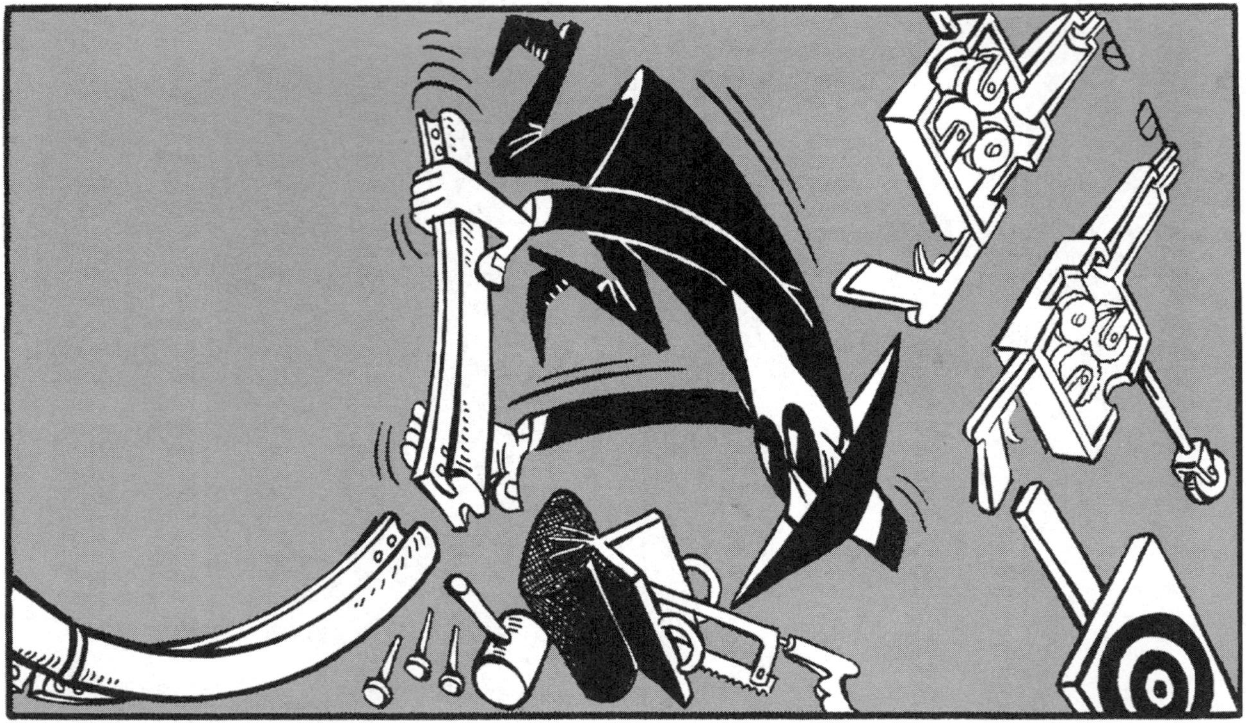

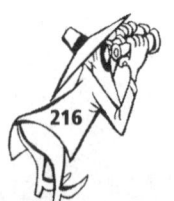

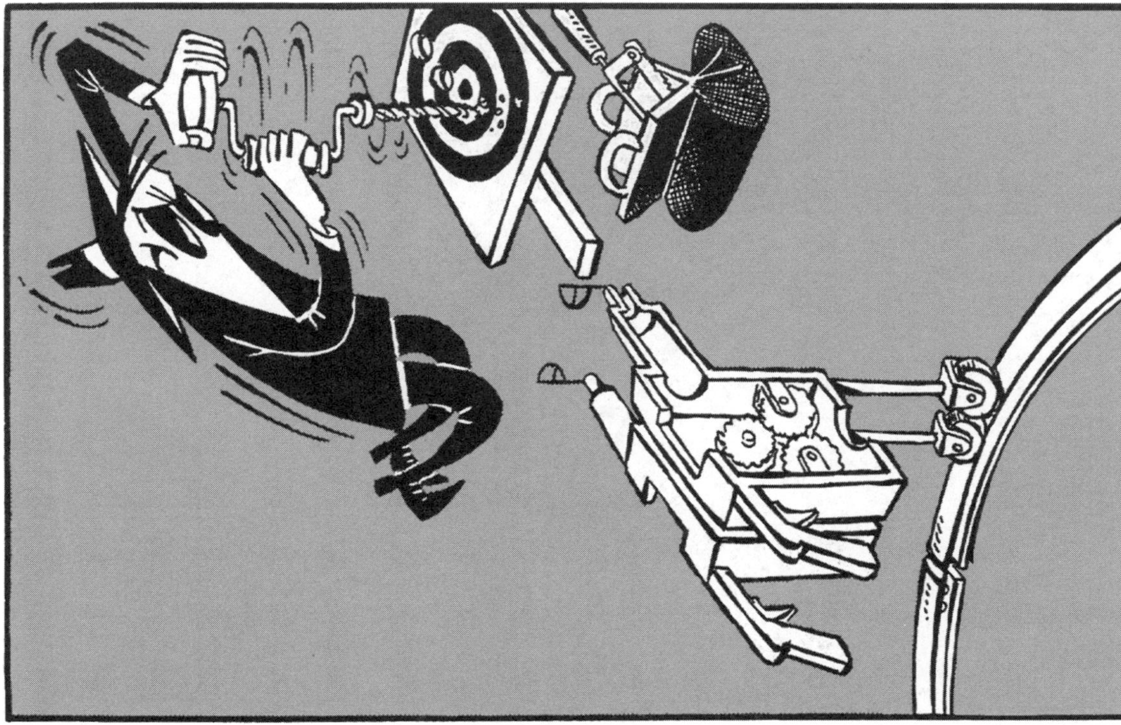

THE SPLITSVILLE MEMORANDUM

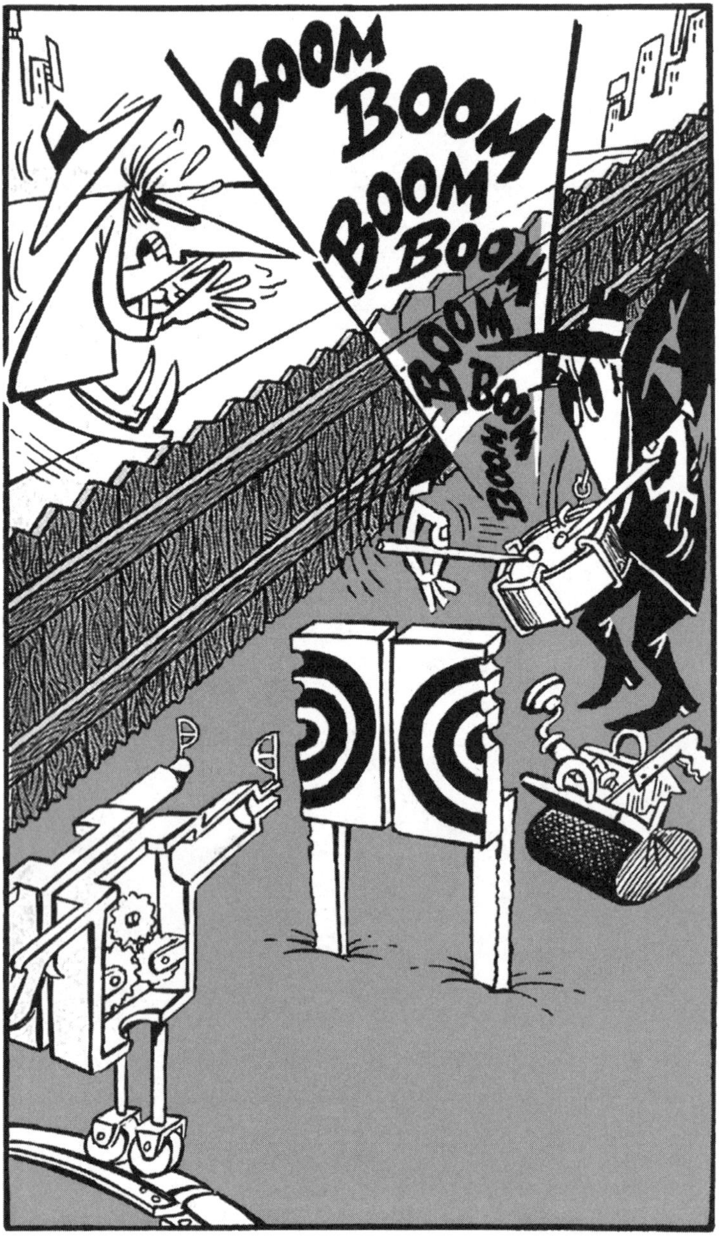
BOOM BOOM BOOM BOOM BOOM BOOM BOOM

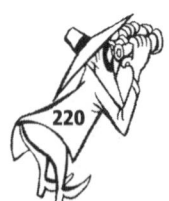

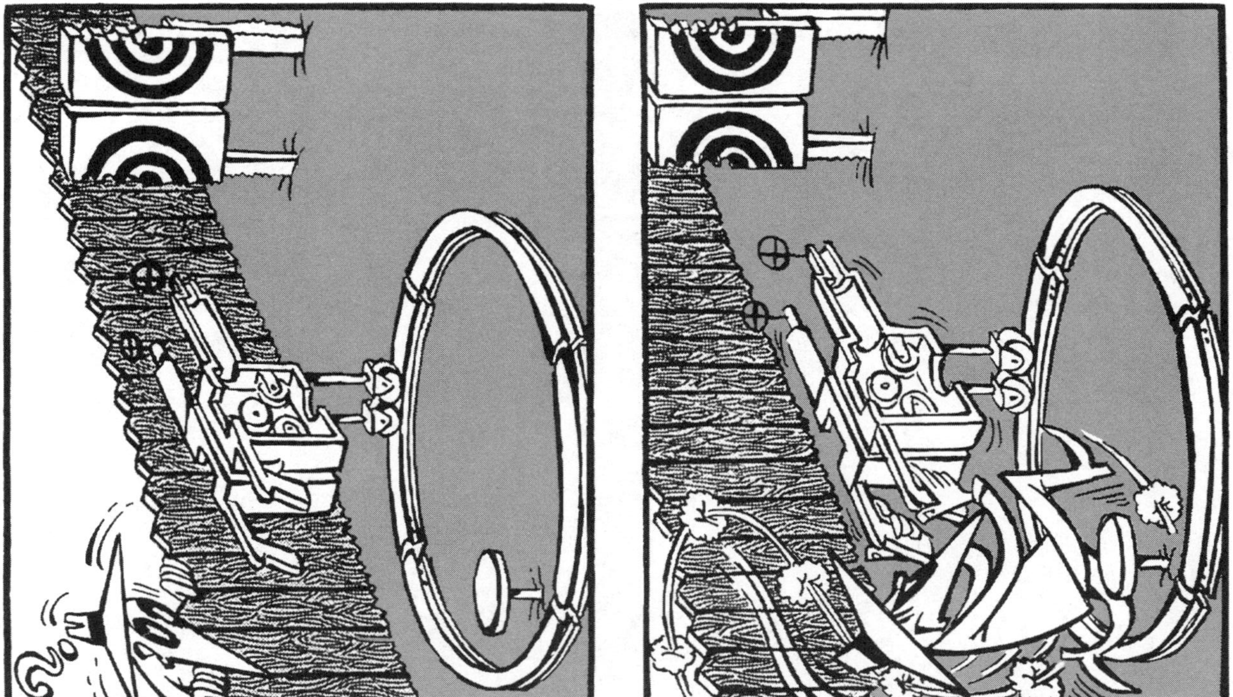

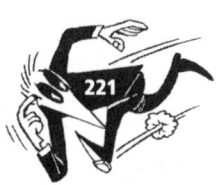

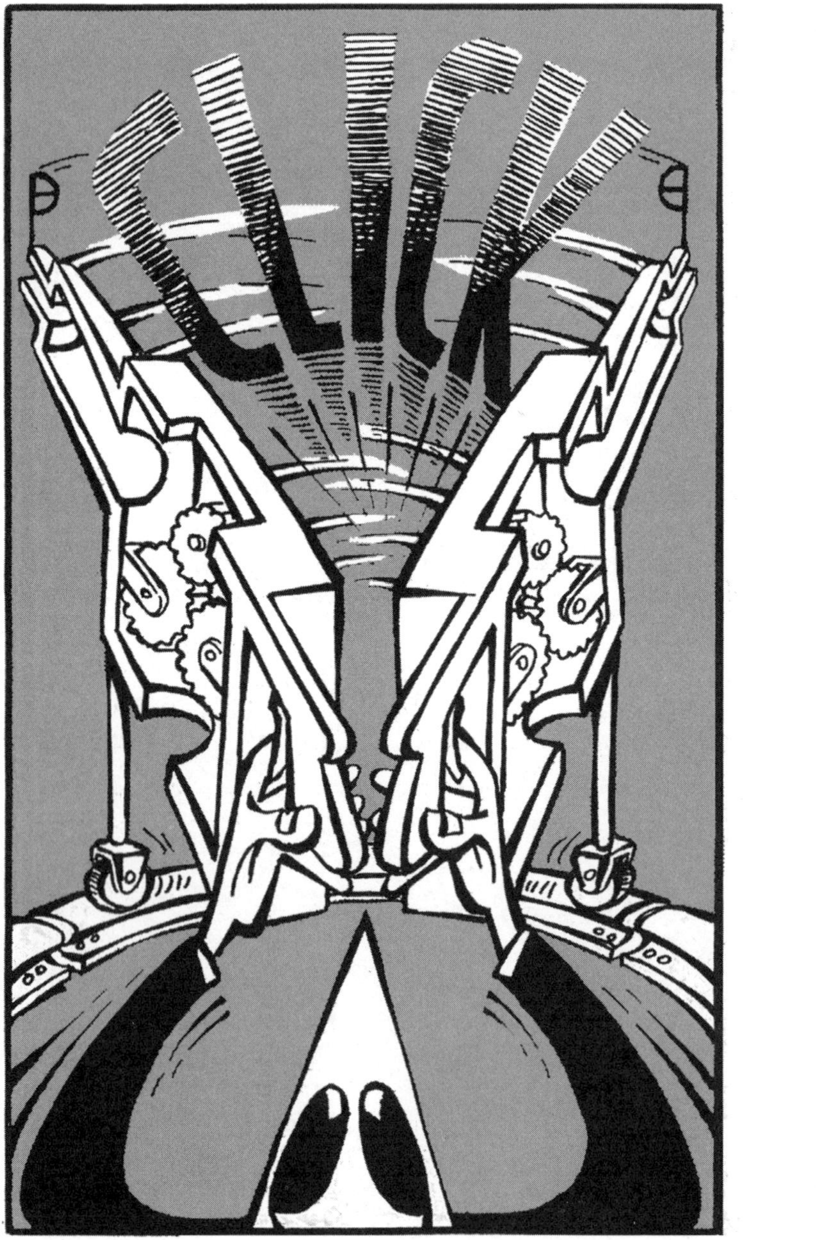
CLICK

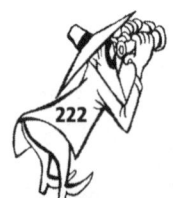

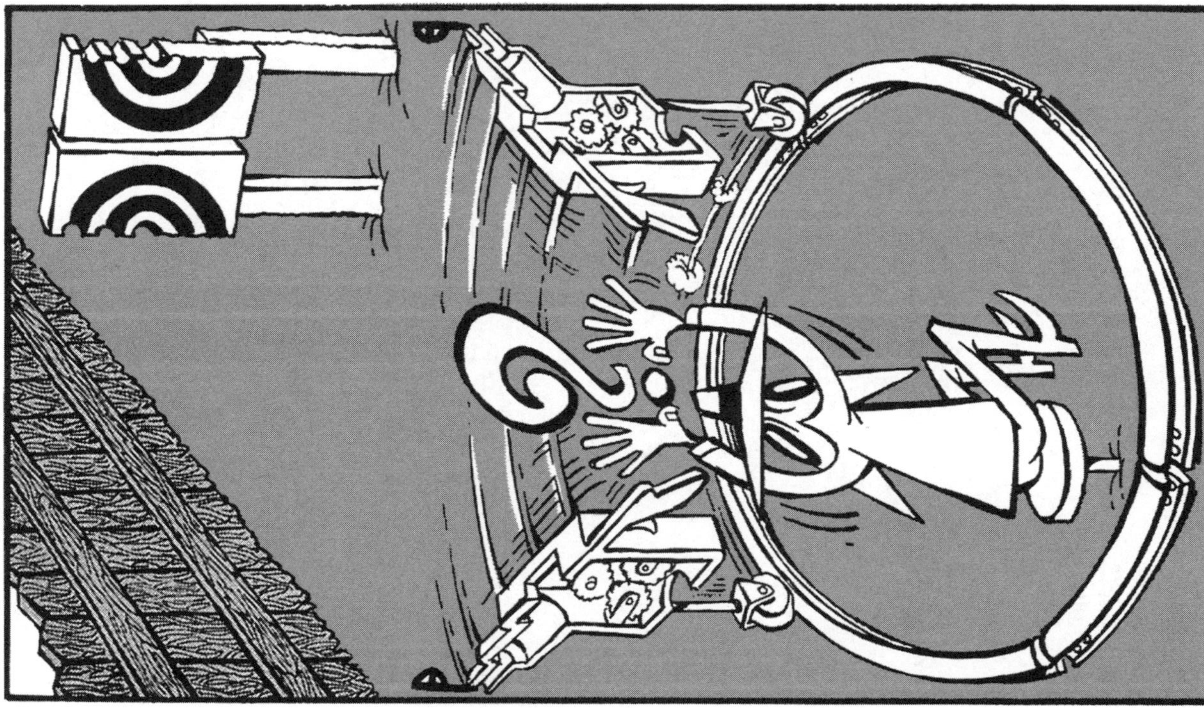

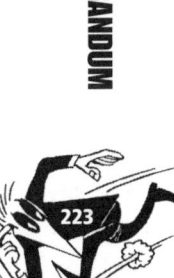

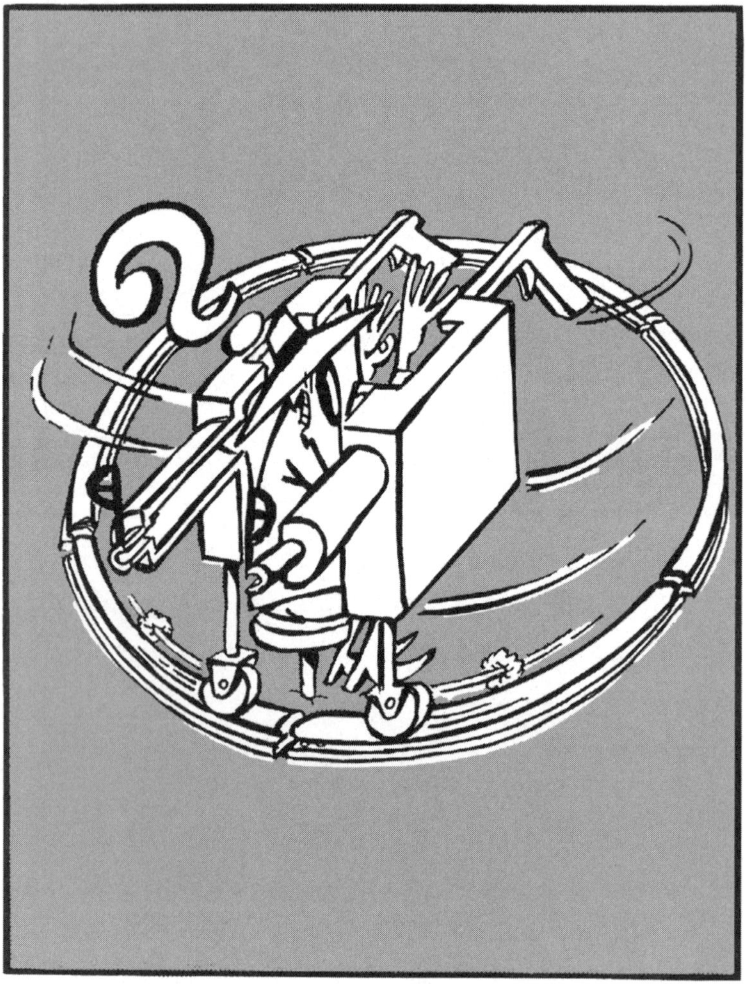

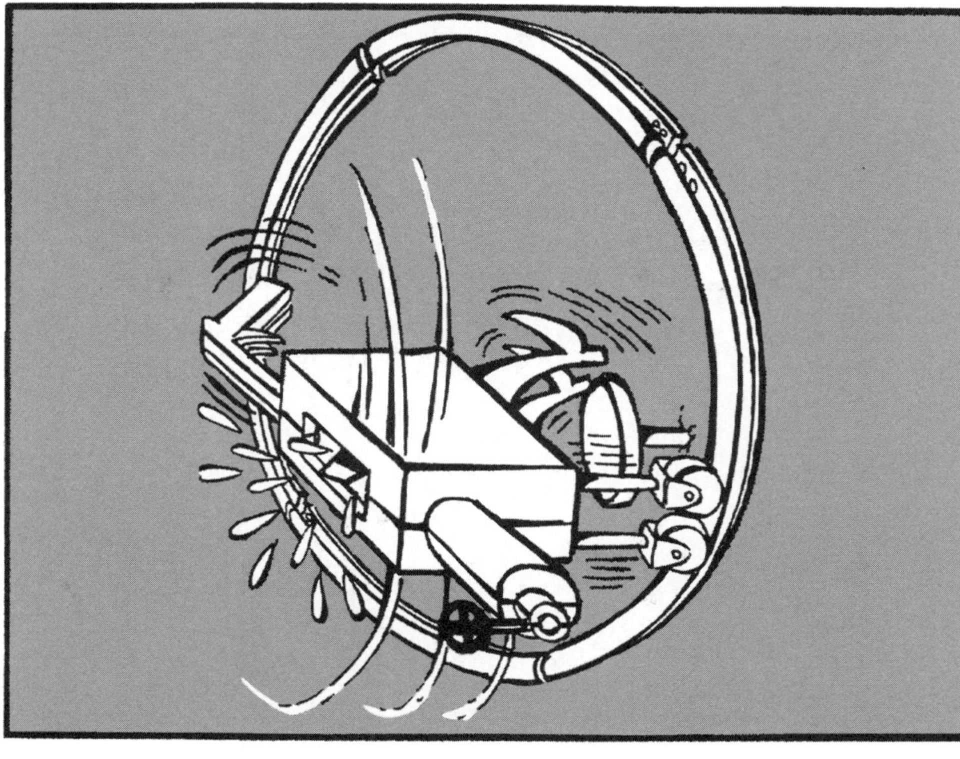

THE SPLITSVILLE MEMORANDUM

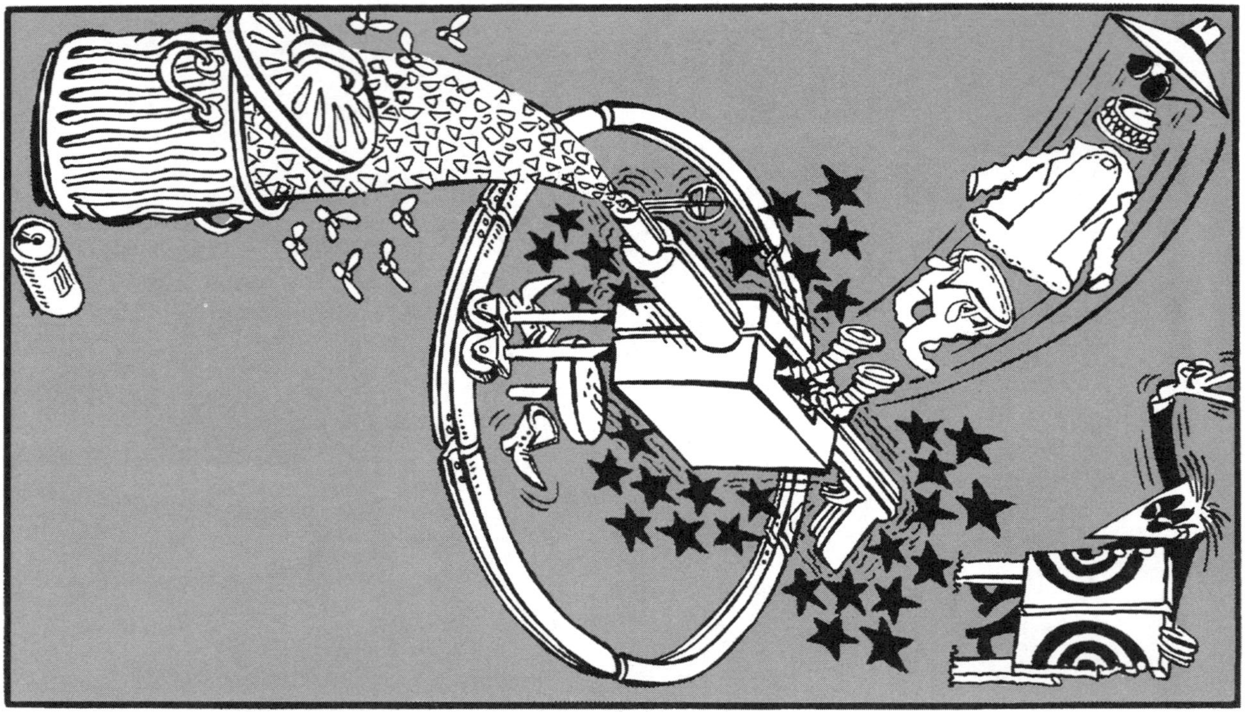

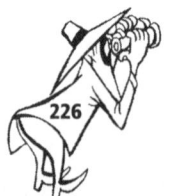

SPY vs SPY

the POOL SHARK PORTFOLIO

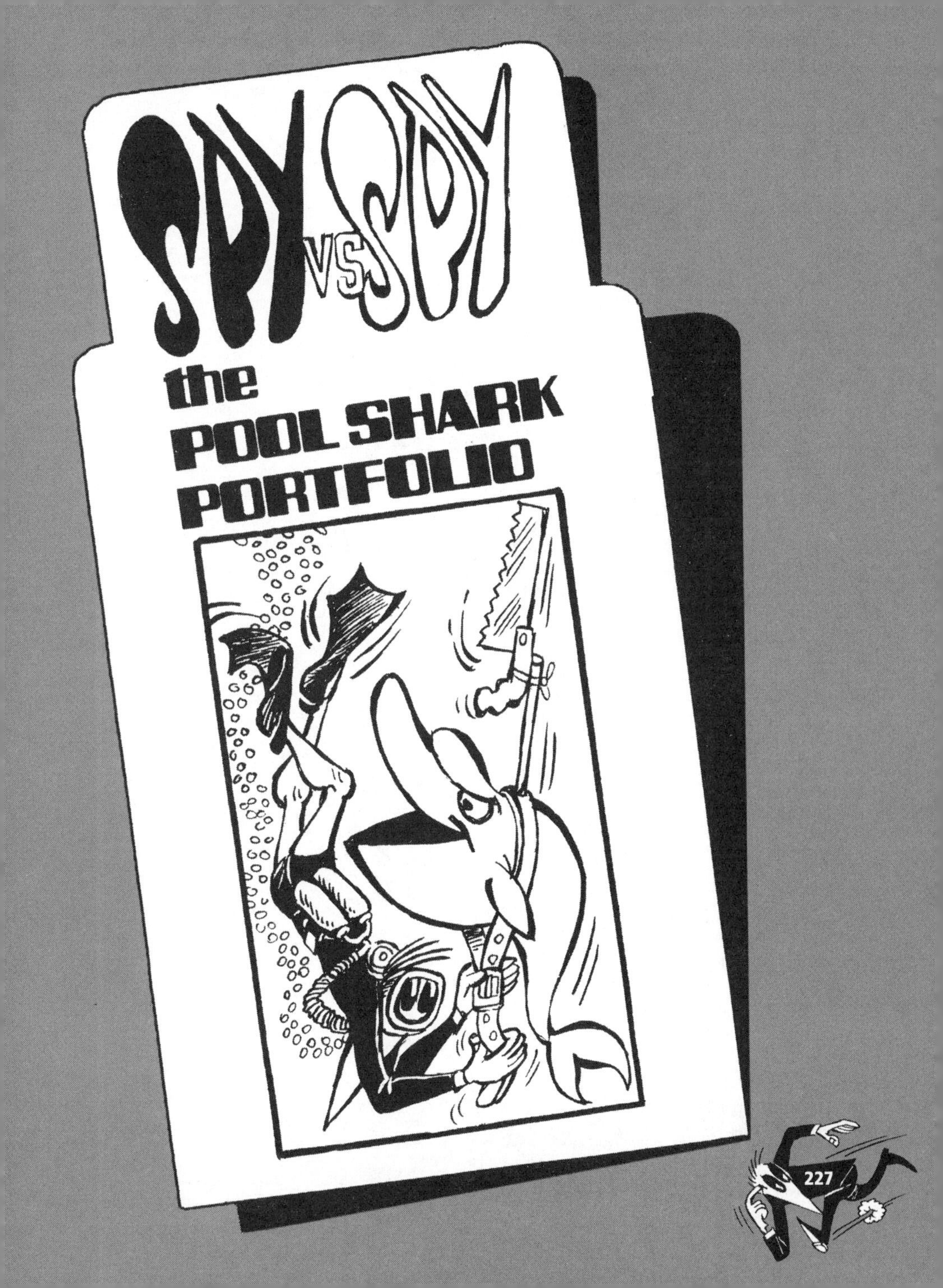

SPY VS SPY

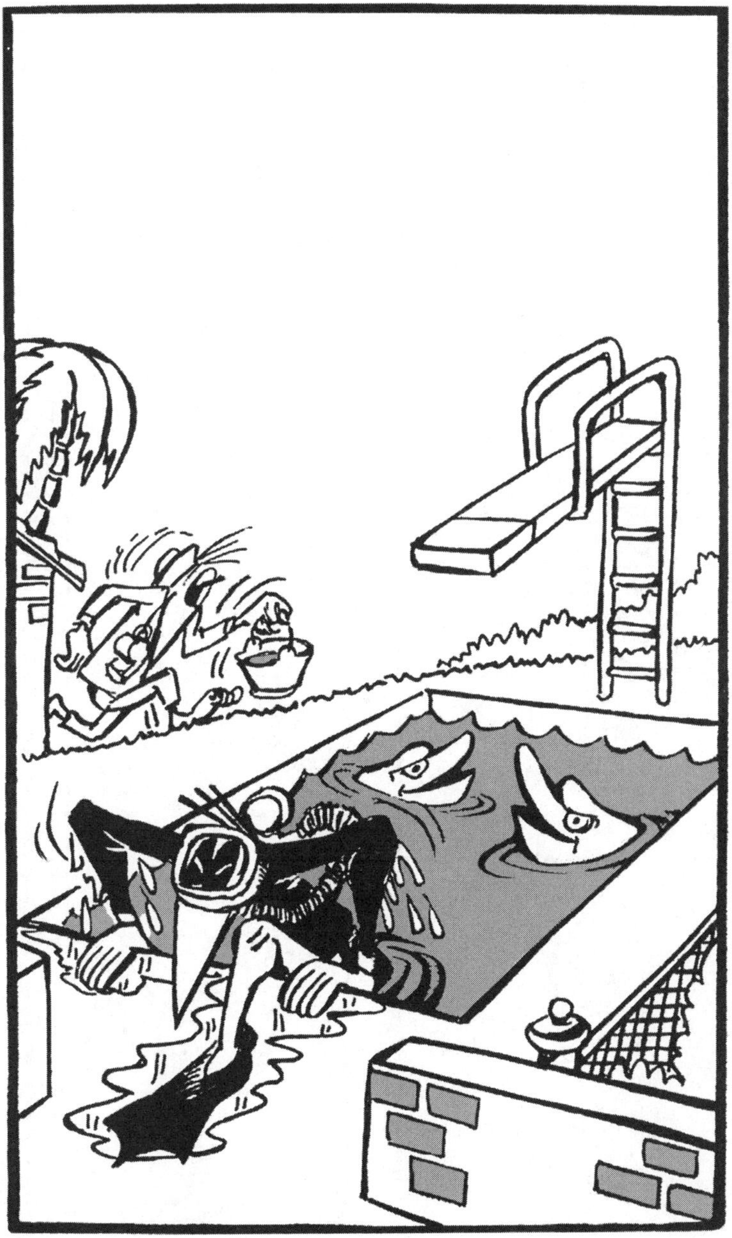

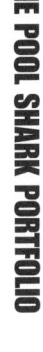

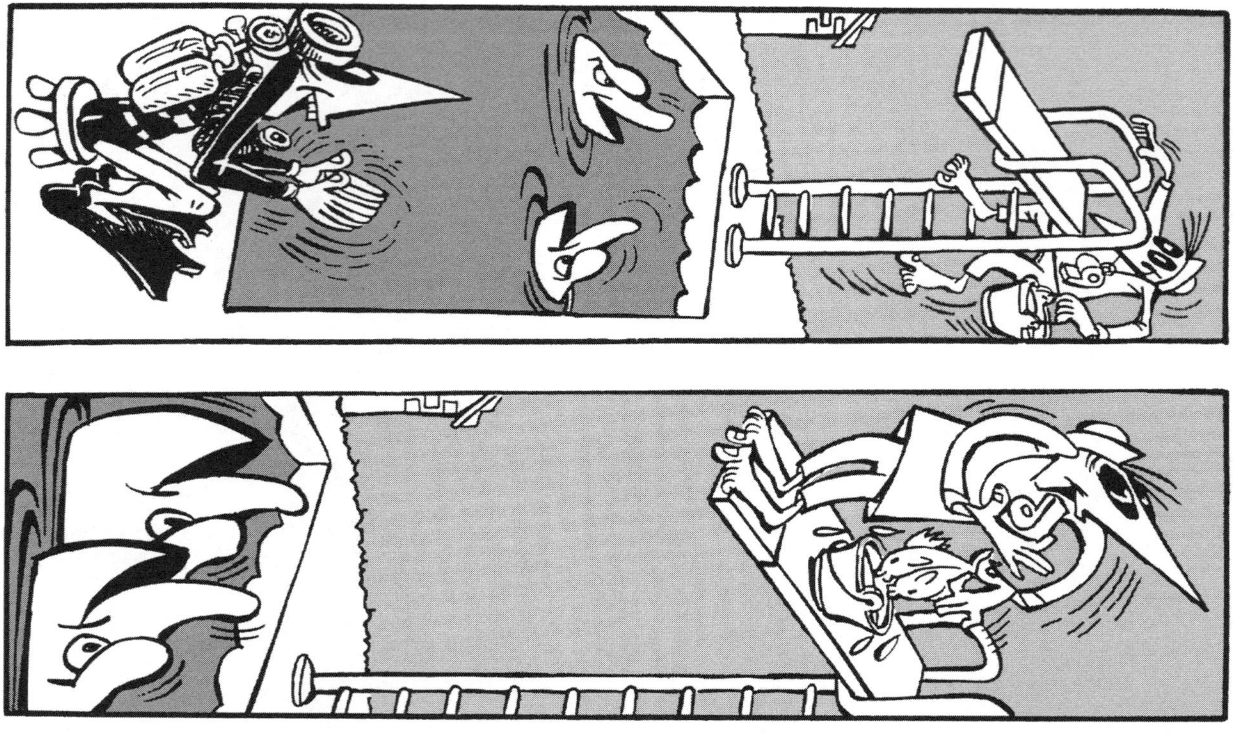

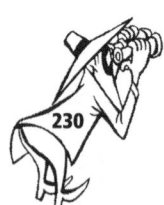

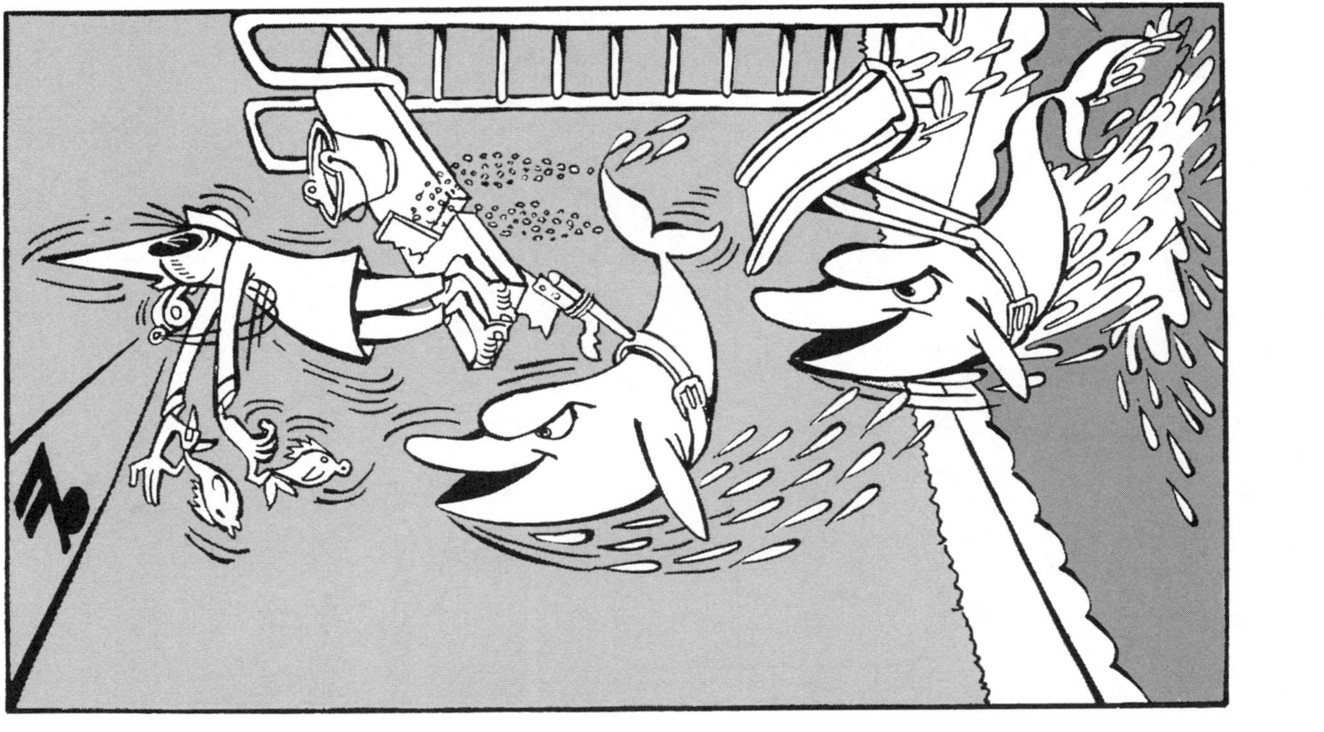

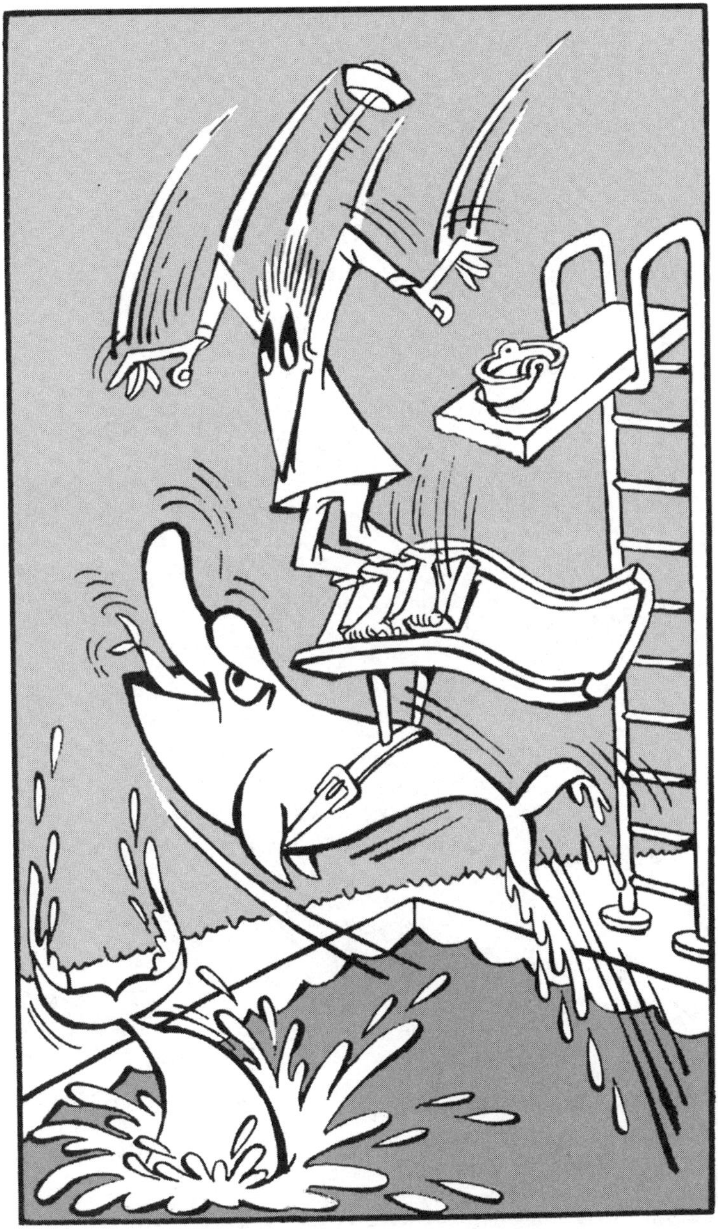

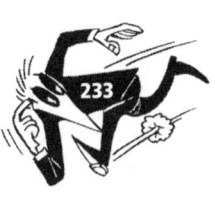

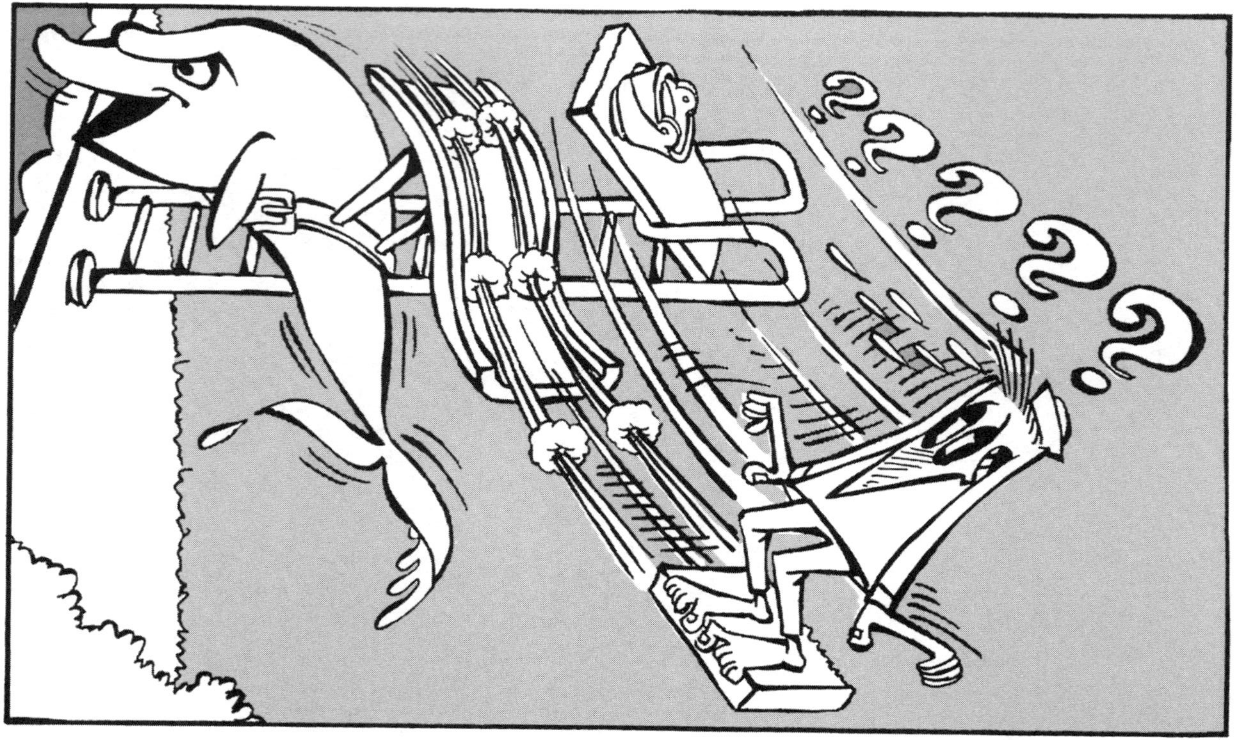

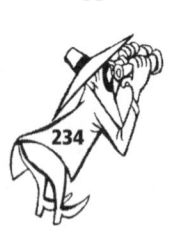

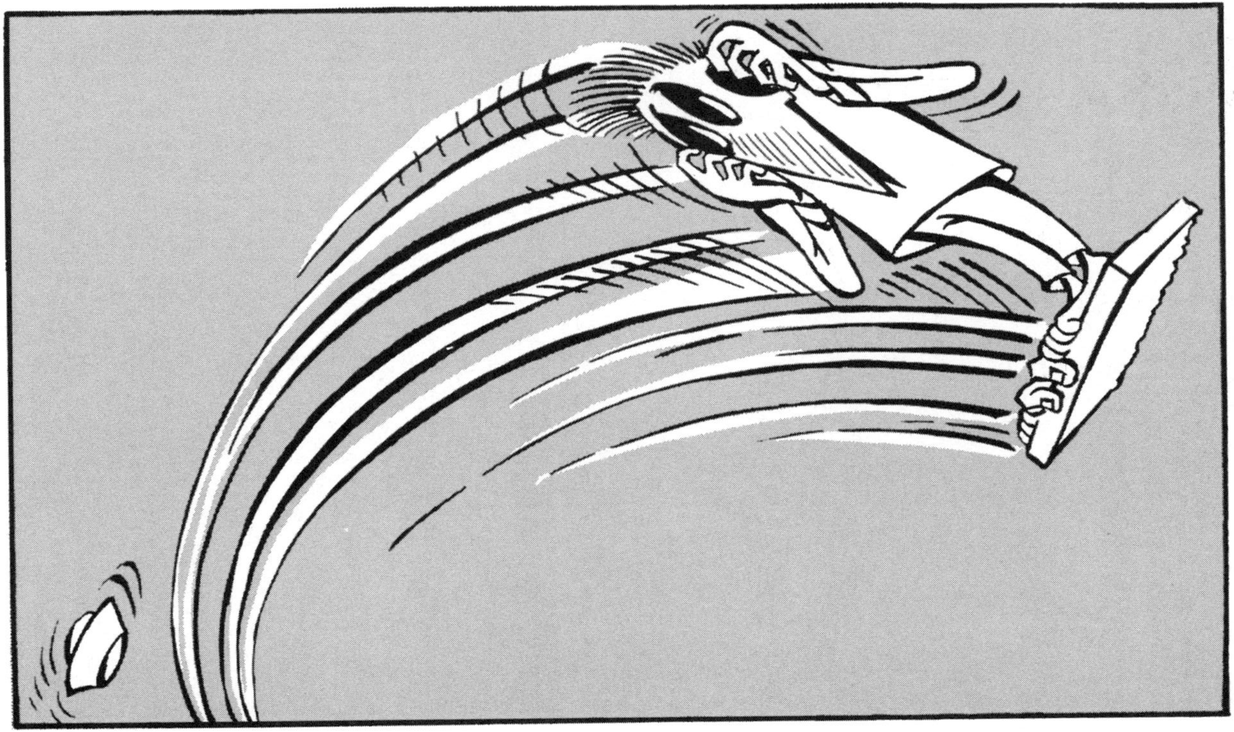

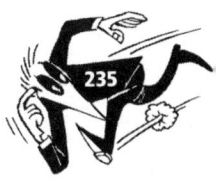

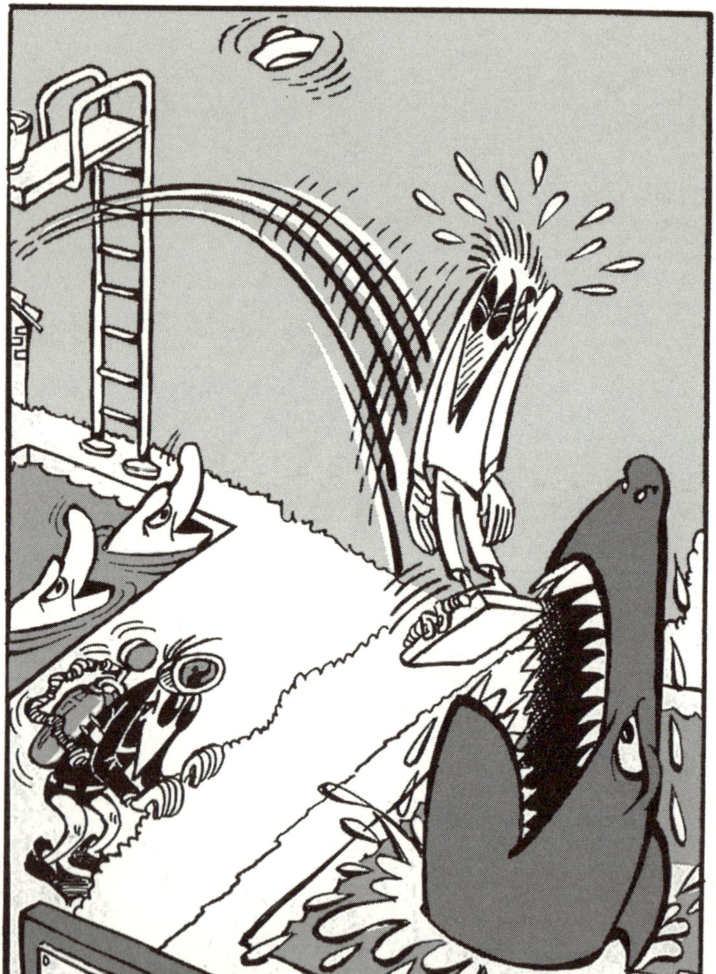
AQUARIUM

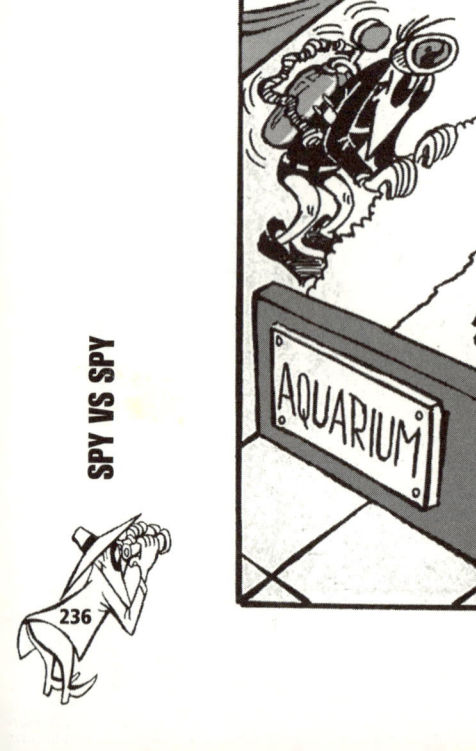

SPY vs SPY

the SHELL GAME REPORT

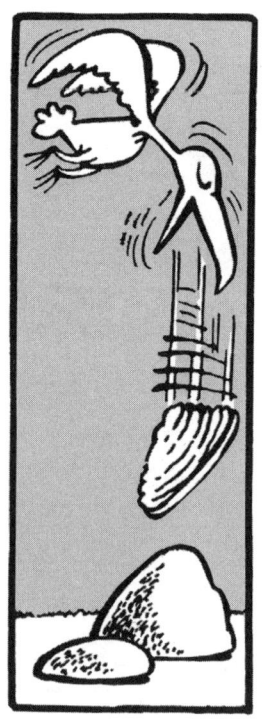

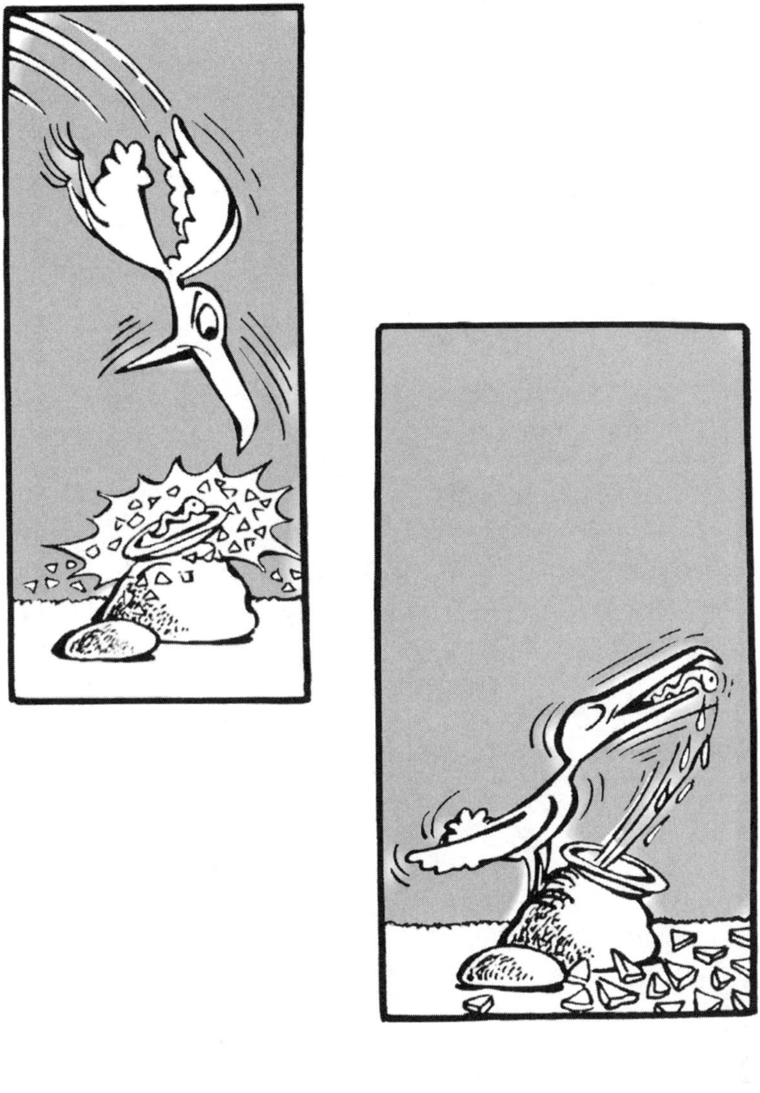

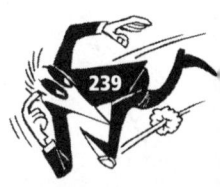

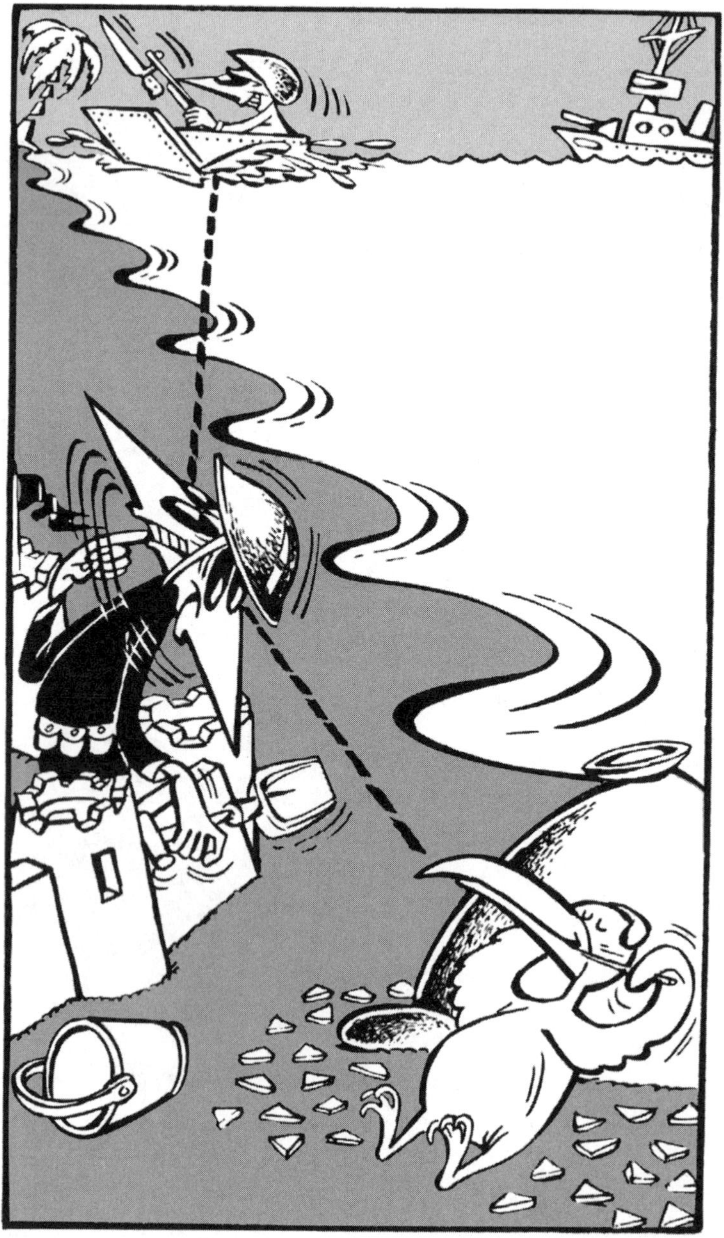

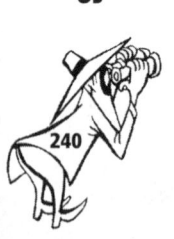

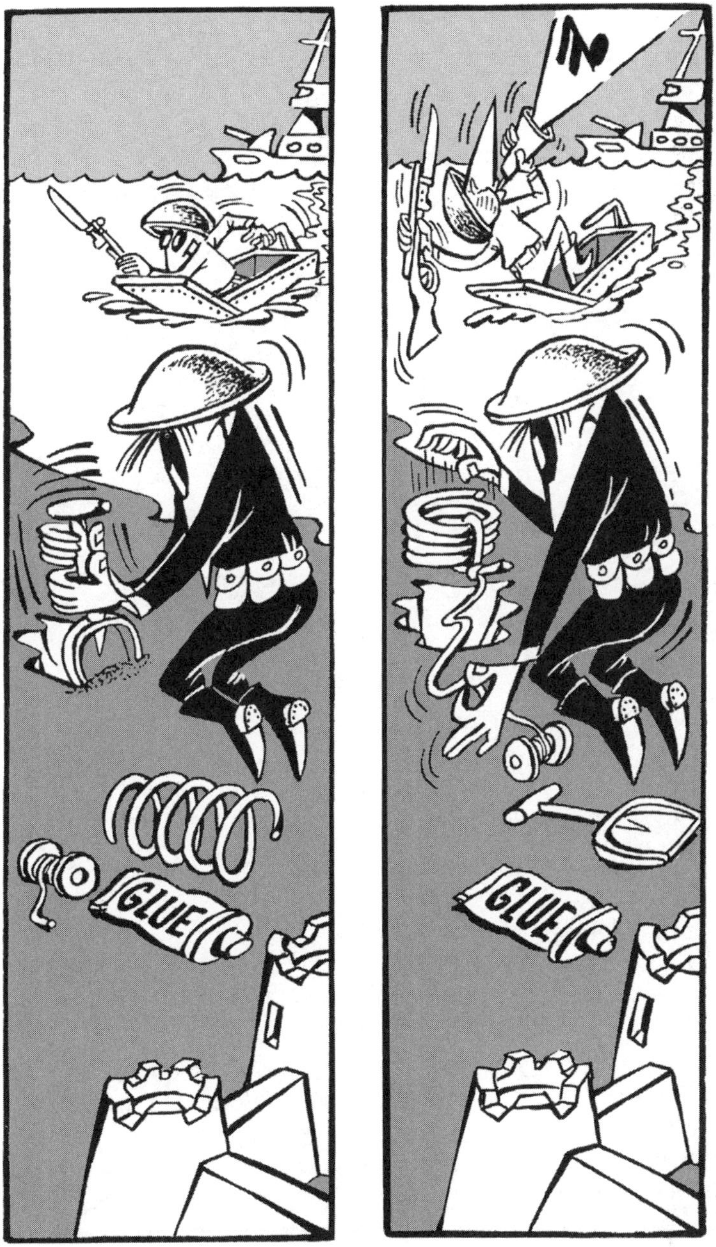
GLUE
GLUE

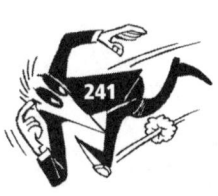

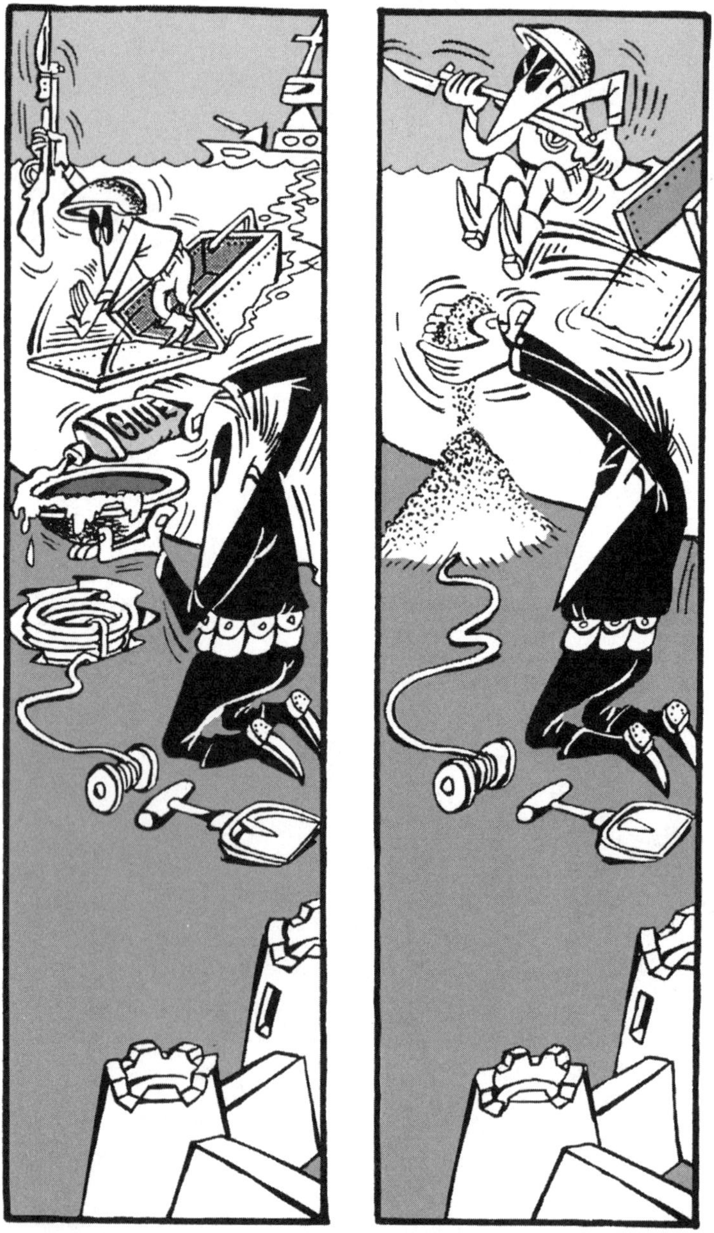
GLUE

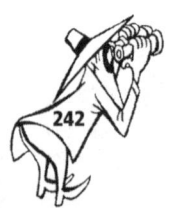

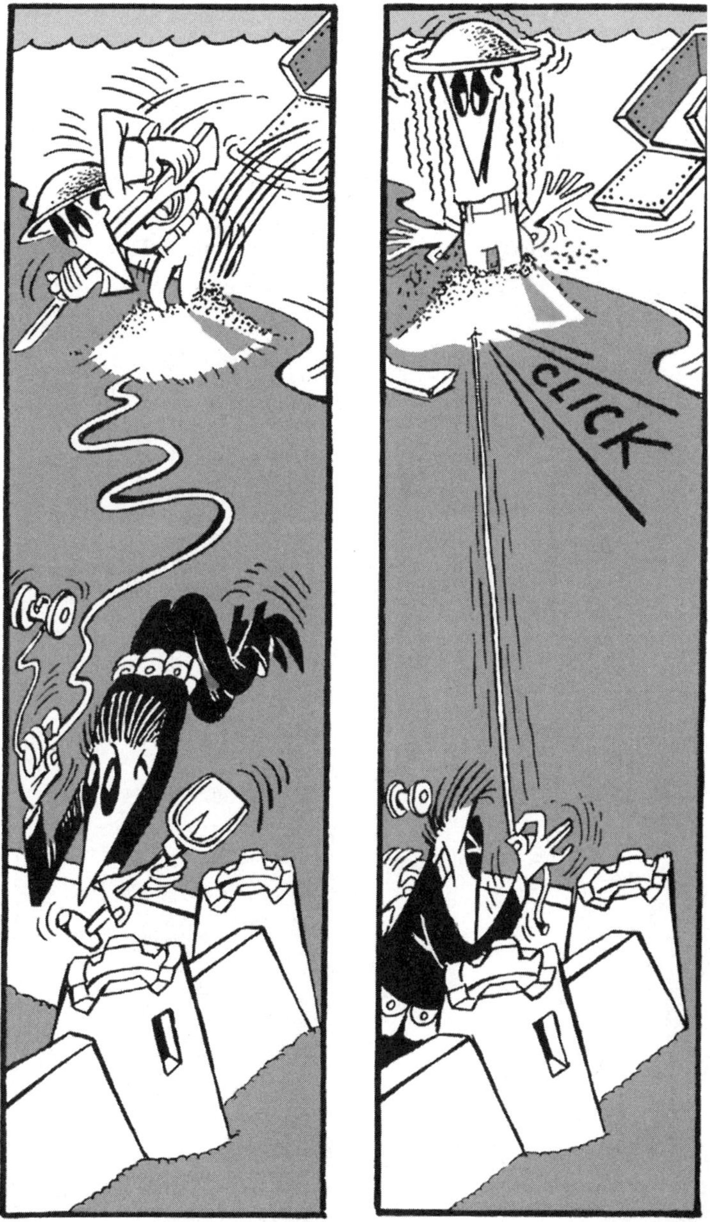
CLICK

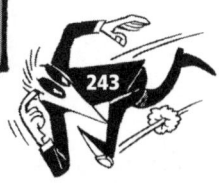

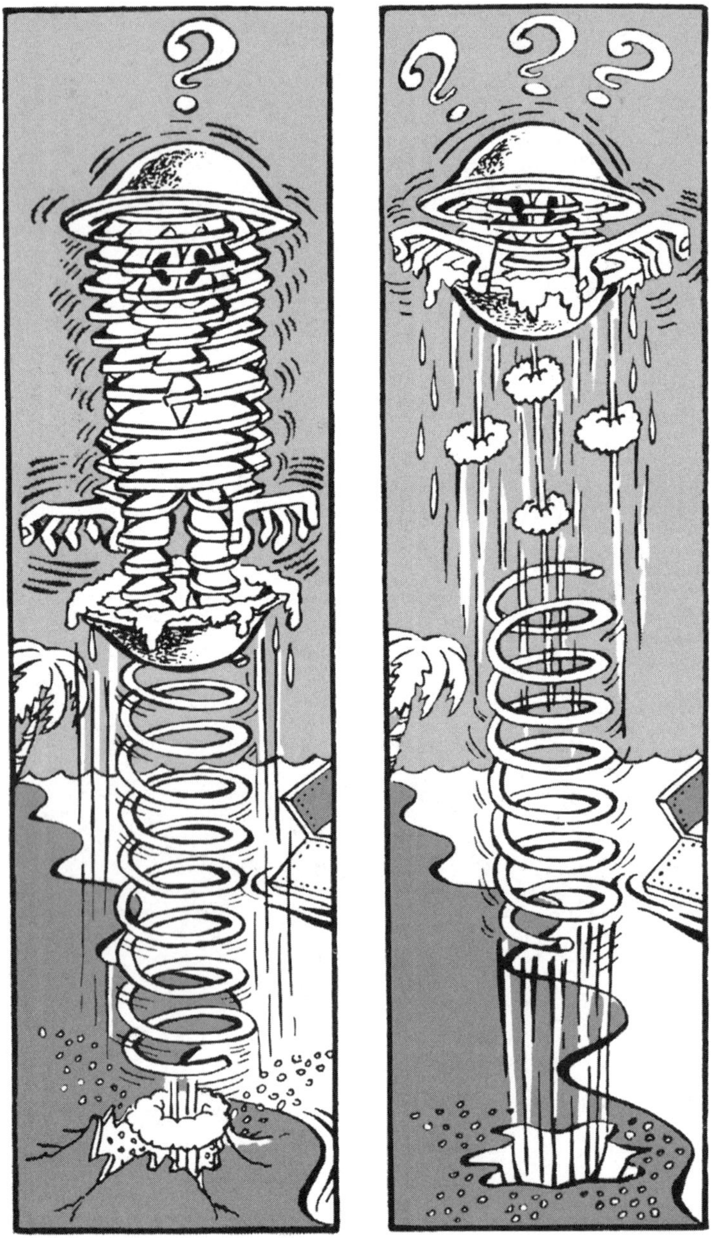

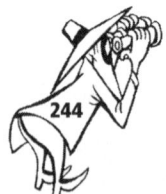

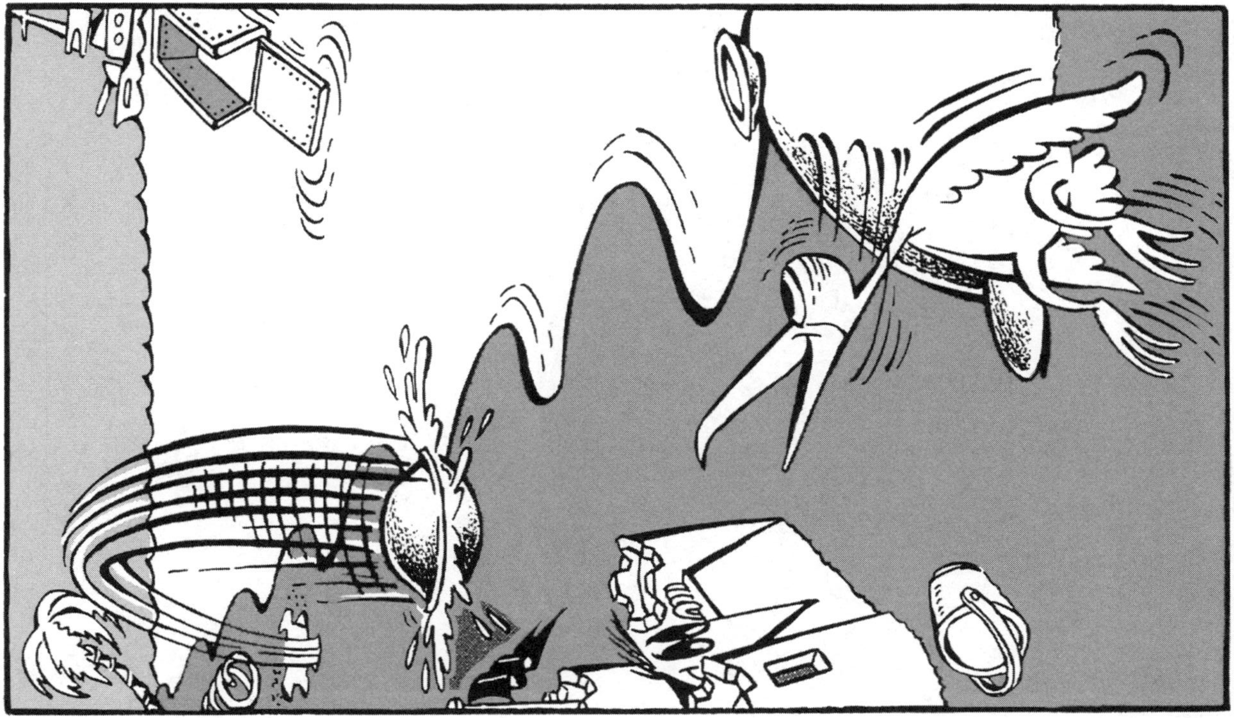

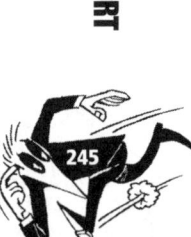

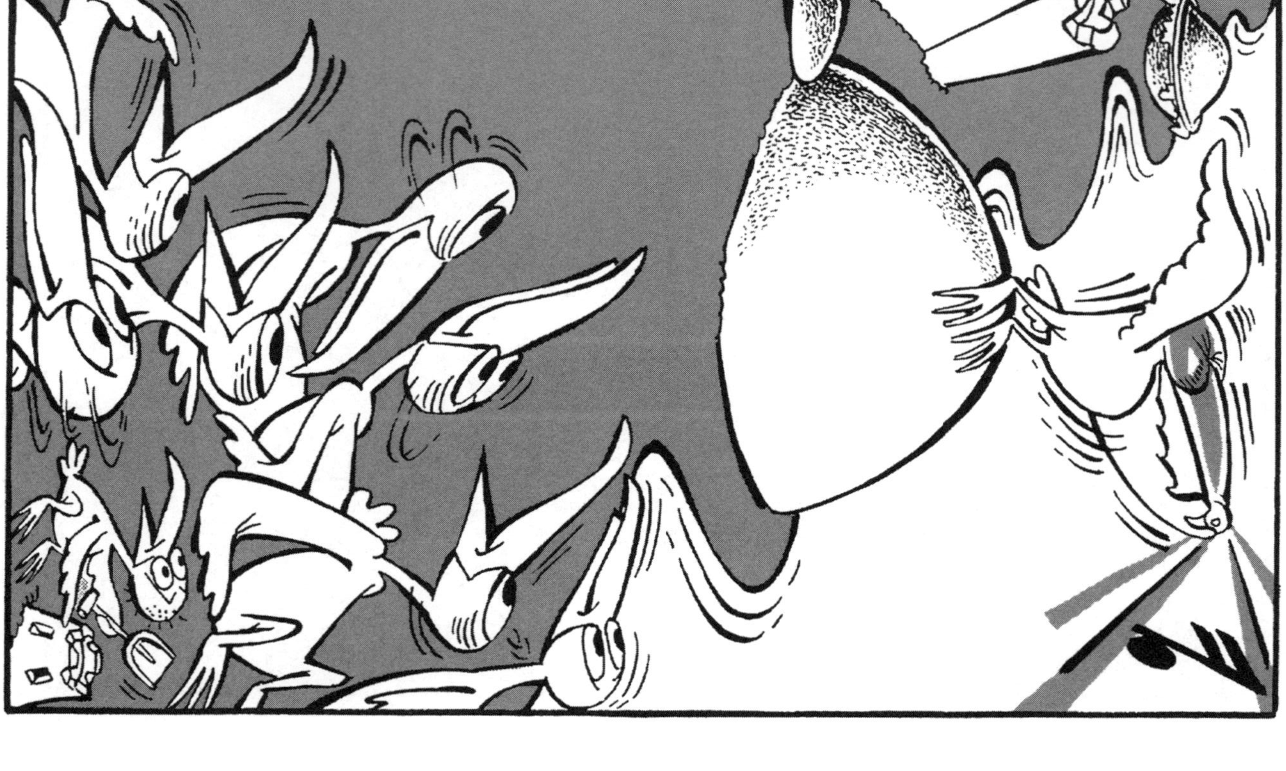

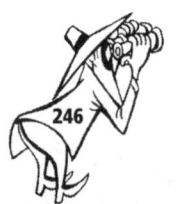

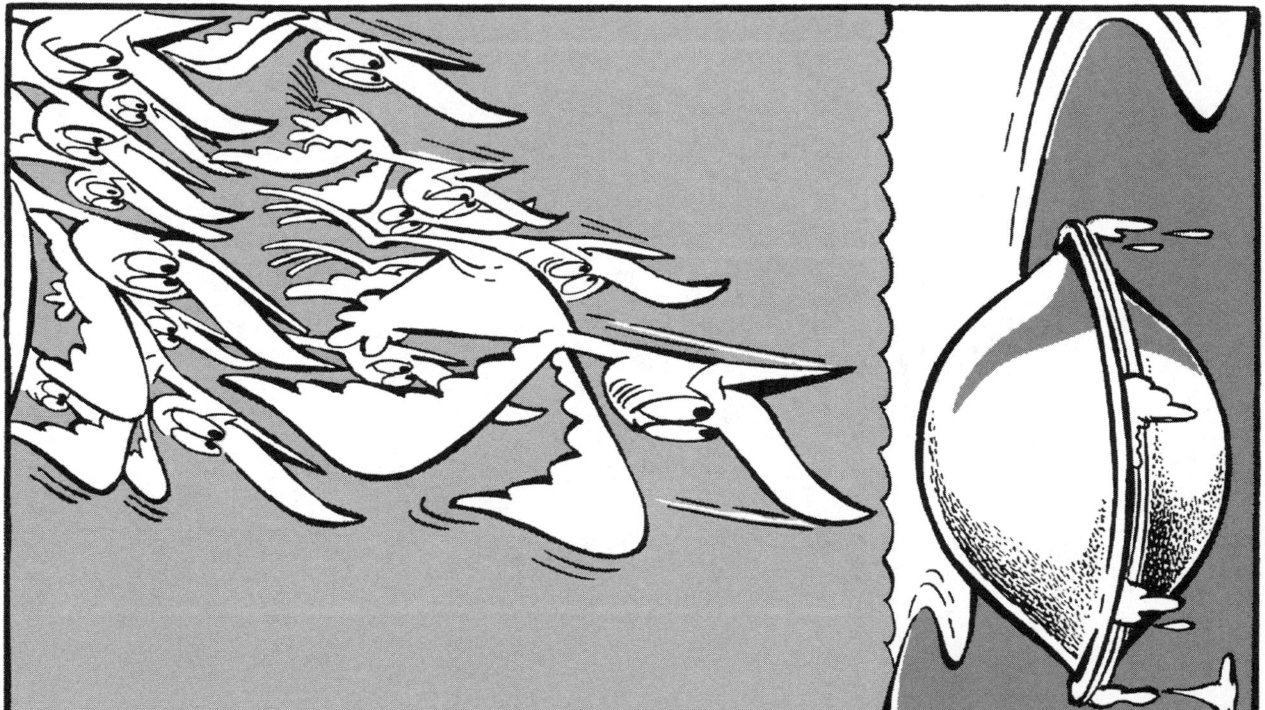

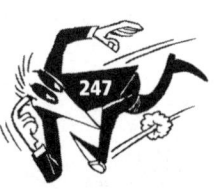

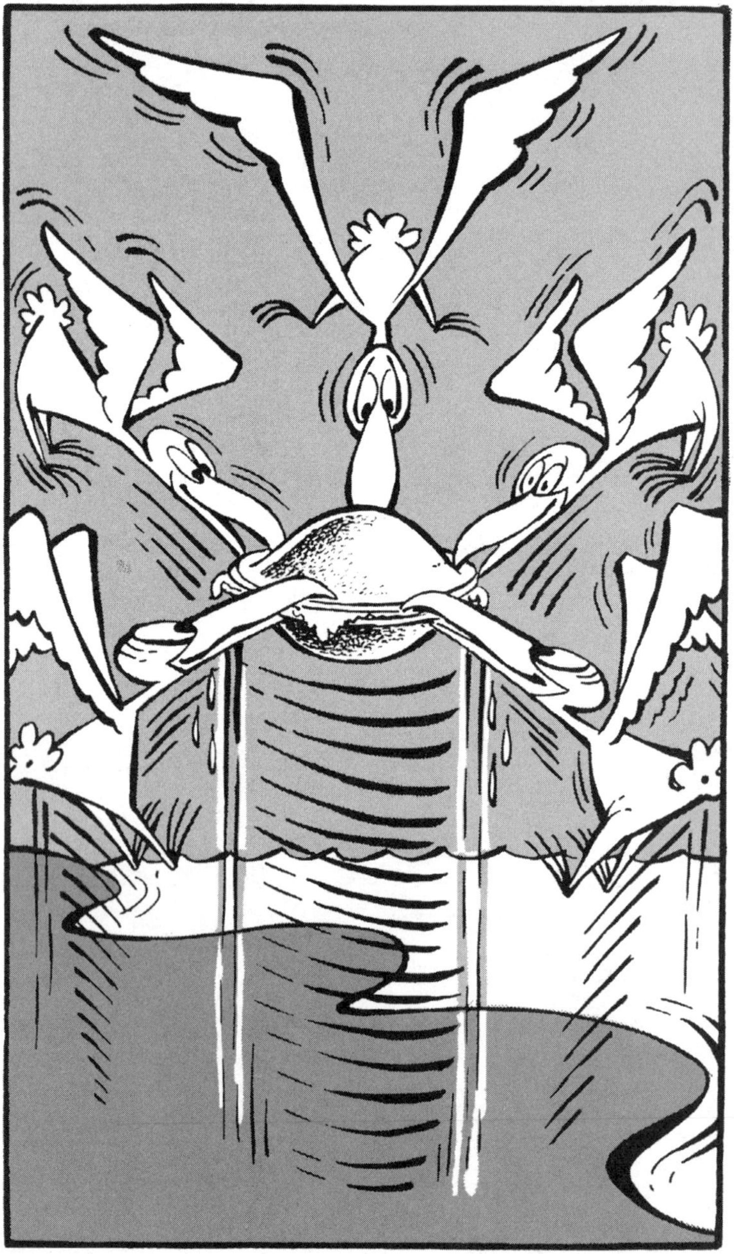

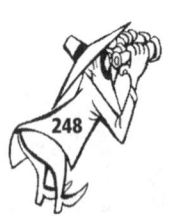

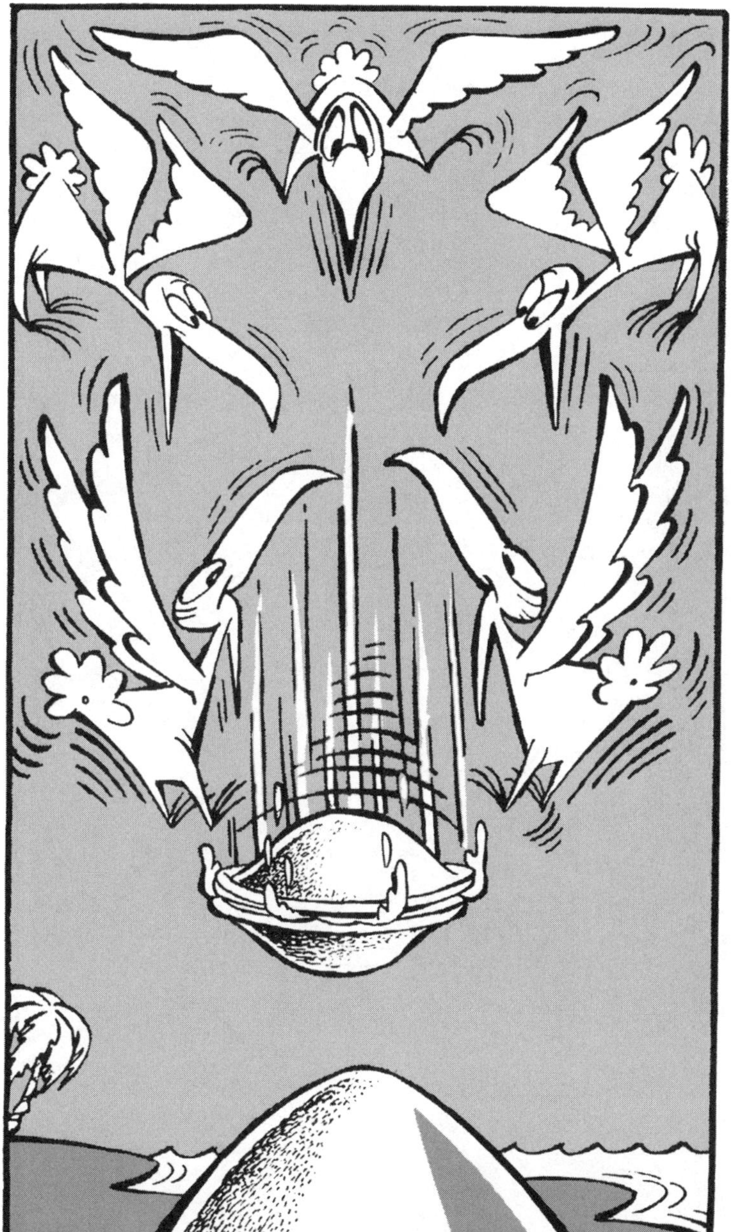

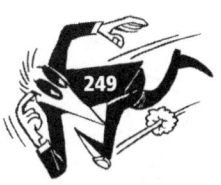

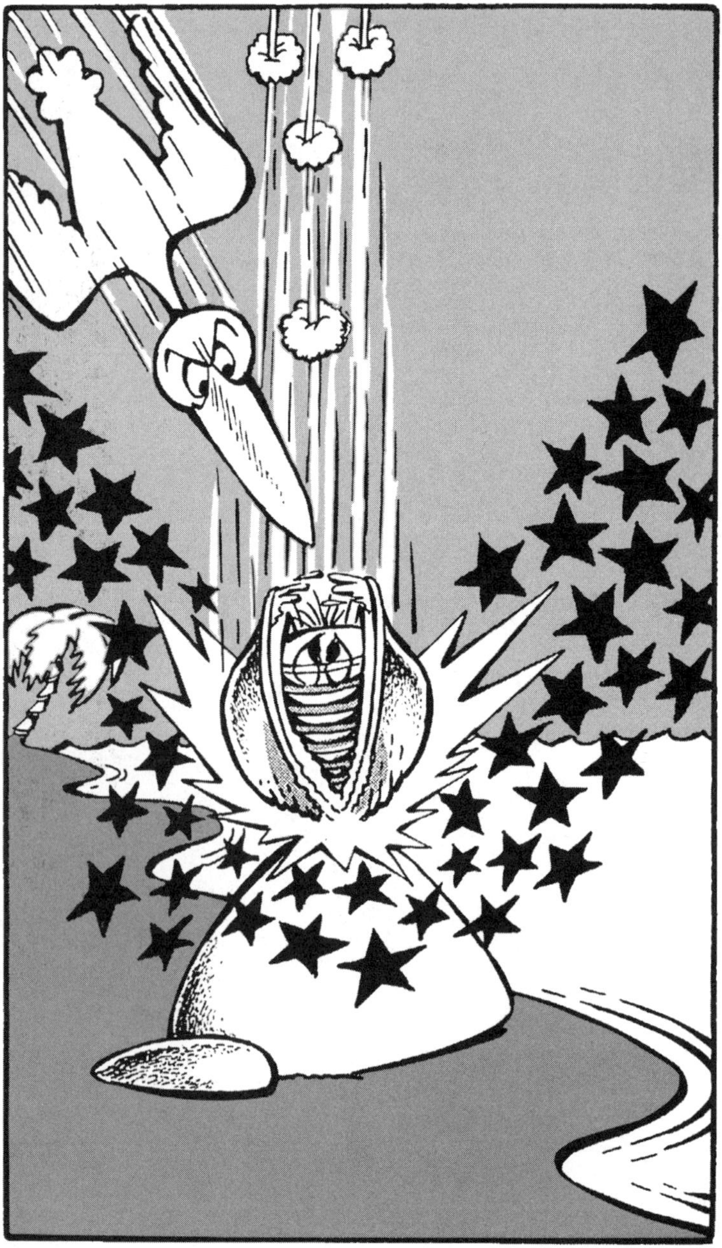

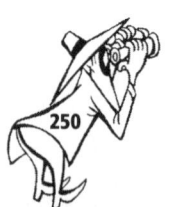

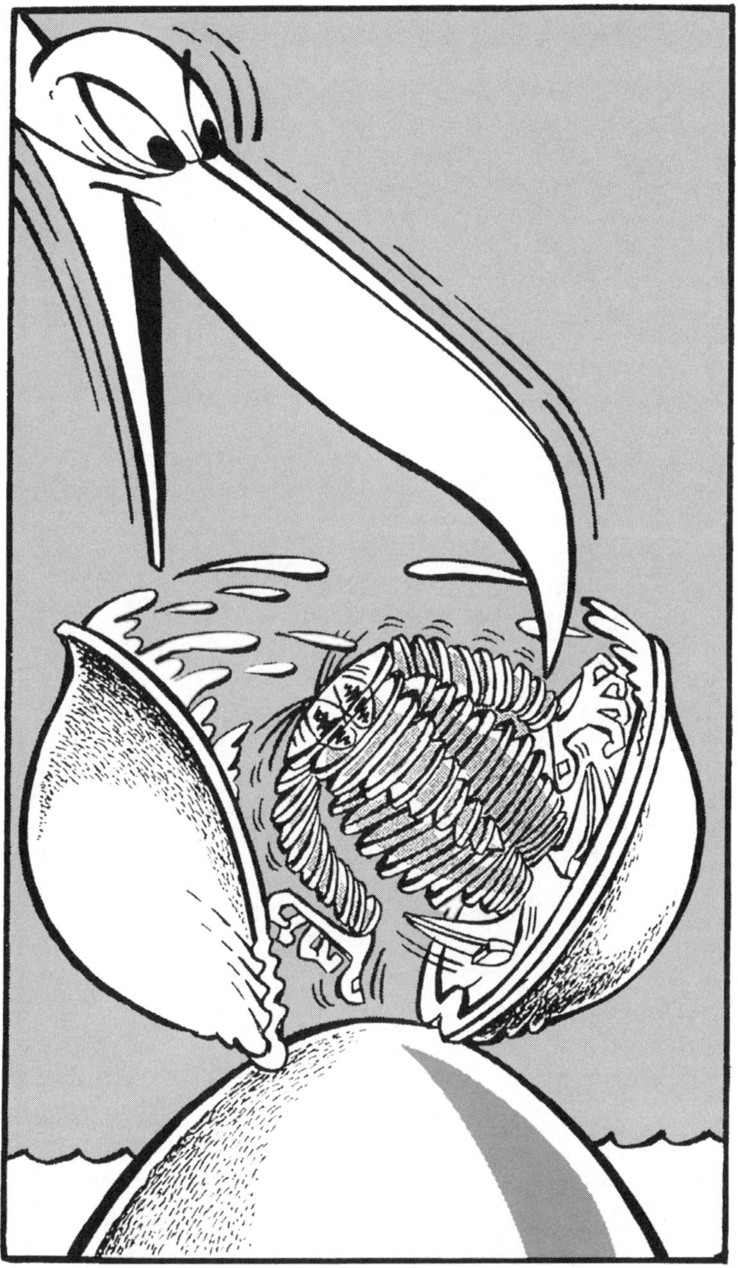

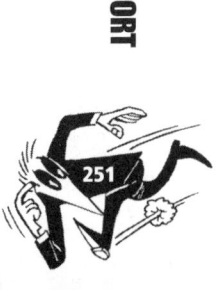

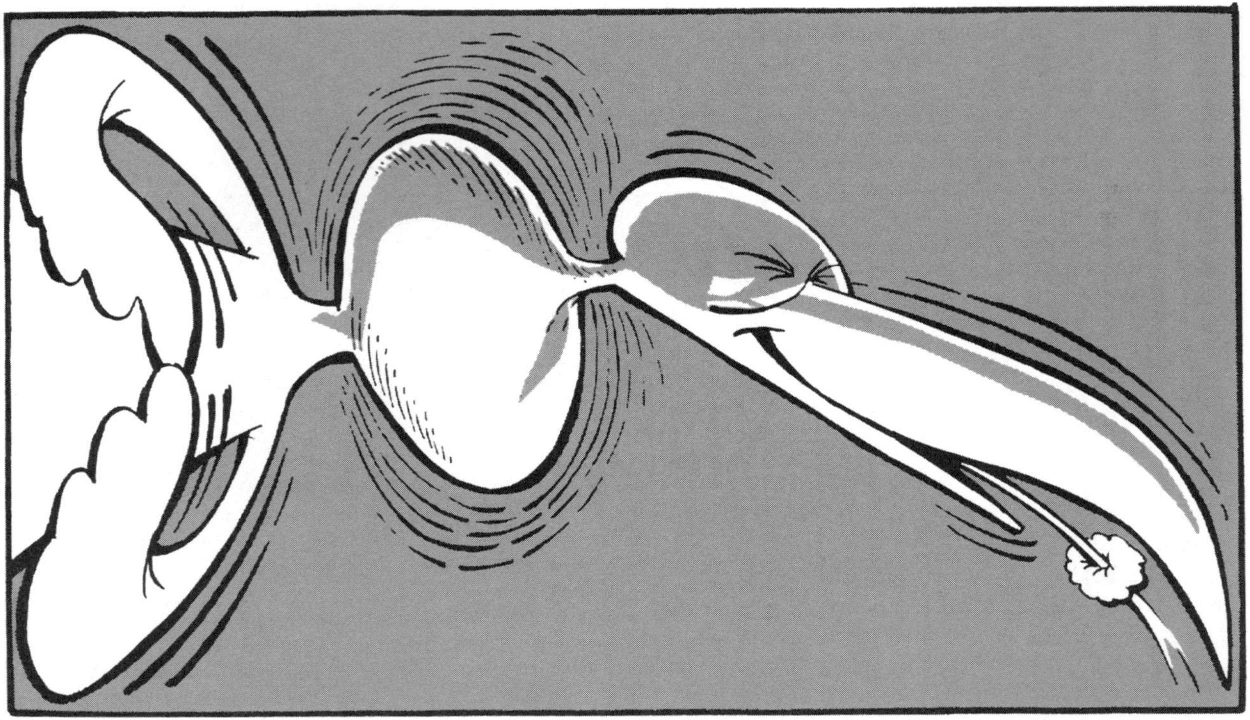

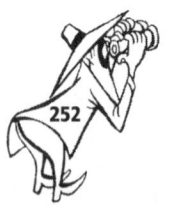

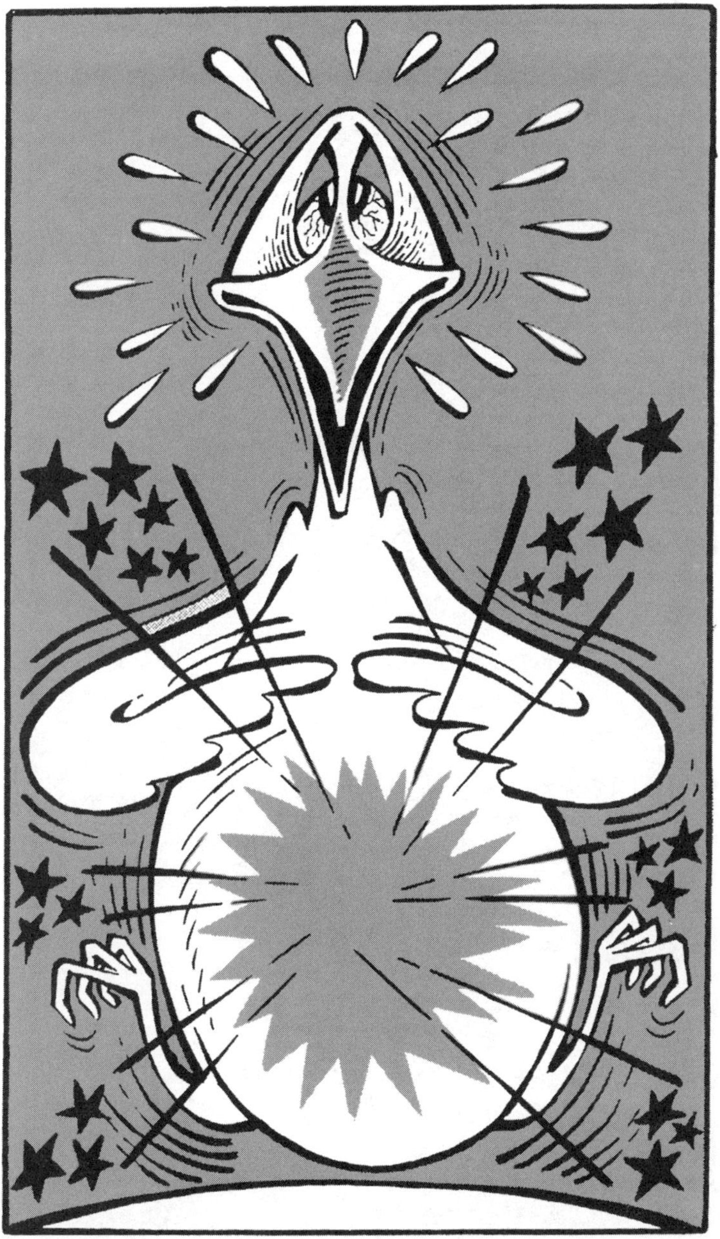

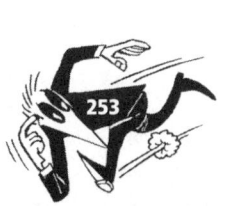

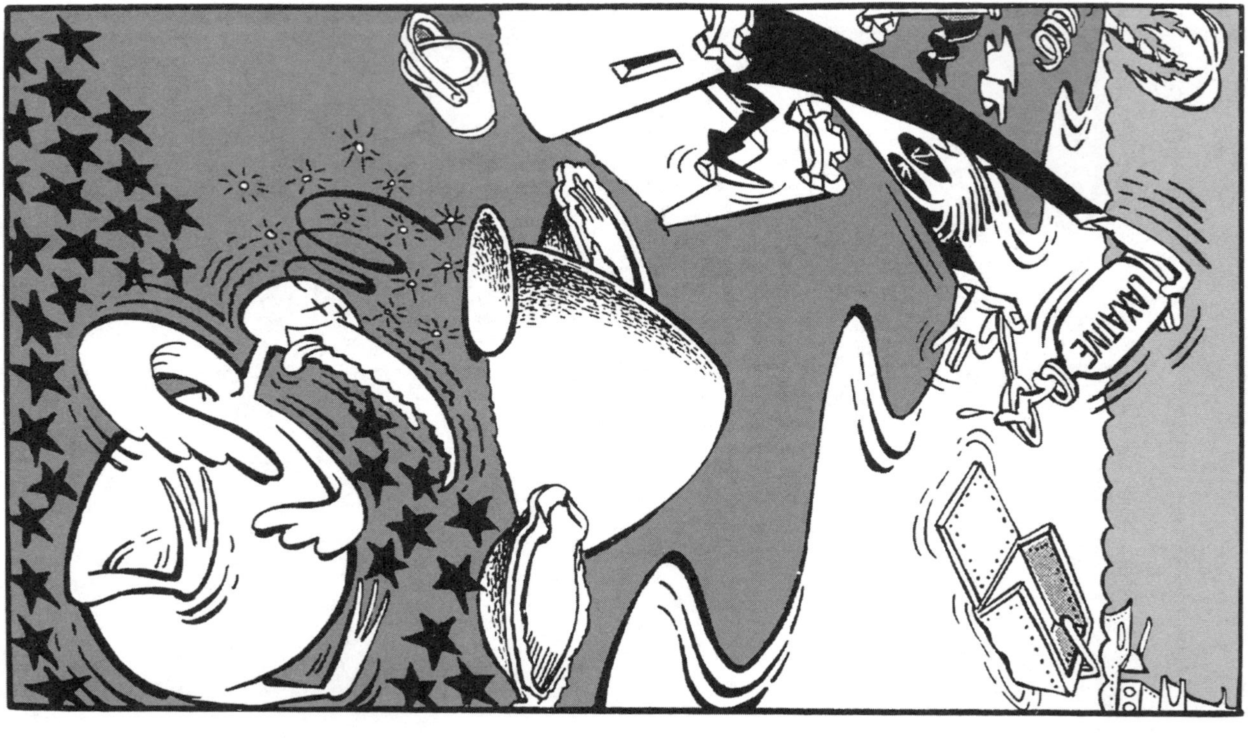
LAXATIVE

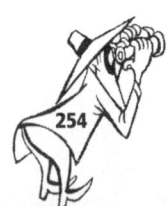

SPY vs SPY

THE ONE THAT GOT AWAY AFFAIR

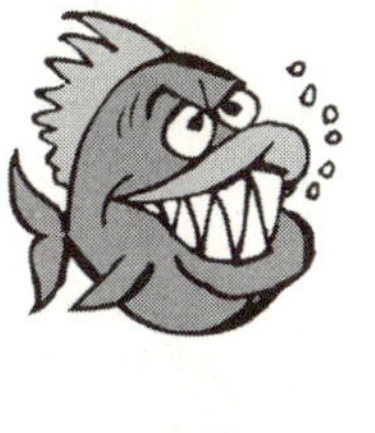

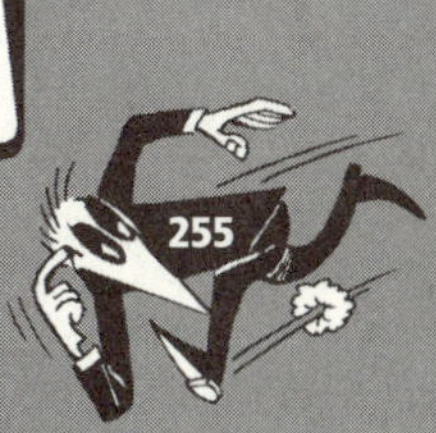

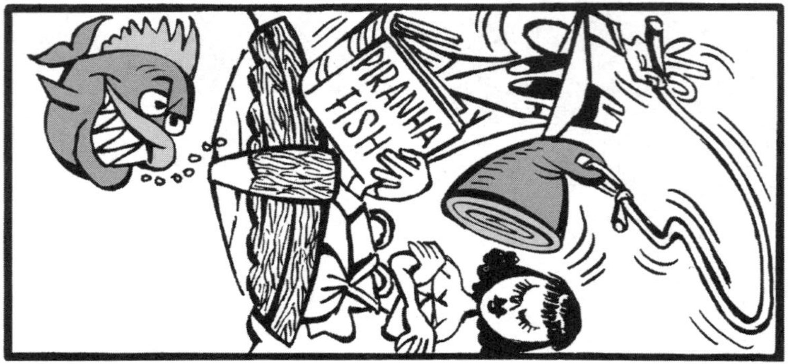
PIRANHA FISH

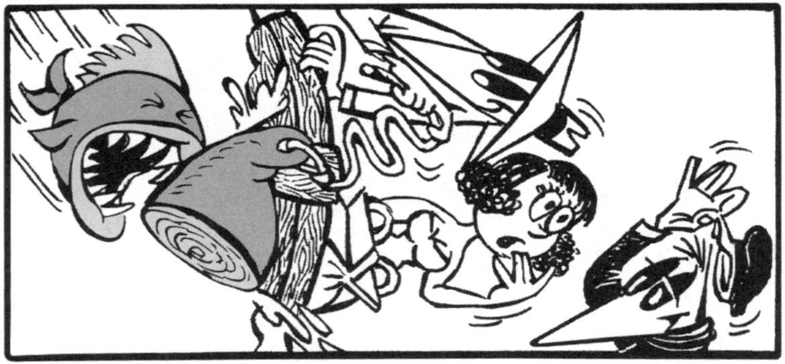

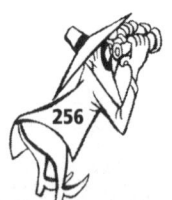

THE ONE THAT GOT AWAY AFFAIR

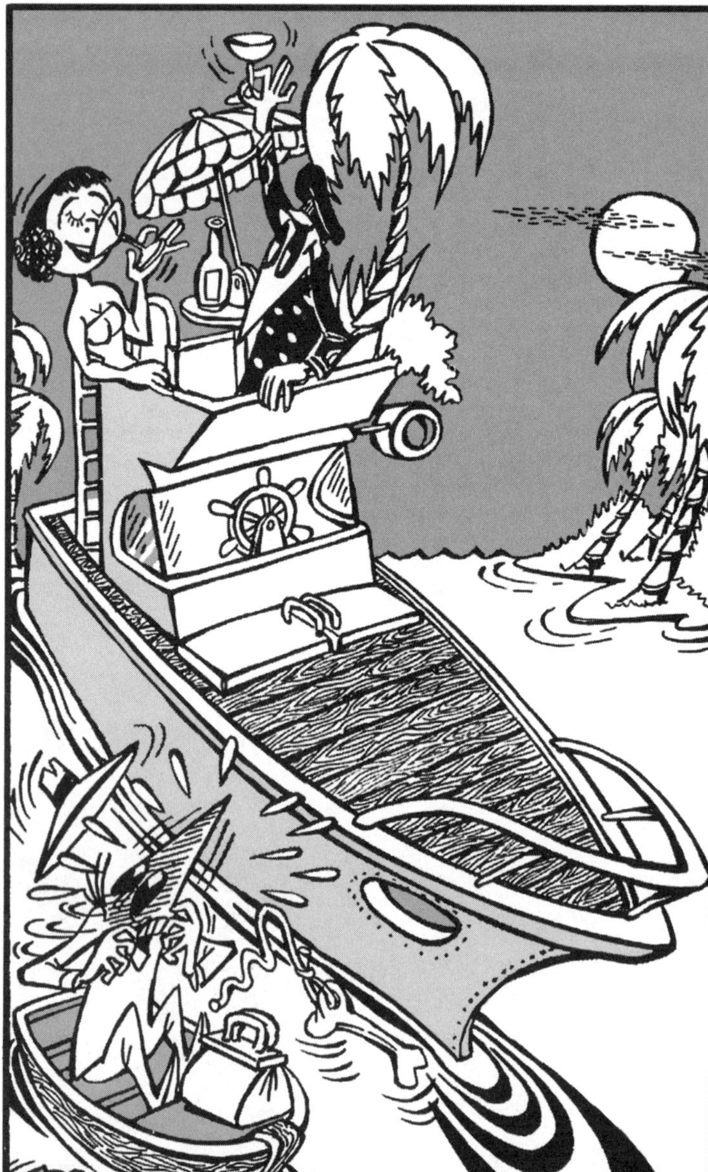

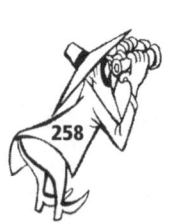

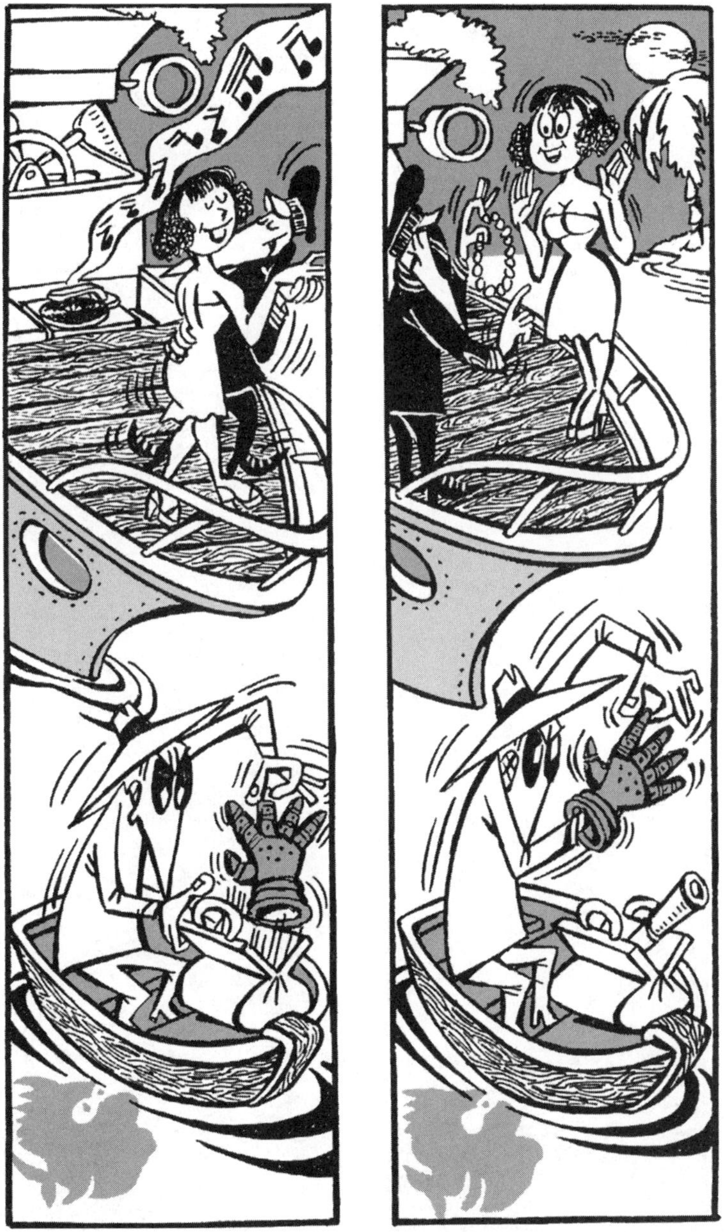

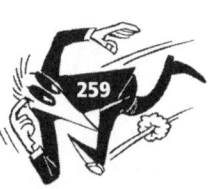

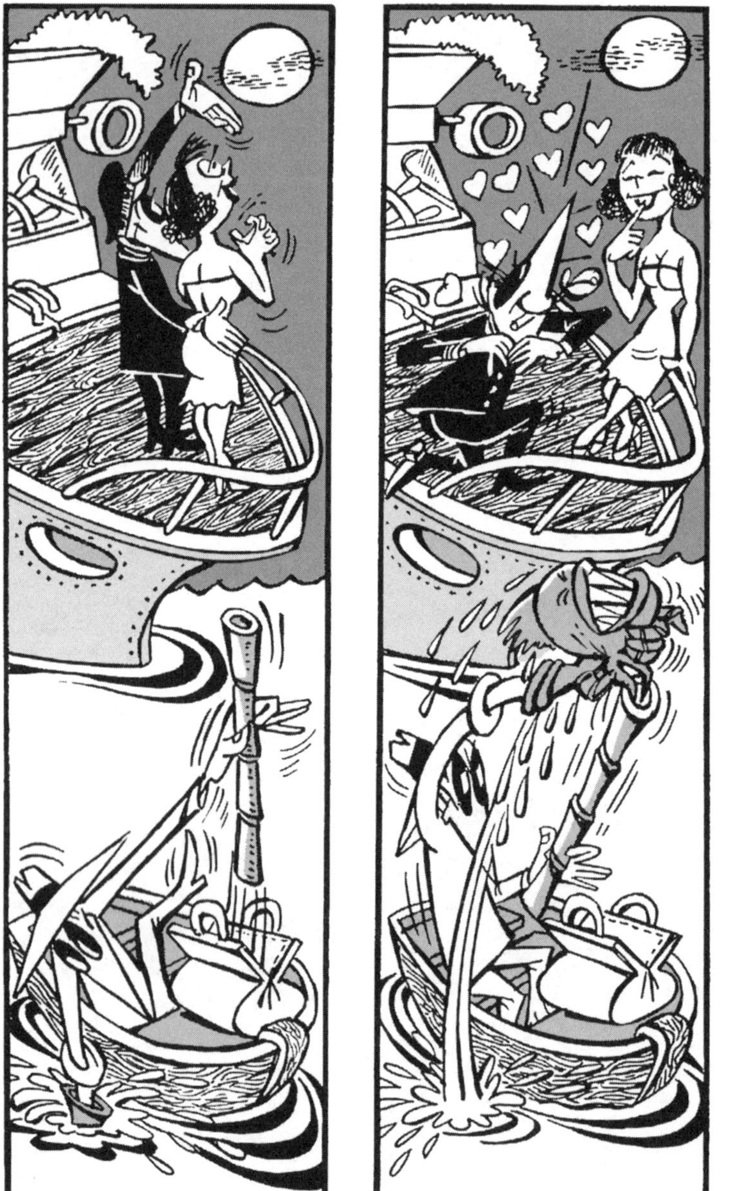

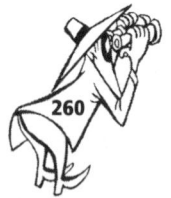

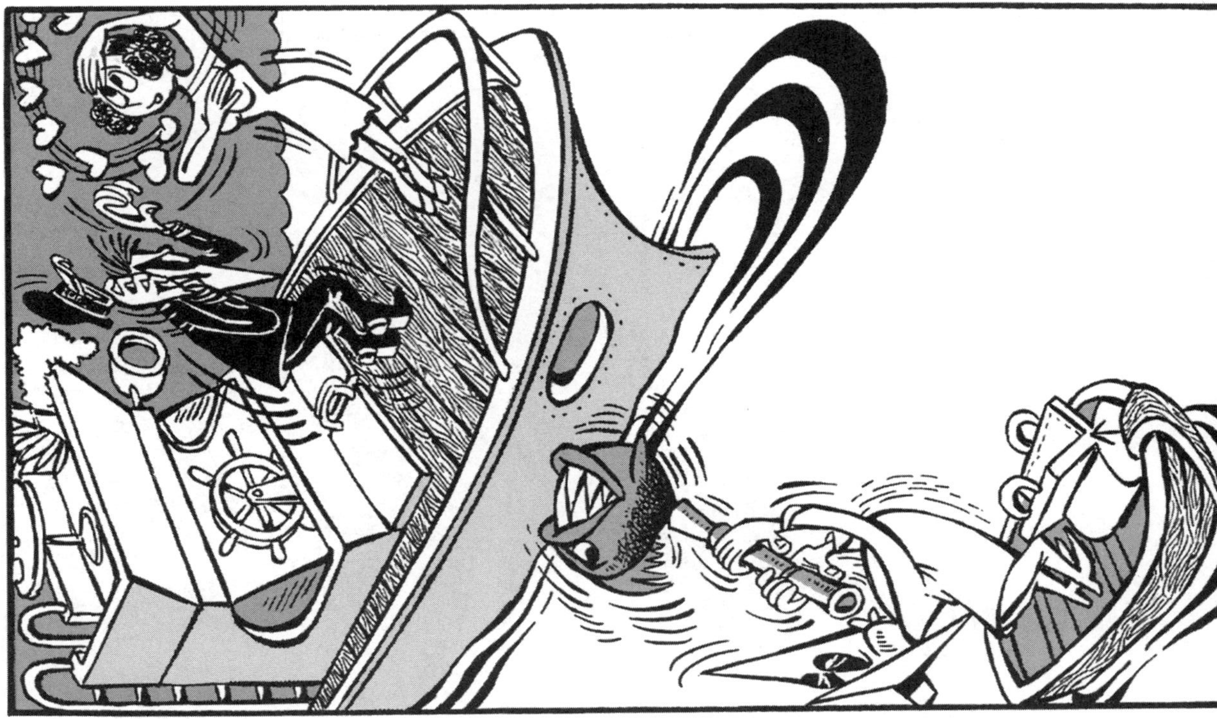

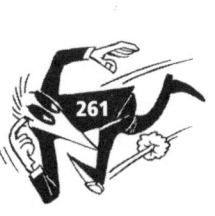

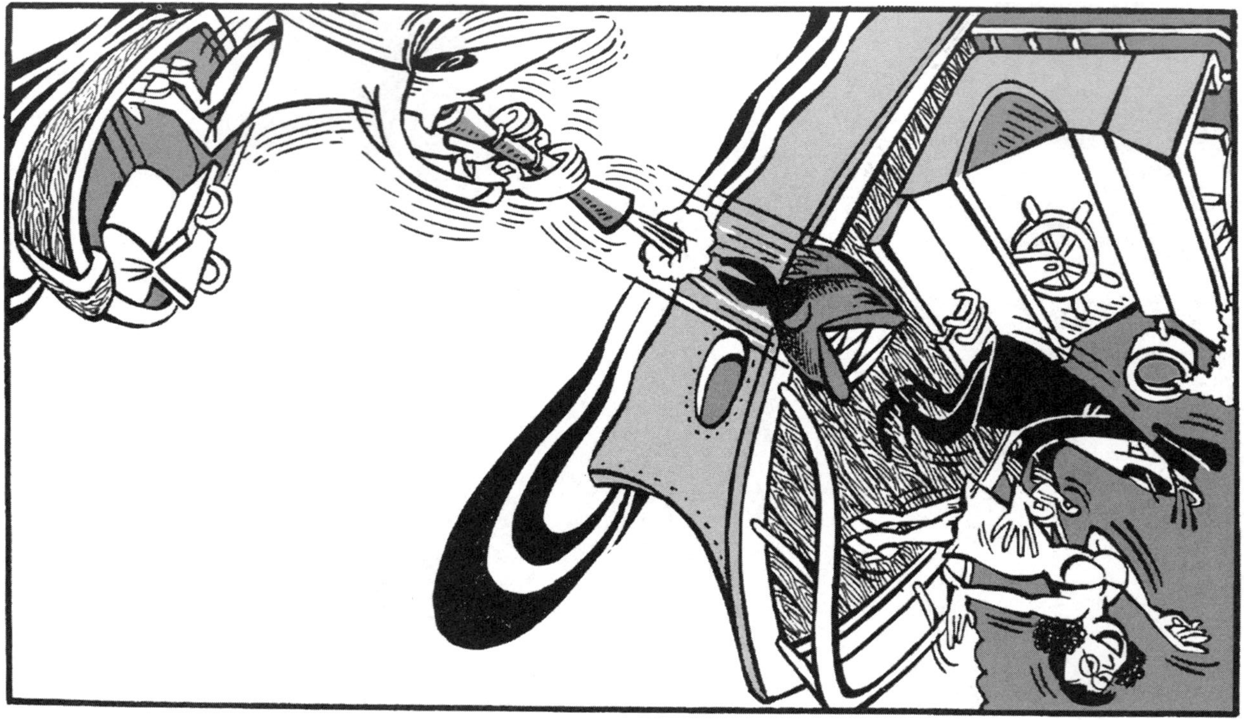

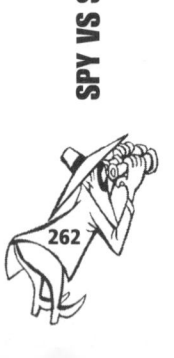

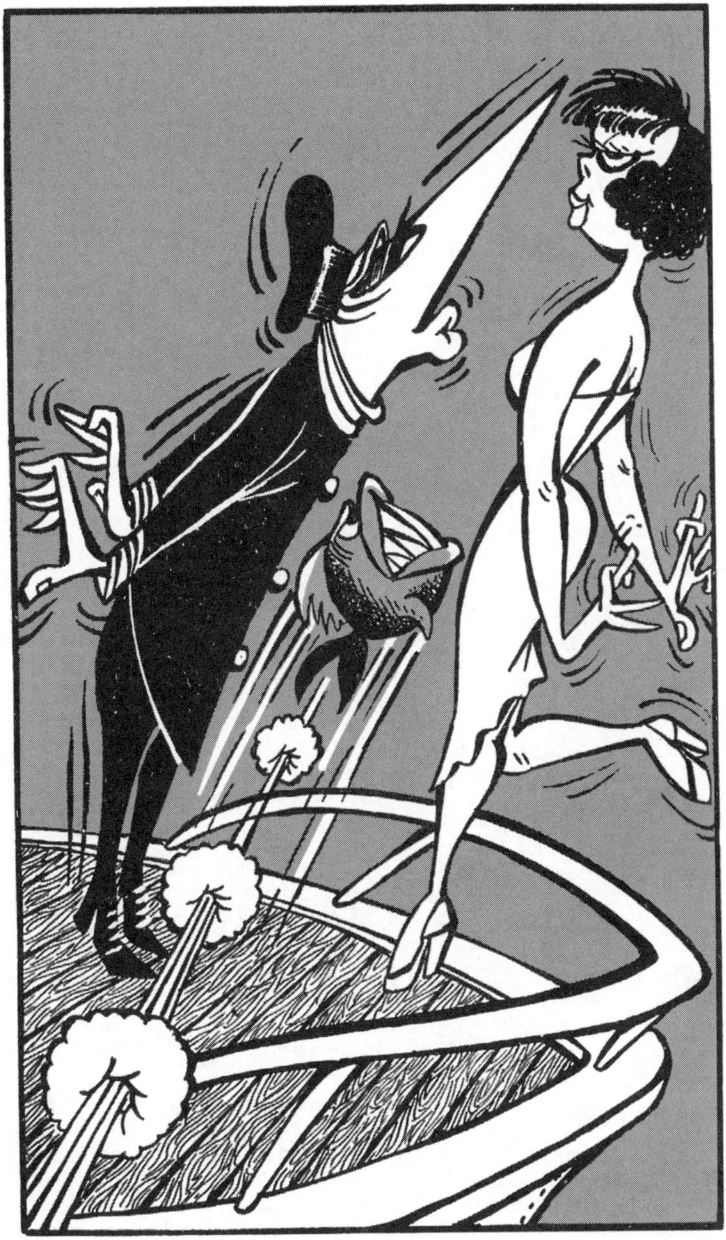

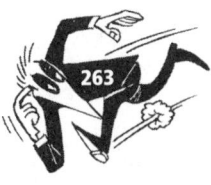

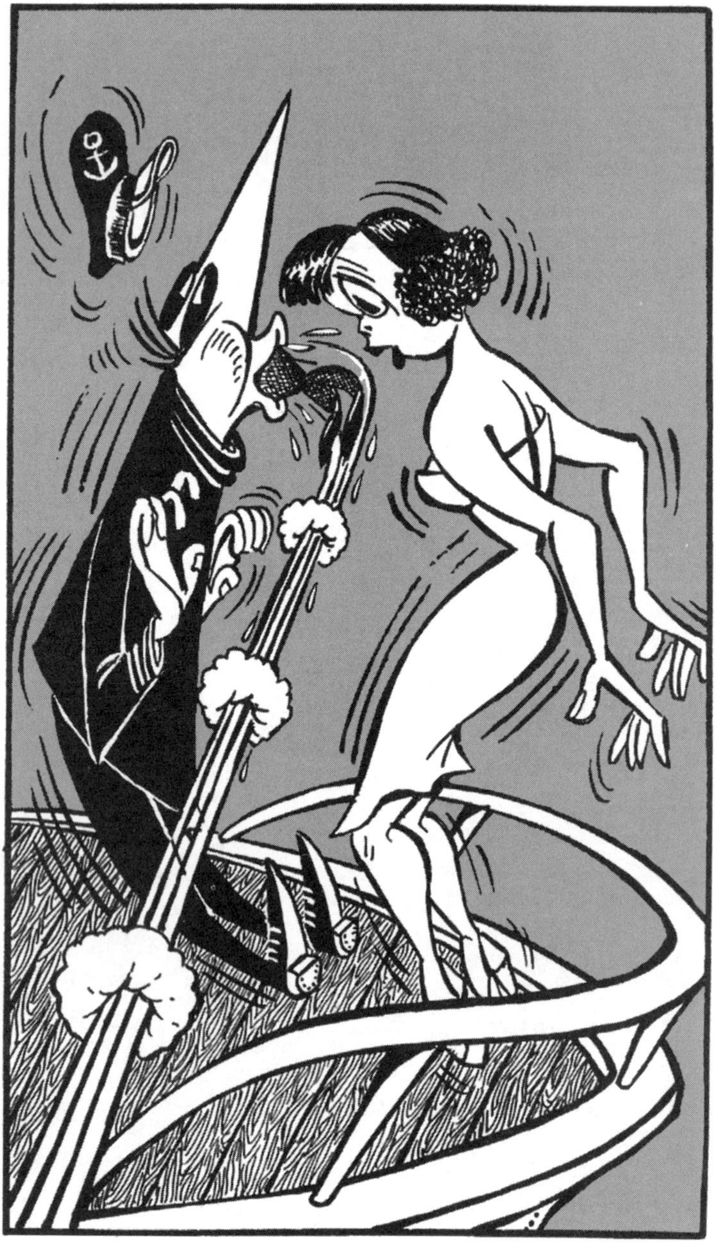

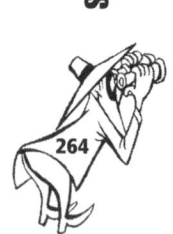

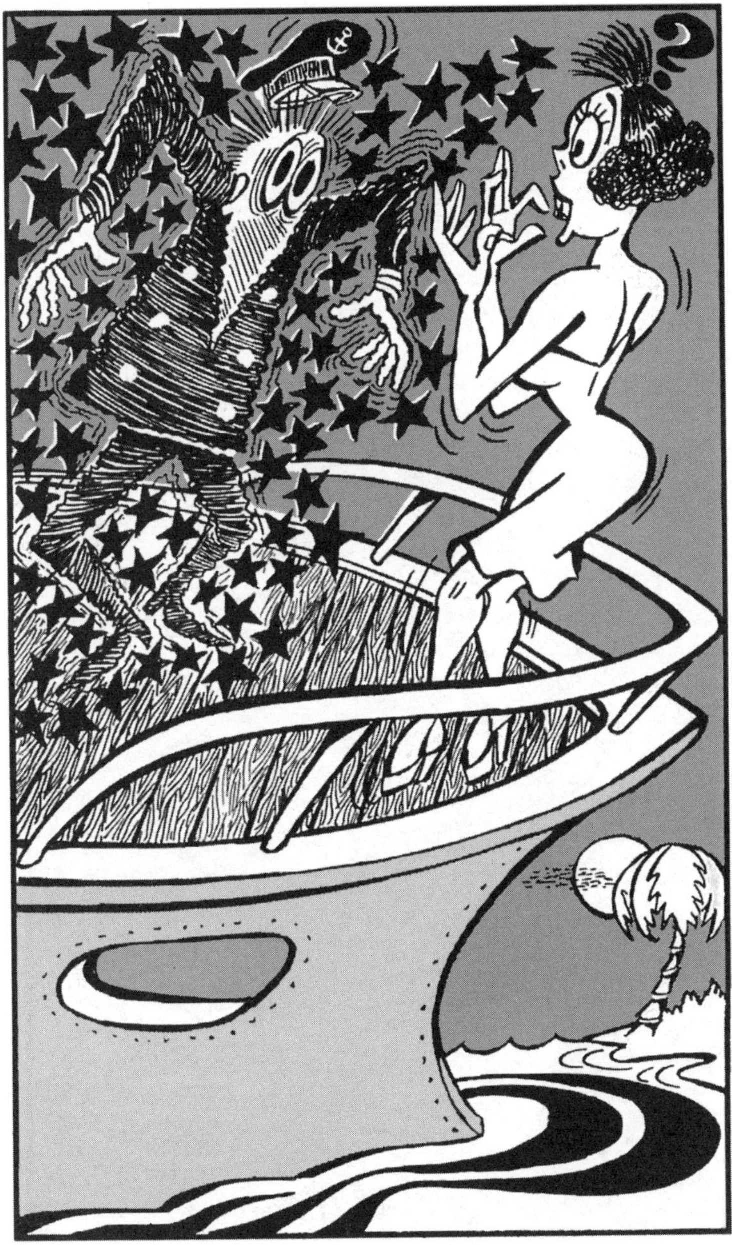

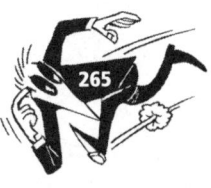

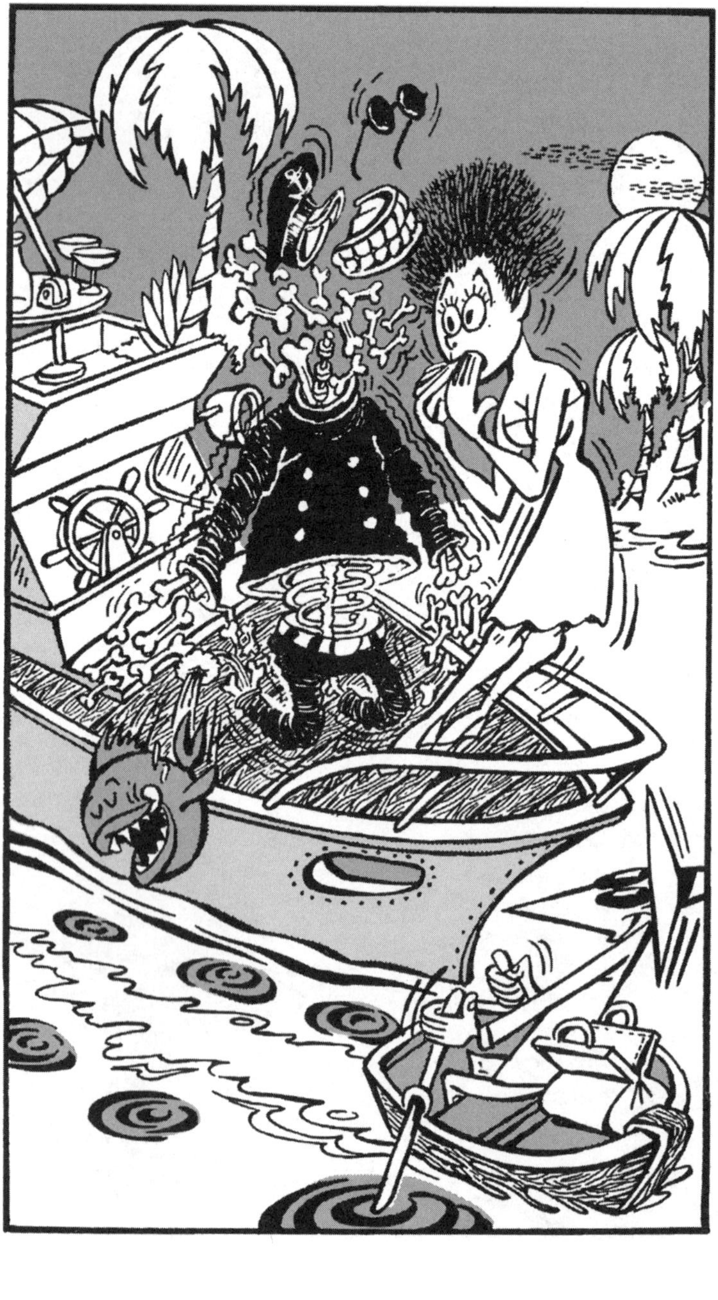

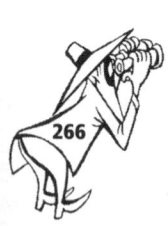

SPY JR. VS SPY JR.

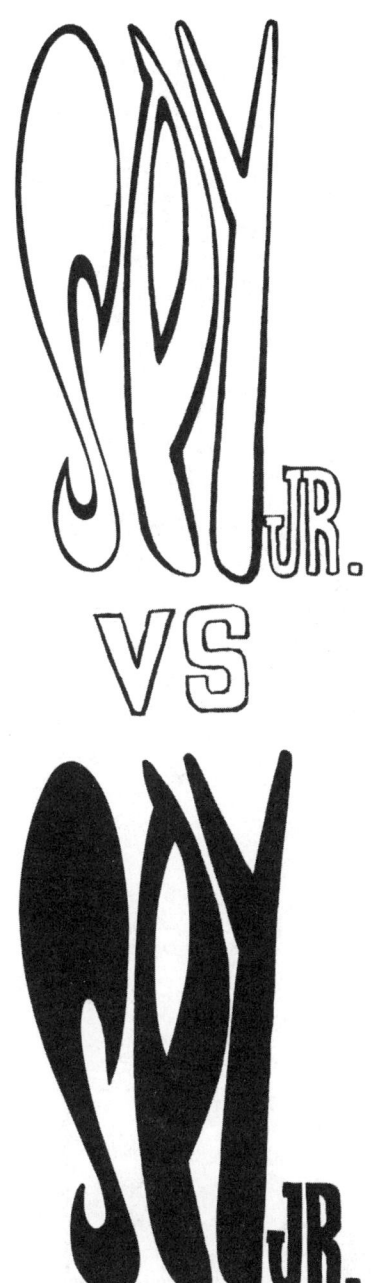

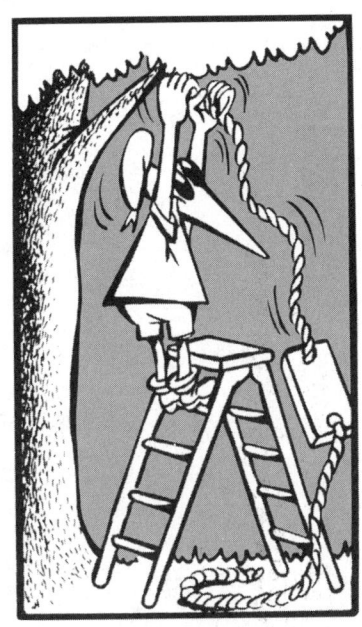

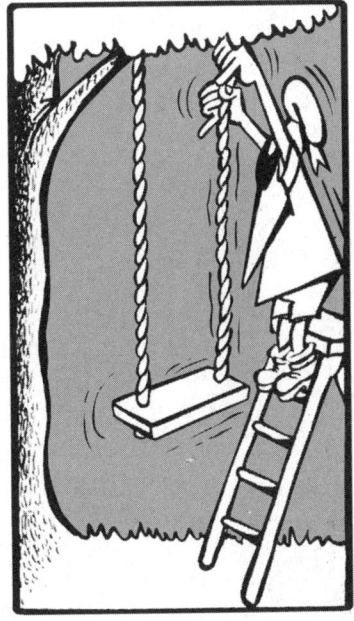

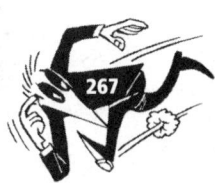

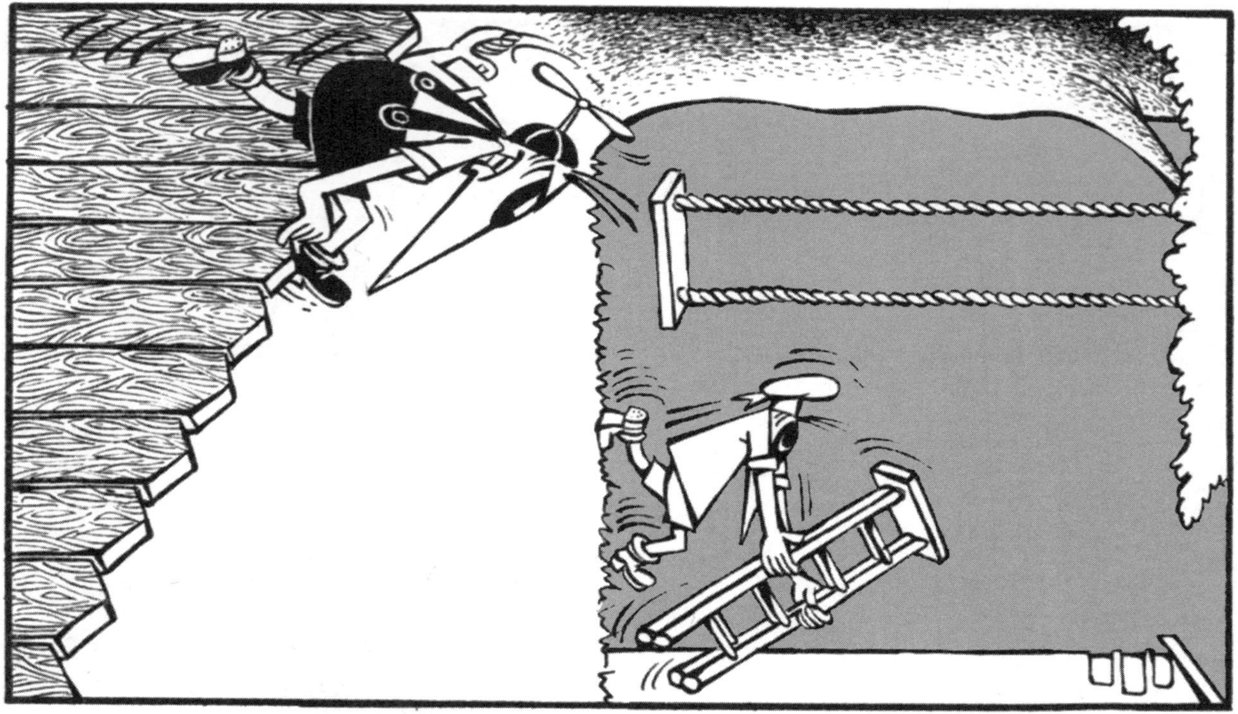

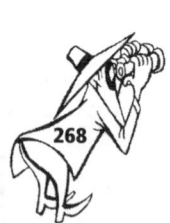

SPY JR. VS SPY JR.

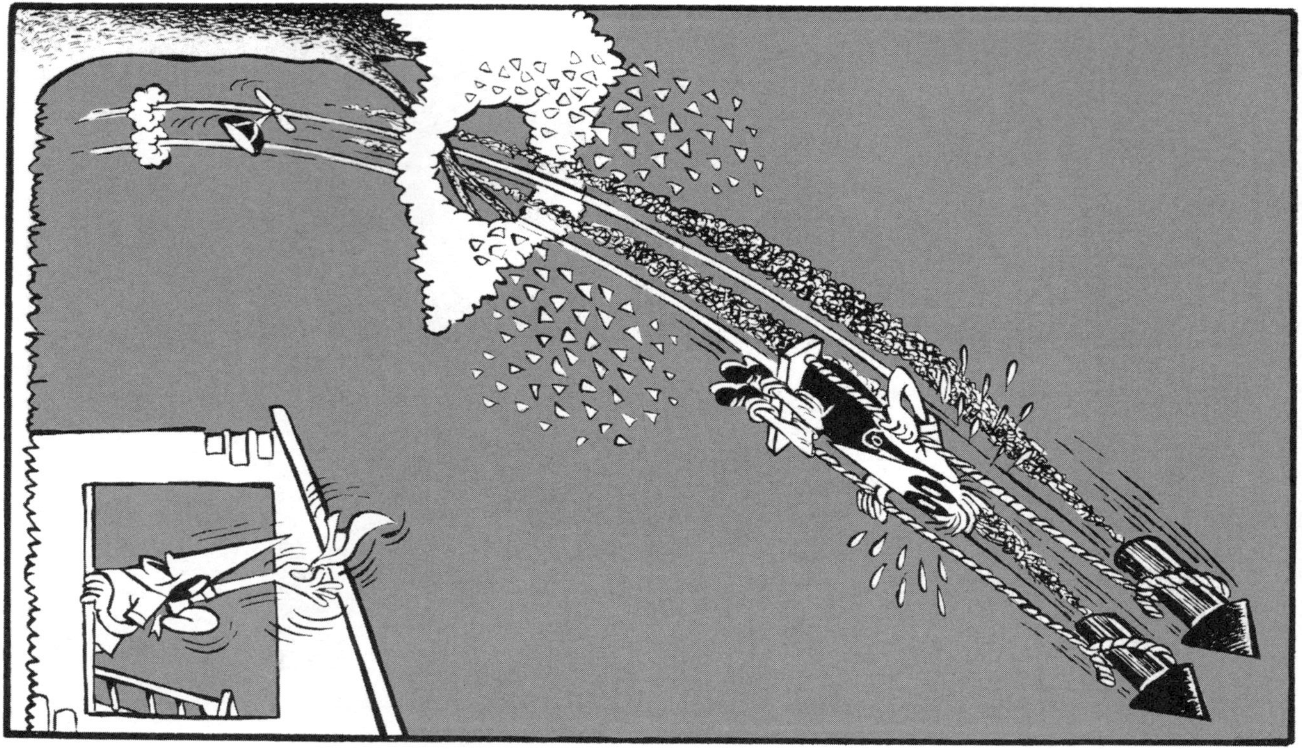

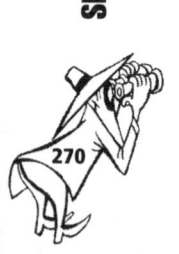

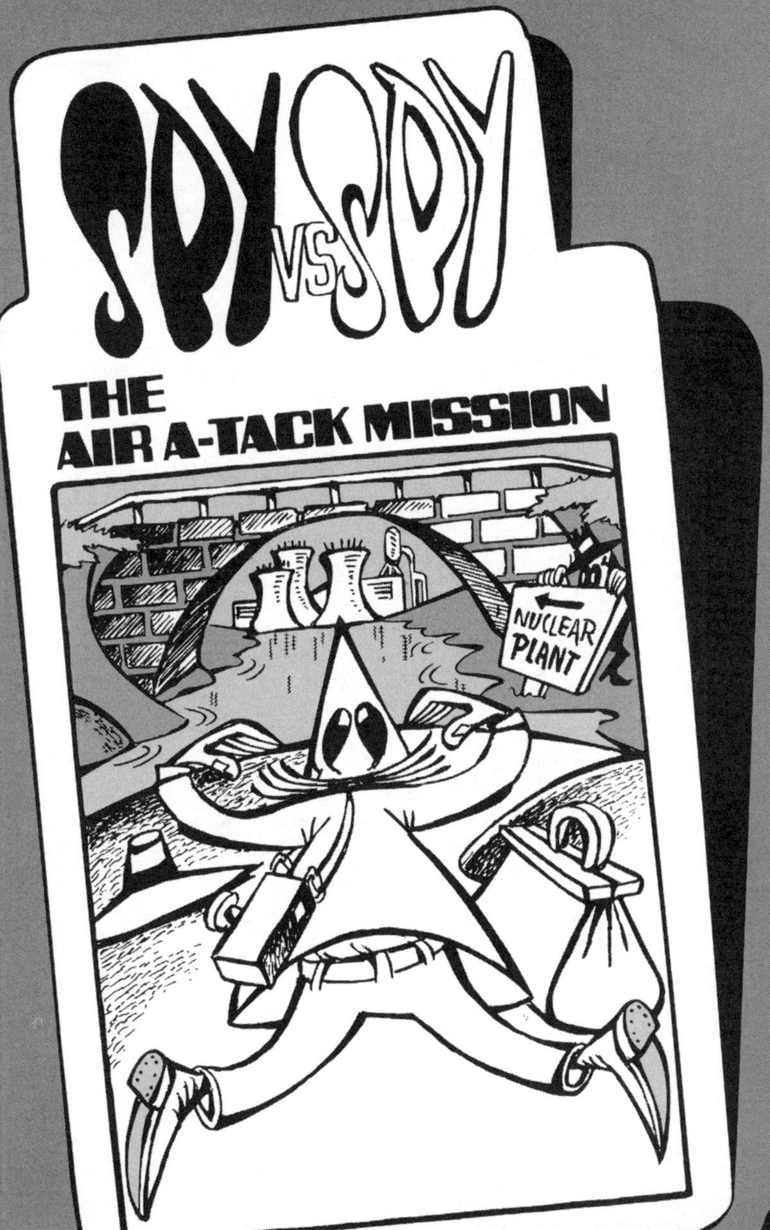
SPY vs SPY
THE AIR A-TACK MISSION
NUCLEAR PLANT

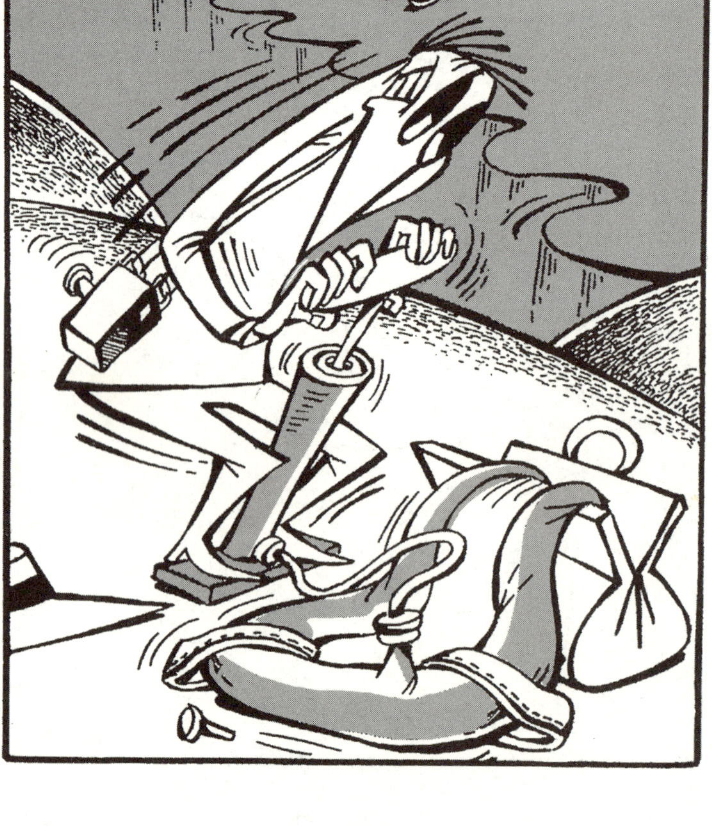

NUCLEAR
PLANT

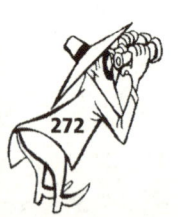

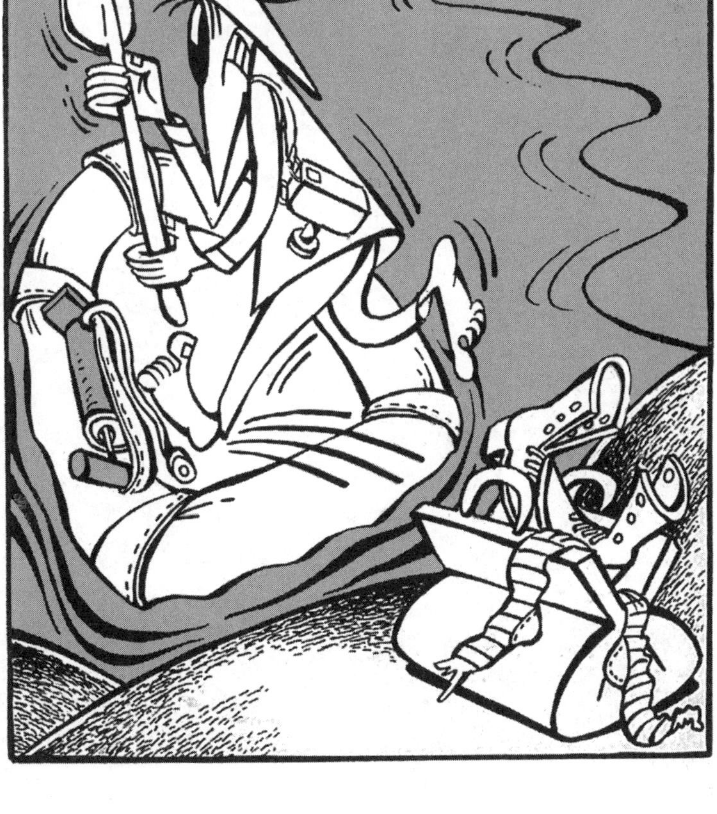

THE AIR A-TACK MISSION

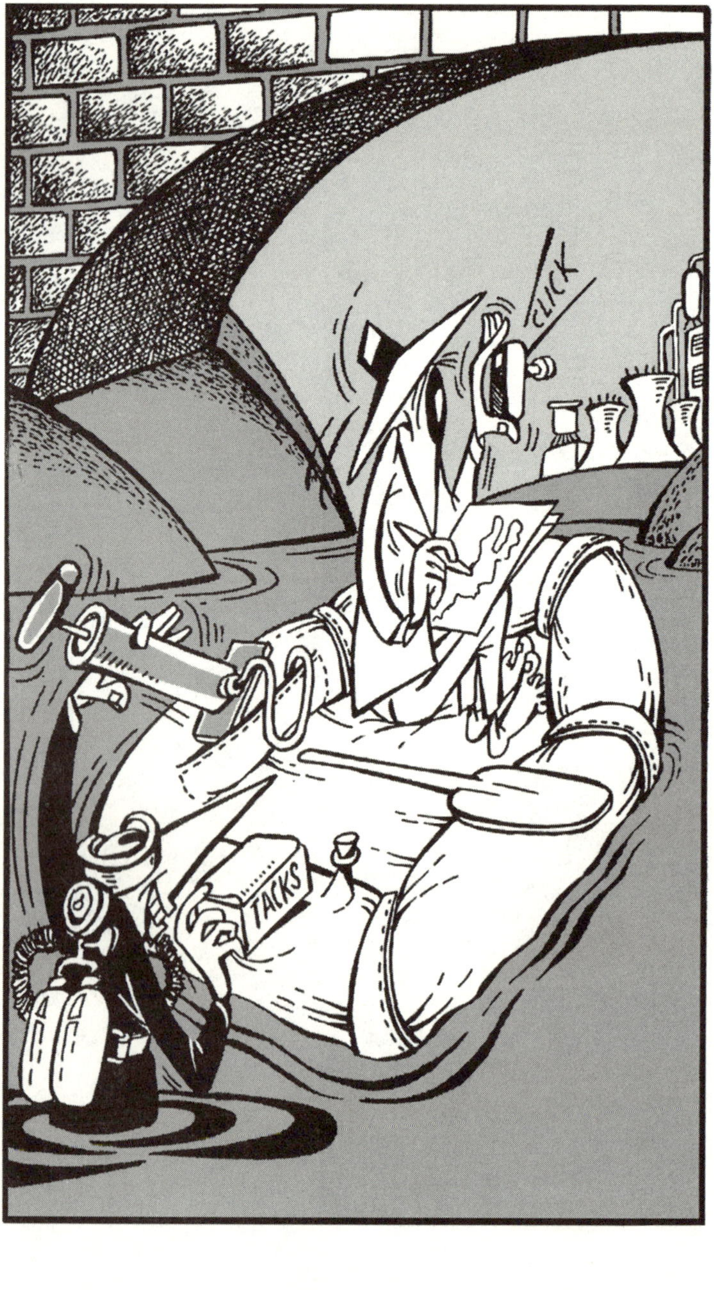
CLICK
TACKS

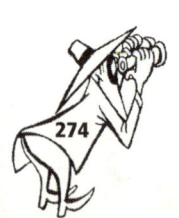

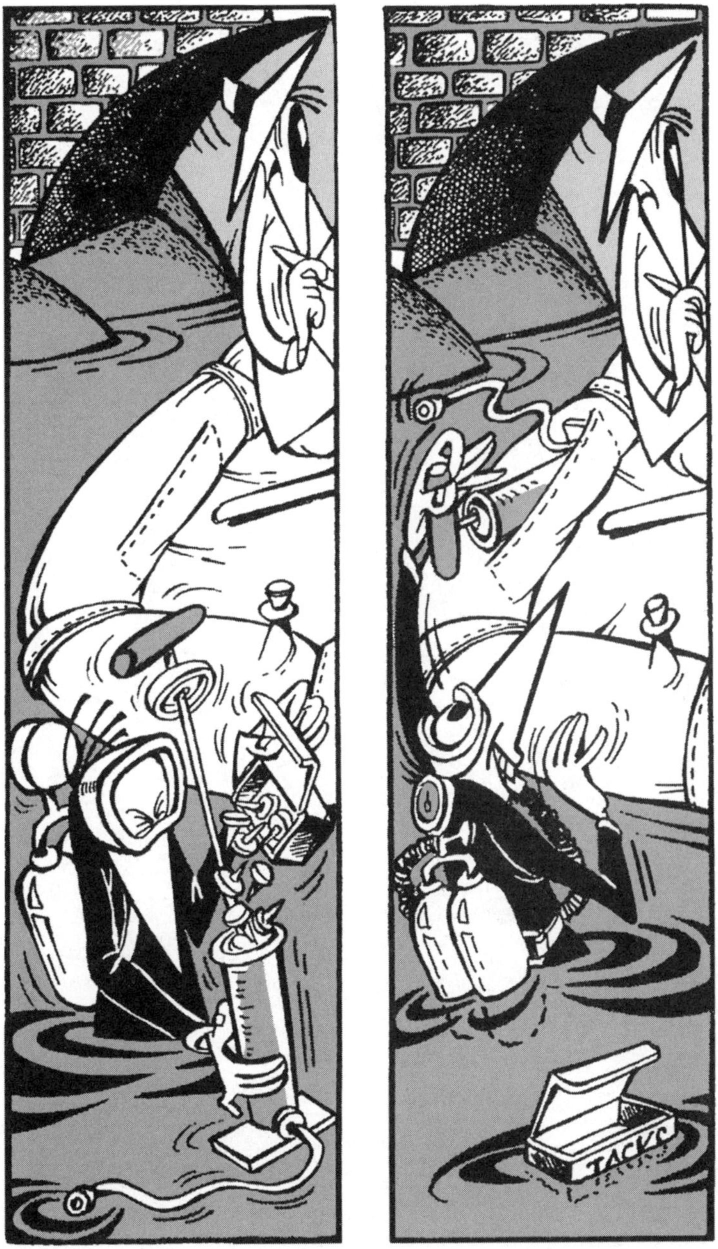
TACKS

THE AIR A-TACK MISSION

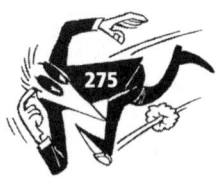

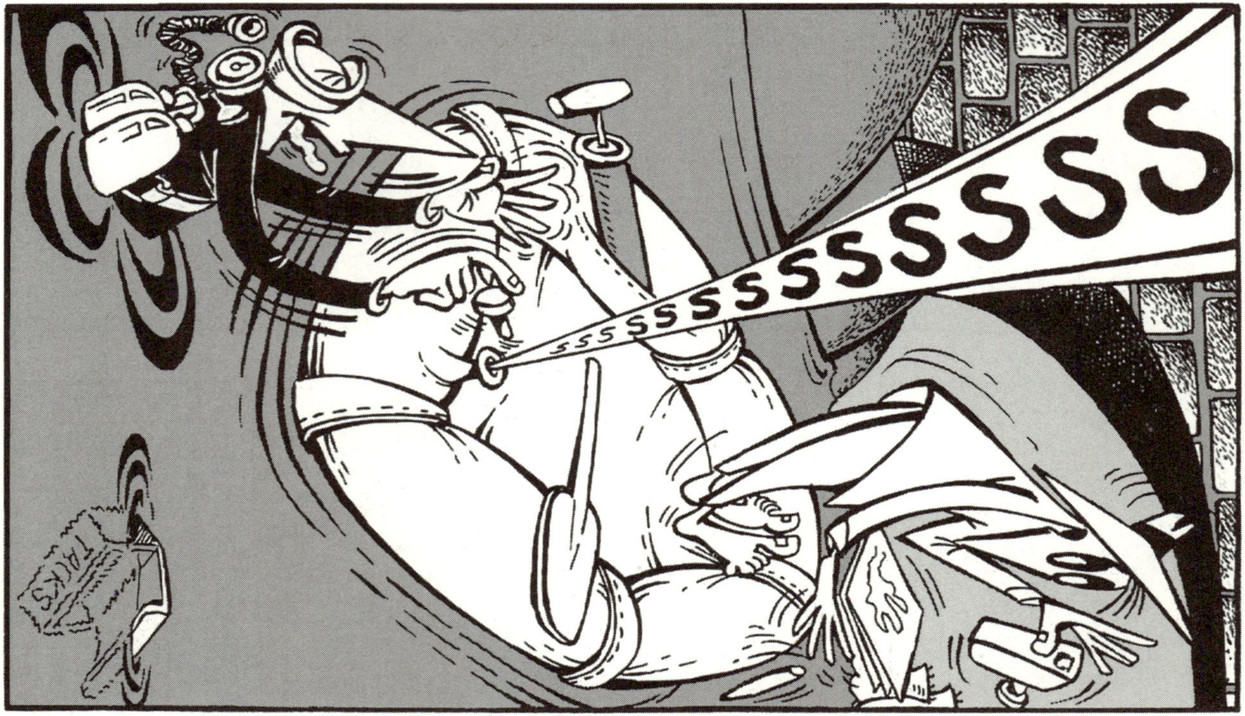
sssSSSSSSSSSS
TACKS

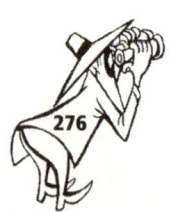

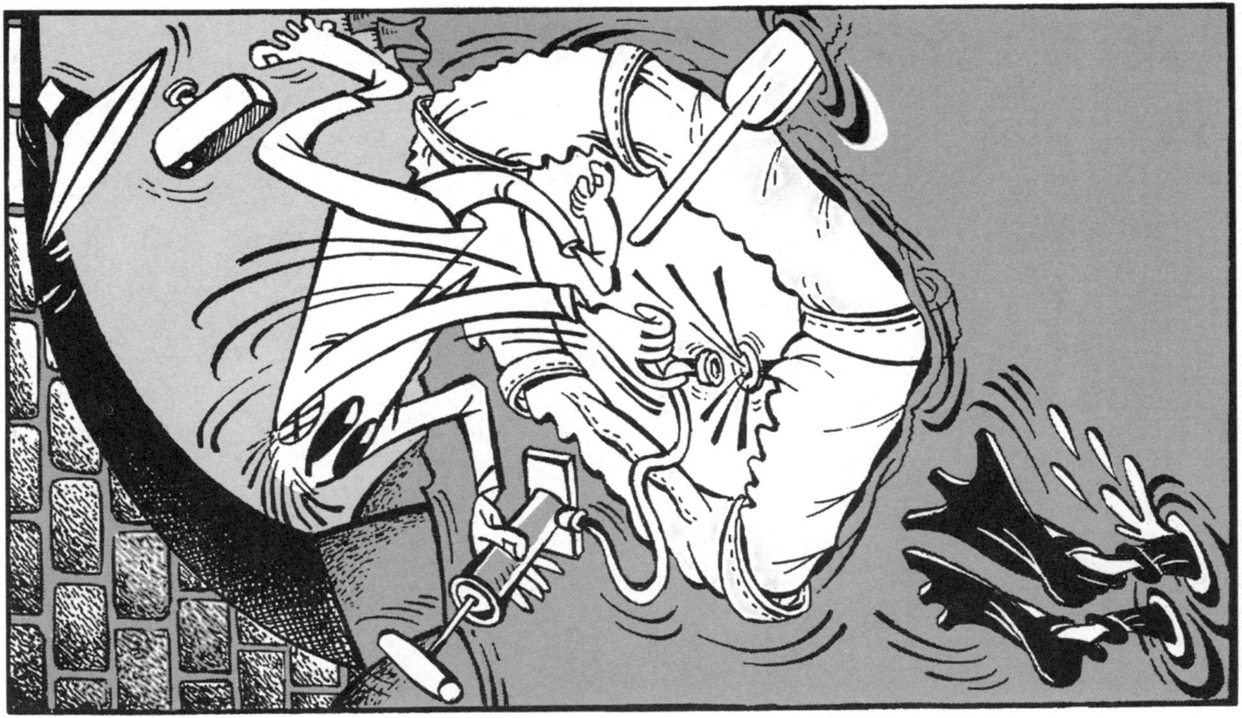

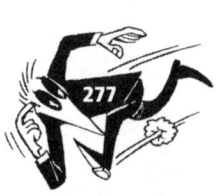

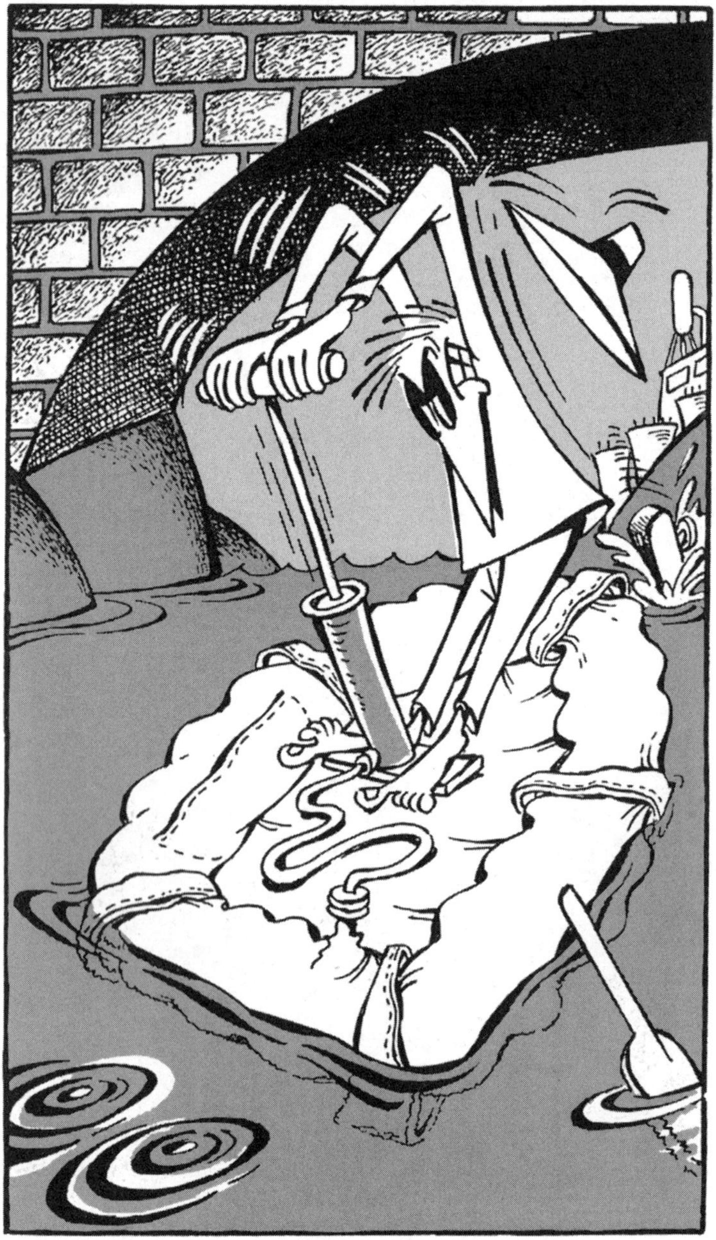

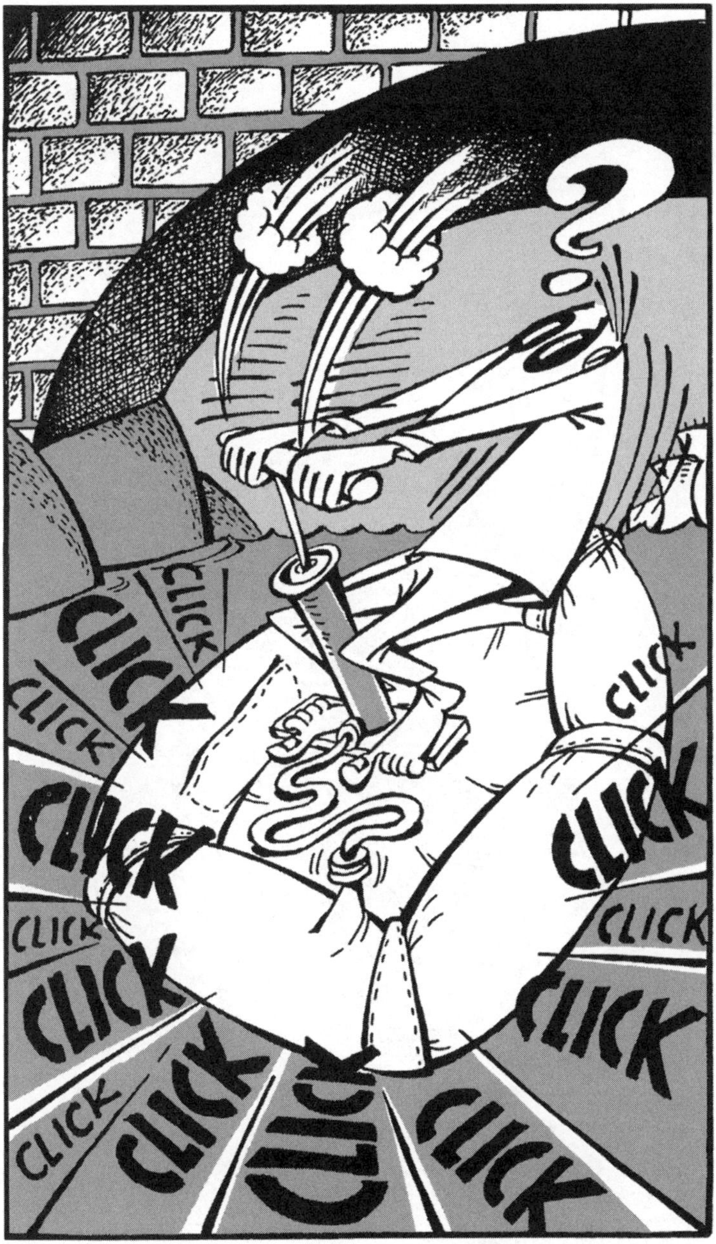
?
CLICK
CLICK
CLICK
CLICK
CLICK
CLICK
CLICK
CLICK
CLICK
CLICK
CLICK
CLICK
CLICK
CLICK

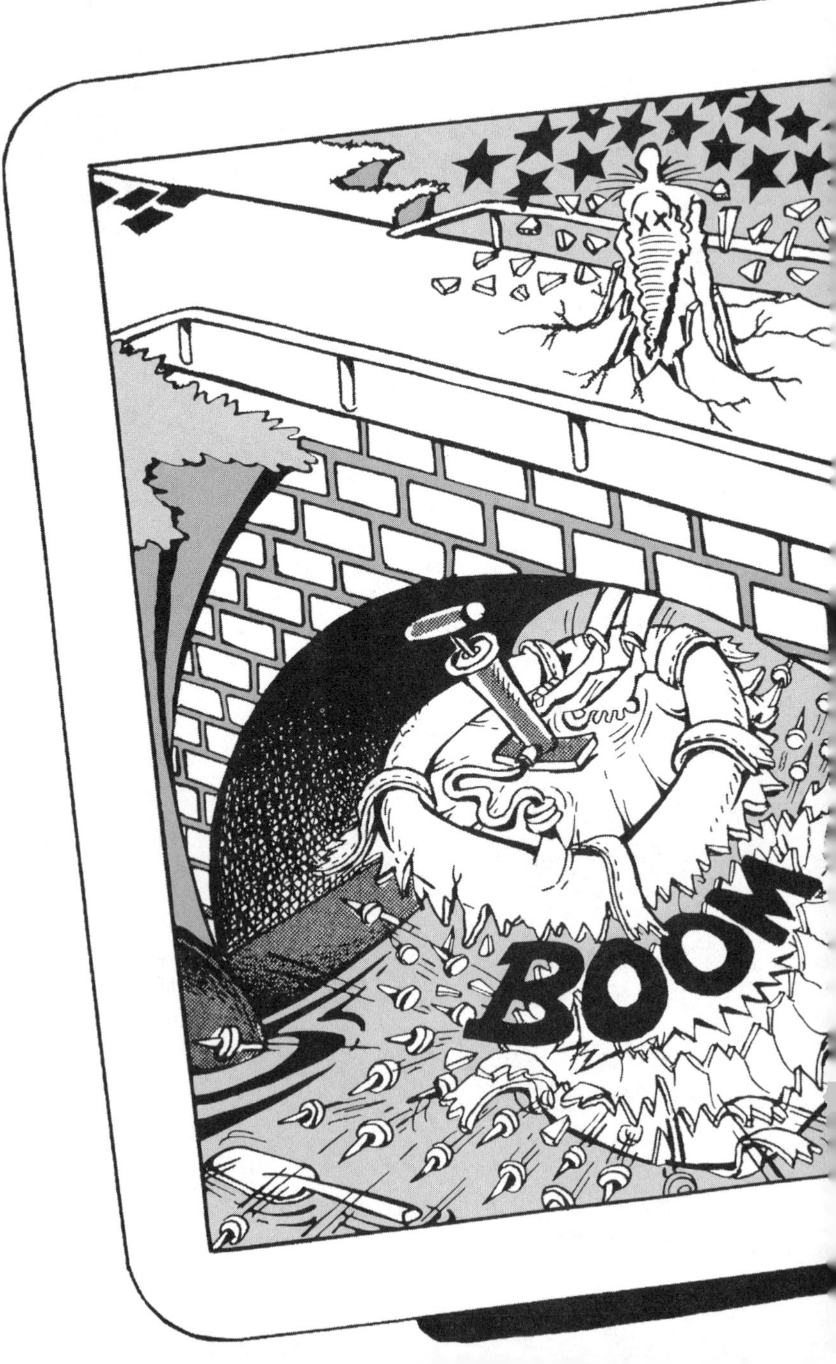
BOOM

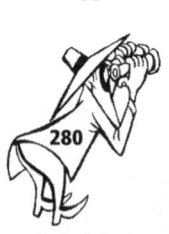

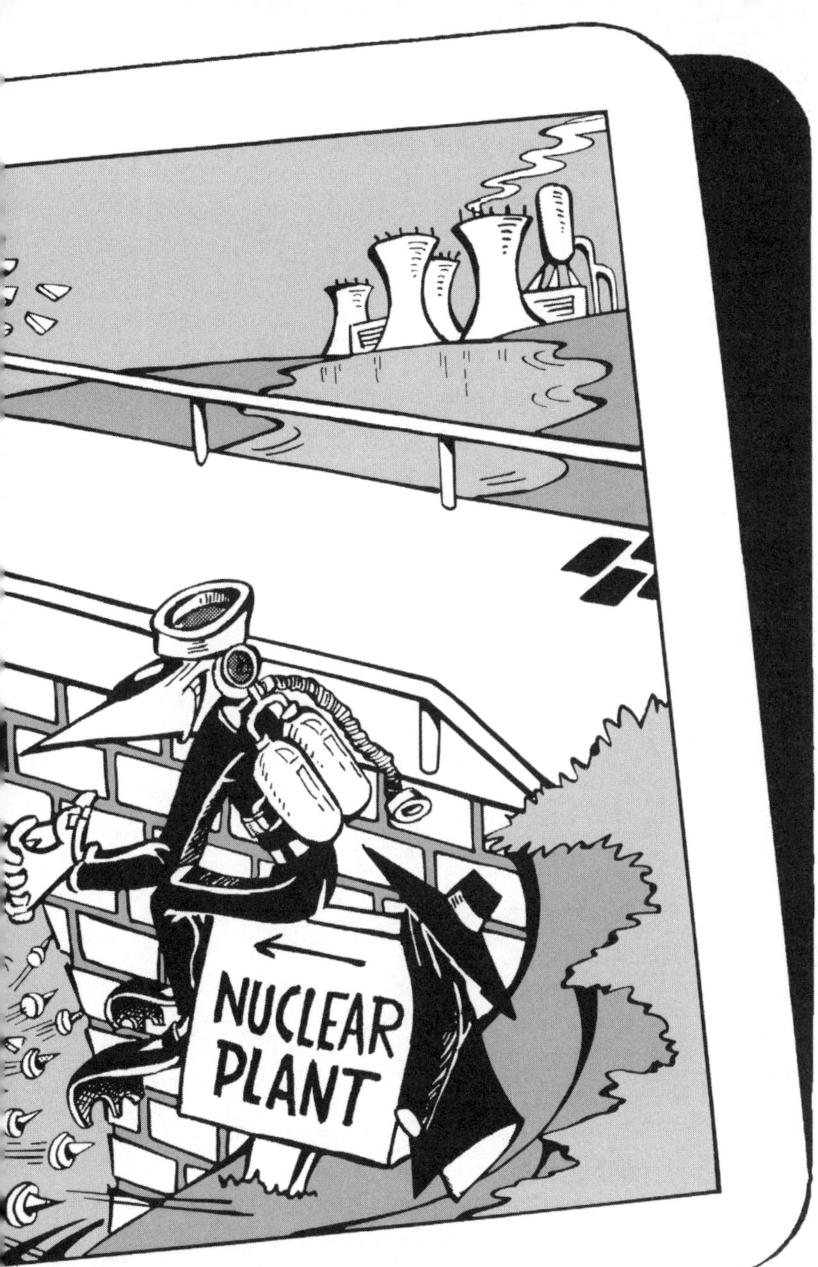
NUCLEAR
PLANT

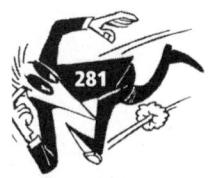

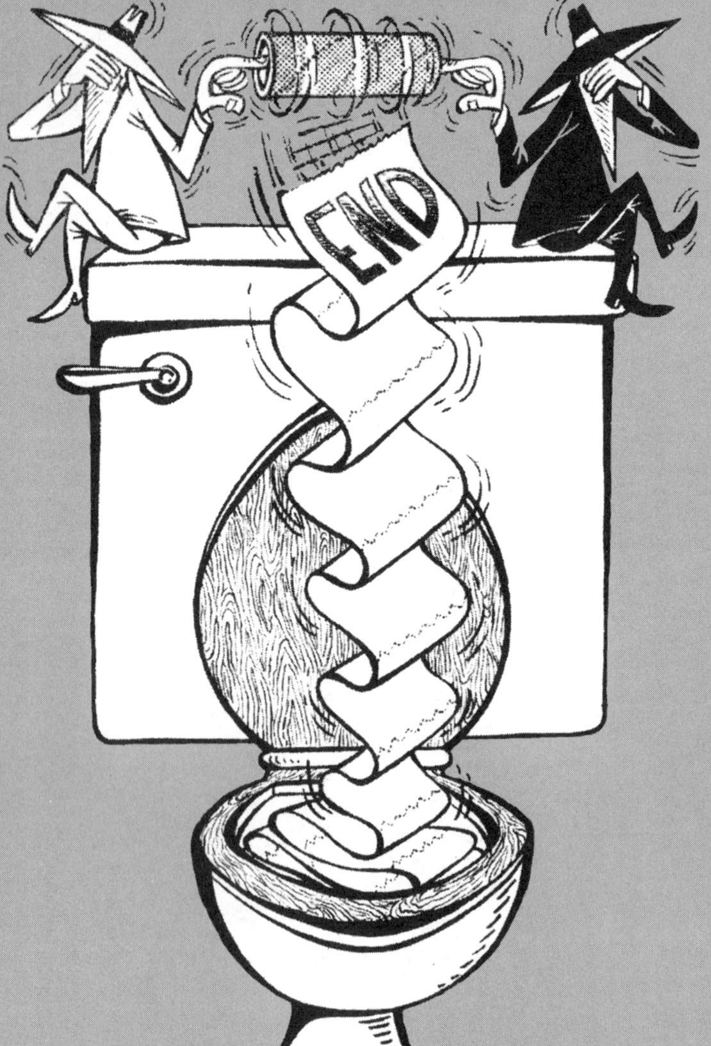
END